EDDIE MATHEWS

and
the National Pastime

Eddie Mathews

and
Bob Buege

Douglas American Sports Publications
1994

The authors gratefully acknowledge the invaluable assistance of the High Point (NC) Public Library, the Milwaukee Public Library, Steve Gietschier, Tom O'Connell, Mike Ploszay, Pam Prouty, Bob Ramstack, Marge Skare, and the Society for American Baseball Research, especially David Vincent.

Copyright ©1994 by Robert D. Buege

Published by Douglas American Sports Publications
P.O. Box 21619, Milwaukee, WI 53221-0619

Publisher's Cataloging in Publication Data

Mathews, Eddie, and Bob Buege
   Eddie Mathews and the National Pastime
      1. Mathews, Eddie, 1931--
      2. Baseball--United States--Players--Biography
      I. Buege, Bob, 1946--
      II. Title
Library of Congress Catalog Card Number 94-71074
GV865.M3M3 1994   796.357'092
ISBN 1-882134-41-9 Hardcover
ISBN 1-882134-44-3 Softcover

Manufactured in the United States of America

PREGAME

I was born during Prohibition, and I've spent most of my life trying to get caught up.

I was also born during the Great Depression, but my life has been anything but depressing. It's had its ups and downs, but mostly ups. I got the chance to do something I loved--play baseball--and get paid for it besides. I never made the kind of money these prima donnas are getting today--notice I said getting, not earning--but I sure can't complain. Baseball gave me all I'll ever need and a lot more. Do I wish I had made the kind of money they're giving these guys today? Of course. Hell, everybody wants more money. But honestly, I wouldn't trade my career for anybody's. When we played baseball we enjoyed it. We ate, drank, and slept baseball. We cared about the game, and we cared about the guys on our team. Except for during the winter when we tried to negotiate a new contract, we never thought about money. We just wanted to play baseball.

The time when I was in the big leagues has got to be the Golden Age of baseball. Just look at who was playing then-- Mickey Mantle and Stan Musial and Ted Williams and Ernie Banks and Hank Aaron and Willie Mays and you can go on and on. Those were ballplayers. And of course there were only sixteen teams then, eight in each league, so the talentwasn't spread as thin as it is today. The ballplayers today are bigger and stronger and faster than we were, but they can't play baseball like the guys in my day. They lift weights and probably stay in better shape today--hell, I know they stay in better shape today--and yet you look and they're always hurt.

But really, I don't want this to sound like some bitter old-timer knocking the game today and saying how great it used to be. I have a lot of admiration for the modern ballplayers. The way the press and the media cover every aspect of your life today, it's got to be tough. You're getting more money, but you've got to deal with agents and bankers and investment brokers and the whole nine yards. We were lucky. We just played baseball. And baseball is a tough game to play. As Ted Williams said, the hardest thing to do in all of sports is to hit a baseball. I think he's right. It was true when I played, and it's just as true now.

If you visit the Baseball Hall of Fame in Cooperstown, New York, you'll find a plaque on the wall saying Eddie Mathews was inducted into that hallowed institution in 1978. It was a wonderful honor. I wish my dad had lived to see it. It would have made him even prouder than it made me. Fortunately, my mom did get to see it.

Being selected to the Hall of Fame was a thrill, a huge thrill, but it was never my goal. The only personal goal I ever set in baseball was to play hard every day and be the best ballplayer I could be. My real goal was to be a part of winning every ballgame I ever played in. We didn't play for statistics or personal glory. We played to win.

One other thing about that plaque in Cooperstown--as flattering as it is, it doesn't say I was the greatest ballplayer ever, because I wasn't. I wasn't the biggest hero--that was Babe Ruth. I wasn't the best hitter--that has to be Ted Williams. I wasn't the best in the league--not with Willie Mays roaming the outfield. I wasn't even the best ballplayer on my own team--a guy named Hank Aaron made us all look ordinary. In fact, now that I think about it, I wasn't even the best ballplayer at the bar after the ballgame--I usually drank with Warren Spahn. I was a good ballplayer who played at the right time and had a hell of a good time doing it. Period.

What I want to do in this book is show what professional baseball used to be like: working your way up through the minors, making the big leagues, playing in all-star games and World Series, the whole nine yards. I started in Class D ball, went through AA and AAA, played on two world championship clubs, coached, managed, scouted, did the whole routine. In order to show how it was, I naturally have to write a great deal about myself. I apologize for that. People who know me can tell you I'm not real comfortable talking about myself--I certainly am not one to dwell on my own accomplishments. Nevertheless, as I write about the game of baseball as I experienced it, along with the ballplayers I had the privilege to play with and against, you're going to get a healthy dose of Eddie Mathews. Please be tolerant.

ONE

Carolina in the Morning

The city of Texarkana straddles the Texas-Arkansas border about ten miles south of the Red River and 25 miles north of the Louisiana state line. Two years after the stock market crashed in 1929, Texarkana was, like much of the country, struggling. The creosote plant, the textile mills, the paint factories weren't hiring. The lucky men who had jobs barely earned enough to feed their families. The cotton farms around Texarkana, both big and small, had seen their markets disappear with the crash. To add to the misery, a yearlong drought put Texarkana on the edge of what came to be known a few years later as the Dust Bowl. Luxuries such as electricity and indoor plumbing were still years away for most of the people in Bowie County. It was tough times in Texarkana.

On October 13, 1931, the only child of Edwin and Eloise Mathews was born on the Texas side of the line. That was me, Edwin Lee Mathews, Jr. My mother's family lived in Iowa, but my dad was a native Texan, from Bonham, Roy McMillan's hometown. Later on the family moved to Texarkana. My grandfather was a railroad man, an engineer on the Texas and Pacific Railroad. After he died, my grandmother moved to Dallas, where most of the other relatives had gone.

Anyway, three days before I was born and four hundred miles to the northeast, the St. Louis Cardinals had beaten Connie Mack's defending champion Philadelphia A's. The star of the Series was The Wild Horse of the Osage, Pepper Martin, from neighboring Oklahoma. I don't know if my dad listened to that Series on the radio--I don't even know if he had a radio--but I'm sure he followed the results of the games with

1

interest. He had played some semi-pro baseball in the Dallas area when he was younger, and he loved the game. Also, considering our location, he had to be rooting for the Cardinals.

My memories of Texarkana are few, and mostly from when I went back there as an adult. In 1935 my dad did what a lot of Americans did during the Great Depression--he packed up and moved his family to California to look for work, living with relatives at first. He did better than a lot of men--he found a job with Western Union. He was a telegrapher and became wire chief. One of his jobs was transmitting the ballgames of the Santa Barbara club in the California State League. He'd telegraph a play-by-play account to a studio, and then a radio announcer would broadcast it as if he were actually at the game.

A few times my dad took me along into the press box at the games he worked, which was great. Really, though, we did not do a lot of things together. We'd go camping once a year, but he wasn'treally an outdoorsman or hunter or anything like that. And he worked funny hours. When he was a wire chief he'd go to work at four in the morning. When he got home he usually took a nap.

One thing he made sure to do every day, though, was play catch with me, usually after dinner. As I got a little older, he and I and my mother would go to work out at La Cumbre Junior High School. They'd take me out there on weekends. My mother would pitch and my dad would shag. I told this at my Hall of Fame induction, and it's true. As I got a little bigger and stronger, I started hitting the ball through the middle at my mother. I found out that every time I did that I got more chores to do at home, so I started pulling the ball. And I became a dead pull hitter from that experience I had as a boy. Eventually my dad became the pitcher and my mom became the outfielder.

Even though we played baseball all the time, my dad never coached me. What he did was build my interest in sports, especially baseball, and make sure I got a lot of experiences, a lot of chances to play. He figured if the ability was there, it would show up if you gave it a chance. I got more chances at Harding Elementary School in Santa Barbara. I played quarterback for the Harding Jeeps (yes, that was our school nickname) tag football team, I played speedball (like soccer), and I took a first place in a track and field meet at Peabody Stadium. Also, as the local newspaper said, the shortstop for the Jeeps softball

2

team was "diminutive Eddie Mathews."

I was still pretty small until high school. By my junior year, though, I was over six-foot and weighed around 185. I was a fullback and linebacker in football, and a third baseman for the Santa Barbara High School Dons. We were the only public high school in a city of about 35,000--there was also one Catholic high school--so we had pretty strong teams in all sports. My coach in both sports was Clarence Schutte. He had played football at the University of Minnesota, and he had the college scouts convinced that I was a "ring-tailed wildcat" as a running back. I had football scholarships offered to me by UCLA, Southern Cal, and some other colleges, but really, the idea of going to college just didn't appeal to me. I would say I was an average student in hign school, but mostly I carried my books home and carried them back to school without looking at them. My real interest was sports.

The sports editor of the local newspaper in Santa Barbara was a man named Homer George. Homer was originally from Georgia. He talked to my dad about arranging a football scholarship for me at the University of Georgia, playing for Wally Butts, but it was never in either my father's or my mind. My dad wanted me to be a big-league baseball player, and that's what I wanted too.

I was selected to the All-Southern California team in both football and baseball in my senior year. In baseball the Dons went to the CIF (California Interscholastic Federation) championship playoff, which was for southern California. We ended up in San Diego playing in Lane Field, the ballpark where the San Diego Padres of the Pacific Coast League played their home games. That night I hit a home run over the rightfield fence and onto Pacific Coast Highway--which was no big deal, Max West and Luke Easter did it all the time--but we got beat. I had been hitting home runs and hitting good, and I noticed that the major league scouts were starting to come around more. In those days we really didn't pay that much attention, but we started getting some inquiries--was I going to college or wasn't I, that type of thing.

This, of course, was 1949, before major league baseball had any kind of draft of free agents. Any ballplayer could sign with any club, so there was a lot of competition. That's how the "bonus babies" came about--guys like Johnny Antonelli and Curt Simmons signed for big money about a year or two before

3

I got into organized baseball. Because everybody was a free agent, the personality of the individual scout became the deciding factor. The only restriction the scouts had was the timing. They couldn't sign or even talk to a high school kid until after graduation. Instead they talked to my parents, said they had an interest, or sent us a letter saying they'd like to talk to us.

The star of the Santa Barbara Dons, 1949. (Author's collection)

In all we heard from scouts for fifteen of the sixteen major league clubs. I think the only team that didn't contact us at all was the Washington Senators. Right at the end, maybe the last week of school, just before I became eligible to sign, that's when they all started coming in, taking us out to dinner--wining and dining us. My dad handled all the actual negotiating, but he and I discussed what we wanted. We were looking for a major league club that had an old third baseman, so I could move up when I was ready; and we wanted a scout that we liked and trusted. Right from the start, that scout was Johnny Moore.

It turned out that Johnny Moore, the California scout for the Boston Braves, had seen me play for the first time back in 1946. I was 14 then, playing for the Santa Barbara American Legion team in a game in San Francisco. Years later, when I was in the big leagues, Johnny told me about seeing me in that game. "You had that beautiful swing," he said, "and it really hasn't changed. Except for opening your stance a little bit, you look exactly the same at the plate now as you did that day in San Francisco."

Johnny Moore was a very, very classy guy and a really nice person. He played ten years in the big leagues--in fact he had just retired a few years before this. He hit over .300 for his career and hit three home runs in a game once when he was with the Phillies. He was also involved in one of the most famous moments in baseball history--sort of. In the 1932 World Series, when Babe Ruth hit what they call his "called shot"-- when he supposedly pointed to the bleachers in Wrigley Field and then hit a home run there to that spot--the Cub outfielder that was standing at the fence with his glove in the air was Johnny Moore. Charlie Grimm played for the Cubs in that game too--in fact, he was also their manager. Anyway, Johnny Moore knew baseball, and he was just the type of person that fit in with our family. Not that there was anything wrong with the other scouts, but Johnny just did a better salesman job.

What really impressed my dad was Moore's honesty. He never tried to flatter me or oversell my prospects. He said I needed experience, that I had potential but I was still a few years away from the big leagues. He also said that Bob Elliott, the Braves' third baseman, was in his thirties and would be about ready to step aside by the time I was ready to move up. Some of the other scouts offered us more money--I think the

5

Pittsburgh Pirates offered something like $30,000--but under the bonus rules at that time, if you signed for more than $6,000 you could only spend one year in the minor leagues. Johnny Moore said that wouldn't be long enough and that by signing for more money I'd actually be hurting myself in the long run. My dad agreed, and we decided to go with the Braves.

Santa Barbara High School had its senior prom on the night of our graduation. The prom was held at the Carillo Hotel. We weren't allowed to sign the contract with the Braves until the day after I graduated, meaning I had to wait until one minute after midnight. While the prom was going on, my parents' house was full of baseball scouts, all waiting for me to come home from the dance. But a little before midnight, my date and I casually danced our way out of the prom, hopped in my dad's car, and drove downtown to the Barbara Hotel. We felt like we were in some spy movie, and we laughed our heads off. We met Johnny Moore in his room at the Barbara, signed the necessary papers, and returned to the dance to share the good news.

At 7:00 o'clock the next morning my parents and relatives were at the train station in Santa Barbara, wishing me a safe trip and a great career in baseball. I was on my way to Chicago to meet the Boston Braves, who would be there playing the Cubs. I wasn't going to play, you understand, just meet the players, hang around the team for a few days, maybe take some batting practice and talk to a few reporters. That would be my introduction to professional baseball. I was scared stiff.

Everything was new to me. I'd led a pretty sheltered life. I'd never really experienced a big city. I don't think I had ever been on a train by myself before. We didn't have TV, so I had never seen a major league baseball game. In those days kids didn't collect baseball cards like they do now, so I couldn't even identify the ballplayers. I knew about Ted Williams and Stan Musial, but not many others. Chicago was the "city of the big shoulders" that we had read about in high school. I was heading into uncharted territory.

The trip went by like a blur. Before I got on the train either my mother or one of my aunts gave me a copy of *Mr. Roberts* to read. That was the first book I had read in a while, and it was one of the funniest I've ever read. By the time I reached Chicago's Union Station, I was relaxed and ready to take on the world. And before long, I had to.

6

No one was waiting to meet me at the train station. My instructions were to report to the Edgewater Beach Hotel. I grabbed my one suitcase, found a taxicab, told the driver where I wanted to go, and sat back to enjoy the drive to the hotel. I felt like royalty, right up until the time the cab pulled up in front of the Edgewater Beach and the cabbie announced, "That'll be twelve bucks!" At first I thought he was joking, but his demeanor told me otherwise.

I said, "What the hell, you been riding me around or something? Twelve bucks?" That might not sound like an outrageous amount today, but in 1949 that was a day's wages for an average worker--before taxes.

"Hey, pal," the driver answered sarcastically, "you're in the big city now." I sure was. We argued a little bit more, but I finally paid him--twelve bucks, exactly. I had never heard of tipping, and if he had asked for one I'm not sure what I would have done. He didn't ask, though, and when he drove away we were both very upset.

Speaking of tipping, I didn't catch onto it for several years after that. I don't know how many years later, my mother had gone east to visit her relatives in Iowa, and after that she met me in Chicago when I was with the Braves. We were in the Edgewater Beach Hotel having dinner. Afterwards when I paid the check, I evidently didn't tip the waiter enough money. He took the bill and then came back and looked at my tip and said, "No, you keep it." I've never been that embarrassed. I ended up giving him some more money. I didn't know much of anything. He did, though, and after that, so did I.

Well, anyway, after I registered at the Edgewater Beach, I spent some time just checking it out. I had never seen a hotel like that! We had hotels in Santa Barbara, but this place was awesome. I was glad the Braves were paying for it. Even at the hotel, though, I didn't see anyone from the ballclub. I just called the number they had given me. It was Duffy Lewis, the traveling secretary. He said, "The bus leaves the hotel at such-and-such a time tomorrow morning"--it was probably ten or eleven--"be on it."

I had packed my baseball shoes, glove, jockstrap, and T-shirt in my suitcase, but I hadn't thought to bring along a duffel bag to take the stuff to the ballpark. The only thing I could think of was to ask the hotel maid for a paper sack. She gave me one, and I reported to the bus the next morning.

Nobody greeted me. In fact, the only thing anybody said to me was, "This is the big leagues, kid, you don't have to bring your lunch." Then they all had a big laugh. I figured out later that the guy who said that was Bob Elliott, the National League's MVP from 1947 and the third baseman whose job I was hoping to take in a few years. At that moment, though, I didn't have the slightest idea who the hell he was.

When we got to Wrigley Field and unloaded the bus, everybody just went up into the locker room, or so I thought. I was just following everybody. Nobody told me anything. But what had happened, as they got to the door, all the coaches, the manager, the trainer, the traveling secretary, all peeled off and went and sat down in the stands, but I followed the players into the clubhouse. When I got in there, Eddie Stanky jumped on me, screaming, "Get the hell out of here!" He didn't tell me why. I just walked outside and saw all these guys sitting, and I said, hmmm. Then they explained to me it was a dissension meeting, just for players, nobody else.

Basically, what was going on was this: The Braves had won the pennant the year before and had lost to the Cleveland Indians in the World Series. Even though they had a real good year, the players thought the manager, Billy Southworth, was getting too much of the credit. They thought Southworth was too tough, that he had too many rules and too many long workouts. The dissension started in spring training and kept building until mid-August, when Southworth took a leave of absence for the rest of the season because of his health. He came back to manage in 1950, but by then the leaders of the dissension, Stanky and Al Dark, had been traded to the Giants.

After Stanky's meeting broke up, the players took the field to practice and I went to the clubhouse to be fitted for a uniform. Actually, fitted is the wrong word. They issued me one that was about three sizes too big. It was so baggy I looked like a fool, and the sleeves were enormous, making it difficult to swing a bat. I should say more difficult.

All decked out in my clown suit, I trudged down the runway to the dugout. The idea was for me to take some batting practice. I naturally didn't have a bat of my own, so I started to pull one from the bat rack at the end of the dugout. As I did, a loud voice snarled, "Get your hands off that bat!" I returned the bat and reached for a different one. Same thing, different voice--"Put that damn thing back!"

Now I wasn't sure what to do. Fortunately, at that moment Tommy Holmes stepped forward and handed me his bat. "Here, you can use this," he said. Again, I didn't know who he was at the time, although it turned out he was the Braves' best hitter and three years later would be my manager. I have to say that, of all the Braves I encountered on my visit to Chicago, Holmes was the only one who treated me half decent.

Finally equipped with a bat, I stepped into the cage to hit a few. Now, batting practice is just what the name implies--a chance to work on your swing, sharpen your eye a little bit. Sometimes a regular pitcher pitches it, sometimes a coach, maybe even a position player or a broadcaster (like Bob Uecker) or a manager (like Tommy Lasorda). At that time the Braves had a regular batting practice pitcher, Si Johnson, but I don't think he traveled with the club. The pitcher I was facing, nameless to me at the time, was veteran righthander Red Barrett. I settled in, took my comfortable stance, and watched Barrett take his windup.

The first pitch was aimed directly at my right ear. I hit the dirt to avoid getting beaned. Okay, the ball got away. Even an experienced pitcher misses his target sometimes. I stood back in, determined to show my unfriendly audience what I was made of, to show them I could swing the bat. Again the ball zeroed in on my head. Again I took evasive action. I looked toward the mound, hoping I suppose for some hint of apology, or compassion. Barrett stood smirking, apparently thinking this was a wonderful joke. His third pitch was identical to the first two. When he finally threw something over the plate, it was off-speed stuff and assorted junk. I made a few awkward swings, hit a couple weak grounders, and that was it. My time at bat was finished. Welcome to the big leagues.

During the ballgame I sat in the grandstand and watched. Nobody from the ballclub talked to me. It was just a different atmosphere than I had expected. I didn't expect any open-arms greetings, but this was more like a fraternity initiation. I think they were putting me through a test or having fun with me or something. It wasn't malicious. It's just the way things were. The veterans didn't really associate with the younger players. When I say associate, I mean drink, go to the bar and have a few pops.

I stayed in Chicago three days, and the pattern was the same. I'd ride the bus to the ballpark, work out with the team, take a little infield, maybe get in a few swings, sit in the stands and watch the ballgame, then go back to the hotel. It was a lonely time, but it was also exciting: seeing Wrigley Field, the crowds, being down on the field. After one of the games I had some time to kill, so I did what seemed natural--I went to a bar. That's what most ballplayers did. I wasn't going to go to the Christian Science Reading Room. I sat down, and pretty soon the bartender brought me a glass of beer. He pointed and said, "It's on those two gentlemen at the end of the bar." I looked and recognized two of the Braves, I think Vern Bickford and Walker Cooper or maybe Earl Torgeson. "They said to tell you to drink it and get the hell out." I did. Three years later when I got to Boston, Torgeson and Bickford and Cooper were still with the club, and we became good friends. But in Chicago, I never got acquainted with *any*body.

There's one other side note about my first brief stay at the Edgewater Beach Hotel. Four nights before I arrived, Eddie Waitkus of the Philadelphia Phillies was shot in a room there by a young woman. He recovered, but that incident became the basis for the novel and later the movie *The Natural.* And yet I never heard about the shooting until three years later when I got to know Waitkus a little bit. Considering the nature of the incident and all the rumors surrounding it, I'm sure all the Braves ballplayers must have been talking about it. But I never knew about it until three years later. Probably just as well.

After three days in Chicago, my contract was assigned to Evansville, the Braves' Class B ballclub in the Three-I League. I took the train and joined them in Danville, Illinois, where they were playing at the time. Once again, I wasn't expected to play there--I was just getting acquainted with the ballplayers. The Evansville Braves were a nice, close-knit group of guys, and they really kind of took care of me. They could see I was going around ga-ga goo-goo. We always went out after the game, pretty much as a group. That's where I got acquainted with Chet Nichols and Pete Whisenant, who became my good friends.

Even though I was only with the Evansville club about a week or so, they assigned me a roommate, or should I say they assigned me as his roommate. His name was Larry Pennell, nicknamed Bud. He was a first baseman. While I was there, he quit. He jumped the team and went home to Hollywood to make movies. And he did, too. I know he was in at least eight or

The Boston Braves who "welcomed" me in Chicago in June, 1949. In the front row, seventh from left, is Bob Elliott, whom I replaced three years later. To his left is Red Barrett. In row two, third from left, is the dissension man, Eddie Stanky. In row three, beginning third from left, are Earl Torgeson, Al Dark, and Tommy Holmes. (Author's collection)

nine different films, including *Seven Angry Men* and *The FBI Story.* He never became a big star, but he found work.

After that he got into television and did even better. The one starring role I know he had was on a show called "Ripcord," in the early sixties. It was about two sky-diving instructors that got into all kinds of adventures. His co-star was Ken Curtis, who was Festus on "Gunsmoke." Larry was also on "The Beverly Hillbillies" a few times. I've run into him a couple times over the years, and I've also seen him on cable. He wasn't as well known as Chuck Connors of "The Rifleman," but he did okay.

Following my short stay in Evansville, I took a train to what was to be my final destination, my first actual hometown as a professional baseball player: Thomasville, North Carolina. I had been assigned to the High Point-Thomasville Hi-Toms of the North Carolina State League. This was Class D ball, the deep, deep minors.

When I got off the train in Thomasville, I saw two things, one that I expected and one that I didn't. The first was that nobody was there to meet me. That I had come to expect. What I didn't expect was this old gal, maybe in her sixties, sitting on a bench near the train tracks, chewing tobacco and spitting a brown streak. That's when I knew I was a long way from Santa Barbara.

I didn't know what to do other than walk to the ballpark. I didn't know where it was, but I sure wasn't afraid of getting lost in Thomasville. It was a pretty small town, famous mainly for making furniture. To remind people of that they had a huge chair right by the train station. I figured if I did get lost, somebody would say, "Hey, there's a strange kid in town." That's how small it was.

The ballpark was called Finch Field. It was located along the highway between Thomasville and High Point, but closer to Thomasville. I took my suitcase and walked over there. And God, it was hot. When I got to the ballpark, they took me over to this rooming house about four blocks from the park, where I checked into a third-floor room. The kids that were working their way up through the minors were pretty much scattered around within other houses and rooms. I met a couple of my teammates who also lived there, Ron Schuettenberg and Ted Alex. Everything seemed pretty nice, but there was a problem.

By the time I worked my way from Santa Barbara to

Chicago to Danville to Evansville to Thomasville, my dad had signed another contract, this one with the Pittsburgh Pirates. The Pittsburgh scout had convinced him that even though I had signed with the Braves, I was still a free agent because I wasn't receiving any salary. The whole $6,000 was a bonus. My dad liked to drink, and this scout got him drunk and got his signature on a piece of paper. So now I had two contracts.

My manager with the Hi-Toms, Jimmy Gruzdis, drove me over to Salisbury, where the Pittsburgh farm club was. They wanted me to sign this Pittsburgh contract. I wouldn't do it. Instead Gruzdis called George Trautman. He was the president of what they called the National Association of Professional Baseball Leagues. In other words, he was the commissioner of all of minor league baseball, all 448 teams. Trautman reviewed my situation and said no, the Pirates did not have any claim on my services. What the Braves had to do was change my contract so $1,000 of it was in salary and the rest in bonus, and that made it all legitimate. Then I was officially a Hi-Tom and part of the Braves organization.

Basically I fit in real well with the Hi-Toms. We had a bunch of nice fellows, a mixture of young guys and older guys. See, in Class D ball you had some young kids, like me, trying to work their way through the minor leagues up to the majors. You also had the other extreme, older guys who had played at a higher level, maybe even the big leagues, who were on their way down but lived in the area and still wanted to play ball. In between you also had some guys who were maybe in their early twenties and still playing Class D. Obviously those guys just didn't have what it took to play in the high minors, let alone the big leagues.

For example, Vann Harrington was a lefthanded hitter that had some pop. He had a good year for us. He played second base, and right at the end of the season he set a record with three home runs in one game. He was an older guy. Now when I say older, that means anywhere from late twenties to early thirties, or on up. Another older player we had was Pete Williams, our shortstop. Both of those guys were good ballplayers, but they weren't going anywhere. They lived in town there and had jobs during the day. Then at night they'd come out and play ball. You had to love baseball to do that because it was hotter than hell, and at the end of the day you were beat. But they did it, and so did some others. Al Jarlett, one of our

13

righthand pitchers, was another one. Even our manager, Jimmy Gruzdis, who was also the club president by the way, did some pinch-hitting for us and might have played a little outfield.

He wasn't the oldest, though. The senior citizen of our club was a guy named Cliff Bolton, a catcher. He was a lefthand hitter, not very big. Cliff was from High Point originally, and he broke into organized ball there. Then he worked his way up and played in the big leagues, mostly with the Washington Senators. He batted against Carl Hubbell in the World Series. Then he worked his way back down and ended up back in Class D in his hometown. He was 42 years old, and he must have caught ninety percent of our games that year. And the most amazing thing was, he led the league in hitting. He couldn't run real well, but he could still drive the ball. He even played for a few more years after that. Cliff was incredible.

We had quite a few good ballplayers. Our outfielders were good--Lou Owens, Chic Petters, Johnny Lybrand. Our home run leader was our first baseman, Herman Niehaus. And we had a pitcher, righthander, worked mostly in relief--his name was Lynn Southworth, and his record in the regular season was 21-1. And then there was a big, tall pitcher we had named Carl Greene. Carl did a good job, but there was one play he never seemed to catch on to. If a guy was stealing second base, Carl would turn around to see if the catcher threw him out. Instead of ducking down, he'd just turn around to look at second base. Carl stood about six-foot four, and he must have got hit right smack in the back about half a dozen times. "Carl, you gotta get down!" we told him, but he kept doing it.

I mentioned two guys that lived in my rooming house, Ron Schuettenberg and Ted Alex. They were both pitchers and both close to my age. Ron was the better pitcher--he won 19 games for us. Ted Alex, though, was the guy I ran around with in Thomasville. We just hit it off from the time we met. He was a little righthander from Greenwich, Connecticut. His dad owned a pool hall, so he grew up playing pool. There wasn't anybody in Thomasville that could beat him. But he kept them strung out so they didn't know that. He could hustle--but not for any bucks. He kept us in hamburgers, though, I'll tell you that. And shoe shines. He was fun to watch. I played at the game, but I was never more than an average player. Ted could play, though. I've tried to find him several times over the years, but he moved out of Greenwich. If you read this, Ted, give me a

14

call--collect.

I think the reason the guys on the Hi-Toms got along as well as they did was our manager, Jimmy Gruzdis. Jimmy was very close to all of us, and he kept everybody happy. I guess we had little petty stuff going on--how come I didn't play tonight, this and that--but we didn't have a lot of extra ballplayers floating around, so we didn't have much problem with that. Looking back on it from forty-some years later, I think probably there was a little resentment from some of the older guys that I came in and was handed the job. I mean, I was the starting third baseman as soon as I got there. But the fact that I started off well and did well for them helped a lot. I hit .363 and I was second on the club in home runs, and I only played half the season. Maybe they thought, who the hell does this kid think he is? But I never had that feeling at the time. Not in the least.

As much as I give credit to Jim Gruzdis, he really didn't teach me much baseball. You learned by experience. If you made a mistake and you were halfway smart, you corrected it. If not, you didn't go beyond Class D. But as far as teaching, everybody was too tired all the time. It was hot, and these guys worked. We just went out there and played, and that was it.

During the day I did nothing. It was too damn hot. There was no air-conditioning anyplace. You just had to kill time whatever way you could. No TV. The big entertainment in Thomasville was the baseball games at night. That was true in every town in our league.

The North Carolina State League had clubs in eight different towns, none more than about seventy miles apart. There was our team, the Mooresville Moors, Salisbury Pirates, Concord Nationals, Landis Spinners, Hickory Rebels, Lexington Athletics, and Statesville--I can't remember what they called their team. Statesmen, maybe? They were mostly mill towns, and each one had a ballpark. Finch Field in Thomasville seated between four and five thousand people, and we often filled it, sometimes beyond capacity. And that was in a town of about 12,000, although High Point was bigger. If you didn't like baseball in Thomasville, you were just out of luck. Waylon Jennings and the gang didn't come in there playing. There was nothing else to do.

We always traveled to out-of-town games in cars, big cars, each one carrying probably six guys. Because the towns

15

were all close, we never stayed overnight. We just drove there, played the game, and drove home. And they always had a cooler in the trunk with beer, waiting for after the game. Always. That was how you relaxed after the ballgame, and that was how you got to know your teammates, how you socialized. It was just a natural part of the game. Everybody drank.

We had fun with the Hi-Toms, which is easy to do when you're winning. The club was in first place when I joined them at the beginning of July, and we won the pennant by 18 games. We were especially tough to beat at Finch Field, where we won 21 straight at one stretch. For the season we set a league record by winning 90 games and only losing 34. It was a real kick. By finishing first we qualified for the league playoffs. The way it worked, the first-place team played the third-place team; the second-place team played the fourth-place team. Then the winners played for the championship.

In the first round the Hi-Toms won pretty easily, four games to one, over the Landis Spinners. We had a game rained out where we were leading 7-0, but it didn't matter. I hit a home run in the tenth inning to win game four. We felt very confident going into the final series.

Our opponents also felt confident. The Lexington A's had finished in fourth place, but that was because they got off to a terrible start. They won their last 13 games of the regular season and then swept the Mooresville club in the playoffs to make it 17 victories in a row before we played them. We cooled them off, though. We took the first three games of the series, mainly with good pitching. I hit two home runs and a double in game three, but we didn't really need them because we won 13-3.

Something happened, though. In game four we got shut out by Hal Wood, which was no big deal. Game five was at Finch Field, and we figured we could end it at home. I had one of my better games that night--two home runs, five RBI's--and with one inning to go we had an 8-3 lead. And then--bang! They got a few base hits, a few runs, a couple more hits, and with two outs they had the tying runs on base. Then there was a high popup out behind third. I went back; Pete Williams, our shortstop, went back; Chic Petters, the leftfielder, came in. Everybody called it; nobody took it. At the last second I reached for it and had it in my glove, but somehow it bounced out. I've never felt worse. I got an error, Lexington got some more runs, and we lost the ballgame. Then we lost the next game at their place, and the series was tied at three games each. Now it was sudden death.

That was on Saturday night. We never played on Sundays, and Monday we were rained out. For me, and I guess for most of the team, that weekend lasted forever. I wanted a chance to redeem myself. After three scoreless innings of the deciding game, I got my chance. I lined a home run to right field to put us ahead 1-0. In the fifth inning we pulled off a triple play to protect the lead, and we still led 1-0 after six innings. They scored three runs against us in the seventh inning, though, and we were losing 3-1 going into the last of the ninth.

That final inning is one I'll never forget. I remember it like it was yesterday. (Actually, I probably remember it better than I remember yesterday. Old age does that to people.) I led off the inning. I bounced one up the middle, kind of off the handle of the bat. The shortstop got to it but couldn't make a throw and I was safe. Cliff Bolton singled through the box, and we had the tying run on with nobody out.

We played it for the tie. Herm Niehaus laid down a sacrifice bunt, maybe a little too hard. The pitcher, Hal Wood, grabbed it and fired to third to try to get me on a force play, but I slid in ahead of the throw. That loaded the bases with no outs. Then, in a scene I still see in slow motion, old Pistol Pete Williams hit a fly ball that sailed way over the 355-foot mark in right-center field. There was joy in Thomasville.

July 12, 1949

From the very beginning, no one really doubted that Eddie Mathews could hit. He made his professional baseball debut on the Fourth of July, 1949, at Holt-Moffitt Field in Lexington, North Carolina. A nervous 17-year-old facing Lexington Athletics' ace hurler Hal Wood, Mathews singled once in four at-bats and handled five fielding chances flawlessly at third base. Mathews' team, the High Point-Thomasville Hi-Toms, lost the ballgame, 4-2, but remained in first place.

Eight nights later, however, a different Eddie Mathews took the field at the Hi-Toms' home park, Finch Field, in a game against the Landis Spinners. The local newspaper was still spelling his name wrong (using two T's), but Mathews was now relaxed at the plate and comfortable in his role as the club's chief power-hitting threat. He lacked polish, he lacked the worldly ways of his veteran teammates (catcher Cliff Bolton was 25 years his senior), but he could play baseball—especially hit.

The Hi-Toms were having an outstanding season, leading the second-place Mooresville Moors by 13 games. What's more, they had won their last 11 home games. Pitcher Jim Hopper of the Spinners knew going in that he would be facing a difficult task; the Hi-Toms, Mathews in particular, proved him right. In the bottom of the second inning, Cliff Bolton tripled. Bolton was a native of High Point, a seven-year major league veteran who had caught for Walter Johnson's Washington Senators and batted against Carl Hubbell in the 1933 World Series. At age 42 Bolton was a phenomenon—he was batting over .400 and would lead the league for the season with a .399 average. After his triple, Mathews singled him home for the game's first run.

With the score tied two-all in the fourth, Mathews emulated Bolton and belted a triple to the base of the fence in dead center, 390 feet away. After one out he scored the lead run on a flyball by leftfielder Mickey McGuire. Then in his next appearance, with two out in the fifth and teammates Vann Harrington and Cliff Bolton on base, Mathews smashed a 400-

18

foot home run far over the rightfield fence to give Hi-Toms pitcher Ron Schuettenberg a 7-2 lead and send Hopper to the bench.

In the last of the eighth Mathews batted for the fourth and final time of the game. Facing relief man Bob Palmer, the Hi-Toms' new hero stroked his second home run of the ballgame, a healthy drive over the right-centerfield fence with the bases empty. It was the rookie's first two-homer performance and a clear indicator of a bright future. For the game Mathews finished four-for-four with three runs scored and five runs batted in. He would finish his abbreviated first season in organized baseball with 17 home runs, 56 RBI's, and a .363 batting average in 63 games. Most important, he would capture the attention of the parent Boston Braves and earn an invitation to spring training in 1950. And by the end of his first season, the *High Point Enterprise*, and a lot of other people, would know how to spell his name.

July 12, 1949

LANDIS	AB	R	H	BI	HI-TOMS	AB	R	H	BI
Barrett, 1b	4	0	0	0	Owens, rf	5	0	1	0
Russell, lf	4	0	3	1	Williams, ss	4	2	2	1
Williamson, 2b	3	0	0	0	Harrington, 2b	2	1	2	1
Deese, ss	4	0	0	0	Niehaus, 1b	4	0	1	0
Chapman, 3b	4	1	2	0	Bolton, c	3	2	1	0
Conwell, cf	3	0	1	1	Matthews, 3b	4	3	4	5
Beveridge, rf	4	0	0	0	Petters, cf	4	0	1	0
Boger, c	3	1	0	0	McGuire, lf	4	0	0	1
Hopper, p	1	0	0	0	Schuettenberg, p	4	0	1	0
Palmer, p	1	0	0	0					
Iacovello, ph	1	0	0	0					
Totals	32	2	6	2	Totals	34	8	13	8

Iacovello popped out for Palmer in ninth.

```
Landis ........................ 0 0 1  1 0 0  0 0 0--2
HI-TOMS ....................... 0 1 1  1 4 0  0 1 *--8
```

E--Harrington, McGuire. 2B--Chapman, Russell, Harrington. 3B--Bolton, Matthews. HR--Matthews 2, Williams. DP--Matthews, Harrington and Niehaus. SB--Harrington 2. HO--Off Hopper, 10 in 4 2-3; off Palmer, 3 in 3 1-3. W--Schuettenberg. L--Hopper. U--Suggs and Horne. T--1:58.

TWO

Ponce de Leon

After the season I flew back to Santa Barbara. My mother worked in a store there, a combination liquor store and delicatessen. I helped out for a month or so during the holidays, pretty much as a delivery boy. My future was uncertain, but I figured I might be invited to the Braves' spring training.

I was. There was no chance of me making the Braves' club, of course. They'd just take a look at me, see how I could do against a big-league curve ball and so forth. Then they'd decide what level farm team to assign me to. I knew I wouldn't be staying in Class D. I expected to play at Evansville, which was Class B. That would be a big step up without getting in over my head.

Needless to say everything in spring training in Bradenton was new to me. I didn't have any idea what to expect. I was just looking around with my mouth hanging open. That's the kind of spring it was, although I had a pretty good spring. The ballplayers stayed in an old hotel called the Dixie Grande. It wasn't the best hotel in town--the year before that the Braves had stayed in a different hotel, a nicer one, but they weren't invited back for some reason. That must have been a wild spring.

I said we stayed in the Dixie Grande, but that's not completely accurate. One of the Braves' players didn't. Sam Jethroe was a rookie outfielder with the club, the first black ballplayer (we said "colored" then) the Braves had ever had. This was three years after Jackie Robinson broke the color line in major league baseball, but in Bradenton, Florida, in 1950, the civil rights movement was still a long way off. It wasn't just the

Dixie Grande--no hotel in Florida would have let a colored man stay there. Sam stayed in a private home across town. It's shameful to talk about now, but at the time I was 18 years old and that's just the way things were. I have to say we never even thought about how wrong that was. Even if I had, I would no more have challenged the system than I would have spoken out against President Truman's foreign policy or budget plan. I was a kid--what the hell did I know?

Spring training gave me my first actual in-a-game look at major league pitching. I would have to say I was impressed. It wasn't just the curve balls, either--the velocity impressed me too. I remember one game where I faced Robin Roberts, and the first time up I hit a ground ball. I didn't think too much of it. They'd told me he was a control pitcher. But the next time up I had a guy on third base with one out, and he notched up about two feet. I mean, he blew me away! I said, "Oh, wait a minute! This ain't fair. You didn't show me that the first time."

I made my debut as a big league ballplayer in an exhibition game against the St. Louis Cardinals in Al Lang Field in St. Petersburg. I don't remember who I faced, but I came off the bench in about the fifth inning, played third base, and went 0-for-2. I think I scored a run, though. I remember the Cardinals beat us. I also remember one other thing about that game. Sam Jethroe became the first colored man to play in a game in Al Lang Field. That was a big deal because it meant the Dodgers and Giants would also be able to play there. Those were the only other National League clubs that had black ballplayers at that time.

I was pretty much in awe of the guys on the Braves at first. It was just the year before last that they had won the pennant and played Cleveland in the World Series. Spahn and Sain carried the pitching load on that club, and here I was, their teammate. Pete Reiser, the former Dodger star and batting champion, was on the team now, too. Vern Bickford was there, Buddy Kerr, Connie Ryan, Sibby Sisti, and a really unforgettable character by the name of Earl Torgeson.

Earl was a neat person, but he had a short fuse. He would fight anybody, anytime, for any reason. In the Dixie Grande Hotel all outside telephone calls had to go through the switchboard operator. So one night Earl was talking on the phone to his wife, and the guy on the switchboard was listening in. This was about one or two o'clock in the morning. Earl heard a click and then he could hear the guy breathing. He said to his wife, "Just a minute." He ran down the steps to the lobby. He leaped over the desk, and the desk clerk took off. Earl chased him outside and down the street, kicking at him as they ran. He kicked the guy's butt, but he sprained his ankle and missed the start of the season. Like I said, he was a neat guy, but he was a character.

After about a week of exhibition games with the Braves, it was time for me to be assigned to a minor league ballclub. I had hit pretty well with Boston actually, but my fielding was not very good. Like I said, I would probably have been assigned to Evansville, except for one person. That person was Dixie Walker.

Dixie had been an outfielder in the big leagues for almost 20 years, starting out as a teammate of Babe Ruth with the Yankees. He played mostly with Brooklyn, where he was "The People's Cherce," helping them win two pennants and leading the National League in batting once. Dixie was a lifetime .300 hitter who knew as much about hitting as anybody. He had recently retired from the Pittsburgh Pirates and been hired to manage the Atlanta Crackers in the Southern Association. He liked my swing enough to convince Braves officials that I could play at the Double-A level. So thanks to Dixie Walker, at the age of 18 and with only a couple months' experience in organized baseball, I became a Cracker.

The Atlanta Crackers had a great history. They had been one of the few minor league clubs without any major league affiliation. That changed in the summer of 1949 when a group of Atlanta businessmen bought the team from the Coca-Cola company. The club president both before and after the sale was Earl Mann, but beginning in 1950, with Mann as an owner, the Crackers had a working agreement with the Boston Braves. That was how I was able to become a Cracker.

Earl Mann had been the club president for about 15 years. He had started with the Crackers 20 years before that, selling peanuts at the games. He worked his way up through the organization and helped achieve Atlanta's reputation as the best baseball town in the minor leagues.

Earl Mann was quite an interesting man, a super-nice guy, very generous with his ballplayers. One time in New Orleans after a ballgame against the Pelicans, Mr. Mann treated the whole team to a dinner party at the Roosevelt Hotel.

That may not seem like much now, but when you're in a strange town, without much money, well, it meant a lot.

Another time I remember I hit a home run to win a ballgame at home, and Mr. Mann called me up to his office and gave me a gift certificate to buy a suit. Well, I had never owned a suit. What was I going to do with a suit? But I went down there and bought a suit. I kept that thing I bet for 15 years.

I'll tell you one other thing to show what type of guy Earl Mann was. He used to sit down near the dugout when we played at home, in Ponce de Leon Park. When you'd hit a home run, he'd throw out a silver dollar when you went around home plate. More often than not you'd pick it up and give it to the bat boy--not that we were that into the money, but it was just a thing that he started--just a way of acknowledging something good you were doing. He was always a thoughtful, considerate man. When I was hired to manage the Braves in 1972, I got several letters of congratulations, and one of them was from Earl Mann.

After I left Bradenton, I reported to the Crackers in Pensacola, Florida, their minor league spring training camp. I still had no way of knowing for sure that I would end up staying in Atlanta, but I had a pretty good camp. I still was pretty crude as far as the fielding, but Dixie Walker thought I could handle it.

On my first day with the Crackers we played an intra-squad game. My first time at bat I faced Hugh Casey. At the time I didn't know who he was--he was just some big, heavy, older-looking righthander who walked on his tiptoes. Later on, of course, I found out quite a bit about him. He had been Dixie Walker's teammate at Brooklyn for a long time, and before that he pitched against the Braves when Babe Ruth played for them. Just a few years before I met him he had been the best relief pitcher in the National League. In the 1941 World Series he threw the famous pitch that got away from Mickey Owen, the third strike that should have ended the game but instead started a Yankee rally.

It was the Yankees who released Casey after the 1949 season and made him a Cracker. That brought him full circle because he had started his pitching career with the Atlanta Crackers. Since the Yankees had released him, Casey was trying to pitch his way back to the big leagues, but he never made it. He had a good year for us, but his major league days were over.

23

The following year he blew his brains out in a hotel room in Atlanta--something about a paternity suit, I think. I didn't really know him too well--as I said, in those days the older players really didn't have that much to do with the younger players.

Anyway, facing Hugh Casey in my first at-bat with the Crackers, I hit a home run. From there things just seemed to fall into place. The third baseman on the club was supposed to be a guy named Rusty Morgan. When I got there they moved him to second base, and I was the starting third baseman. Obviously Dixie Walker liked me. And I must say everybody on the club liked him. We had a real comfortable feeling on the club, a lot like at Thomasville. Dixie made everybody happy by canceling calisthenics in favor of more batting practice. "You never can get in too much batting practice," he used to say, and nobody argued with him. Dixie could still hit. He did some pinch-hitting for us and even played a little outfield.

After we got to Atlanta, I roomed with two other Crackers, George Uhle and Harry MacPherson. We rented a small house together within walking distance of Ponce de Leon Park. I think we roomed together because we were the only single guys on the ballclub. Nobody had a car or anything, so we did a lot of walking.

Both Uhle and MacPherson were a little older than I was, maybe four or five years older. Harry had been in the Boston Braves organization for a while. He had pitched one inning for the Braves back during the war, when he was about 18 years old. He was a wiry little righthander with a mediocre fastball but a real good curve. He was a real nice guy, too.

Uhle was a pitcher too. He was actually George Uhle, Jr., and his dad had been a pitcher in the American League in the 1920's and '30's. His dad won 200 games and pitched in a World Series. His biggest contribution to baseball, though, was that he developed the original slider. I think he named it, too. He was bothered by arm trouble throughout his career, and George Junior had the same problem. In fact, that's how he ended up with the Crackers. In spring training he had been pegged as one of the Braves' starting pitchers, along with Spahn, Sain, and Bickford. He had had a real good year at Denver the previous season. But because he was having arm trouble and Boston is cold and damp in the spring, the Braves left him in Atlanta to get his arm in shape while they traveled north. George went to

24

Cleveland for some treatments during the season, but it didn't seem to help. He stayed with the Crackers until about the middle of the season and then went back to Denver in the Western League. His arm never fully recovered, and he never got to pitch in the majors.

On the last weekend before the Southern Association season started, it was traditional that the Brooklyn Dodgers, on their way north from spring training, would play a three-game exhibition series against the Crackers. It was a chance for the Atlanta ballplayers to play the major leaguers, although the Crackers usually got their butts kicked. The series the previous year--I wasn't there, of course, but I sure heard about it--made history. Jackie Robinson and Roy Campanella played for the Dodgers. Robinson had already played for Brooklyn for two years, but playing in New York City was hardly the same as playing in Georgia. There had never been a colored ballplayer in the Southern Association. Until 1949 no colored ballplayer had ever played against white ballplayers in the city of Atlanta. Before the series opener the Grand Dragon of the Georgia Ku Klux Klan announced that 10,000 people had signed a pledge to never attend another baseball game at Ponce de Leon Park if a game was played there with "mixed races." Despite the threat both Robinson and Campanella played, in violation of the unwritten "Jim Crow law," but there was no violence. Overflow crowds attended all three games.

The only time I remember the fans in the South ever getting on anybody because he was black was Jackie Robinson. They would sit up in the stands and go, "Caw, caw--blackbird!" That type of thing. But by the time I was with Milwaukee and Aaron and the rest of the guys, I didn't hear any of that. By that time all these old-timers that had gotten on Jackie Robinson were all gone. It was pretty much of a new breed.

In our series with the Dodgers, we also drew big crowds, and a lot of the people were black. I don't recall any Ku Klux Klan activity, though. In those days the seating in the ballpark was still segregated--blacks sat only in the bleachers along the third base side. But after they filled the so-called "Negro seats" for the Dodger series, they just roped off "white" areas and sat there, or stood in roped-off areas in the outfield. There was no big deal or racial fights; the ballgame just went on. The crowds were at least half black, eager to see Robinson, Campy, and Don Newcombe. The best thing I did against the Dodgers was hit a home run off Newcombe, but they whipped us all three games.

At the start of the league season, we didn't know what kind of club we were going to have. Most of us didn't have enough experience to know a good team from a bad one. They had a sports editor there in Atlanta named John Bradberry, and right before opening night he called us a "ragamuffin" team, said we were "the most patched-up, inexperienced Atlanta Cracker team in 50 years." Maybe he was old enough to know that, but we sure weren't. He picked us to finish fifth, but who cares? We had a new manager in Dixie Walker and a mostly new lineup. The way ballplayers come and go in the minor leagues, any kind of prediction is crazy. It's not even an educated guess.

Double-A ball, which the Southern Association was, was close enough to major league level--not close, but close enough--that you had ballplayers going in both directions, up and down. For example, Hugh Casey had pitched in the big leagues for nine years and hoped to go back; Chet Hajduk, our first baseman who broke his wrist in the spring, had pinch-hit in 1941 for the White Sox, but he knew he was never going back. Ellis Clary had been up for several years in the mid-40's but never got back. Plus we had at least eight or nine young guys like myself who made it to the big show in the next three or four years: Don Liddle, Art Fowler, Bob Thorpe, Gene Verble, Dick Hoover, Jim Rivera, and a few others. There was a lot of turnover.

Other clubs in the Southern Association were just like ours, of course. We had a few old guys pitching against us that year. Floyd Speer of Little Rock was 37, twice my age; Bobo Newsom of Chattanooga was 43; and Earl Caldwell of Birmingham was 45 years old. Old Earl was a side-armer who pitched in the National League before I was born. He still had some stuff, though. He struck me out in the opener.

Speaking of the opener, we were playing the Birmingham Barons in Ponce de Leon Park. Just like at Thomasville, we played almost all night games. That was a good idea most of the summer because it's hot in Atlanta. But in spring--this game was in mid-April--it gets cold at night. That night it was 34 degrees, and the fans were wearing parkas and covering up with blankets. The stands were only about half full because of the temperature. Birmingham was the team to beat that year in the Southern Association, or so everybody thought. They had

26

five guys in their lineup--Fred Hatfield, Joe DeMaestri, Karl Olson, Norm Zauchin, and Charlie Maxwell--within a year or two of making the big leagues, plus a pitching staff that included Leo Kiely and Boo Ferriss, both Southern League all-stars who had good major league careers.

We beat them that night, though, and I got my first hit as a Cracker. I hit a home run off Bobby Brake that put us ahead to stay. After that we scored a couple insurance runs that were set up by a beautiful double steal by Ralph Brown and Jim Rivera. I think Ralph ran a country store for a while and then became a sheriff someplace in Georgia. Rivera played a little first base for us, and later he became one of the best base-steal-ers in the American League. He only stayed with the Crackers for a couple weeks and then got sent down to Pensacola. Jim had some tough times. He had served five years in the Atlanta Penitentiary for criminal assault, although he said he was innocent. I got along with him real well in the time I knew him.

The winning pitcher in our opening game--he pitched the complete game--was Art Fowler, who became a very good friend of mine that year. For some reason we just hit it off, and we did a lot of running around together. Art is one of these Ernest Hemingway characters. He's fun to be around. He had a good career in the big leagues pitching for Cincinnati and the Angels. He had an older brother who pitched a little in the big leagues. Art is well-known now for being Billy Martin's pitching coach wherever he managed. He and Billy were just about inseparable. With the Crackers Art promised Dixie Walker that he'd win 20 games if he gave him enough starts. He ended up winning 19, I think, unless he won another one in the playoffs. He was our best pitcher for the year. Right after the All-Star game he announced that he wasn't going to lose another game all year. Then he pitched a one-hitter in his next start. He did lose a couple more, but one was the night his son was born in South Carolina and he was kind of distracted because he could not be with his wife that night. Art had a hell of a year.

After our opening series with the Barons, we took the train to Birmingham and played three games in their park, Rickwood Field. That was my first real road trip as a ballplayer. Rickwood Field was an interesting ballpark to play in. It's still standing today, I think, the oldest ballpark in the country. It was modeled after Forbes Field in Pittsburgh, and it was a good park for me to hit in. Left field and center field were deep, but right field was only about 335 feet. It also had railroad tracks running past the fence out beyond right field, just like in Ponce de Leon.

When we got to Birmingham, I was wondering if I'd ever get another hit. I only had one hit in our first series--that home run on opening night. And I had two errors in one of those games. I was so green that I had never experienced a slump before, not that a couple games is a slump. I remember telling George Uhle I was ready to pack up and head back to Santa Barbara. I was just a hot-headed kid, 18 years old. George talked with me and settled me down, told me how good I was, blah blah blah, and convinced me to stay. That first night in Rickwood, I hit two long home runs, and after that I was fine; everything fell into place.

One time later in the season we were playing at Rickwood again, and Art Fowler was pitching. It seems to me it was a day game, and God, it was hot. Along about the seventh inning our pitching coach, Whitlow Wyatt, went out to the mound and said, "What's the matter, Art?" because Art was really flushed. He looked like something was wrong.

Art said, "I've had it. This is too much. I feel like I'm gonna faint."

Wyatt pointed up toward the flagpole and said, "If you look up there, there is a breeze."

Art looked around and said, "Yeah, but I'm not pitching on top of that flagpole." Wyatt went back to the dugout. Art threw one more pitch and--Bang! He collapsed right on the pitching mound. They helped him to the clubhouse. He was all right, though, once they got him some ice, and maybe some bourbon to dilute it.

Birmingham was hot, but our hottest moments of the season came from Mobile--not the city, and not because of the temperature and the humidity. We just never got along with the Mobile Bears. I'm not sure why. They weren't near us in the standings or anything. We just didn't like them.

The first time they came into Ponce de Leon Park, we played them in a Sunday afternoon doubleheader, in early May. In the first game their pitcher was a guy named Chuck Eisenmann. He was throwing a spitter. We could all see it. Whitlow Wyatt, our pitching coach, was really screaming about it, and pretty soon so was Dixie Walker. I guess Eisenmann did not like that, or maybe all of a sudden he lost his control, but

28

anyway he threw one up and in on Ralph Brown, our center-fielder. In those days beanballs really weren't--they were brush-backs or whatever--but Ralph hit the dirt, and when he got up he was steaming. He took his bat and kind of flung it, not at anybody, just in disgust. Then he yelled some things at the pitcher.

Well, while they were cussing at each other, Wyatt walked out of the coaching box and retrieved the bat and threw it toward the pitcher. I don't really think he was trying to hit him; it was more or less of a warning. When that happened, a riot broke out! Both benches emptied, and it was crazy. It seemed like everybody on the field was punching and taking punches. I got hooked up with the Mobile manager, a guy named Chervinko. I nailed Chervinko, and then I got in another beef with a player--I couldn't tell you his name.

Meanwhile the police were all out on the field. Really, though, they let us go at it. They didn't try to break anything up particularly, at least for a while. Finally after we'd all had some pretty good pops and been hit with some too, they broke it up. And of all people, the umpires decided I was the guy they were going to throw out. They could have thrown out both teams. Everybody was fighting. We lost the ballgame, too, but we won the second game and I hit a home run.

A week later we played the Bears again, this time in Hartwell Field in Mobile, but there were no more fights. It was more the opposite. We spent most of the time laughing. What happened was, the Mobile team wore shorts during the ball-game. It was kind of an experiment, the first time anybody in the Southern Association wore them. The idea actually had started about a month before that in the Pacific Coast League. Fred Haney's team, the Hollywood Stars, were the first ones to wear shorts. It was Fred's idea. He said his players would be able to run faster in shorts. Be able to, or have to, Fred? Anyway, the Hollywood and Mobile clubs were both in the Brooklyn Dodger organization under Branch Rickey, so the Bears experimented with them, too.

Well, we had a field day! You never heard so much bench jockeying in your life. In those days the ballplayers wore sliding pads. Those guys had to put these sliding pads on underneath the shorts, so it made their butts about twice as wide. And every once in a while the sliding pad would slip down below the shorts and hang out. We had a great time teasing them. They didn't

29

like it, but they were too embarrassed to say much. Nowadays kids and basketball players wear these Spandex things hanging out under their shorts, but in those days we had never seen anything like that.

We didn't get into it that day, but a few months later we had a rematch of our brawl with the Bears. It was back in Atlanta, and it was another doubleheader. We were coming to bat, and as the teams passed each other, Whitlow Wyatt made a comment to their pitcher, Marion Fricano, because Fricano had been giving our pitcher, Don Liddle, a lot of abuse. When Wyatt said that, he was overheard by Chuck Eisenmann, who had been coaching first base. Eisenmann said something and then took a swing at Wyatt.

That's all it took. Pretty soon everybody was on the field, fighting and punching. This time Dixie Walker decked Chervinko. The whole thing went on for ten minutes, and then the police finally stopped it. But after everything had calmed down, old Whitlow had Eisenmann in a headlock, a choke hold, and he would *not* let go of the guy. Four cops tried to pull him off, but they couldn't. Finally one of the cops took his billyclub and said, "If you don't let go of this guy I'm gonna whack you, Whitlow!" So Whitlow finally let go of the guy because everybody knew everybody, even the cops. The one guy that got thrown out of the game was Eisenmann, for tossing the first punch. And the only one that really got hurt was Whitlow, who got spiked by somebody.

The Crackers were not just a bunch of fighters, though; we could play. We got off to a good start and pretty much stayed in front all season. One of the reasons we got off to such a good start was Ebba St. Claire, our catcher. Ebba was really a piece of work.

Ebba had been in the Pittsburgh organization at one time, with the New Orleans Pelicans. Dixie Walker was with the Pirates then, so they met in spring training. After that Ebba quit--he left and went to Canada and played semi-pro for a year. Now he was back, and thanks to Dixie, he was hitting the lights out. Dixie taught him to slow his swing down, to go to the opposite field instead of pulling everything and trying to hit home runs. As a result Ebba hit over .400 for the first couple months. Then he gradually tailed off and ended up at .280, but he drove in over a hundred runs for us. He really carried us in the early part of the year.

30

Usually the Crackers beat the pants off the other team.
This is Ralph Brown, Hank Ertman, Ebba, and me.
(Atlanta Journal-Constitution)

Ebba had his little quirks, though. For example, he was very superstitious. He had a thing about bird feathers. He used to go around the playing field before the game and pick up any feathers he found on the ground. And things always seemed to be happening to him. One day he fouled a pitch back over the grandstand and broke the windshield of a car--and it was his car! And then a few days later he sprained his ankle. He must have missed a feather that week or something. Ebba played a few years with the Braves, but he never really had a lot of success. When we were in Milwaukee he opened up a little restaurant, kind of a diner type. I think he called it "The Home Plate." He had us come out there and sign autographs and sign the walls, but the restaurant never went over for him either.

31

Another big reason for our success was Ellis Clary. Ellis had played a few years with the St. Louis Browns. He was on the same team as Pete Gray, the one-armed ballplayer. Ellis didn't start the season with us. He came over from Chattanooga after a few weeks and did a great job at second base. He was a feisty little guy. We got him after Chattanooga suspended him because he went after the umpires after a ballgame. He tried to talk to them and they locked the door of their dressing room, so he kicked the door down. The owners didn't like that, so they got rid of him. That was their mistake.

Ellis started a hell of a fight in a game in Atlanta. He was a tough little monkey. A guy hit a double and pulled what they do now all the time. The guy went around first base, and when he came into second, he had his hands up in a victory signal, plus he was doing a little dance--a little hotdog move. Ellis just walked up and knocked the guy's front tooth out. He never did that dance around Ellis again.

Ellis is an interesting guy, but he's had some health problems. I used to run into him quite a bit when I was scouting. He was a scout, too. One day he had a heart attack. As they were taking him off in the ambulance, he told a fellow scout that was there, "Get the mileage," because we all got mileage when we were scouting. He was fun. He's been a lifelong friend.

Ellis and Ebba were both selected to the All-Star team for us, Ebba unanimously. So was Art Fowler, and so was our shortstop, Gene Verble. And so was I, although not as the third baseman. I was selected as the "extra infielder." As it turned out, though, the Crackers were in first place at the all-star break, so we played the all-stars from all the other clubs, and we hosted it. They gave each of the players a gold watch. We had a huge crowd, so they roped off part of the outfield and people stood out there and watched. Ebba drove in three runs and we won the game. But that's not the real story.

The big story of the game was our pitcher--Whitlow Wyatt. Old Whit was 43 years old and hadn't pitched in five years since he was with the Phillies, but he was our starting pitcher against the All-Stars. The year before that they had passed a rule that every team had to have at least one player on the All-Star team, just like the major leagues. This year New Orleans didn't have anybody. The league president, Charlie Hurth, decided it wasn't fair to drop anybody who had been chosen, so he let them add one extra player, the guy from New Orleans. To be fair he also let Dixie Walker add one more to our roster, so Dixie added Whitlow.

As soon as Dixie announced who his starting pitcher would be, some of the writers around the league started moaning, saying it was wrong, that it would make the game a farce, and so forth. So what did Whit do? He pitched four innings and only gave up one run. In one inning he had the bases loaded and two out, and he struck out the league's leading hitter, Pat Haggerty. He did so well that some people suggested Dixie should add him to our roster for the rest of the season. Dixie just said, "I can't think of better way for a man to make his exit from baseball than Whit just did."

Whit was very popular in Atlanta before that, and the All-Star game just added to it. He had a farm outside of Atlanta that he worked during the day, and then he came to the ballpark for the games. They had a Whitlow Wyatt Night for him during the season. The people from the little town where he lived presented him with a wristwatch and a shotgun. Practically the whole town showed up.

Whit was not only a nice guy but also a tough guy. When you'd see him in the clubhouse with his shirt off, he had three scars across his back by his shoulder blades. We didn't know why until one day somebody asked him about it. He'd had a bad back or shoulder that was hurting his pitching, he said. Whoever he went to took a red-hot poker and just laid it on his back three times across there. He had three scars maybe ten inches long and an inch wide, in a pattern right across his back. That was what he went through just to try to keep his arm, to keep pitching. Guys would try anything. One year George Uhle used horse liniment. He'd put that stuff on and start perspiring, and nothing else could hurt any worse than that. If your arm went you were out of work, so pitchers would try anything.

One of the reasons I was voted to the All-Star team, and one of the reasons I was chosen Rookie of the Year in the Southern Association, is that I hit some fairly long home runs. That really isn't a big deal; we all hit them. But fans, and especially sportswriters, get excited about long home runs. When you talk about Mickey Mantle, you talk about the 565-foot home run he hit out of Griffith Stadium in Washington. Or with Joe Adcock, you talk about the one he hit into the centerfield seats at the Polo Grounds, or the one he hit over the

33

grandstand at Ebbets Field. Well, I hit some with the Crackers.

The one that seemed to get the most attention, the one that everybody I've talked to since in Atlanta claims to have seen, was the one into the magnolia tree. See, Ponce de Leon Park had kind of a funny shape. The scoreboard was out in left center, and it had to be 500 feet away. You could never hit one over it. Center field was deep too, and to the right of dead center there was no fence. There was a steep slope, and up the slope was a big magnolia tree. I hit one early in the season that landed in the magnolia tree. That got people talking.

About a month after that, I hit one in Joe Engel Stadium in Chattanooga that the writers said was one of the longest ever hit there. It was over the right centerfield fence, which was 420 feet away and twenty-some feet high, and it cleared it by about ten feet. But that ball was a fastball. See, to hit a long ball you need bat speed and strength and all that, but you also need some velocity on the pitch. Otherwise it's harder to hit for distance. Little Rock had a pitcher by the name of Floyd Speer, an older guy. He was in his late thirties, and he didn't have much arm left. He threw me a blooper pitch one time, and I almost screwed myself into the ground trying to hit it. Then he threw me a couple more and I was able to time it. I hit the last one about as hard as you can hit a ball. It went for a home run, but only over the second row of signs in Atlanta. You just don't get the distance off the slow stuff.

The only home run I hit that actually earned me any money was in Memphis. The Memphis Steam Laundry was located next to the ballpark, and they had a deal--if you hit their big brick smokestack, you'd win a thousand dollars. I missed that thing by about ten feet. I don't know if anybody ever did hit it. I hit the roof of their building, though, so I won $200. The next night when I came up to bat the first time, they stopped the game and awarded me a check.

I'll mention one other home run. In Pelican Stadium in New Orleans, I hit one over the centerfield fence, which believe it or not was closer than either foul line, but still well over 400 feet. They said I was the first one to do it since Ted Williams, which was flattering but was really neither here nor there. But the guy I hit it off was an 18-year-old lefthander from Los Angeles just two months out of high school. His name was Paul Pettit. He had signed a $100,000 bonus contract with the Pittsburgh organization, one of the first bonus babies. He was a

34

tall kid with a strong arm, but he wasn't ready for Double-A ball. Because of the bonus rule, though, he had to be moved up quickly through the organization. The following year he was with the Pirates, but he developed arm trouble. A couple years later he was washed up, trying to make it as an outfielder and first baseman in the Pacific Coast League. His total number of wins as a big league pitcher--one. I never regretted signing for only $6,000.

One factor that affected the home runs was the ball. In those days they used what they called a "97" ball. It was the same size, but it was wound differently, and you'd get another 10 or 15 feet with it. It would be like today if you used an aluminum bat, you'd get a little extra distance with it. They used the "97" ball in the Southern Association and I think the Texas League. Whether it was cheaper or what the reason for it was I don't know, but you could hit it farther.

As my home run total increased, so did the number of opinions about my future with the Braves organization. The Braves' scout in the southeast part of the country, Gil English, said, "Ed Mathews is a great prospect, but he'll never go to the big leagues as a third baseman. They'll have to switch him to the outfield." Jake Flowers, the president of the Milwaukee Brewers, the Braves' Triple-A farm club, said I had a swing like Johnny Mize, with "a great follow-through." Harry Jenkins, the director of the Braves' farm system, called me "the best prospect in the Southern Association in the last ten years."

I usually didn't pay all that much attention to what the so-called experts said. Just in case, though, I had Dixie Walker around keeping an eye on me, making sure I kept my mind on the game and my head didn't start to swell up. Dixie was asked by a sportswriter what he thought of my future in baseball. Dixie paused to think for a minute, then drawled, "He has a peculiar way of throwing." Dixie was very important to me.

Not everything that happened during that season was positive. In New Orleans in late June I was playing third base and a guy named Bob Ganss was batting. I was playing in fairly close, I suppose because he wasn't one of the league's better hitters, or maybe I was expecting him to bunt. Later in my career I usually played a deep third base because I had a strong arm and I could make the plays. Anyway, Ganss just ripped one that skipped off the grass on one hop and smashed into the middle of my face. I couldn't even react quick enough to get my glove up. I guess that's why they call it the "hot corner."

I dropped down like I'd been shot. Blood started pouring out of my nose as if somebody opened a faucet. Believe me, it hurt like hell. They got an ambulance and transported me to New Orleans Hospital. I was sure that when they washed the blood away, they'd find a new nostril. George Uhle rode in the back with me and tried to keep my spirits up. I spent the next several days in the hospital while the club went on to Mobile. Nobody flew in those days; a few days later I took the train back to Atlanta to join the club there. It was just a broken nose, but I missed six days in all.

After I started playing again, I began to have trouble with my feet. I was a mess. I had to cut my shoes so I could get my feet in them to play. I didn't know what the hell it was, and we didn't really have a team doctor--more like a trainer. Finally, I said, "This is ridiculous," and I went to see a doctor who sometimes worked with the ballplayers. He asked me what had happened to me. I said, "Well, I broke my nose, and when I left the hospital they gave me shots of penicillin."

He still at that time--this was 1950--didn't know that somebody could be allergic to penicillin. People didn't know about allergies in those days. He didn't really do anything for me--I just kind of got over it gradually. A little while after that for some reason--I don't think it involved baseball--I got another shot of penicillin. The same thing happened, and at this point they realized I was allergic to it. In those days they never asked if you were allergic to anything--they just hit you with whatever they thought would help.

Late in the season I got hurt again, but not seriously. Bert Flammini of Nashville threw me a high inside fastball, and as I spun out of the way I caught my spikes or something and twisted my knee and ankle. I only missed a couple days, but one was the Crackers' home finale. Earl Mann had designated that as "Ty Cobb Night." Cobb and his wife came in from their home in California. The mayor and the lieutenant governor were there, and Mrs. Cobb pulled a cord and unveiled a huge plaque honoring Cobb.

They had a big pregame ceremony, and we were all out there. It was very exciting for us. Cobb was not a very emotional-type guy--he didn't come into the dugout and start "Hi, hi,..." and slap people on the back. But we did get to meet him. He wasn't feisty or anything. He was just a quiet man. I

36

know he enjoyed it, and so did we. A few years later when I was with the Braves I got a letter from Cobb. He mentioned that night and the fact that I didn't play in that game. But he said he had watched me play and he admired my skills. Receiving that letter was a thrill. It's one of my most prized possessions.

The ballgame that night was satisfying too, even though I wasn't able to play. We finished our home season with a victory, and our pitcher, Charlie Gorin, just graduated from the University of Texas, threw a one-hitter against Nashville. And as a final touch, the losing pitcher was my old beanball buddy from Chicago, ex-Brave Red Barrett, now on his way down.

A week later we clinched the pennant and finished our season on the road, four games in front of Birmingham. The playoff structure was the same as the year before at Thomasville, so we played the Memphis Chicks and Birmingham played Nashville. We swept Memphis four straight. I had a really good series. Nashville, meanwhile, surprised Birmingham and beat them in five. That was bad news for us.

For some reason the Crackers had had trouble with Nashville for years. Until we won a game there in July, Atlanta hadn't beaten Nashville in their park in two years. Their ballpark was the most unusual I ever saw. It was a freak. It was called Sulphur Dell, and it really was a big hole in the ground. It got its name from the smell of a dump that used to be across the street. The playing field was below street level, so you can imagine how hot it got there without any breeze. The fans sat so close to the field that you could hear them chewing. The strangest feature, though, was right field. There wasn't any.

They had about a 25-foot hill in right field. It started only a little ways beyond first base and gradually went up. Then it went up at about a 45-degree angle for a ways and then leveled off about half way up. There was a little ledge that the rightfielder could actually stand on if he wanted to, but it was only about ten feet wide at the most. Then it slanted up again at about 45 degrees to the top, to the fence.

The rightfielder had to play so shallow that if you hit him a line drive one-hopper, he could throw you out at first. That's what happened to me. I hit a really hard grounder between the first and second basemen, and Paul Mauldin, their rightfielder, picked it up and threw me out. Another time Dixie Walker was playing right field there, standing on the ledge. He tried to charge a base hit, but his feet got tangled. He rolled head-over-heels down to the bottom, and the batter got an extra-base hit. It was wild.

Whether it was their crazy ballpark or the Nashville jinx or what, I don't know, but they beat us in five games. Each game they beat us was by one run. I hit a couple home runs in the first few games, but in the last two I started feeling very sick. The final game went 14 innings, but I had to be taken out in about the fifth or sixth inning. I was so weak I couldn't stand up, and I had a high temperature. It turned out I had pneumonia. I don't know how I got it. If I knew I wouldn't have done it.

April 18, 1950

On the eve of the 1950 Southern Association season, sports columnist John Bradberry of *The Atlanta Constitution* called the Atlanta Crackers "a ragamuffin outfit." He derided the club as "the most patched-up and inexperienced Atlanta Cracker team" in half a century. Among the reasons he cited was the fact that the club's regular third baseman, Rusty Morgan, had been shifted to second base. The change was made to accommodate a muscular 18-year-old third base prospect named Eddie Mathews, whose total professional experience consisted of 63 games in Class D the previous summer.

Mathews' third at-bat on opening night showed why he was in the lineup. The young slugger blasted a tie-breaking home run over the last row of signs beyond right field in Ponce de Leon Park. His team never trailed after that. Mathews went hitless the next night, but the Crackers still beat the heavily-favored Birmingham Barons for the second straight time. The following night, however, Mathews made two errors and again went 0-for-4 as the Barons beat the Atlantans. The despondent teenaged slugger entertained thoughts of returning to his home in California. Fortunately he was dissuaded from leaving by his roommate.

Having beaten the Barons twice in the opening three-game series in Atlanta, Mathews and the Crackers hit the road for a three-game set in the Barons' home park. Rickwood Field in Birmingham was the first concrete and steel minor league ballpark built in America. It opened in August of 1910, a month and a half after Comiskey Park, but it was patterned after Pittsburgh's Forbes Field. Rickwood was home to both the Barons and the Negro Southern League version of the Barons. Cracker manager Dixie Walker made his home in Birmingham, and Eddie Mathews wasted no time in showing that he felt at home there as well.

In the top of the first inning of the Barons' home opener, Atlanta first baseman Ralph "Country" Brown lined a single to right with two out. Mathews then put his team ahead 2-0 with a home run into the rightfield bleachers off Barons' righthander Jim Atkins. It was Mathews' second hit of the season and his second home run.

Leading 3-2 after three innings, the Crackers blew the game open with a five-run burst in the fourth, helped by some shoddy fielding by the Barons. Catcher Ebba St. Claire started the inning by grounding to second baseman Fred Harrington, who booted the ball. Rusty Morgan rifled a double to right field, but Charlie "Paw Paw" Maxwell muffed it, allowing Morgan to reach third and St. Claire to score. Cracker pitcher Al Henencheck, making his first start in the Southern League, then singled home Morgan with the eventual winning run to make it a 5-2 ballgame.

Birmingham skipper Pinky Higgins went to his bullpen and brought in Red Swanson, who retired Gene Verble. Dixie Walker, however, in one of his occasional appearances in the Atlanta lineup, laced a run-scoring two-base hit. Then with two out, Mathews provided the exclamation point with his second towering home run of the night, scoring his manager ahead of him and making the score 8-2.

Before the night was over Mathews added the first non-homer base hit of his Cracker career, a single in the top of the sixth. His teammate Leon Culberson contributed a two-run home run in the eighth inning, and thanks to four and one-third innings of strong relief by Norman Brown, the Crackers had a 10-4 victory and an early share of first place. The main topic of conversation, though, was Atlanta's 18-year-old power-hitting third baseman. Eddie Mathews was actually being compared by some people with such legendary Southern Association sluggers as Babe Barna, Chuck Workman, and Swish Sawatski. Mighty big shoes for a young man to fill.

April 18, 1950

ATLANTA	AB	R	H	BI	BIRMINGHAM	AB	R	H	BI
Verble, ss	5	0	1	0	Harrington, 2b	4	0	0	0
Walker, rf	5	1	2	1	Hatfield, 3b	3	1	1	1
R. Brown, 1b	4	1	1	0	Maxwell, rf	3	0	2	0
Mathews, 3b	5	2	3	4	Lavigne, lf	3	0	0	1
Rivera, cf	4	1	2	0	Zauchin, 1b	5	0	0	0
Culberson, lf	5	1	1	2	Olson, cf	4	1	1	0
St. Claire, c	5	2	2	0	DeMaestri, ss	4	0	1	1
Morgan, 2b	3	1	1	0	Mathis, c	4	1	1	1
Henencheck, p	3	1	1	2	Atkins, p	1	1	1	0
N. Brown, p	1	0	0	0	Swanson, p	2	0	0	0
					Damman, ph	1	0	1	0
Totals	40	10	14	9	Totals	34	4	8	4

Damman singled for Swanson in ninth.

```
ATLANTA ..................... 2 1 0  5 0 0  0 0 2--10
Birmingham ................. 1 0 1  0 1 0  0 1 0-- 4
```

E--Harrington, Maxwell, N. Brown, Morgan. 2B--Walker, Atkins, Morgan, St. Claire. 3B--St. Claire, DeMaestri. HR--Mathews 2, Mathis, Culberson. DP--Verble, Morgan and R. Brown; Harrington and DeMaestri; Verble and R. Brown. Left--Atlanta 6, Birmingham 10. SB--Rivera. BB--Off Henencheck 5, Atkins 2, Swanson 2, N. Brown 2. SO--By Henencheck 2, Atkins 2, Swanson 1, N. Brown 6. HO--Atkins 8, with 6 runs in 3 innings; Henencheck 4, with 3 runs in 4 2-3. WP--Swanson. Balk--Atkins, Henencheck 2. W--N. Brown (1-0). L--Atkins (0-1). U--Girard, Delmore and Fields. T--2:36. A--14,067 (paid).

THREE

In the Navy

I was a pretty sick puppy dog, but I really didn't know how sick. I just didn't know what the hell was wrong. I was really dragging, but it's so hot in the South in the summer that you can't tell if it's the heat or if it's you. During the season there had been other times when we all felt tired and kind of listless. In fact, for a while my roommates and I were even drinking Hadacol.

At that time Hadacol was real popular. It was one of these old tonics, a patent medicine that you take for anything and everything. A state senator from Louisiana invented it and sold it all throughout the South. His name was Dudley LeBlanc, and he made millions of dollars peddling that stuff. Later he got in trouble for making false advertising claims about it. George and Harry and I helped the senator make his fortune--we bought a case of that stuff and starting drinking it to try to keep our energy up. We'd take a little shooter of it every day. We didn't know at the time that it had a high alcohol content or we might have drunk more of it.

What I had, though, Hadacol wouldn't cure. On the train ride back to Atlanta I decided I'd better get checked out. The doctor that worked with the ballplayers took a look at me and put me in the hospital in Atlanta. While I was in the hospital, I had a friend of mine buy me a car. He wasn't a ballplayer, just an acquaintance I'd made in Atlanta. I had never owned a car before and didn't know much about them, but he supposedly did, so he did the shopping. He bought me an old black Ford coupe. When I got out of the hospital, I packed up my few belongings and took off for Santa Barbara.

41

I shouldn't have, though. I wasn't feeling very good the whole time. I had gotten some pills and all that crap to take, but they didn't help much. I probably should have stayed in Atlanta for another couple weeks. To add to my misery, the stupid car was giving me trouble, heating up on me all the time. I managed to make it to Dallas, where my dad's relatives lived. I stayed there a few days, trying to recuperate, and while I was there my cousin's husband, Monty, took the car apart and redid the radiator. That's what was wrong with it. After that I drove to California, across the desert Southwest, in my broken-down old Ford jalopy, just like the family in *The Grapes of Wrath.*

I was still sick when I got to Santa Barbara, but it was good to be home with my family. After a week or two I gradually recovered, and I took a job at the lumberyard in town, but I knew it would only be temporary. A few months earlier the North Korean Communists had crossed the 38th parallel and invaded South Korea. President Truman had responded by sending U.S. air and naval forces to support South Korea. The war seemed very distant to me, but I knew it was about to change my life. I had just turned 19, prime draft age.

In those days the draft board would tell you when your number would be coming up. You could know in advance when you were going to be drafted. I had a group of buddies from high school, six or seven of us, that all knew we were going to be drafted before the time when I was supposed to play baseball again. For some strange reason--don't try to figure out young minds--we didn't feel like we wanted to go in the Army. It would have been a shorter tour of duty--three years instead of four--but the whole bunch of us decided we would enlist in the Navy together. I guess it just sounded better. We enlisted there in Santa Barbara--no waiting, immediate seating--right after Christmas. They didn't really give you a physical until after you were in. We were sworn in together and sent to the Naval Training Center in San Diego.

When we had enlisted, they promised us we could all stick together. As we became a little more aware of how things work, though, we found out they had lied to us. They just told us that to get us to enlist. Everybody got split up. One guy went to electronics, one guy got sent to communications, and so on. And I ended up playing baseball.

Before I enlisted I never contacted the Braves organization, and they never contacted me. They never advised me in

42

any way, like saying, "Go in the Army. Get drafted. Your tour of duty will be shorter, and you'll be playing baseball sooner." I was entirely on my own. But what happened, after boot camp, the Navy found out that I had played some professional baseball. For all I know the Braves might have told the Navy. I don't know. But when it came time to "ship out," they wouldn't let me. My buddies all shipped out, and I was still in the training center.

Our commander, it turned out, was a big sports buff. He wanted the best football team and the best baseball team in the 11th Naval District, which included the Marine Corps and the Navy. He said, "You're going to be here for the rest of your tour, so you might as well play baseball." I said no.

"I told those guys I was going to ship out with them," I said. "I'm not going to play ball."

They told me I was going to either play baseball for the Naval Training Center baseball team or be sent to Camp Elliott, an old Marine barracks in San Diego. Camp Elliott was really a pit--nobody wanted to go there. It was used as a disciplinary measure. They sent people there who weren't exactly conforming. I still refused to play ball, so I shipped out with a few other non-conformists to Camp Elliott. They basically said, "You're going to stay out here until you decide to play baseball." So now after a few weeks everybody started to leave, and that's when I said, "Okay, I'll play baseball." I figured otherwise the next thing would be bamboo splints under my fingernails.

After I had been playing ball for a short time with the training center team, Pete Whisenant showed up and joined the team, too. I had met Pete in Evansville when I was with them briefly in 1949. It was a happy surprise to see Pete. He had enlisted in North Carolina. As we got moved around into the baseball company, he and I worked together. You know, we did not just play baseball. We still had our duty orders and responsibilities. We ended up taking care of the pool hall and the base bowling alley. We'd go in and swab it down every morning and wax it and polish it. I guess you call it special service. We put in our day before we went out to play baseball. That was our contribution to the war effort.

Before a ballgame one day I suffered my only service-related injury. We were warming up, and three guys in the outfield thought they were going to be funny. I was at third base, and they all threw balls at me at the same time and then yelled, "Hey, Eddie, turn around!"

One of the balls caromed off the bridge of my nose. I was transported to the infirmary on the base to get it treated. This medic or whoever he was said, "We're going to set this."

I asked him, "Aren't you going to give me something?"

"No," he said, "in the Navy we use a term called intestinal fortitude," and he went "djjttt" and tried to put it in place. It didn't straighten out. I ended up taking a leave for a week to have a plastic surgeon in Santa Barbara straighten it out. He did a number on it.

The quality of baseball we played in the service was actually pretty good. I'd say it was about on a Double-A level, pretty much the same caliber as with the Atlanta Crackers. We had some good ballplayers, even though most of them didn't pursue it. A few of them tried, but they didn't quite make it. I tried to keep track of some of them, but we lost touch over the years. Those guys, of course, stayed in the service for four years, and most of them went to war.

The Marine Corps guys that we played against also had some good ballplayers. I got acquainted with some of them. After the baseball season ended I was working in Santa Barbara in the store where my mother worked. Ralph Kiner got married to Nancy Chaffee, the tennis star, in the Episcopal Church right across the street from the store. I didn't see the wedding, but I snuck in the back door of the reception to catch a glimpse. I just started looking around, and who did I run into but this marine I had played ball against and gotten to know. He said, "Yeah, I'm still in. I'm on a leave." Then he said, "Hell, if you're in the service, you'll do anything not to go over to war, particularly if you're a marine."

I didn't have to go to war. I played on the training center's baseball team for most of their season. Then one day I received orders to report to such and such a place. I went there and they told me I was being discharged. What had happened was, my father had gotten very sick. He had developed tuberculosis and been hospitalized. As an only child, I was now the sole support of the family. My mother had contacted the Red Cross, who helped her obtain a dependency discharge for me. It took about a week to process, and I was out.

After my discharge the team went on to win the 11th Naval District championship without me, which shows how

44

valuable I was. Whisenant finished the season, but shortly afterward he also received a dependency discharge. Later they sent me a little championship plaque for winning, even though I wasn't there at the end.

Actually I was a little embarrassed that I got special privileges because I was a ballplayer and also that I got discharged after only six months, even though I wanted out. All of my buddies that enlisted with me came back after four years and started telling horror stories about what they had gone through--and I was lucky. They all went to war. Bob Bates, who is my closest friend, spent three years on a destroyer over in Korea. He did the whole nine yards--the shelling and the shooting match and everything. He had a rough tour. If I had stayed in for four years, there's no way I'd have accomplished what I did in baseball. Things just fell right for me, like an outhouse mouse.

After my discharge I returned to Santa Barbara for a couple days, visited my dad, and then flew to Milwaukee to resume my baseball career. Why Milwaukee? Good question. No one ever told me why. Harry Jenkins, the Boston Braves' farm director, just sent me a message saying I should report there, and voila! I was a Milwaukee Brewer. Ballclubs in those days didn't offer the ballplayers a lot of explanations, especially not 19-year-old minor league ballplayers, and frankly, I didn't ask.

Kids growing up today would have a hard time understanding the "good old days." I never questioned somebody in authority who told me what I was supposed to do--well, hardly ever. Whether it was my dad or my manager or the Braves' farm director, I did what they told me. I was just happy to be doing something I liked, playing professional baseball. I just hoped I could do well when they asked me to do something.

When I joined the Brewers, it was like when I had joined the Hi-Toms in mid-season--they were a very good ballclub, in first place, on their way to a pennant. Milwaukee's manager was Charlie Grimm, and he was wonderful. He had managed the Chicago Cubs to three pennants, so his baseball credentials were beyond question. Most of all, though, Charlie loved to have fun. He used to say, "Here's a bat and a ball and a glove. Go out and have fun." That was his philosophy of managing. Charlie loved to drink beer and play the banjo and sing songs in a phony German accent. I'm sure he was the most popular man

45

in Milwaukee.

I was treated very well by the Brewers' players and by the organization, although I wasn't there very long. I was only with them for about three weeks, not even long enough to learn the names of the streets in the city. I lived downtown, at the Towne Hotel. The only ballplayer they had that I knew when I first got there was Bob Thorpe, who had played with the Crackers. I didn't play very much--just did a little pinch-hitting. One main reason was named Billy Klaus, known rightly as "the best-fielding third baseman in the minor leagues." The other reason was, I was out of shape.

I had been playing ball in the Navy, but that was all--playing the ballgames. Because we played after we finished our work details, we never had either the time or the interest to work out, to train, to really get in physical condition to play our best. And you don't get in shape by waxing the bowling alley. I suspect the Braves organization thought I could play at the Triple-A level, at Milwaukee, because I had done okay at Atlanta the year before. When they saw the shape I was in, they sent me back to Atlanta. That's where I went after my three weeks with Milwaukee. And as if to prove their decision was correct, in my first at-bat after rejoining Atlanta, I hit a triple. When I got to third base, I could hardly breathe.

I have two vivid recollections of that brief stay in Milwaukee. The first one is the ballpark. I had seen quite a variety of parks in my young career--big and small, new and old, even ridiculous like Sulphur Dell--but Borchert Field in Milwaukee was unique. The only word I can think of to describe it is ramshackle. The whole stadium was wood, and it looked like it had been built a hundred years ago out of used lumber. The only metal in the whole structure was probably the nails, although as old as it was, they may have used wooden pegs instead.

"Borchert Orchard," as the natives called it, had a wooden grandstand that extended down both foul lines. Depending on where you sat, you could see either left field or right field, but not both. The centerfield fence took a good poke, but the foul lines were short, 266 feet each because the park was built into one city block, completely surrounded by houses. About a third of the grandstand had no roof--it had been blown off in a windstorm years before and never replaced. That ballpark would have looked bad in Class D, let alone Triple A.

46

They had great fans, though. The ballplayers couldn't say enough about them.

The other vivid memory I have of that first Milwaukee experience was my one moment in the sun there, my only contribution to the Brewers' pennant. In the last inning of a ballgame against the Minneapolis Millers, in the second game of a doubleheader, I had a pinch-hit grand slam home run off Dave Barnhill. After the game most of the ballplayers and some fans were in this tavern kittycorner from the ballpark. People were buying me beers faster than I could drink them. Charlie Grimm came in and shook my hand and said, "Nice going, kid. We're sending you to Atlanta." Then he drank a beer with us.

The Brewers went on the road that night in the general direction of Atlanta, so I accompanied them, first to Indianapolis, then to Columbus. My last night with them I pinch-hit for Virgil Jester and singled in a run. The following morning they took off for Toledo and I took the train to rejoin the Crackers. I was back in familiar territory, but I felt like a stranger, the new kid at school. It was an entirely different ballclub. Hank Ertman was still there, Don Liddle, and a couple other guys, including my old running mate, Art Fowler. Ebba was gone, though, and so was tough little Ellis Clary, back with Chattanooga. And my roommates, Harry MacPherson and George Uhle, were gone, and since there was only a month left in the season, I took a room by myself at the Ponce de Leon Hotel, right near the ballpark.

I didn't like that as well as having roommates. George and Harry and I always got along real well. Besides that, there was another advantage. George had gotten some work done on his teeth, and he got to know the dental hygienist. They started dating, and she turned out to be a neatness fanatic--like Felix from "The Odd Couple." Whenever she came over to see George she used to clean the apartment. She didn't stop there, though. She used to stock up the refrigerator while we were on the road. We'd come back and there would be ham and cheese and bread and milk and beer and cigars and every damn thing you could think of. And while we were at the ballpark, she'd come over and straighten everything up. It was terrific--she was a wonderful girl.

Then George broke up with her. Well, Harry and I didn't want to see her go. I must have spent at least a month trying to get them back together again. I'd go and tell her how much

47

George liked her, and so she'd come back, and then he'd get rid of her, and then I'd have to try to get her back again. I guess she finally got tired of it, but I hated to see her go. George and I always laughed about that.

George and I had some good times together. One night in New Orleans we were out on the town with Hank Ertman, three young kids with time on their hands and nothing between the ears. We ended up on Bourbon Street in one of those come-on joints that have a back room partitioned off where you sit and drink with the girls. Theoretically these are not prostitutes; you just buy them drinks and stuff like that. Ertman had his option check with him, and he talked them into cashing it in this den of iniquity. The champagne was flowing, and we dropped a bundle with these honeys.

At the end of the evening, we made our way back to the St. Charles Hotel, which had an excellent name but was only half air-conditioned--and naturally we were in the wrong half. With the heat and humidity, we woke up the next morning with some god-awful hangovers. George still claims that Hugh Casey, who was his roommate on the road, saved his life. Casey went out and brought back a big bottle of aspirin and a huge bucket of ice cubes.

In 1950 the Crackers had been a first-place club all season. Everything seemed to work for us. The club I was joining now was in sixth place and struggling to get up to .500. They had some hitting--Jack Dittmer and Chuck Tanner in particular were having good years, and Hank Ertman was near .300. Don Liddle was having another good year pitching, but the pitching overall was down. Hugh Casey was missed in the bullpen. The whole chemistry of the team seemed different.

Dixie Walker was the manager when I got back, but he had just returned a few days before I did. Dixie had been suspended at the end of June for arguing a call at home plate in a game with (who else?) the Mobile Bears. The umpire called the Mobile runner out but then reversed himself and claimed interference by the catcher. A huge argument followed, during which Crackers pitcher Joe Reardon swallowed his chewing tobacco and had to receive medical treatment. Dixie called the umpire every name he could think of and then pulled his team off the field.

Because the Crackers would not return to the field, the game was declared a forfeit. The president of the Southern

48

Ponce de Leon Park, home of the Crackers. (Atlanta Journal-Constitution)

Association fined Dixie $100 and suspended him for 90 days, which would have been the rest of the season. Whit Wyatt took over the managing duties while Dixie was on suspension. Dixie appealed the suspension to minor league commissioner George Trautman, and finally after a month he lifted the fine and cancelled the suspension.

The fans and the ballplayers were mighty glad to have Dixie back, so they had a Dixie Walker Night for him just after I rejoined the team. The players chipped in and bought him a new hunting rifle. The fans and local businesses presented him with a television set and a bird dog. Dixie's parents were both there, too. His father, also called Dixie, had been a pitcher with the Washington Senators way back when Walter Johnson was just getting started. It was a nice tribute to Dixie, and besides that, we won the ballgame.

We didn't win enough of them, though. We finished below .500, 76-78, in sixth place. The Little Rock Travellers, the last-place club in 1950, finished first. Whether you're sixth or fourth or whatever really doesn't matter, of course. Because we were out of contention anyway, the parent club, the Braves,

49

called up Hank Ertman and Jack Dittmer before our schedule was completed. I stayed till the end, then got called back up to Milwaukee for the playoffs.

For the third straight year I was in post-season play. I was beginning to think it was normal, just like the New York Yankees. I arrived in time for the opening series against the Kansas City Blues, which was the Yankee farm club. In a best-of-seven series, just like the World Series, we beat them in five games. I say we--I never left the bench except for pregame warmups. They didn't need me--they had an outstanding club, probably one of the best minor league ballclubs ever. Just in the infield they had George Crowe at first, Billy Reed at second, Billy Klaus at third, Buzz Clarkson at short, plus Gene Mauch wherever they needed him. Those guys all played in the big leagues. Clarkson was the heaviest shortstop I ever saw, but he could hit the ball a ton. He was a real favorite in Milwaukee.

In the outfield the Brewers had Bob Thorpe, my team-mate from the Crackers in '50; Luis Olmo, who played quite a few seasons in the majors; and a guy named Jim Basso, who had the best power on the team. And then the pitchers--Ernie Johnson was the best in the American Association, plus they had Virgil Jester, Bert Thiel, Dick Donovan, Murray Wall, Charlie Gorin, Dick Hoover. Those were all quality pitchers. And Al Unser, the catcher (not the race car driver), was the league's most valuable player.

After Kansas City the Brewers had to beat the St. Paul Saints to make it to the Little World Series, which we did, four games to two. I pinch-hit a few times--in each of the games we lost, plus I walked and scored in the final game, which we won. The only reason I got in was the score--we beat them 17-2, so Charlie Grimm cleared the bench.

The Little World Series was for the Triple-A championship, between the winners of the American Association and the International League. In theory, then, it was to determine the best minor league club in the country and the world, although the Pacific Coast League disputed that. The Brewers' opponents were the Montreal Royals, the Brooklyn Dodger farm club managed by Walt Alston. This was the same team that a few years earlier had produced ballplayers like Jackie Robinson and Roy Campanella.

The series with Montreal was exciting, a real World Series atmosphere. The trip to Montreal was my first time outside the United States, and it was unbelievably coldup there. They postponed two ballgames because it was so cold. Milwaukee lost the first and third games, then won three in a row to take the title. The only time I left the bench was in game two in Montreal. In the ninth inning I was announced as a pinch hitter. Then the Royals changed pitchers and brought in their ace lefthander, Chris Van Cuyk. I never got to face him--Charlie sent in a pinch hitter for me. Coincidentally, six months later I finally got to bat against Van Cuyk, when he was pitching for the Dodgers, and I got my first major league hit off him.

The final game of the Little World Series was played in Borchert Field, and it was crazy. The Royals took a 10-2 lead in the third inning, but the Brewers fought back and won the game, 13-10. The winning hit was a bases-loaded triple by ex-Dodger Luis Olmo. The pitcher who gave up that triple was a lefthander by the name of Tommy Lasorda.

In the clubhouse afterwards, amid all the happy screaming and celebrating, Charlie Grimm announced loudly, in true Charlie Grimm fashion, "This is the greatest thrill of my life!" It wasn't mine. I hadn't really done anything to help them win, although I liked being there better than swabbing the pool hall. The ballplayers voted me a small share of the championship money, which was generous. I also ended up with a belt buckle. The ballclub gave everybody a belt buckle for winning the pennant. That thing must have cost about ten cents. The Braves organization was not known for--let's just say they were not big spenders. I was to be reminded of that fact more than once in the years ahead.

July 22, 1951

In late June of 1951, Eddie Mathews received his discharge from the United States Navy. On July 10 he joined the Milwaukee Brewers, the Triple-A affiliate of the Boston Braves. Charlie Grimm's Brewers boasted a talented lineup, maybe the best in baseball outside the major leagues and hardly in need of an inexperienced, teenaged third sacker. Mathews tried his hand at pinch-hitting a few times, but mainly he warmed the bench, bided his time, and waited to be returned to the Atlanta Crackers.

The Brewers stood in a virtual tie with the Saint Paul Saints for the American Association lead as they began a Sunday doubleheader with the Minneapolis Millers. A vocal crowd turned out at Milwaukee's decrepit Borchert Field to try to boost the local heroes into first place. Their beloved Brewers had taken the first two games of the series from the Millers and had won their last four games.

The opener matched Milwaukee's sidearming righthander Ernie Johnson against the dancing knuckleball of Minneapolis' Hoyt Wilhelm. The game shaped up as a pitchers' duel, and it was. The visitors manufactured their only run in the top of the first with a bunt single, a stolen base, an infield out, and a two-out single by Neil Sheridan. It looked like one run was enough as Wilhelm allowed the Brewers just three singles and no runs through eight innings.

In the last of the ninth Ernie Johnson was due to lead off, but Mathews was sent in to bat for the light-hitting hurler. He grounded to the second baseman for the first out. Third baseman Billy Klaus was quickly retired for the second out. With two strikes on Bob Thorpe, though, Wilhelm hung a

52

knuckleball and Thorpe smacked it into the left centerfield bleachers to tie the game. Reliever Virgil Jester shut out the Millers in the tenth, and with a man on second and one out in the bottom of the tenth, local favorite Buzz Clarkson pinch hit for shortstop Gene Mauch. The pudgy Clarkson bounced Wilhelm's first pitch between the third baseman and shortstop, and George Crowe lumbered home with the winning run for Milwaukee.

The second game looked a lot like the first. The Millers finally eked out a run in the fourth on a base hit, a walk, a sacrifice, and an infield out. Meanwhile Frank Fanovich held the Brewers scoreless on five hits until the sixth inning. Then his luck ran out. He walked second baseman Mark Christman. Mauch rapped a doubleplay ball to the shortstop, but he kicked it. Fanovich then nicked catcher Al Unser with a pitch to load the bases with nobody out. With pitcher Dick Donovan scheduled next, Grimm sent pinch-hitter extraordinaire Buzz Clarkson to the plate.

Clarkson was hoping to repeat his first-game heroics, but he never got the chance. Fanovich walked him on four pitches, forcing in pinch-runner Murray Wall with the tying run. Fanovich fanned Klaus, but then Thorpe hit a ball off his fists that blooped behind second for a feeble single and a 2-1 lead, with the bases still loaded. The unfortunate Fanovich was replaced by a new pitcher, Dave Barnhill. The next batter was supposed to be rightfielder Luis Olmo.

Olmo had played six years in the big leagues, interrupted for over three years by a suspension for playing in the outlawed Mexican League. He was a righthanded hitter, though, in the twilight of his career, so Grimm played a hunch and the percentages and summoned Mathews for another pinch-hitting attempt. The decision paid off handsomely. Mathews clubbed a high fly ball far over the rightfield wall for a grand slam, putting the Brewers ahead by a 6-1 score. Virgil Jester later gave up a solo home run to Dixie Howell of the Millers, but Mathews' slam proved to be the difference in a 6-2 win. The Brewers had their sweep, and Mathews had his first hit and only home run in the American Association.

July 22, 1951

Second Game

MINNEAPOLIS	AB	R	H	BI	MILWAUKEE	AB	R	H	BI
Rufer, ss	4	0	0	0	Klaus, 3b	4	0	1	0
Milne, lf	4	0	1	0	Thorpe, lf	4	1	1	1
Hofman, 2b	4	1	3	0	Olmo, rf	3	0	1	0
Sheridan, rf	2	0	0	0	Mathews, ph	1	1	1	4
Lucadello, 3b	2	0	0	0	Wooten, rf	0	0	0	0
Gilbert, 1b	2	0	0	1	Crowe, 1b	3	0	2	0
Kropf, cf	3	0	0	0	Basso, cf	3	0	1	0
Sokol, c	1	0	0	0	Christman, 2b	1	0	0	0
Howell, ph	1	1	1	1	Wall, pr	0	1	0	0
Fanovich, p	1	0	0	0	Jester, p	0	0	0	0
Barnhill, p	0	0	0	0	Mauch, 2b	4	1	1	0
Natisin, ph	0	0	0	0	Unser, c	1	1	0	0
Bowman, pr	0	0	0	0	Donovan, p	2	0	0	0
					Clarkson, ss	0	1	0	1
					Montag, ph	0	0	0	0
Totals	24	2	5	2	Totals	26	6	8	6

Wall ran for Christman in sixth; Clarkson walked
for Donovan in sixth; Mathews hit home run for
Olmo in sixth; Montag hit by pitched ball for
Wall in sixth; Howell hit home run for Sokol in
seventh; Natisin walked for Barnhill in seventh;
Bowman ran for Natisin in seventh.

```
Minneapolis .....................  0 0 0   1 0 0   1--2
MILWAUKEE .......................  0 0 0   0 0 6   *--6
```

E--Gilbert, Rufer, Sokol. 2B--Crowe, Hofman,
Basso. HR--Mathews, Howell. S--Christman, Fanovich,
Lucadello. Left--Minneapolis 7, Milwaukee 10. BB--
Off Fanovich 4, Donovan 3, Jester 1. SO--By Fanovich
6, Donovan 5, Jester 1. HO--Fanovich 6 in 5 1-3;
Barnhill 2 in 2-3; Donovan 4 in 6; Jester 1 in 1. HBP
--By Fanovich, Crowe and Unser; by Barnhill, Montag.
W--Donovan (2-2). L--Fanovich (2-5). A--4,038.

FOUR

Rocket Man

When it came to their ballplayers, the Boston Braves threw nickels around like they were manhole covers, but they did spend money in other ways. A couple years before I signed my first contract, the Braves left on a road trip, and when they came back the whole playing field in their ballpark had been lowered by a foot and a half. Why the hell they lowered the field I don't know, but Lou Perini owned a construction company-- maybe business was slow that week.

Beginning in the latter part of January of 1952, the Braves' front office dreamed up another way to spend Perini's money. Their costly brainchild, a promotional scheme worthy of Bill Veeck or maybe P.T. Barnum, was dubbed "The Rookie Rocket." What they did was charter a Pan American-World Airways B-23, a converted bomber, and fly around the country-- actually, the Caribbean plus the U.S.--to visit 18 of the Braves' hottest minor league prospects, the potential big-league rookies. They stocked the plane--excuse me, rocket--with seven intrepid travelers: Braves' publicity director Bill Sullivan; Red Marston, a veteran Boston radio announcer; and five Boston sportswriters, one of whom was nicknamed "Thirsty" and all of whom were worthy of the name.

The way this thing worked, the writers would visit each prospect, in some cases watch him play, interview him, attend some kind of banquet in his honor, and then write a column about him for their particular newspaper. One of the writers also wrote for *The Sporting News,* plus the wire services picked up reports. Sullivan carried an old wire recorder, and Marston phoned in radio reports and interviews. The idea was to create a million dollars worth of publicity for the Braves and jack up their sagging ticket sales. The success of the project can probably be gauged in the 282,000 total attendance for 1952, their worst since World War II. It was a wild idea, though. This was *Travels with Charley* a decade before John Steinbeck thought of it.

As you may have guessed, I was one of the rookies that the rocketeers chose to visit. Almost all of the others were guys who had been my teammates in Atlanta or especially in Milwaukee. The tour was scheduled to reach Santa Barbara after about a week and a half, just past the middle of the itinerary. We followed the news reports with interest and waited impatiently for "The Rocket" to strike California.

After leaving Boston, the Braves' bomber flew to Miami, then on to Havana to see my Crackers and Brewers teammate Bob Thorpe. At the airport in Havana, Thorpe was waiting for them. He was easy to spot because, as Al Hirshberg of the *Boston Post* said, "Outside of Thorpe, the only people at the airport who didn't have mustaches were women." Thorpe was playing for the Cienfuegos team, managed by Billy Herman, who later became a coach with the Milwaukee Braves when I was there. And lo and behold, who should be the best pitcher on Thorpe's club but my old nemesis, Red Barrett, who also, believe it or not, was singing in a nightclub in Havana. That guy sure got around!

In Havana the Boston writers attended a luncheon for Thorpe and managed to take in a ballgame, as well as a generous supply of daiquiris, which one of them referred to as "not a drink in Cuba, but an essential dietary ingredient." These guys were all, as I remember them, Ernest Hemingway types. They all drank, they all were fun people to be around--and they must have had a blast on that trip.

After Cuba they flew to San Juan, Puerto Rico, where they watched five of the champion Brewers who were spending the winter playing in the Puerto Rican League, including Don Liddle, George Crowe, and Billy Klaus. They also saw my Cracker teammate Jack Dittmer. The Braves had suggested that Dittmer and I both play winter ball; Jack took them up on it, but I wasn't interested. I returned to Santa Barbara and went to work in the store where my mother worked.

The rocket stop before mine was Los Angeles. The subject of interest there was Ernie Johnson, the pitching star of the Brewers' recent Little World Series victory. Johnson had won five playoff games for the Brewers to go with his 15-4 record during the regular season. Ernie was from Vermont, but he spent the off-season working for the Los Angeles Post Office. They had a luncheon in his honor at the Hotel Biltmore, attended by his wife and parents and my friend Johnny Moore.

Finally, on February 1, the Rookie Rocket touched down in Santa Barbara. That night at the Carillo Hotel we had a fancy dinner with probably a hundred or so people. There was really no main speaker or anything. A lot of different people got up and said a little something, who they were and what they were doing. The people were asking me questions, which scared the shit out of me. I just said I was looking forward to the next year. Two or three of the sportswriters got up and explained what was happening in Boston.

My former football and baseball coach, Clarence Schutte, got up and said a few words, how good a guy I was and all that happy stuff. When I was in high school, Coach Schutte was tough--mean and nasty. He literally would hit you over the head. We were all in awe of him. Now that I was out of school, though, it was altogether different. He was a hell of a lot of fun to sit and yak with. That's the way I've found a lot of people are, people in a position. They have to maintain a certain stature or whatever you call it. Once they get their tie and coat off, you find out they're a lot of fun to be with.

The unfortunate part of the evening was that my dad couldn't be there. He was too sick with tuberculosis. He would have loved every minute of that dinner. My mom, though, was the hit of the night. The sportswriters all got a big kick out of her. They said she was "vivacious and charming," and they were right. She was and still is. She was going strong all night. She and I both thought it was a really nice affair. It was no big deal, but at that time in my life and in the city of Santa Barbara, everybody got kind of excited about it.

The next morning on the way to the airport, the sportswriters stopped at the store where my mother and I were both working. They just pulled in to say goodbye before they got on the plane. One of them, John Gillooly, looked over in the corner where there was a huge bottle of scotch.

"Look at the size of that thing," he said. "I've got to have it." He bought it to take back on the plane.

The other writer that I remember vividly from that visit

is Al Hirshberg. Hirshberg wrote a book about me way, way back in the early fifties, I suppose around the end of that same year. The only reason I know about the book--because he never even asked me a question--is that it turned up in some libraries and people were starting to say, "Hey, I read your book." I looked through it, and it wasn't really all that accurate. When I say I never talked to him about it, well, I talked to him because he was one of the reporters that traveled with our club. But I never talked to him in regard to a book. What the hell, though, he was a good guy. We enjoyed all of the writers. They treated my mother and me very well.

From Santa Barbara the Rookie Rocket headed north to the state of Washington to intercept Gene Conley, the minor league player of the year, who was one of the few Braves rookies I hadn't yet played ball with. After that the Rocket criss-crossed the northern half of the United States: Denver, to meet Virgil Jester; Shawano, Wisconsin, to locate second baseman Billy Reed (Shawano, a town of maybe 5,000, had no airport so they flew to the nearby metropolis of Clintonville); St. Louis, for breakfast with Harry Hanebrink; Evansville, Indiana, to catch my Navy buddy, Pete Whisenant; and on east to New Jersey and Pennsylvania and finally Boston. The country's first long-range rocket (this was five years before Sputnik and the space race) covered 11,000 miles and cost Lou Perini more than he was paying his whole infield. I don't know if it helped the ballclub, but it sure made a bunch of young ballplayers feel important.

A month after the Rookie Rocket took off from Santa Barbara (I never did actually see the thing), I reported to the Braves' spring training camp in Bradenton, Florida, to try to make the club. My chances looked mighty slim. I had really only played baseball for two months the previous year, and with the Triple-A farm club in Milwaukee I rode the bench while Billy Klaus played third base. Now Klaus was in spring training with me, and both of us took a back seat to Bob Elliott, although Elliott was not there--he was back home in California, holding out for more money.

I ran into the Commissioner of Baseball one day. I mean, I really ran into the Commissioner of Baseball. Several of us were shagging fly balls in the outfield at old Ninth Street Park, which is where we played in Bradenton. That was part of our workout to get our running in. For some reason three guys were

Ninth Street Park in Bradenton, Florida. (Frank Stanfield photo)

Inside Ninth Street Park. To the right of the white building (our clubhouse) is where I ran into Ford Frick. (Frank Stanfield photo)

59

standing in the playing field and talking near the clubhouse: publicity director Bill Sullivan, who I knew from the Rookie Rocket; a writer for the Associated Press named Whitney Martin; and the new Commissioner, Ford Frick.

Well, Johnny Cooney was hitting fungoes to us, and one of them went over near the leftfield line. I put my head down and went charging after it. I kept my eye on the ball and tried to backhand it. The next thing I knew I was lying on the ground with blood all over me. I had caught the ball and somehow hung on to it, but my face hit Sullivan in the back of the head. He was sprawled unconscious on the grass. The Commissioner was sitting on the ground wondering what the hell hit him. I was spitting out blood, and the first thing I said was, "There goes my nose again!"

Somebody on the club drove both Sullivan and me to a doctor nearby, a Dr. Broderic Jones. He basically told Sullivan he'd be okay, he just had a bruised leg, and after he poked around at my snout he sent me to a specialist. Actually, it was not too serious, so I was playing baseball again in a couple days. It hurt like hell, but at least I had the distinction of being the only ballplayer ever to knock the Commissioner on his can, which I'm sure a lot of guys would like to have done.

I never really got to know Ford Frick. I suppose that out of all the things he ever did in 14 years as Commissioner, he's best remembered for the asterisk he demanded when Roger Maris broke Babe Ruth's single-season home run record. Frick had been a friend of Ruth's, so a lot of people thought he was unfair to Maris, which of course he was. That decision and his general do-nothing attitude made him unpopular with quite a few people.

One of the people who didn't care for Frick was the previous Commissioner, Happy Chandler. He had been a Senator and Governor of Kentucky before he became Commissioner, and of course he was Commissioner when Jackie Robinson broke the color line. Happy Chandler had a memory for people that was unbelievable. I met him three times, probably five years apart. Each time, as soon as he saw me, it was, "Hey, Eddie, how are you?" He was impressive.

Many years later Chandler was asked about Ford Frick, and he said, "There was a vacancy when I left the office, and the owners decided to continue with it." He was quite a guy. He went into the Hall of Fame the same year as Hank Aaron.

After I recovered from my unscheduled meeting with the Commissioner, I returned to the business of trying to make the ballclub. I was rooming with Pete Whisenant at the Dixie Grande, so I felt very much at home. Elliott was still holding out, so I got a lot more chances. The other thing that really helped me was that the Braves brought in Billy Jurges to work with me on my fielding. Billy had played many years with the Cubs and Giants, mainly as a shortstop but also at third base. He was an outstanding fielder, and he taught me a lot. He tried to get me to stay down low, not to stand up so straight. He made me bend my knees to get the glove closer to the ground. That made a big difference.

Every day before the workout and after the workout, Billy would work with me. I don't know how many ground balls I took and how much time I put in. Billy always stressed the rhythm of fielding a ground ball. He said most grounders come to you the same way, with the same rhythm, so you have to concentrate on the routine ones and learn the rhythm. The other ones, the hard smashes or the slow rollers, you pretty much do by instinct. Billy worked with me for about three weeks and then went back to Virginia. I think he had a miniature golf course there. You've heard of the Gold Glove Award--before Billy worked with me, I got the Golden Chest Award. Knock 'em down, throw 'em out.

My fielding came along gradually. I don't think I really became a good fielder until about 1955. My hitting, though, was different. I felt comfortable as a hitter much earlier. Paul Waner, the great Pittsburgh Pirate hitter, came to Bradenton and volunteered to work with our hitters. Paul watched me hit a few and then told Tommy Holmes, our manager, "We can't improve on that boy's swing. Just let him hit." And he never tried to change my swing.

He did help me as a hitter, though. One time I was standing with Paul. He had the bat just sitting on his shoulder. We were talking about his theory of hitting. His theory was a quick belly-button. You've got to be quick in through there.

I asked Paul, "What was your stance?"

He said, "I'm in it." After a few seconds, he added, "I can't do anything until he throws it, can I?"

That's exactly what he told me, so I listened. I'm not saying that everyone should do that because Yastrzemski had a different stance, and Musial had a different stance. Everybody's got their own stance, but I decided to relax until they threw the stupid thing. That was my stance. As the pitcher cranked up, I cranked up. That's the lesson that Paul Waner taught me, that worked for me. I had a loosey-goosey approach to hitting, relaxed and taking my time. I don't try to tell anybody else that. I might tell them that story, but I don't try to say, "This is the way you've got to stand to be a good hitter." You do what works. Everybody's an individual. Hank Aaron hit cross-handed in the minor leagues--and it worked! Of course, Hank Aaron could hit in a dark broom closet.

Paul Waner and I became good pals, and his brother Lloyd, too. I rode to the Hall of Fame with Lloyd once, us and our wives. All the way from Syracuse to Cooperstown, two and a half hours, I heard nothing but Paul Waner stories. I never had such a good time. Paul was heavy duty.

One story about Paul that I know is true, because I happened to be there, was the time I was standing with Duffy Lewis, our traveling secretary. Paul came along and said, "Thanks a lot, Duffy."

Duffy said, "Don't thank me. But next time you order the Breakfast of Champions, make sure it's Wheaties."

What Paul had done, he'd called up room service and ordered a six-pack of Budweiser at six in the morning. Room service said, "Wait a minute," and they called the front desk, who got hold of Duffy. Duffy just said, "Give him the six-pack."

Duffy was a classy guy, a sharp dresser, and one of my biggest backers. He had been a great ballplayer with the Red Sox around the time of the First World War. He was part of one of the greatest outfields of all time, with Tris Speaker and Harry Hooper, when Babe Ruth was pitching for them. Even before spring training started, Duffy told a reporter I had a chance to become one of the all-time great hitters, as good as Shoeless Joe Jackson and Babe Ruth. Not bad for somebody that hadn't made the big leagues yet.

Duffy also gave me the greatest backhanded compliment I ever received. He told a story about the time he was managing in the Pacific Coast League. Somebody in the San Francisco Fire Department sent him a ballplayer that he said couldn't miss--just a great prospect, but a little inexperienced. It turned out to be Tony Lazzeri, the future Yankee second baseman. Well, the first couple weeks Lazzeri was there, all he did was strike out. He couldn't hit the ball. Duffy called up his friend in the fire department and said, "Look, I can't use this guy. All he does is strike out."

His friend said, "Sure, but doesn't he look good striking out?"

Duffy thought about it and said, "You're right, he does look good striking out." And he kept him on the club.

And the punchline was, "That's why Mathews reminds me of Lazzeri--he looks so good striking out."

That season I would remind him of Lazzeri a lot. I struck out 115 times, more than anybody in the league. Until expansion, that was the most strikeouts ever by a rookie in either league.

Batting in Bradenton, 1952. (Frank Stanfield photo)

Despite striking out a lot, though, I was having a decent spring. Then as we broke camp and began to work our way north, playing in the minor league towns along the way, a sequence of events occurred that changed my season. First, I hit a home run off Robin Roberts in Jacksonville, my first of the spring. The next day Monte Irvin of the New York Giants, the batting star of the 1951 World Series, broke his ankle. Six days later Bob Elliott, still a holdout, was traded to the Giants to fill the vacancy left by Irvin. In the span of a week, I went from Rookie Rocket prospect to the starting third baseman of the Boston Braves, pretty much by default.

As opening day approached, we barnstormed our way north with the Brooklyn Dodgers, playing against them in ballparks I knew from the Southern Association: Hartwell Field in Mobile, Sulphur Dell in Nashville, and Engel Stadium in Chattanooga, where Warren Spahn and Ernie Johnson combined for a no-hitter. Eventually we reached Boston, where we played the Red Sox in the so-called "City Series," first in Braves Field, then in Fenway Park. This, of course, was my first look at Boston's major league ballparks; except for my visit to Wrigley Field, these were the first big-league parks I'd seen.

My first game in Braves Field was a dandy. We won the game, I know, and I hit a double, but the most memorable part of the day occurred in the outfield. For some reason Tommy Holmes put Earl Torgeson, our first baseman, out in left field. Earl had always played first base. I don't think he had ever played the outfield before, but apparently Tommy wanted to see what Earl could do out there. Sam Jethroe was our centerfielder. What happened was, Vern Stephens hit a fairly tall flyball toward left center. Earl came running over, and he was yelling, "I got it, I got it."

Sam came around behind Earl to back him up, and the ball hit Sam right on top of the head, about three feet away from Earl. Sam came back in to the dugout and said, "I'm not playing with that man in the outfield anymore."

Earl couldn't stop apologizing. He admitted that it was his fault, that he didn't know the position. As he said, "I was out there with nothing but a glove and a prayer."

Sam was funny. He could run faster than anybody, but he wasn't a great fielder. One time he was chasing a fly to deep center field, and he turned his back toward home plate. When he turned around to look for the ball, it hit him right in the mouth. Another time we had to pick him off a chicken-wire fence. It was in an exhibition game going north, I think in Lynchburg, Virginia. He went after this ball, and as he went to catch it he hit this chicken-wire fence and got stuck there, hanging like a scarecrow. We had to go and pick him off.

To tell the truth, I don't know what it was like in Boston for Sam. A lot of the time he was the only black player on the club, and on the road he didn't have a roommate. He must have felt sort of isolated, but he never said a word about it that I heard. I was a rookie--I was in such a fog anyway. Plus the grownups and the young kids didn't associate much. Sam was only in his third year in the big leagues, but he was older. He had been a catcher for the Cleveland Buckeyes in the Negro American League. He had to be at least 30.

Sam did do a couple things that pissed off some of his teammates. Against the Dodgers we were losing by one run in the ninth inning, bases loaded, two out, and Sam was the batter. I was on second base at the time. The count was three-and-one. The pitch came in and it was up around his eyes, not even near the strike zone. All he had to do was stand there with the bat on his shoulder, take the walk, and force in the tying run. Besides that, Charlie had the take sign on. Instead Sam swung at the pitch and missed it. On the next pitch he popped a flyball to Duke Snider and we lost the ballgame. Grimm really blasted Sam for that one. He told the reporters that even a Little Leaguer wouldn't have done that.

A couple weeks later we were playing the Dodgers again. The score was tied after seven innings. In the top of the eighth the Dodgers scored two runs to take the lead, but you could see it was going to rain any minute. We had already had two rain delays, and it had gotten really dark and threatening. We could see lightning--everybody knew it was going to pour. All we had to do was stall a little bit, not finish the inning, the Dodgers' runs wouldn't count, and we'd end up in a tie and play a doubleheader the next day. The first two batters took their time but both made outs. Now Sam came up. He jumped right into the batter's box like he had a train to catch. I yelled to him from the dugout, "Take your time." He could have cleaned his spikes or stepped out to check the sign. Instead he swung and grounded out to Pee Wee Reese to end the game. About one second later the sky opened up, and it poured. The umpire called the game about a half hour later.

A few days after "the rainout that wasn't," the *Boston Globe* reported that it was a foregone conclusion Sam would not be back with the Braves in 1953. Newspapers write a lot of crap, of course. The next year Sam went through spring training and traveled to Milwaukee with the club. The day before the season started, though, Sam was optioned to Toledo. He never played for the Braves again.

When I first arrived in Boston, I needed a place to live. I went with one of our coaches, Bob Keely, to a place called Madam DuBarry's Home. I know, it sounds like a whorehouse, but it was a three-story house owned by a lady called Madam DuBarry. She rented her house out to ballplayers. I think there were four or five of us who lived there, within striking distance of the ballpark. The only room that was available at the time I got there was on the third floor. It had one window, about the size of a shoebox. There was no air-conditioning--you can forget that.

The room was small, but it was clean. I don't really remember how it was furnished. What I remember is the damn humidity. Atlanta's hot with some humidity, but my room at Madam DuBarry's was like the Black Hole of Calcutta! I would lie there at night and sweat. Then one of the ballplayers told me a trick--wet your sheet in the bathtub and put it over you. It helped, but I've never spent a summer like that. That was my first experience with New England humidity.

After I had a place to live, I reported to Braves Field to get issued a uniform. Shorty Young, the clubhouse attendant, found me one that fit pretty well, and I took it. In those days none of the uniforms really fit. They were all baggy, but that's just the way it was. I had number 41 on my back. I didn't request any particular number--Shorty just grabbed a uniform and handed it to me. I didn't care about the number or even if it had a number. I was just happy to make the ballclub. I know some guys got all worried about their number. When Hank Aaron got his first number he wasn't happy with it. He wore number 5 during his rookie year, which had been Sam Jethroe's number. Hank wanted two digits for some reason, so the next year he changed to number 44. To me numbers on the uniform didn't matter. With the Hi-Toms I wore number 7. With the Astros I wore number 11. With the Crackers I don't even remember what number I had. Who cares?

My first impression of Braves Field was that it was a big, cold cement arena. Later, after I had played there awhile, I thought it was a big, cold cement arena. Left field had a huge electronic scoreboard. The wind usually blew straight in the batter's face from center field, right off the Charles River, which made it a tough place to hit home runs.

We had very few fans--we sometimes had more pigeons than fans. In the rightfield bleachers there would be a group, every day, of about 40 or 50 guys that would gamble. They would gamble on popup, strikeout, ball--every pitch they'd make bets. You could see them passing the money around. I never met any of them. This is what I saw them doing. The ballclub didn't win too often, so I guess the fans had to have something of interest, whether it was gambling or just enjoying the fried clams at the concession stands.

Near the ballpark there were a couple of places that some of the ballplayers used to go to hang out. Sometimes we'd go to the Kenmore Hotel, which is where the visiting teams stayed. Another place was the Vendome Hotel, a big, older hotel right down the street from the Kenmore. The main reason we went there was Joe Taylor, a trainer for the ballclub, also tended bar at the Vendome. Joe ended up being my best man and a real close friend. He'd buy us drinks or whatever, so we spent some time in there. I was running around with Chet Nichols a little of the time, but we didn't have a favorite place. We actually didn't do much running around, mainly because we didn't have any money.

Speaking of money, one of the new experiences for me was getting meal money every day. With Atlanta they used to feed us when we traveled, usually at the place we were staying. If not, they'd give us a couple bucks. We didn't eat all that well, but you didn't hear a whole lot of complaining. Most of the ballplayers had been in the low minors where it was worse.

George Uhle told about when he broke in with the Pony League in 1944. When they were on the road they got one dollar a day. They had to look for restaurants that would give them a break. On one road trip they weren't going to leave until noon, so they got their meal money and it was only 50 cents that day because they were only going to be on the road a half day. That's how it was in the minors.

When I started in Boston, we could go in and sign at the hotel we were staying at and the ballclub would pick up the tab. But then the guys were starting to eat T-bone steaks for breakfast and T-bone steaks for lunch, so then the club said, "No way." That's when we started getting five bucks a day. That wasn't too bad then, but if you ate a lot of hot dogs, you had enough left over to buy beverages.

One of the gimmicks the Braves came up with to try to build more interest in the team in 1952 was a television program. During March and April, at 6:15 every Thursday evening you could tune in WNAC and enjoy "Baseball in Your Living Room." It was no threat to Milton Berle or "I Love Lucy," but it attracted a certain amount of attention among Bostoners starved for entertainment. In the beginning the show was nothing more than instructional films or little clips of spring training workouts. One of them was called "Accent on Youth," and it showed some of the potential rookies--Billy Klaus, Jack Cusick, Billy Bruton, and me, among others. Later on they started to do interviews with different players. One of the people interviewed was so entertaining that he ended up being on every week as the moderator. It was Earl Torgeson.

Earl was a natural comedian. He didn't really tell jokes, but he had a way of saying just about everything that made it funny. But Earl had another side of his personality, too. As I mentioned, he had the shortest fuse of anybody, and not just with nosy hotel night clerks. His temper was legendary. I don't know if any player has ever gotten in more fights than Earl.

At the start of July we were playing the New York Giants one night in Braves Field. Earl had been having a feud with Giants catcher Sal Yvars for a while because he said Yvars set up too close behind home plate. He told Sal to quit crowding him, but Yvars wouldn't move back. So what Earl started doing was, as he'd follow through with his swing, one-handed, he'd bring the bat around and hit Yvars with it. Sal said to him, "If you do that again, I'll break your bat."

Earl got a base hit, but as he let go of the bat he kind of flipped it backward and hit Yvars. Sal was angry. He picked up the bat and slammed it across home plate a couple times and cracked the handle. Earl didn't see that, but an inning later, as the teams changed sides, Whitey Lockman, the Giants first baseman, said to Earl, "I think Yvars broke your bat."

That got Earl upset. He went to the bat rack and, sure enough, the handle was cracked. Earl went crazy. He took off his glasses like Clark Kent turning into Superman--actually, Earl looked a lot like Clark Kent--and took off for the New York dugout. Sal was sitting there putting on his shinguards and did not see what was coming. Earl just pounced on him and caught him with a good punch above the eye. Then they both went down on the bottom of the dugout. Half our team followed Earl over there, so now there were all these people in the dugout. It was so crowded you couldn't even swing. Everybody was just trying to break it up. It ended pretty fast.

68

The fight might have spread or gone on longer except that Leo Durocher, the Giants' fiery manager, was sitting in the stands at the time, on suspension. A doctor came out of the stands, out of the crowd, and looked at the cut on Yvars' head and stopped the bleeding. Yvars had to stay in the game because he was the only New York catcher that was healthy. Wes Westrum was hurt at the time. Torgeson got kicked out, Yvars finished the game, and we lost to the Giants. After the ballgame Yvars went to the hospital and got some stitches.

Even with colorful characters like Earl Torgeson, our club had trouble drawing crowds, beginning on opening day. We didn't even have 5,000 people in the seats for the opener--because it was cold, they said. To tell the truth, though, I didn't care who showed up. It was my first game in the big leagues; I was just numb. A lot of that game is a blur. I remember the governor of Massachusetts threw out the first ball. I also remember my first at-bat--second inning, one out, nobody on base, facing lefthander Preacher Roe, the old spitballer and junk thrower. He walked me, which was fine. First time at the plate and I got on base. Jack Cusick got a base hit and I was on second, only one out. Scoring position. Careful not to take too big a lead, get picked off.

Warren Spahn struck out. Two down now, up to Billy Reed, the leadoff batter. Lefthand hitter. He reached out and punched a single to the opposite field. I hit third flying, head down, just clipped the inside corner of the bag, good turn. My run was the lead run, the first run of the new season. Andy Pafko was in left field, trying to cut me down at the plate, but I had good speed, 20-year-old legs. Pafko had a 31-year-old arm. In full stride, I looked toward the plate for a sign--do I score standing up, or do I score in a cloud of dust? What I saw was Campanella, reading the inscription on the baseball. He calmly put the tag on me. I was out by 20 feet. Okay, so it's not Hollywood.

The story of that game was the story of our season--not many fans, Spahn pitched a good game, and we lost to the Dodgers. We lost the first three games of the year to the Dodgers. Brooklyn had an excellent club, and we couldn't beat them. We won three games against them all year and tied one.

And poor Warren Spahn--he lost 19 games for us. Charlie Grimm didn't pitch him at the end of the season because they didn't want a 20-game loser. But it had nothing to

Out by a mile in my first game, second inning. (UPI/Bettmann)

do with Spahn--it was the terrible ballclub we had. In a ballgame with the Cubs, Spahn set a record with 18 strikeouts in 15 innings. He pitched the whole game for us but lost, 3-1. For 14 innings he gave up one run and didn't give up a walk until the last inning, but the only run we scored was a home run that Spahn hit himself. Finally he lost in the 15th on a triple by outfielder Hal Jeffcoat (I'll have more to say about him later on). Poor Spahnie, though--four days later he pitched another complete game and struck out 11 but lost by that same score, 3-1. How the hell are you going to win for a ballclub that can't score any runs?

Something else happened to Spahn. On one of our trips into Chicago he received a threatening letter from some wacko. They had armed guards keep an eye on him the whole time we were in Chicago, but nothing came of it. Apparently some nut was upset because Spahn had hit the Cubs' leading hitter, Frankie Baumholtz, with a pitch in an earlier game.

After going hitless in the opener, I got my first hit in the big leagues the next day--two of them, actually--off Chris Van

Cuyk, a tall, mean lefthander, the same guy that I almost batted against in the Little World Series with Milwaukee. The Dodgers got 20 hits and kicked the crap out of us, and the Braves made seven errors--none, I'm happy to report, by yours truly. In the early part of the season my fielding was real solid. Tommy Holmes commended me several times for my glove work. My hitting, though, was another story.

Every ballplayer that's ever played in the big leagues can tell you about his first home run. Mine was in Shibe Park in Philadelphia. It was a three-run job off lefty Ken Heintzelman in my fourth ballgame. I had struck out a couple times earlier in the game, but this time I hit a 1-1 fastball that went over 400 feet to right center. The home run raised my batting average to .188. The season was young, but base hits were scarce. I was panicked because I expected to go up there and hit .300 and do a good job. I quickly learned that it's a hell of a lot tougher in the big leagues, a big jump from Double-A.

Four days later I struck out for the 13th time. At that point I had a grand total of four base hits, and my batting average was lower than my blood pressure. In that ballgame, though, in the Polo Grounds, I finally started to hit a little bit.

That was the game in which Hoyt Wilhelm made his first appearance. In fact, in his first time at bat, against Dick Hoover, he hit a home run, which was a 260-foot opposite-field blooper that would have been an easy out anywhere but the Polo Grounds. At that point he and I were tied with one home run apiece. I hit one off him later in the game to move ahead of him for good. From that day until he retired in 1972, he never hit another one. That day at the Polo Grounds, though, he had the last laugh because the Giants beat us and Wilhelm was the winning pitcher.

We had a lot of losing days. After a month and a half our General Manager, John Quinn, had seen enough. We lost a doubleheader to (who else?) the Dodgers in Brooklyn on Decoration Day, which is what Memorial Day was called then. Quinn fired Tommy Holmes and promoted Charlie Grimm from Milwaukee. I felt bad for Tommy. He always treated me well, from that first day in Chicago when he let me use his bat. But Tommy was too much of a gentleman.

One day Vern Bickford was pitching in Boston, and he was getting bombed. Tommy walked out to the mound to take him out. I walked over from third base, and I heard Bickford say, "You're not taking me out."

Tommy said, "Vern, I want to take you out."

Vern repeated himself. "You're not taking me out."

Tommy said "Okay" and turned and walked back to the dugout. The next pitch Vern threw was a home run.

Here comes Tommy again. He said, "This time I'm really taking you out."

Part of the problem was that Tommy had played with those guys, and they just didn't give him the respect that some stranger would have gotten. Charlie was no stranger either, of course, since some of the guys, including me, had played for him in Milwaukee.

The only thing Charlie did that I didn't like was bench me sometimes and put in Buzz Clarkson or Sibby Sisti at third base. He did that a few times "to take the pressure off," he said, when there was a lefthanded pitcher working. To me that was baloney. First of all, how could I learn to hit lefties when I was sitting on the bench? And second, I wasn't that bad against them. I hit about a third of my home runs off lefties that year. It's true that certain southpaws gave me a lot of trouble--guys like Curt Simmons and Vinegar Bend Mizell--but they gave everybody trouble. By the middle of August, though, I was hitting better and playing every day.

As for being replaced by Sibby Sisti, well, nothing against Sibby, who was a good guy--a pretty serious guy, a straight shooter--but he was not any great hitter. He batted .212 that year. And in the field, Sibby had perfected the art of missing the ball and rolling when he probably should have caught it. He went down on the ground more times trying to get to a ball than anybody I've ever seen.

One smart move Charlie made, however, was bringing Johnny Logan with him from Milwaukee. Johnny became a terrific shortstop for the Braves. He led the league in fielding that year and the next two, and he was a good clutch hitter, too. Johnny and I hit it off right away. He was real sociable. We had some interesting times together.

One time Johnny and I were walking down the street and two sailors jumped on us and tried to beat us up, right in broad daylight in Boston. I don't think they were trying to rob us; I guess they just didn't like our looks. As it turned out, though, the sailors got beat up. Logan was pretty handy, a little bit like Billy Martin was.

72

In Milwaukee I usually hit behind Logan--he hit second and I usually hit third. That's basically how I ended up in some fights on the field. I'd have to follow him whenever he started a fight because I was in the on-deck circle.

Johnny was a neighbor of mine in Milwaukee for years. He had a certain ritual--he'd get up in the morning, at ten o'clock he was at the Athletic Club, then he'd have some soup and maybe a sandwich, and then take a nap. That was every single day, just like that.

One day I walked into Logan's room, and he was writing a letter. I said, "What are you doing, catching up on your correspondence?"

He said, "No, I'm writing a letter, can't you see?"

He was the Yogi Berra of the National League when it came to language. Instead of being a darkhouse shortstop, he was a "blackhorse" shortstop. He was funny.

About a week before the end of the season we played our last--*the* last--game in Braves Field. Of course nobody had the slightest thought that it would be the final game there. In a pregame ceremony a bunch of Little League kids from Martha's Vineyard presented Charlie Grimm with some fish they had caught, but once the ballgame started it was the Braves, not the striped bass, that stunk. We got the stuffing kicked out of us, once more, by the Dodgers. Relief pitcher Joe Black, who had never started a ballgame, pitched a complete game against us. I scored the last Braves run in Braves Field. Big help.

The Braves finished the season with a three-game series in Ebbets Field. We went there with a nine-game losing streak and immediately made it ten. Nobody wanted to be there, of course. Everything was already settled. The Dodgers had won the pennant; the Braves had wrapped up seventh place. We did not even have a full team at the end. Charlie had let a few guys go home that weren't going to pitch or play.

Because the game didn't matter, the ballpark was empty of fans--there were maybe a thousand people there--but jammed with reporters and cameramen fawning over the National League champs. Only one media person came near our dugout, and that was radio announcer Dizzy Dean. He saw Charlie Grimm and decided to give him the needle.

"Hey, Charlie, how come there's no photographers around your club?"

Charlie paused for a second and said, "Well, Diz, we all

had our pictures taken at spring training."

The next day we beat the Dodgers big. I hit three home runs and ex-Cracker Jack Dittmer hit one for only our third win over Brooklyn all year. Then on Sunday we played part of our finale.

I say part of it because we never got a chance to finish. For eight innings everything was perfectly normal, which is to say we were losing. Then with two out in the top of the ninth and nobody on base, Logan walked. I was the next batter. Jim Hughes threw me a fastball, and I banged it off the scoreboard in right field for a double, scoring Logan with the tying run. Sid Gordon made the third out. The Dodgers didn't score in the ninth, so we went into extra innings.

You should have heard my teammates when I got to the dugout. "What the hell are you doing?" was one of the milder reactions.

"We wanna go home!" was another. Some hero.

We played the tenth inning and then Al Barlick, the home plate umpire, left to catch a train to wherever he lived. He just left, even though the game was still going. We played two more innings. In the bottom of the twelfth Tommy Holmes, now a Dodger outfielder, grounded into a fielder's choice for the third out. The umpires looked at each other and called the game on account of darkness. It was ten minutes to five in the afternoon. It was broad daylight. The sun was out.

One complication had presented itself right before the end of the season. In anticipation of my return to Santa Barbara, I had bought a car. We had a Pontiac dealer in Boston named Ed Foote, and he gave me a good deal on a Pontiac convertible. I think it cost me $1200. It was really a beautiful car.

I parked it outside the ballpark before one of our last home games. When I came out there was a note on the windshield. It was from a gal that everybody called Bullpen Annie. All the ballplayers knew who she was because she was always hanging around. She would lounge around wherever there were ballpalyers. She was a wart. Anyway, her note said, "I'm pregnant, and I need some money," and she signed it.

This I did not need. I didn't even know the girl. (I know, that's what they all say.) My mind was racing at a hundred miles an hour, but when I was able to think clearly, I took the note to General Manager John Quinn.

"I don't know what this is all about," I told him, "but here it is."

John Quinn made some phone calls, and they sent a lawyer and a detective over to see her. They made her sit down and sign a statement saying she was trying to extort money from me, and that was the last I heard of Bullpen Annie. That was my first experience--actually, my only experience--with what I've seen going on with women and ballplayers in recent times. In those days there was not much hanky-panky going on. But as I got older, particularly when I was managing, I found out that, like the song says, "Girls just wanna have fun" when ballplayers are around. I don't know why that girl picked on me. I sure didn't have any money in those days.

I did have a shiny blue Pontiac convertible, though. As I drove it across the country to my parents' home, my thoughts were on playing ball in Boston in 1953. I knew our attendance had been awful; I had heard that Lou Perini lost a ton of money. But I also knew that Perini was a Bostonian, that he had said he was keeping the club in Boston. "What do I have to do," he asked, "sign an agreement to satisfy some people that I'm not selling or moving the team?"

September 27, 1952

The last ballgame the Boston Braves ever won was the penultimate game of the 1952 season, a Saturday affair staged at Brooklyn's Ebbets Field. The Dodgers had already clinched the pennant; the Braves had been mathematically eliminated in August, had now lost ten straight, and had clinched seventh place. The game was historic but not important. Fewer than 5,000 Flatbush fans showed up to watch it. In relative privacy, Eddie Mathews, not yet old enough to vote, inscribed his name in the record book of major league baseball.

Approaching the end of his rookie season, Mathews ranked second on the club in home runs with 22, many of them tape-measure blasts that drew admiring remarks from sportswriters and fans throughout the league. He had poled at least one homer in every National League park except Ebbets Field.

In other departments, though, he mirrored his team. At game time, his batting average weighed in at .237, and he had struck out more times than anyone else in either league.

Mathews added to his leading strikeout total in the first inning. Facing Joe Black (15-3), who was tuning up for his starting assignment in game one of the World Series, Mathews swung and missed strike three. The next time, though, in the third inning, with two runs in and Boston pitcher Virgil Jester on second base, Mathews timed a 3-2 curve ball from Black and gave it a ride. The ball cleared the 30-foot rightfield fence, crossed Bedford Avenue, and hit a filling station on the first bounce. Dodger outfielder Dick Williams, on the disabled list and just parking his car, caught the ball as it caromed off the garage. The Braves led, 4-1, and would never trail.

The next time Mathews stepped into the batter's box, in the top of the sixth, Joe Black was in the shower, the Braves led 5-2, and tall Ben Wade was on the mound. Mathews took a strike, then smashed a belt-high fastball over the 344-foot left side of the Schaefer's Beer scoreboard, a longer poke than his previous homer, to make the score 6-2. To prove it was no fluke, he repeated the feat in the eighth inning off Wade, this time ripping a slow, hanging curve over the rightfield fence for his third home run of the day. In the 77-year existence of the National League, the Braves' young third baseman became the first rookie to hit three home runs in one game.

With one out in the ninth, Mathews came to bat again with a chance to join the truly select company of hitters with four homers in a game. Only four players in the twentieth century had accomplished that feat, most recently Gil Hodges in this same ballpark just 25 months previous. Billy Loes was now pitching, and because the game meant nothing in the standings, the Brooklyn fans were screaming for a home run. The Dodgers tried to cooperate—catcher Roy Campanella told Mathews, "We're gonna give you one right down the middle, kid." Mathews didn't believe him and took the pitch—right down the middle. Eventually he grounded out to Pee Wee Reese at shortstop. Virgil Jester blanked the Dodgers in the ninth, and the Braves won, 11-3.

Naturally all the postgame talk was of the Braves' young slugger. Boston captain Walker Cooper opined, "He might become one of the greatest...when he learns how they're trying to pitch him. He's not even a good hitter right now."

Perhaps the most insightful and prophetic remarks, though, came from the man who finished the ballgame as the Dodgers' rightfielder—Tommy Holmes, who four months earlier had been Mathews' manager. Of Mathews, Holmes said: "The biggest factor is he doesn't scare. He has hitting guts. In another year he might be the best third baseman in the league."

September 27, 1952

BOSTON	AB	R	H	C	BROOKLYN	AB	R	H	C
Jethroe, cf	5	0	2	3	Cox, 3b	3	0	1	1
Logan, ss	4	0	0	3	Morgan, 3b	2	0	0	0
Mathews, 3b	5	3	3	5	Reese, ss	3	0	0	6
Gordon, lf	5	0	0	6	Snider, cf	4	2	2	3
Torgeson, 1b	3	1	0	10	Robinson, 2b	1	1	1	9
Burris, c	4	1	0	5	Bridges, 2b	1	0	1	0
Daniels, rf	1	3	0	1	Campanella, c	3	0	1	4
Dittmer, 2b	3	2	2	5	Lembo, c	1	0	0	2
Jester, p	2	1	1	0	Pafko, rf	3	0	0	0
					Holmes, rf	1	0	0	1
					Hodges, 1b	4	0	0	10
					Amoros, lf	4	0	2	2
					Black, p	1	0	0	1
					a-Walker	1	0	0	0
					Wade, p	1	0	0	0
					Loes, p	0	0	0	0
					b-Nelson	1	0	0	0
Totals	32	11	8	38		34	3	8	39

a-Flied out for Black in 5th.
b-Grounded out for Loes in 9th.

```
BOSTON ..................... 0 0 4  0 1 1  1 4 0--11
Brooklyn ..................  1 0 0  1 0 0  0 1 0-- 3
```

E--Jethroe, Jester, Black, Robinson, Morgan. RBI--Snider, Pafko, Dittmer 4, Mathews 4, Jethroe 2, Jester, Lembo. 2B--Snider. HR--Snider, Mathews 3, Dittmer. S--Logan, Jester 2. DP--Reese to Robinson to Hodges. Left--Boston 2, Brooklyn 7. BB--Jester 3, Black 2, Wade 3. SO--Jester 5, Black 1, Wade 3. HO--Black 5 in 5; Wade, 3 in 3; Loes, 0 in 1. R-ER--Jester 3-3, Black 5-5, Wade 6-4, Loes 0-0. PB--Burris. W--Jester (3-5). L--Black (15-4). A--4,903.

FIVE

Heroes' Welcome

The news took us all by surprise. We had seen speculations and rumors in the Boston newspapers a few times during my rookie year--"Braves may move to Milwaukee," and so forth. We knew Milwaukee wanted a club, but Mr. Perini insisted he loved Boston. Near the end of the season he told a reporter, "I'll give the fans in Boston two years to show me they want the Braves to stay here." Two years.

Then all winter nothing happened. Spring training started as usual. We had some new ballplayers in camp: Andy Pafko from the Brooklyn Dodgers, Joe Adcock from Cincinnati, Del Crandall and Johnny Antonelli and Bob Buhl from the Army. Spirits were high. We figured Boston might be able to move up to the first division if everything worked out.

And then came the news. *The Sporting News* printed an anonymous report that the Braves were moving to Milwaukee in time for the 1953 season, which was only a month away. A Milwaukee baseball reporter named Sam Levy asked Perini if it was true. His answer was, "I can't confirm it, and I can't unconfirm it." When he didn't deny it, everybody knew it was true.

What had happened was the St. Louis Browns' owner, Bill Veeck, tried to move his club to Milwaukee, which had just built a new stadium. Because Perini owned the rights to Milwaukee, though, with the minor league Brewers there, he had to agree to move his minor league team. The city of Milwaukee started to pressure Perini, including threatening an antitrust suit. Veeck then made an announcement that he was moving the Browns to Baltimore. The next day Perini told the press officially, "We are moving the Braves to Milwaukee."

The Bostwaukee Braves at change-over time, March, 1953. Some caps have the old "B," some the new "M."
(Frank Stanfield photo)

Even though the move seemed sudden, I assume Perini and his brothers and John Quinn had been considering it for some time. If you look at our ballclub in 1952, we had some older players, but we also had some young kids, like Logan and Dittmer and me, who probably weren't quite ready for the big leagues. You don't bring a bunch of kids up to the majors and decide "We're going to lose" unless you have something in the back of your mind. Perini was a shrewd man--he didn't just fall off a turnip truck in spring training and say, "Oh, we're gonna move." There had to be conversations a lot further back.

After Perini's announcement the National League owners had their little meeting in St. Petersburg. Of course they approved the move. They would never turn against one of their own, and they all liked Lou Perini. A little while later somebody came around to the ballplayers and started passing out baseball caps, dark blue like the old ones but with a big M on the front. That was how we got the word. The uniforms stayed the same because they just said "Braves."

Nobody ever held a team meeting and said, "This is what's happened, here's what happens next." All the information just kind of sifted down. We got the word, but nobody like the general manager ever gave us the details. I guess they figured it was too late, that we already knew.

The move didn't mean anything to me. I didn't have any ties in Boston. As far as I remember, no one on the team lived in that area, so actually the players were kind of excited about going to Milwaukee. We'd had a dismal season--no attendance, no nothing--and I guess everybody felt, hey, the grass is greener on the other side. Warren Spahn had opened a restaurant, a little diner, about half a block from Braves Field, so he might have been upset. Mostly, though, while I wouldn't say the ballplayers were enthusiastic, we figured maybe it wasn't a bad deal. Nobody worried about it.

Perini had every reason to move the Braves, as I've said. He was losing money in Boston. But he never said it was money that caused the move, and it's true. He was a sportsman in the real sense. He became one of the Braves' owners as a hobby. He certainly didn't need money. He and his brothers owned a heavy construction company that built huge dams and projects of that scale. They had built a tunnel that carried water from above Niagara Falls for a hydroelectric plant.

There was a story about the Braves' signing of Johnny

Antonelli to a bonus contract. Antonelli's father owned a building construction company, and he told Perini, "I own two steam shovels. How many do you have?"

"I'm not sure," Perini responded. "I think about fifty."

Perini did not need the money. I'm not saying he didn't want to cut his losses, but he said what he missed in Boston was "the roar of the crowd." He quickly found it in Milwaukee.

When our train pulled into the Milwaukee Road depot, we knew we were not in Boston anymore. Every man, woman, and child in Milwaukee had turned out to meet us at the station, or so it seemed. Actually the crowd was only--notice I'm saying only--ten or fifteen thousand, which was more than we drew in Boston for a three-game series. These people received the thrill of watching us step off the train onto the platform, and they were overjoyed by it.

I guess you could say our reception started as soon as we left Chicago, heading north for our new home. Our train had two special passenger cars just for the players and team officials. All throughout the two cars was a squadron of reporters, some of them tape-recording interviews to be broadcast later on the radio in Milwaukee. Between conversations with the writers I played cribbage with Dave Cole.

"Fifteen-two, fifteen-four, and a double run of three makes--right, I was with the Brewers in '51 but I didn't--yeah, that grand slam in Borchert Field..." It was wild.

Or at least it seemed wild until we got off the train. Then things got really wild. You would have thought World War II just ended! They had Earl Gillespie, the Braves announcer, doing a live radio broadcast. They had people with cowbells and drums and noisemakers. A drum majorette wearing a big Indian headdress ran out of the crowd and threw her arms around Charlie Grimm. Charlie blushed, and then he and Lou Perini shook hands with some of the local officials. Then they led the way and the ballplayers followed as we walked along a red carpet that stretched all the way through the depot and out to the street. Along the way were rows of young women wearing Indian feathers and short outfits. It was cold and windy--this was Wisconsin in April--and we all had on top coats, but these girls--young women, I guess I should say--had nothing covering their legs but had big smiles on their faces. I felt welcome already.

On the street was a long row of convertibles. Two

81

Fred Miller and Lou Perini wave to the crowd during the 1953
welcoming parade. (Miller Brewing Co.)

ballplayers got into each car, with one of the feathered young
ladies in between, and we had a parade to our hotel, which was
maybe a mile away. All along the route the people were packed
three or four deep and screaming and waving like we were
heroes or something. Factory whistles and aerial bombs were
going off. As we passed a big department store people were
throwing confetti on us from the upper windows. I knew how
Lindbergh must have felt, but I didn't know what we had done
to deserve all this.

After we got to the Schroeder Hotel, we had more
interviews and some speeches, with the crowd cheering every
sentence. Then they took us inside to this big ballroom where
they had--I'm not kidding--a Christmas tree surrounded by
presents. Everybody on the ballclub received all kinds of
stuff--a wallet, fishing lures, cufflinks, gift certificates, theater
passes, you name it. Even underwear. We couldn't figure this
out. We were absolute nobodies.

That afternoon we worked out and had our first look at
our new ballpark, County Stadium. They named it that because
that's who paid for it--the taxpayers of Milwaukee County. It

was the first major league stadium built with lights, and if I'm not mistaken it was the first one in the big leagues built with public money. Of course it cost less to build than some ballplayers make now in one year. But I don't want to start on that--the whole subject of player salaries today makes me want to puke. As far as the ballpark, it didn't look quite finished, and I thought it had a tough background for hitting. Later they planted trees beyond the centerfield fence, the so-called "Perini's Woods," and that helped.

On the night of our arrival in Milwaukee, the city fathers held a big rally at the Milwaukee Arena to have the team officials and the ballplayers introduced. It was a terrible night outside, hailing and sleeting, but once again we had a great time inside. People treated us like we were a conquering army or something. The governor gave a little talk, and the mayor, and Lou Perini, and Charlie Grimm, and who knows who else, and then they introduced the ballplayers. We were seated at a long table across the front of the stage. They introduced each of us by name, one at a time, and the people went nuts. To tell the truth, though, I don't think they knew who most of us were. Maybe they knew Spahnie, and of course Andy Pafko because he was from Wisconsin, plus some guys had played for the Brewers. But it didn't matter to those people--we all got a huge ovation.

What we soon found out was that the people of Milwaukee couldn't do enough for us. Our money was no good anywhere in town. A car dealer named Wally Rank provided all of us with cars to use. He used that for advertising purposes, but we didn't care. We each had a brand new car to drive around. Wally was a wonderful friend to us. Later on he even went on road trips with us. And gasoline--Clark gas stations gave us all we wanted. We didn't even have to tell them who we were because everywhere we went people recognized us. Free dry-cleaning, free food--you name it, we got it.

Right from the beginning the ballplayers made a lot of public appearances. In that way we were able to put something back into the community. We were never compensated for those appearances. The publicity director would make all the arrangements and then say, "We need three or four guys to visit the Veterans' Hospital," or "St. Jahoozis Church is having a smoker or a sports night," and we'd go. No problem. Most of the time we enjoyed ourselves. The people were great to us. We did

83

hundreds of those appearances. I'd say the Catholic Church were the champs. They always had something planned.

As we started doing public appearances, I realized I did not have enough clothes for that role. The only suit I owned was the one Earl Mann bought me in Atlanta, so I went to a clothier in town and got fitted for a new one. It was a nice suit, two pairs of pants. When I went to pick it up, they wouldn't take any money for it. I said, "Cut it out, I have to pay for it."

"Just give us an autographed picture to put on the wall," the man said. And that's all he would take. That type of thing went on for years.

When we first got to town, we didn't have houses or apartments to live in, so a bunch of us rented rooms at the Wisconsin Hotel, right downtown. Logan lived there, I think Adcock, probably a dozen of us in all at one time. As the season progressed, we were getting all kinds of stuff given to us. One of the big items, a real big item, was cases of beer from Miller Brewery. They were the major sponsor on the radio broadcasts. For every game a pitcher won, he got a case of Miller High Life. If you hit a home run, you got a case of Miller High Life. They'd deliver it right to your room at the hotel. Well, I had 27 home runs at the All-Star break, and that was just me. We had to rent another room just for the beer because besides Miller there were other breweries--Blatz, Schlitz, Pabst...

It wasn't only businesses that treated us that way. One night Bob Buhl and I went into a little neighborhood restaurant and ate dinner. When we came out there must have been 300 kids out there. Somebody had spotted us going in and spread the word. We started signing autographs, and this one kid said, "We live right across the street, and my dad says to come over and get away from this madhouse." It was tempting. Then he said, "He's made his own wine in the basement." We walked over to this guy's house and sat down there and had a hell of a good time with the family.

About a month after the season started, busloads of people started showing up from the Dakotas and Iowa and all over Wisconsin. Milwaukee isn't that far from Chicago, but all of a sudden it was like they had opened up a whole new territory for baseball. Fans even followed us on road trips. Six hundred "Braves Boosters" took the train to Brooklyn for a series at Ebbets Field. And after we returned home at the end of our first road trip, 7,500 people were waiting for us at the train station.

To say that the Milwaukee fans took us to heart would be a gross understatement.

Another promotion that fans took part in was a "Best of the Braves" competition. Blatz Beer sponsored it. Fans would fill out ballots for whoever they thought was the best ballplayer or their favorite ballplayer. If they attached a ticket stub, their vote counted triple. The fans didn't win anything for it, but whichever ballplayer was chosen "Brave of the Week" got something. We could choose from a big list that included golf clubs, TV set, wristwatch, all kinds of stuff. At the end of the season, the top vote-getter of the Braves would receive a brand new Cadillac. I had sold my Pontiac by then and I'd need a car to drive back to California. I thought driving up to my parents' house in a shiny new Cadillac would be a real kick.

Well, I had my best year in 1953. I hit .302, drove in 135 runs, led the majors with 47 home runs, and finished second to Roy Campanella in the Most Valuable Player voting. But Andy Pafko was still playing good ball for the Braves. And what happened, I wasn't into a religion or I didn't have anything particular going for me, but Andy was a Lutheran. The fans had a special night for Andy, as they did for a number of us, and over 10,000 Lutherans showed up. At that point I said, "I'm not going to win that voting." And I didn't. Andy won it. He got the Cadillac, and I ended up buying a Mercury to drive home in. The Lord works in mysterious ways.

The fans treated us great, and in return, we played good baseball for them. The night before the home opener they had a gala dinner for us at the Elks Club, with the usual dignitaries plus Commissioner Ford Frick (this time I kept my distance) and National League President Warren Giles. That's also where I first met one of my future fathers-in-law, August A. Busch, Jr., the head of the Busch Brewery who had just bought the St. Louis Cardinals. The next day we played the Cardinals and beat them in ten innings. The Cardinals' first base coach was my old friend, Dixie Walker. I didn't have a good day personally--I struck out my first three times in County Stadium--but it didn't matter because Billy Bruton won the game with a home run.

Despite the opener in Milwaukee, I really got off to a good start, which was unusual for me. I hit six home runs in our first eight ballgames. One reason for the improvement, a big reason, was that I had changed my stance. In Boston I hit with a closed stance, like Stan Musial. But I was no Stan Musial.

Because of that stance I had a blind spot in my swing. I wasn't seeing the high-inside pitch very well, so I was striking out a lot. To correct that I moved my right foot back a little bit and pointed it more toward right. It made a huge difference.

As the season went along, the Braves really started to surprise people around the league. We had been so pathetic in Boston that nobody expected much from us. But we had new players, with Pafko and Adcock and Crandall and Bruton and Pendleton and Buhl. We had a much better attitude, and the fans helped with that. What we really had, though, was great pitching. In the first half of the season, Spahnie was winning, and so were Burdette and Antonelli and Buhl. And the one who surprised a lot of people was Max Surkont.

Old Max had done a pretty good job in Boston, but in Milwaukee he won nine of his first ten ballgames. The fans loved him, too, especially the Polish fans. One night against the Cincinnati Redlegs Max set a record with eight strikeouts in a row. What happened was we scored six runs in the first inning, and it was a rainy night. The Reds decided their best chance was to stall until the rain cameand hope we couldn't finish the game. Rogers Hornsby was their manager. He did everything he could to delay the game. The fans were booing like crazy.

In order to slow things down, every batter that the Reds sent to the plate was taking. They were under orders not to swing until they had two strikes on them. Max would get two strikes and then throw them a spitball and strike them out. Once the count went to two strikes, you knew Max would throw the spitter and, bang, punch 'em out. And it worked eight times in a row. We drank some beer that night.

Max was a pretty good beer drinker. Beer and Polish sausage, that's what he liked. The fans gave Max a ton of Polish sausage. They also had a special night for him and gave him a $1,000 savings bond, and they gave his little boy a fancy tricycle. After Max retired he ran a tavern. He was a good guy. The funny thing about Max, though, was that he always wanted to know how much everybody was making. That bothered him. You'd get your paycheck and open it and look up and there was Max, standing and looking over your shoulder.

Of course, Max was not unique in that regard. A lot of people are curious about what other people earn. These days they publish player salaries in the newspapers, but when I was playing it was much more secretive. During spring training I was sitting with Walker Cooper and Vern Bickford, having a beer. They said, "Kid, what did John Quinn do to you?"

I said, "What do you mean?"

Vern said, "Everybody knows how tight-fisted that Quinn is. How much is he paying you?"

Well, I had hit 25 home runs in '52 and finished second in the Rookie of the Year balloting, which I felt was a pretty good year. I had made $5,500--that was the minimum salary. When I went to talk to John Quinn about my new contract, he said, "We're going to give you $10,000."

I thought it over for a second and said, "Okay." What the hell. I didn't know how much I should get or how much anybody else was getting. So I signed the contract.

And that's what I told Bickford and Cooper. I said, "Well, he's giving me $10,000."

They said, "You've gotta be nuts!" Now here's how naive I was. They said, "Go back and tell him you're not happy with that."

So I did. I said, "Mr. Quinn, I don't think you were fair with me."

Quinn said, "Oh, you've been talking to Vern Bickford and Walker Cooper."

"I'm not going to say who told me," I said, "but I know that I should be making a little more than this."

He said, "Okay, I'll give you $12,000." Just like that.

I said, "Do you think that's fair?"

"I'll tell you what I'll do," he replied. "I'll put a clause in there that if you hit 30 home runs, I'll give you an extra $2,000."

So that's what I ended up at. I hit 47 home runs, so I made $14,000. He never wrote down the little incentive clause. It was strictly a verbal agreement, but he honored it.

I was hitting home runs at a pretty good clip, the ballclub was winning, and the fans were setting attendance records. It was great to be young and a Milwaukee Brave. We had an excellent month of May and took over first place, ahead of the Brooklyn Dodgers. We stayed in first all through June and stayed neck-and-neck until the All-Star Game in mid-July.

The voting of the fans made me the youngest starting infielder the National League All-Star team had ever had. The game was played at Crosley Field in Cincinnati, and the National League won, 5-1. Warren Spahn was the winning pitcher. Playing alongside guys like Stan Musial and Ted

Kluszewski and Roy Campanella was a thrill, but I didn't get any hits. In fact, I didn't get a hit in an All-Star game until 1959, when I hit a home run off Early Wynn. I did score the first run in this game, though, after getting hit by a pitch from Allie Reynolds. Yogi Berra and Casey Stengel claimed I didn't try to avoid the pitch, but they lost the argument.

The most memorable part of that All-Star game for me was batting against Satchel Paige. My last time up--I played the whole game at third base--I faced Satch, and he surprised me. I wasn't getting cocky, but I was having a good year, and Satch had some miles on him. I didn't realize he could still get it up there the way he did. I was standing there waiting for the local, as Campy would say, and he sent me the express. He got it up there pretty darn good, and I popped it up to Phil Rizzuto.

Even before the All-Star game, but especially after it, I was getting a lot of fan mail, much of it from young ladies. I was probably averaging between 50 and 100 letters a day, sent to Eddie Mathews, in care of County Stadium. It was flattering and it was fun, but it got to be more than I could handle. I always believed that each of those people was entitled to a response, and I couldn't keep up. I hired a gal out of the front office, one of the secretaries, to help me answer it.

What I would do--they didn't know what a return envelope was in those days--I had a bunch of postcards printed up with my picture on them, so as my helper opened the letters, I would sign the cards. She'd put the stamp on and send them back. Of course postage was a lot cheaper in those days. You could mail a postcard for a penny. But the club never paid for any of that.

In addition to the mail, I started appearing in articles and on the cover of national magazines. I wasn't used to all that attention. I enjoyed it, don't get me wrong, but it was distracting and to a certain extent embarrassing. I've always liked my privacy. I enjoy being with people I like, but when all the reporters and photographers start coming around and wanting stories or wanting me to pose for pictures, I get uncomfortable. I'm sure I didn't deal with all the attention as well as I might have. I was very young and not very sophisticated or experienced. Some writers began to call me surly or moody. I never tried to be, but that became my reputation.

In mid-season before a ballgame at County Stadium, they had a little ceremony in which sportswriter Sam Levy presented me with a leather-bound copy of the *Saturday Evening Post*. The magazine contained an article he had written about me. His article was very nice, very complimentary, but the ceremony was for Sam Levy, not for me. He wrote the article, not me. But that was fine.

Then near the end of the season I was chosen by *Look* magazine as their "All-American third baseman." Between games of a doubleheader I was supposed to come out and receive a watch from *Look* in honor of that recognition. In the opening game, though, I made a couple errors. The Redlegs scored four unearned runs against Johnny Antonelli and beat us. When Charlie Grimm went out to take Antonelli out of the game, some of the fans booed Charlie. They thought it was my fault, not Antonelli's, and it was. Then they booed me for the last three innings of the game. I think that was the first time in my life I was ever booed by the crowd.

In later years I learned not to let the crowd bother me, but that's not easy, especially when you're 21 and it's never happened before. Now between games they wanted me to go out and receive a watch. I said, "I'm not going out there. They just got through booing the hell out of me." And I didn't go. Sid Gordon chewed me out for not going out--and he was absolutely right--but I wouldn't go.

To show you what kind of fans Milwaukee had, though, the newspapers were full of angry letters after that incident, critical not of me but of the fans who had done the booing.

"What happened to a kid like Mathews shouldn't happen to Stalin. Anyone giving Grimm and Eddie the boo should hang his head in shame," one letter said.

Another was equally supportive: "For those few rude and unappreciative people, I wish to publicly apologize to Charlie and Eddie."

The Milwaukee Braves' fans were the best I've ever been around.

One of the inevitable results of being a home run hitter is that sooner or later somebody is going to compare you with Babe Ruth. If you hit a long home run, or if you hit two in one game, or if you hit ten in the first three weeks, people start talking about Babe Ruth. Even when I was playing Double-A ball in Atlanta, some people were saying I was the next Babe Ruth, and all that happy stuff.

During spring training of my rookie year, Earl Torgeson

started calling me Babe, mostly I think because I looked so young. Fortunately, the name never stuck. With Milwaukee a few teammates called me that too once in a while, just kiddingly. As the season went on, though, more and more sportswriters started asking me: "Can you break Babe Ruth's home run record?" During the 1950's that always seemed to be the big question the writers posed--who can break Ruth's record? First Ralph Kiner went through it, and later Mickey Mantle and Willie Mays, and finally Roger Maris. Nineteen fifty-three was my year to deal with the legend of the Babe.

I never even thought about Ruth's record. Being the next Babe Ruth was never a goal of mine. I never set goals. I never said, "This year I've got to hit 45 home runs" or anything like that. I just went out every day and did the best I could. Break Babe Ruth's record? Who cares? Babe Ruth made baseball. If I broke his record, or if anybody did, would that make us better than Babe Ruth? Give me a break. Look what happened to poor Roger Maris--he lost all his hair.

At the end of August, in a doubleheader at Forbes Field in Pittsburgh, I hit three home runs, which raised my total for the year to 43. At that point and for the rest of the season, one of the Milwaukee newspapers started putting a little box called "Eddie Mathews' Home Run Count" in its sports section every day. It had a little sketch of an Indian in a headdress, swinging a baseball bat lefthanded. It also showed my season total, how many games had been played, and how many Ruth had hit at that point in his record year. After that doubleheader in Pittsburgh, I only hit four more, so Babe didn't have to roll over in his grave.

After the All-Star game the Dodgers gradually pulled ahead in the standings and won the pennant by a wide margin, with the Braves a solid second. Regardless of the standings, however, the Dodgers were always our bitterest rival, along with Cincinnati and, to a lesser extent, the Cubs. When Chicago came up to County Stadium, we used to like to watch the fights in the stands. With the Dodgers, the action was always on the field. We had two near-fights, neither one amounting to anything, one in Brooklyn and one in Milwaukee. Both involved my buddy Lew Burdette. In Milwaukee Burdette knocked Campanella down twice and then struck him out. Campanella claimed Lew called him a "nigger," but I never heard Lew say that. Campy started toward the mound with his bat in his hand, but the umpire and Del Crandall stopped him. Whenever we played the Dodgers, somebody got knocked down or beaned or words were exchanged. But after it happened, it was over.

The Braves' most notorious fight of the year happened after a doubleheader loss in Brooklyn, but the Dodgers weren't involved. Bickford and Cooper and Logan and I were in a bar on 42nd Street about three doors down from the Commodore Hotel, where we always stayed in New York. We were talking about the ballgames, like we always did. The Dodgers' last out had been a line drive at Logan. Johnny said, "It was a curve ball."

Bickford said, "It was a fastball."

"It was a curve ball," Logan said. "I was looking right in there. That's why I moved."

Bickford said, "You're full of it. I'll bet you a hundred dollars it was a fastball."

So they bet. They went to a public phone and called Del Crandall. He didn't drink, so he was in his hotel room. Crandall said, "It was a curve ball."

Bickford took a hundred dollars out of his wallet. "Here's your hundred dollars."

Logan said, "I don't want it."

Bickford said, "Take it or I'll take you out in the alley and beat the crap outta you." He threw down the money. Logan wouldn't pick it up, so they went at it. It didn't last very long, and it was very one-sided. Like I said, Logan was handy. Later that night Burdette and I were sneaking into the hotel, and we saw Bickford again. He looked like he had been in a stick fight without a stick. Logan really worked him over. Nothing more was ever said about it, though.

Bickford's hundred dollars was picked up off the floor by a guy he knew, who mailed it to him later. Vern didn't like Charlie Grimm, so he told them to trade him after the season. They sold him to the Baltimore Orioles, and six years later he was dead of cancer at age 39.

Besides the Dodgers, we also had some donnybrooks with the Redlegs throughout the year. On the last day of the season at Crosley Field, we decided to settle it. We had a track and field meet before the ballgame. We had contests in running, hitting for distance, throwing for accuracy by the catchers, and some others. The winning catcher was Frank Baldwin, my old teammate with the Crackers, which was interesting because he

91

only caught six games in the big leagues. The foot race was a sweep for the Braves: Bruton first, Pendleton second, and me third. The Reds must have had Ed Bailey and Ted Kluszewski running; I don't remember anymore. And finally the hitting for distance contest--after 47 home runs to lead the major leagues, I finished dead last. I didn't hit a ball past the infield. The winner was Andy Pafko. I guess he deserved the Cadillac.

Our first year in Milwaukee was an amazing success. We set a league attendance record and finished in second place, surpassing everybody's expectations. When the season ended, we all went our separate ways. Charlie Grimm went to his farm outside of St. Louis. Bob Buhl and George Crowe went to play winter ball in the Caribbean. Ernie Johnson went back to work at the Los Angeles Post Office. Jack Dittmer went to sell cars for his dad in Elkader, Iowa. Several guys stayed in town to work for local breweries. And Edwin and Eloise Mathews' boy took off on the most exotic trip of his life--barnstorming in the "Land of the Rising Sun."

We were called "Eddie Lopat's All-Stars." Lopat was a lefthanded pitcher on those New York Yankee teams that won five World Series in a row. They had just won the fifth one a couple days before we left. Why the team was named for Lopat I don't know. He may have been a good friend of Frank Scott, who organized the trip. Scott had been the traveling secretary of the Yankees at one time, and then he quit and became an agent and promoter. He signed up all the ballplayers for the trip, and a guy named Yetsuhega, who owned a trucking company in Hawaii, sponsored it, along with the Mainichi newspapers in Japan.

In those days a lot of ballplayers would go on barnstorming tours after the season to pick up some extra cash. Ruth and Gehrig and the players of that era did it, and it continued until the late fifties or early sixties. Sometimes the teams were all black. After the '53 season Billy Bruton and Jim Pendleton of the Braves played on Roy Campanella's barnstorming team. They would go out for a month or six weeks and travel around the country playing in areas that didn't normally get to see major league baseball. Sometimes, as in our case, the barnstorming team would travel overseas. While we were in Japan, the New York Giants were over there too. They even took Ford Frick along with them, but he found his way back.

Eddie Lopat's All-Stars was billed as "the greatest array

of major league stars ever to visit Japan." That may just have been promotional hype, but we did have a good ballclub. Warren Spahn had originally signed to play on the team, but he had some surgery right after the season and couldn't go along. Even without Spahnie we had a terrific pitching staff: Lopat, of course, plus Robin Roberts and Curt Simmons of the Phillies and Mike Garcia and Bob Lemon of the Cleveland Indians. I figured out that all together those five guys won 994 games in the big leagues. Roberts and Lemon are now in the Hall of Fame.

To back them up we had ten other ballplayers. That did not allow many substitutions in case of injuries. We had a scare, too. Eddie Robinson suffered a kidney stone attack in Honolulu on the way over, but he pulled through it. Anyway, we had Robinson at first base; I was at third; Harvey Kuenn, my roommate for the trip, was at shortstop; and a pair of second basemen, Billy Martin and Nellie Fox. The outfield had no extras, just Hank Sauer, Jackie Jensen, and Enos Slaughter. Finally we had two catchers, Yogi Berra and Gus Niarhos. Gus was never a regular in the big leagues, but he had played behind Yogi in New York for a few years.

The way the tour worked, we started out in Colorado playing four games in Pueblo and Denver against a ballclub that Paul Richards put together, mostly guys from the White Sox, which he managed at the time. That was fun playing in that high altitude. The ball really carried. I hit a bunch of home runs there, and one of them, they said, went 500 feet. Then from Colorado we flew to Hawaii, where we played against an armed forces team and then several games with Roy Campanella's Negro All-Stars. Don Newcombe was in the Army at the time, but he got a furlough and pitched for Campy's team and beat us in Honolulu Stadium. They had a real good ballclub.

Hawaii was paradise. We hated to leave. Jackie Jensen's wife was there with him. He had been an All-American fullback at the University of California, and he married Zoe Ann Olsen, the Olympic diving champion. Jackie was a pretty straight shooter. In fact, he didn't even want to fly. He was scared to death of flying. But Zoe Ann was a party girl. She would go out with Billy Martin and myself and whoever else, and he would go back to the hotel and go to bed while we went out on the town. She was a hell of a gal and still is.

While we were in Honolulu, Billy Martin managed to get

a date with one of these hula dancers. She was on the stage, and he was waiting for her to finish her act or dance or whatever it was called. He was going to go backstage. The whole team was in the audience, watching the show. As he started to go backstage, this Hawaiian bouncer wouldn't let him back there to get his date. Billy acted like he was going to turn away from him, and then he stretched the guy. He came back around and just coldcocked him. Then he went back and got the girl and left.

From Honolulu we hopped a Pan Am jet and flew to Tokyo. From the moment we landed at Haneda International Airport, we were in a different world. Thousands and thousands of screaming Japanese people were all around our plane. They had a huge welcoming ceremony for us, very ritualistic and formal. There were translators for us, but we still didn't catch all of what was going on.

Right away they started giving us gifts. Every time we turned around, someone was giving us a gift. I brought home boxes of gifts six feet long. They packed everything up for us and shipped it for us. In Japan in those days very few people

Welcome to Tokyo. I'm behind the flower girl, left of the rear banner.
(Author's collection)

Motorcade from Tokyo Airport. I'm in car number two.
(Author's collection)

spoke English or understood what we were trying to communicate. But they just kept smiling and bowing and giving us gifts the whole time. Wherever we went they had geisha girls or girls in beautiful costumes or shows or something special.

After the welcoming ceremony at the airport, they had a parade to our hotel, kind of like in Milwaukee. Each ballplayer rode in a separate convertible, so we had a procession of fifteen cars plus a few extra ones for the local officials. But unlike Milwaukee, the people along the parade route were all over the cars. They crowded in so tight the cars could barely move. The drive from the airport was supposed to take less than a half hour, but it took ten times that long. I didn't think we were going to make it. Try to picture the Pope in a motorcade with no police or security guards.

When we finally reached the Nikkatsu Hotel, they had mounted police and regular police to control the crowd. We checked in and then they escorted us to a rally at the Nichigeki Theatre (I looked it up). A Hawaiian-born singer whose name I didn't catch--they called him "the Eddie Fisher of Japan"--introduced each of the ballplayers to the crowd. He announced that the first American ballplayer to hit a home run would receive an expensive Nikon camera, and the first one to hit one completely out of the park or hit the scoreboard would receive a motorcycle. Then it was time for more gifts.

The next day we played our first game on Japanese soil, at Korakuen Stadium in Tokyo. Of course we had pregame festivities. First we had a home run hitting contest. Yogi and I hit two each, but Jackie Jensen won it with five--he was probably more rested. Then the U.S. and Japanese army bands both played. After that, helicopters dropped bouquets of flowers to each of the managers. Finally, another helicopter hovered very low over the field and dropped the first ball. It stirred up so much dust that the game was delayed for a while.

When we finally got to it, the ballgame turned out to be embarrassing. The Mainichi Orions, the fifth-place team in Japan's Pacific League, defeated "the greatest array of major league stars ever to visit Japan" by a score of 5-4. We scored three runs in the ninth to tie it, but they beat us in the bottom of the ninth. Hank Sauer hit a home run in the ninth to win the Nikon camera.

We played 12 games in Japan, and that was the only one that we lost. The slow pitching by the Japanese pitchers bothered me at first, but I ended up hitting seven home runs in the 12 games. Hank Sauer hit 12, including one that went out of the park and earned him a motorcycle to go with his camera. Most of the games weren't close, so we were able to try different things and have some fun: Yogi played the outfield, and Jackie Jensen pitched seven innings in one game. The only controversy in any of the games came when Yogi got kicked out for arguing balls and strikes--and it was our umpire. We had brought along Johnny Stevens, an American League umpire, and he ran Yogi.

There were two things about playing in Japan that I really got a kick out of. One was when you would hit a home run--the first baseman would bow to you, the second baseman would bow to you, the third baseman would bow to you...The other thing was the sound of the crowd. There was no clapping, no cheering. If something good would happen, they would hit their hands together three times, and that was it.

My only bad experience on the whole trip had nothing to do with the Japanese. Some of my teammates talked me into chewing tobacco. Nellie Fox was with us, and of course he could get up in the morning and put a big wad of that stuff in his face and it didn't even faze him. Well, I tried it, but I must have swallowed some. It trickled down or something, but boy, I thought I was going to throw up a lung. Nellie Fox, by the way, died at the age of 47.

One other memory of Japan stands out in my mind, or somewhere else. We played some of our ballgames in Tokyo, but most of them we played in the outskirts. You could always tell when you were getting near the town because you could smell it. They used human dung for their fertilizer. I don't think I would ever get used to that aroma.

After Japan we flew to Okinawa for two games against U.S. servicemen. We finished the tour in the Philippines, in Manila, playing a team from Japan. While we were staying in Manila, we took a trip out to see the military cemetery there. That was awesome! Just as far as you could see there were crosses, all lined up. Manila was as poverty-stricken an area as I have ever seen. Also, we saw ships in the harbor that were sunk or partially sunk in the war.

Across the street from our hotel in Manila was a big park. Billy Martin came running into the bar where we were, and he said, "Jeez, you oughta see over in that park. There's all kinds of women!"

The guy that was with us from Manila, who was acting as our guide, said, "You don't want to fool with them. Those are Benny girls."

Billy said, "What's a Benny girl?"

The guide said, "Those are guys dressed up like women."

Billy just shook his head and said, "Oh, brother!"

Billy, Harvey Kuenn, Bob Lemon, Eddie Robinson--
those are all guys I got to know on that trip. I had met a couple
of them in spring training, but I never got to talk to them much
or really knew them before. When you get a group of guys
together for that period of time, certain people click. Those
guys remained my friends ever since. And besides that, we made
about $4,000 apiece on that trip.

Flying back to San Francisco, I said "Sayonara" to one of
the best times of my life.

July 27, 1953

The agony of the Korean War came to an end on July
27, 1953, with the signing of a truce agreement at Panmunjom.
Meanwhile, halfway around the world in Cooperstown, New
York, Milwaukee-native Al Simmons celebrated his induction
into baseball's Hall of Fame. In Milwaukee, hundreds of loyal
fans jammed the train station to welcome home their beloved
Braves to begin a 21-game home stand. Charlie Grimm's club
had lost three straight to the front-running Dodgers. Had the
Braves won all three they would have come home a game out of
first; as it was, they barely clung to second, a game ahead of
the Phillies.

The Braves' opponents on this Monday evening were
Leo Durocher's New York Giants. It was Durocher's 48th birth-
day, but he should have known it was not his day when the
team bus broke down between their hotel and County Stadium.
The New York ballplayers were finally transported in station
wagons provided by the owners of a nearby nightclub called the
Blue Dahlia. Once the ballgame began, matters only got worse
for the visitors.

Warren Spahn, the Braves' ace (12-4), was staked to a
one-run lead in the third inning on a Jack Dittmer single, a
sacrifice bunt by Spahn, and a base hit by shortstop Johnny
Logan. In the next inning, though, the Braves exploded. Sid
Gordon hit a hard grounder to Giants' shortstop Daryl Spencer,
but the ball skipped right between his legs for an error. New

York hurler Jim Hearn uncorked a wild pitch, advancing Gordon to second, and Gordon tagged and moved to third on a long fly by Andy Pafko. Joe Adcock walked, Del Crandall singled home Gordon, and Dittmer ripped a single off Hearn's glove to load the bases. When Hearn missed the strike zone with his first two offerings to Spahn, Durocher called in Marv Grissom from the bullpen.

Grissom was no better. His first two pitches completed the base on balls to Spahn, forcing in Adcock and making the score 3-0. Billy Bruton singled in two more runs, and Logan's short single loaded the bases. Grissom was removed; Al Corwin came in to face Eddie Mathews. Until fifteen days earlier, Mathews had never hit a grand slam in the major leagues. On Corwin's 3-2 pitch, Mathews slammed his second, far into the rightfield bleachers. Spahn now had a nine-run cushion.

In the sixth inning Milwaukee parlayed two walks, three singles (one by Mathews), and a fly ball (next season it would again be considered a sacrifice fly) by Adcock to add three more to their total. Mathews then capped the evening's offense in the eighth with another home run, this one deep into the Braves' bullpen off Monte Kennedy. As a reward for his twin blasts, Mathews was permitted by Charlie Grimm to enjoy the last inning from the dugout. Veteran Sibby Sisti finished the game at third base. Spahn remained masterful and posted the 30th shutout of his still (relatively) young career, and the final score was an embarrassing 13-0.

Mathews' two home runs and a single raised his batting average from .299 to .303 and increased his major league leading home run count to 32. With 59 games remaining, Mathews was exactly even with Babe Ruth's 1927 pace, a fact widely trumpeted by the sportswriters. Mickey Mantle had not yet become a home run phenomenon and Roger Maris was eight years in the future, so Mathews was now the media's designated Ruth-chaser.

July 27, 1953

NEW YORK	AB	R	H	BI		MILWAUKEE	AB	R	H	BI
Lockman, 1b	4	0	3	0		Bruton, cf	3	2	1	2
Dark, rf	4	0	1	0		Logan, ss	5	1	2	1
Thomson, cf	4	0	0	0		Mathews, 3b	5	3	3	5
Irvin, lf	2	0	0	0		Sisti, 3b	0	0	0	0
Rhodes, lf	0	0	0	0		Gordon, lf	4	2	1	1
Spencer, ss	4	0	1	0		Pendleton, lf	0	0	0	0
Thompson, 3b	2	0	1	0		Pafko, rf	4	0	2	0
Hofman, 3b	2	0	0	0		Thorpe, rf	0	0	0	0
Williams, 2b	4	0	1	0		Adcock, 1b	3	1	1	1
Westrum, c	2	0	0	0		Crandall, c	4	1	2	2
Calderone, c	2	0	0	0		St. Claire, c	1	0	0	0
Hearn, p	1	0	0	0		Dittmer, 2b	5	2	2	0
Grissom, p	0	0	0	0		Spahn, p	2	1	0	1
Corwin, p	1	0	0	0						
Kennedy, p	1	0	0	0						
Totals	33	0	7	0		Totals	36	13	14	13

Hofman flied out for Thompson in sixth; Pendleton
ran for Gordon in eighth; Thorpe ran for Pafko
in eighth.

```
New York ....................... 0 0 0  0 0 0  0 0 0-- 0
MILWAUKEE ....................... 0 0 1  8 0 3  0 1 *--13
```

E--Spencer. 2B--Williams, Pafko. HR--Mathews 2. S--
Spahn. DP--Spencer, Williams, and Lockman 2; Mathews,
Dittmer, and Adcock. Left--New York 8, Milwaukee 7. BB--
Hearn 2, Corwin 2, Kennedy 3, Spahn 2. SO--Corwin 2,
Kennedy 2, Spahn 7. HO--Hearn 6 in 3.1; Grissom 2 in 0
(pitched to 2 in fourth); Corwin 5 in 2.1; Kennedy 1 in
2.1. R-ER--Hearn 6-5, Grissom 2-2, Corwin 4-4, Kennedy
1-1, Spahn 0-0. WP--Hearn. W--Spahn (13-4). L--Hearn
(6-6). U--Pinelli, Engeln, Boggess, Roberts. T--2:47.
A--28,380.

100

SIX

I Fought the Law

Only a fool would leave the warmth and comfort of sunny southern California in the middle of January and travel to snowbound Milwaukee, Wisconsin. My plane touched down at Milwaukee's General Mitchell Field, and I caught a cab to the Pfister Hotel. The occasion of my wintry visit was the First Annual Diamond Dinner of the Milwaukee chapter of the Base Ball Writers Association of America.

Along with teammate Billy Bruton, I was receiving an award from the writers, Billy as the Braves' rookie of the year and myself as the team's most valuable player. I didn't have to make a speech, thank God, just say how much I appreciated the award and blah blah blah. I left the speech-making to the dignitaries and regular speakers: Lou Perini, Charlie Grimm, the mayor of Milwaukee, and so forth. Over filet mignon and baked Alaska, we heard the featured speaker, President Clarence Miles of the Baltimore Orioles, tell how the Orioles hoped to duplicate the Braves' recent success in their transformation from the St. Louis Browns to the Orioles.

The whole affair was very cordial. We laughed at Ripper Collins' stories about the old Gas House Gang in St. Louis (we found out that Pepper Martin never wore an athletic supporter or any underwear). I saw my roommate from the Japan trip, Harvey Kuenn. I met my new teammate, Danny O'Connell, just traded to Milwaukee by the Pirates a few weeks earlier. Everybody had a good time yakkin' and frakkin', and since I was staying there at the hotel, I didn't even have to go outside afterwards and freeze my tail.

One other person I spoke to after dinner was our general

manager, John Quinn. John figured that would be an appropriate time to sign me to my new contract. "Eddie," he said, "I've been thinking about your contract." I had been too, but it wasn't on my mind that evening. "You had a pretty good year." Pretty good year! I led the majors in home runs and drove in 135 runs. "I'm willing to give you a $5,000 raise. That'll make it $17,000."

The figure stopped me. Mathematics was not my best subject in school, but something didn't add up. "That's not a $5,000 raise," I corrected him. "I made $14,000 last season."

"Sure," he said, "but $2,000 of that was the bonus I offered you for 30 home runs."

John Quinn did not miss a trick. He had a well-earned reputation for squeezing people. He did it with everybody, even Spahn. "That's not enough," I told him.

Then he got a little testy. "How much did you have in mind?"

So here I am. What am I going to ask for? I still didn't know how much anybody's salary was. I pulled a number out of the air--"I want $35,000," I said.

"Are you out of your mind?"

"No, that's what I want," I insisted.

"Well," he said, "that's not even a possibility." Then he went to schmooze with the big-wigs.

The next morning Lou Perini offered me a ride to the airport in his limousine--Mr. Perini, the chauffeur, John Quinn, and myself. Quinn started in again about my contract.

"Have you reconsidered the offer I made last night?" he asked me.

"No," I said, "I want $35,000. I signed originally without a bonus. I worked my way up from Class D. I played for the minimum salary. I took what you gave me the following year. Now I've hit a lot of home runs and batted .302, and I think it's time I got a pretty decent salary. I think $35,000 is fair."

Quinn's face said no, but before he could respond, Mr. Perini turned around in the front seat and said, "Eddie, I think you're right. Give it to him, John."

That irritated John Quinn so bad that I had trouble with him for the next two years. From then on, though, I was always able to talk to Lou Perini--not that I talked to him much--but whenever we ran into each other, he was always a super-nice guy. One year he was at spring training, and he was talking about his business. He did a lot of business up in Canada, and he was talking about a stock he was going to buy. Well, Perini was a sharp businessman and a millionaire many times over, so when he talked--like the old E.F. Hutton commercials used to say--people listened.

"I'll give you a tip," Perini said. "Invest in Mid-Chibougamau Mines, Ltd., in Canada."

I knew nothing about the stock market, but what the hell. Perini did. The company, this Mid-Chibougamau Mines, was involved in Canadian copper fields. None of us had much money to invest, so we didn't exactly jump in, but I put a couple grand down. I called my mother, and she put in a couple thousand, too. The stock got switched around to where it was called Consolidated Dennison. It fluttered around a little bit, and then we lost everything.

But Lou Perini and his brothers, Charlie and Joe, were all good guys. Basically they weren't baseball people. They turned it over to John Quinn, and John was a baseball man. But he could make shoes squeak, he was so tight. He was a very, very tough salary negotiator. And they were making a ton of dough. I could understand in Boston, when they were drawing crap, he might have to hold the line. In Milwaukee, though, drawing two million or two and a half million people, and paying almost nothing for the stadium, it didn't make sense. They didn't want to pay anybody. And it wasn't Perini--it was John Quinn. Nobody was making money--not me, not Spahn, not Aaron. Even today if you asked Hank Aaron, I'll bet he would laugh at what they were paying him back then.

Hank joined the Braves in spring of 1954. We had heard about him before he arrived. He had played second base with Jacksonville in the Sally League and torn up the league with his bat last year, but we didn't know about that. Major league ballplayers paid no attention to what was going on in the bush leagues. What we did know was that Hank had played winter ball in Puerto Rico with Caguas Guayama, which was the same team my roommate, Bob Buhl, played on. Everybody who saw him play--Ben Geraghty, his manager at Jacksonville; Mickey Owen, his manager in Puerto Rico; Buhl--everybody agreed Aaron was a great prospect, a can't-miss ballplayer. What we mainly knew was that the front office was all excited about him.

Buhl told us that John Quinn had called down to Puerto Rico and asked how Aaron was doing. Everybody, of course, raved about Hank, what a great prospect he was. Somehow Quinn ended up talking to Buhl. Bob said the same thing, Hank was terrific, but then he said, "If you don't get him off second base he's going to kill himself."

Quinn said, "What do you mean?"

Buhl said, "Well, he's not a second baseman. Why don't you put him in the outfield?"

Then Quinn asked Bob, "How about his hitting? What do you think he'll hit?"

"Honestly," Bob said, "he'll probably hit .280-something his first year in the big leagues and probably .300 after that."

"Is he that good?" Quinn said.

"Yes," Bob said, "he is."

Right after that Mickey Owen, the manager down there, put Hank in the outfield. He apparently got orders from higher up. And of course, Buhl's judgment of how Aaron would hit in the big leagues turned out right on the money. I don't think Hank has ever forgotten that.

Hank's plane landed in Tampa, so Buhl and I drove over from Bradenton to pick him up. He was a skinny kid, very nervous and shy. He was quiet and kept to himself pretty much at first. Gradually, though, he fit in with the rest of the club as he became acclimated. We didn't learn about it until much later, but Hank had had some rough experiences, racial experiences, during his year in the South Atlantic League with Jacksonville.

It's hard to explain what the racial situation was like in spring training in the '50's. Certainly Hank knew what to expect after growing up in Alabama and playing ball in Jacksonville. I don't think we understood it, though--we meaning the white ballplayers. There was never any racial problem on the ballclub, not in the sense of name-calling or fighting, but I'm sure the black ballplayers were treated differently and felt they were treated unfairly. They stayed in a boarding house in a different area of town, as Sam Jethroe had, while we were at the Dixie Grande. Hell, they couldn't drink at the same fountain or go to the same bathroom.

Really, it sucked--it was brutal. Read Hank's book and you'll get some idea of how difficult it was for him and for all the black ballplayers. For myself, I don't know if I didn't realize it when we went north on the train and the colored players could not even sit in the same car, even though there were black waiters working there. We had to get food and take it back to them. If I have one regret in my life, it would be that I didn't realize what it was like for a black person down there in the South, that I didn't try to take a stand.

I think the Chase Hotel in St. Louis was the last hotel to integrate of the ones we stayed at. We'd go to St. Louis, and Hank and the other black players would have to go to a different hotel. The rest of us just said, "Well, that's the way it is." We just rolled over and played dead or looked the other way. I deeply regret that--not that I could have made a difference, but I could have spoken out.

At the time of spring training, Aaron was assigned to Toledo, which was Triple-A. The gap between Class A, which is what Jacksonville was, and the big leagues, especially in those days, was enormous, even as talented as he was. I don't think Hank expected to make the club with Milwaukee. After about two weeks, though, Bobby Thomson broke his ankle, so the job in the outfield belonged to Hank.

Thomson had come over from the Giants in a trade that, according to Donald Davidson, was made at three in the morning at Toots Shor's saloon. We knew Bobby and what he had done, hitting the famous home run in the playoff in '51, and he was a hell of a nice guy. He fit right in with us. It was so easy with that ballclub. There weren't any strangers or outsiders. Everybody was treated the same. Bobby was a little more sensitive--I don't think he was used to the agitating and kidding that we did. When I say agitating, I mean giving somebody the business, giving him a hard time, just to stir things up and stay loose. It wasn't malicious or mean, just to get a reaction and keep things lively. I guess the Giants didn't do as much of that as we did because Bobby hackled up a few times at first. He got used to it, though. If he hadn't gotten hurt, he would have helped us, but I don't think as much as Hank did.

Thomson was brought in by the Braves to fill the vacancy in left field created when they traded Sid Gordon to Pittsburgh in the Danny O'Connell deal. I really hated to see Sid leave. He was a good pal, a veteran who took an interest in me and looked out for me when I was wet behind the ears. For some reason pitchers used to knock Sid down almost every time he got up to bat, or at least pitch him in tight. They thought it intimidated him. I don't know where he got that reputation because he was a damn good hitter.

Home run congratulations from Bobby Thomson in early
spring training, 1954. (Frank Stanfield photo)

Sid brought in a businessman from Cleveland and introduced him to me. What the businessman had in mind was a
couple of batting ranges where people could hit against pitching
machines. They'd get in a batting cage and set the speed they
wanted--major league, minor league, softball, little league, whatever. Sid helped me figure out if these things were a good idea, if
the financial arrangement was going to be any good. We decided

106

to go ahead with it.

The first "Eddie Mathews Bat-A-Way" opened on a chilly spring weekend in 1954 on the southern edge of Milwaukee. It had ten "Iron Mike" machines and a big field so the batters could hit it as hard as they wanted. We gave out autographed pictures and had a few local celebrities or personalities: former Green Bay Packer Don Hutson, announcer Earl Gillespie, and a local disk jockey named "Coffee Head" Larson. Sometimes some of the Braves would go out there and take some swings. We got some pretty big crowds.

One time when I was out there a guy swung and missed, and the ball hit the net behind him and rolled down near his feet. He reached down to pick up the ball, and the next pitch hit him right in the head. We never got sued, though. We opened the second "Bat-A-Way" on the north side later on in the summer. That one had to be torn down after a couple years because they were building an interstate highway. The original one lasted quite a few years, but gradually the interest died out and it was closed. We had a lot of fun with those things, though.

Early in my career a number of baseball people were convinced that third base was not my best position, and I'm sure I gave them reasons to believe that. Rogers Hornsby said I'd never be good at that position because my hands were too small. Tommy Holmes thought I might be an outfielder until the day I smacked into Ford Frick and reorganized my nose. If I hadn't made the Boston club in '52, I would have played with the Milwaukee Brewers, and Charlie Grimm had threatened to turn me into a first baseman. Fortunately I managed to avoid all that foolishness and stay at third base, where I had always played and belonged--until four games into the 1954 season. Then Billy Bruton caught a virus.

This was some virus. Whatever it was knocked him out of the lineup for two weeks. Thomson was already out with his broken ankle. On opening day Andy Pafko had been beaned by Joe Nuxhall and was still recuperating. That left our outfield crew shorthanded. Charlie Grimm put Danny O'Connell at third base, which was where he had played with the Pirates. Then he put me in left field and Jim Pendleton in center field and moved Aaron to right. I suppose you could say I made a rightfielder out of Hank. I should get some credit for that.

I definitely did not want to play the outfield, but what was I going to say--"I want to quit"? Or "Give me my release"? I wasn't like that. If the manager said "Squat," I just said "How much?" I was never the type of player to go and complain to a sportswriter or create a problem with Charlie or with the team. I didn't really know what playing left field would be like. Once I got out there, though, I found out very quickly that I didn't like it.

To me there's no question that third base is a tougher position than the outfield, just as shortstop is a tougher position than third base. Of course catching is tougher than any of them. But I found out I didn't like the outfield position, and it didn't like me. I played ten games out there, made two errors, batted less than my weight, and was in a 1-for-22 slump when Billy finally came back and saved my career. We were in last place when he returned.

When I got back to third base, there was still one thing missing. The commissioner had just made a rule that we could no longer leave our gloves on the field while we were at bat. That was always kind of fun. It had a certain flair to it. After the third out you'd turn around and--zzzztttt--sail your old rag out onto the outfield grass. And I don't ever remember tripping over anybody's glove. After that they started making us pile them on the side, so, what the hell, we just took them back into the dugout. I don't know why they ever changed that.

After Bruton returned we won a few, but we were still in seventh place after losing a Sunday afternoon game to the Cubs. That night I was invited to dinner at Bob and Joyce Buhl's house. They had just moved into a rented house after living in a hotel for a while, so after dinner we had a few beers to celebrate. The next day was an off-day before traveling to Brooklyn. We didn't have to catch the train until the afternoon, so we stayed up late just talking and laughing and sipping Milwaukee's famous beverage. All very innocent. It was almost 3:00 A.M. when I finally headed back to my apartment on the east side of Milwaukee.

Just a short distance from Buhl's house I approached a stoplight. Either I saw it too late or I was driving a little too fast, but I didn't stop until I was about halfway through the intersection of 76th and Blue Mound Road. There was no traffic at that time of night, so I looked around and then just kept going on through. The next thing I knew I saw a police car come out of nowhere with his red light going, but facing in the opposite direction. As he started to make a U-turn, I shut my lights off and took a right.

I went down about three blocks with my lights off. I did not see any lights in the rearview mirror, so I turned left, put my lights on, and went back to Blue Mound Road. There was the son of a gun sitting and waiting for me. He must have known that this was a creature of habit, that I wanted to get someplace, and that I was going to come back to get there. And he was right.

He approached my car and asked to see my driver's license. I handed him my license. "This is a California driver's license," he said. I already knew that.

He studied the license for a minute and then asked, "Are you Eddie Mathews?" My name was on the license. I just nodded. "I didn't recognize you," he said kind of apologetically. "I haven't been out to any of the ballgames." Ah, a glimmer of hope.

"I know it was a damn foolish thing to do," I said ingratiatingly, fishing for a stern warning.

"Will you follow me to the station, please?" No hope.

At the Wauwatosa Police Station I was booked, and the arresting officer, Howard Haag, asked me, "Were you drinking?"

"I had a few bottles of beer at some friends' house," I told him honestly, "but I'm not drunk."

He agreed. "Do you want to post bail?"

I didn't have my checkbook, and my wallet contained maybe twenty or thirty dollars. He released me without bail and told me to be in court at 8:30, about five hours away. He said if I missed my court appearance they would issue a warrant for my arrest.

"I'll be there," I assured him.

And I was, even a little early. I was in a foul mood when I got there, though. I had only slept a few hours, and I knew the front office would be upset when my little indiscretion hit the newspapers. As soon as I entered the courtroom, a photographer aimed his camera at me. "You take my picture and I'll break your arm," I explained.

He did snap the picture, but before I could snap him, the judge said, "None of that here."

This was hardly the Manson trial. The whole proceeding, the Honorable Edgar A. Bark presiding, lasted maybe four minutes. Sgt. Haag told what had happened, I pleaded guilty, and that was it. I didn't have an attorney, and there was no prosecutor. Except for the judge, the officer, the photographer, a reporter, and me, the courtroom was empty. No other cases were scheduled that day. Obviously Wauwatosa was not a high-crime area in 1954.

"Do you have any explanation to offer, Mr. Mathews?" Judge Bark asked.

I shook my head. I was fined $50 plus $4.15 in costs. We walked downstairs to the police station and I wrote out a check for the fine. As I did, the judge walked over and handed me an autograph book. "It's my daughter's," he said. "She's a big Braves fan."

I signed it. We had a nice chat about the Braves, and Sgt. Haag said I should get a Wisconsin driver's license. We all shook hands, and I went home to pack for our eastern road trip. The newspapers carried the story on page one in Milwaukee, but except for a sportswriter named Oliver Kuechle, they just laid out the facts and that was it. Kuechle did a pretty good number on me, but most writers in those days didn't make a big issue out of everything the way they do now. I got a little bad publicity out of it around the country, but it wasn't like a drive-by shooting or anything. When I went into Ebbets Field the following night a few people had sirens that they cranked up. We had some laughs with that. The incident was embarrassing, but what the hell--things happen.

A few weeks later, though, while we were in Pittsburgh, I received the news that I had been expecting and dreading. My dad was near death out in California. I flew back home on a Friday night. The flight was a kaleidoscope of emotions and thoughts. I loved my dad, very deeply. I had been told he could go at any moment. I wanted very much to see him again, to talk to him, but at the same time, I felt bad about leaving the Braves. Baseball meant everything to me. I felt a responsibility to it. My parents had raised me that way. I hadn't missed a single ballgame since we moved to Milwaukee.

My dad had been sick for over three years, since I went in the Navy. Even before that his health had been kind of frail, plus he was a pretty good drinker, and I think that contributed to his problem. When I was playing in Boston, he got out of the hospital for a while and went to visit his mother in Texas, but while he was there he got very sick again. When he came back that time, he didn't have a chance. Forty years ago tuberculosis was nearly impossible to treat. They couldn't do much for him except try to make him comfortable. Whenever I had visited him after he got sick, I felt empty and helpless. Flying home to see him one last time, I felt the same way.

When I got there he was all drugged up and completely out of it. He didn't know we were there. My mom and I and most of the relatives were at the hospital that whole weekend. We went home for a little while and then went back all day Monday and half the night. It was an awful time, with people crying and just waiting around for him to die. About three o'clock in the morning I couldn't stand it any more.

"Jesus, Mom," I said, "is he going to die or isn't he?" He was suffering, and we were suffering. About a half hour later, he passed away.

I had made the arrangements, and we buried him two days later. I said, "Mom, Dad would want me to go back and play baseball," so I left. She had her sisters there with her, so she was okay.

One of the saddest things about my dad's illness and early death is that he was never able to see me play big league baseball. He would have been so proud. He might have seen me on television, but I'm not even sure about that. I had my mother back east to see me play, but he was too sick by that time to make the trip. My mom even came down to Atlanta when I was a Cracker. I tried to get my dad to come, but he said he didn't feel up to it. Of course, we didn't know he was going to die, or I would have insisted. That's bothered me a lot, but I guess there was nothing I could have done about it. All I could do was play baseball and give him reason to be proud. I rejoined the Braves at Connie Mack Stadium and hit a home run off Steve Ridzik.

Shortly before my dad died, the Braves had returned from our first eastern road trip of the season. We had left in seventh place, right after my arrest, but we came home in first place, riding a nine-game winning streak after sweeping five games from the Cubs. The train station was mobbed with people, a couple thousand at least. This had happened before, but in the past it was always an organized civic function, with speeches and the whole nine yards. This one was entirely unplanned. These were just ordinary fans who thought they would come out on their own and welcome the Braves back to town. The Milwaukee people were unbelievable! Later on in the

111

year they organized a group that followed us for a whole road trip--Brooklyn, Philadelphia, and New York.

A couple days after our latest "Welcome home," I was leaving my apartment late one morning. I was living at that time in the Royal Plaza on Prospect Avenue, overlooking Lake Michigan. I shared the apartment with Joe Adcock, the only other bachelor on the club. A reporter had asked me in April if I had any marriage plans, and I told him, "I haven't found the right girl yet, but I'm getting tired of hotel life and looking at four blank walls." I didn't know it yet, but Adcock was about to lose his roommate.

As I approached my car, I saw someone standing behind it. A pretty girl was fumbling with a map, obviously confused. I walked over and gallantly asked, "Can I help?"

She pointed to the map and said, "I don't know how to get over to here," and she named a place I had never heard of.

I said, "Well, I really don't either, but would you like to come to the ballgame tonight?"

She brought a girlfriend of hers to the game, and I left tickets for them. We met after the ballgame. Her name was Virjean, and she was from Marshfield, a small town in central Wisconsin, about a hundred and fifty miles from Milwaukee. She was a student at the state college in Eau Claire, which is the town where Hank Aaron and Billy Bruton started their careers. Virjean was studying to be a school teacher.

We started seeing each other, and we both knew right away that this was something very special. Within a couple months, out in Santa Barbara, my mother made the announcement to the Associated Press: Virjean and I would be getting married after the baseball season. My mom flew to Chicago while the Braves were playing there, and she came back to Milwaukee with me to meet Virjean. To keep it as simple and private as possible, we agreed on a civil ceremony to be held soon after the World Series.

Despite some ups and downs, the Braves fully expected to be playing in the World Series that season. We put together some great winning streaks, winning nine in a row once and ten in a row three different times. From late July up until the middle of August, we won 20 of 22 games to get back in the thick of things. I had ten home runs during that stretch, and I was really seeing the ball well. Then in Chicago, on the same weekend my mother flew in, Hal Jeffcoat split my finger open.

112

My mother and I enjoying the hospitality of the Miller Inn.
(Miller Brewing Co.)

See, in those days, we had knockdowns. If a batter was having a lot of success against a pitcher or against his team, the pitcher would knock him down. He wouldn't necessarily hit you, but he would throw inside or near your head. Like Sal Maglie-- that's why they called him "Sal the Barber." He would throw one near your chin, not to hurt you but to back you off the plate. Maglie was very good at it. Now his teammate Marv Grissom was tougher--if he hit you, that was T.S. Eliot. He didn't give a shit. But to pitch you've got to be able to come inside. We pretty much accepted that fact.

Hal Jeffcoat, though, was really a nasty son of a gun. He hit Don Zimmer of the Dodgers in the face and damn near killed him. He got me three balls and one strike and then tried to stick one in my ear. Now, in my entire career I never got hit in the head with a pitch, and I never left my feet. I had the ability to lean, duck, or squat--or sometimes just get hit. Willie Mays exploded--he went down. Hank Aaron was similar to me. It's not a matter of courage; it's just the way an individual gets out of the way of the ball.

113

In 1962 in Philadelphia, I froze on a pitch for some reason. I don't know if I lost it or what, but it hit me right on the neck. The funny thing was, if it had been an inch or so in any direction, it would have been damaging, but it hit so flush that the sucker didn't even hurt. It just kind of rolled down my shoulder, and I went to first base. The pitcher was a guy named Dennis Bennett. I'll never forget that.

Getting back to Jeffcoat, though, the pitch was aimed directly at my head. As I ducked out of the way, I sort of stuck my hands and the bat up in the air. The ball jammed my middle finger against the bat and split the finger wide open. It bled like a stuck pig. I had to leave the game and go to Illinois Masonic Hospital. There was no fracture, but I needed some stitches. I was out of the lineup for 13 days. I missed our series against the Giants and Dodgers, the two clubs ahead of us in the standings. I didn't return until Labor Day weekend. On Sunday, the day before Labor Day, Hank Aaron broke his ankle in Cincinnati and was done for the year. That day and the following day in Chicago I got nine straight hits, one short of the National League record, and the guy who stopped the string, on a flyball to right field, was good old Hal Jeffcoat.

Actually, I may have been the first victim of the "*Sports Illustrated* Jinx." The week before Jeffcoat shattered my finger, my picture appeared on the cover of the premiere issue of that most famous of sports magazines. The picture was a side view of me swinging at a pitch, with Wes Westrum of the Giants catching and Augie Donatelli calling balls and strikes. The background shows the first base grandstand at County Stadium at a sold-out night game. It's a beautiful photograph. They sent me a copy, and I have it on my wall at home.

The idea of the "*Sports Illustrated* Jinx" developed over the years, I guess. One example was in 1957 when Roy McMillan of the Cincinnati Reds appeared on the cover late in the season, and of course the Braves, not the Reds, won the pennant. A couple months after that the Oklahoma football team was on the cover. They had won 47 straight games, and the heading was "Why Oklahoma Is Unbeatable." The following week they lost to Notre Dame. More recently, in 1987 the SI Baseball Preview issue featured the Cleveland Indians and said, "Believe It! Cleveland Is the Best Team in the American League." Of course, the Indians finished with the worst record in baseball.

114

There were lots of other cases, some of them far more serious. In the mid-'50's a young woman skier was on the cover at the time she ran into a tree and was paralyzed for life. Later on, a figure skater who had just been on the cover died in a

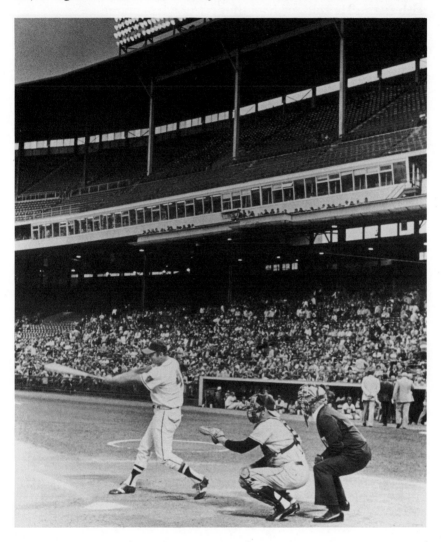

Recreating the original Sports Illustrated cover, 25 years later.
(Milwaukee Sentinel photo)

plane crash in Europe. My injury pales in comparison, but I may have started the trend.

The photographer who took the picture of me that was

on the cover used to live in Pismo Beach. There's a famous photography school in Santa Barbara, and he donated the camera that he used to take that picture. They called me to see if I would be part of the ceremony, so I went up and had lunch with them. He told me how that cover came about.

He said he took about 150 shots of different players and turned them all over to the editor. The editor chose that particular photograph because he said it was timeless--you don't really see anybody's face, and it doesn't emphasize an individual, but rather a scene that's repeated thousands and thousands of times every year. Years later we went back and recreated the scene, with Westrum and Donatelli and myself. The picture came out nearly identical.

Meanwhile, back in the pennant race, with Aaron out of the lineup our chances of catching the Giants were slim. Six days later in Brooklyn they diminished even further when Don Newcombe hit Joe Adcock on the wrist with a fastball and ended his season. We had to settle for third place. While the Giants prepared for the World Series, Virjean and I went to the Milwaukee County Courthouse the day after the season ended and began our life together by tying the knot in the County Clerk's office.

Because both of us like our privacy, we did everything we could to keep reporters and cameramen away from the wedding ceremony. In a baseball-crazy town like Milwaukee, though, that was not easy. Actually the decision to get married on that Monday was a last-minute deal to keep the press from finding out. They were expecting it in October, so we figured moving it up would make things simpler. However, getting married on the spur of the moment is not easy--and she wasn't even pregnant.

To help with the legal arrangements, I had an attorney by the name of Harry Zaidins. On Monday morning we found a doctor to perform the blood test for syphilis required by the state of Wisconsin. Then my attorney got the judge, Circuit Judge Harvey Neelen, to agree to sign a waiver of the five-day waiting period required after an application for the marriage license. We gave them the necessary information for the application, and they typed it right away. By that time the news of our presence was starting to filter throughout the courthouse, and we were beginning to attract a crowd. Harry Zaidins got Judge Neelen to perform the ceremony in the clerk's office instead of going to his courtroom, and he also kept the photographers away until afterwards. The only "outsider" was a newspaper reporter. I told him, "If this weren't my wedding day, buddy, I'd kick your butt." I would have, too. I wasn't always understanding with the press.

Once we got underway, the ceremony took about three minutes, and it went okay. Virjean had on a pink dress and a little pink hat, and she was as pretty as ever. I'm sure I looked dashing in my best suit. The bridesmaid was Virjean's best friend from Marshfield. My best man was Joe Taylor, the Braves' assistant trainer and my old bartender buddy from the Boston days. A typist in the courthouse put on a record of "I Love You Truly." The judge said his piece, I kissed the bride, and we managed to sneak out a side door and avoid most of the photographers and spectators. We ran to my car and made our getaway, Joe Taylor driving, Virjean and me in the back.

The plan was for Virjean and me to drive to California and meet up with Eddie Lopat's All-Stars. They were going to fly to Hawaii and then go back to Japan again. That would be our honeymoon trip. We thought it would be a lot of fun and romantic too, plus I would earn some money to start off the marriage. But as the poet said, "The best laid plans of mice and men..." or something.

What happened was, about a week or two before the end of the season, I came down with a big-time case of jock rash. We're talking industrial strength here. After four days of driving to California, I was so raw I could hardly sit down, let alone play baseball. I told Virjean, "There's no way I can go to Hawaii and play ball. In fact, I might even go in the hospital with this stuff." And I did. I had to cancel out of the Eddie Lopat All-Stars.

As it turned out, Eddie Lopat couldn't go either because of an ulcer. Whitey Ford went, and Del Crandall, and Duke Snider, and they went over and the guy that promoted the tour stole all the money and ran. None of the ballplayers got paid except for their air freight. There were some lawsuits, but they never did collect their money. The novelty of barnstorming baseball teams had worn off, and they never went back.

As for the honeymoon, we didn't really have one. We took a few short trips just in California, but that was all. We got shut out. The final score was Jock Rash 1, Honeymoon 0. So much for romance.

In 1953 Eddie Mathews had led the major leagues in home runs (with 47) and home run percentage while batting .302. Almost overnight he earned a reputation as the most feared slugger in baseball. His fielding skills, though, were suspect. That same year he made 30 errors at third base, tops in either league, and compiled the second-worst fielding average (.939) in the National League.

The next year Mathews' home run total declined (to 40) although his home run percentage actually increased (he played in 19 fewer games). His batting average also dipped slightly, to .290. He was, however, a better ballplayer. His improvement can be measured in his fielding statistics: in 1954 he committed 57 percent fewer errors (13), led the league in double plays by a third baseman (28), and compiled the second-best fielding average (.966) among league third basemen. His improvement was well demonstrated in a ballgame in Philadelphia on August 3, 1954.

The Braves were in the midst of a hot-and-cold season. In May they had won ten straight games, catapulting them from sixth place to first place as they entered June. After falling as far as fifteen-and-a-half games out, they started another ten-game winning streak against the Phillies on July 22. That streak ended in a tough 13-inning, 2-1 loss in Brooklyn on August 2, two days after Joe Adcock had slammed four homers and a double in Ebbets Field. Now they were in Connie Mack Stadium hoping to begin a new streak and gain some ground on the Giants and Dodgers.

The game matched two struggling veteran hurlers, nearly-38-year-old Murry Dickson and relative youngster Warren Spahn, a frisky 33. Dickson was en route to leading the league in games lost for the third year in a row. He showed why in the top of the second inning when he gave up a home run to Andy Pafko. In the bottom of the inning Spahn showed why he was sporting a mediocre 10-10 record (although he would finish 21-12) by allowing a tying solo shot to rookie outfielder Danny Schell.

The Phillies might have taken the lead in the fourth but for a fine defensive play by Mathews. Catcher Stan Lopata slammed a low line drive toward left field, but Mathews lunged to his glove side and grabbed the ball in the webbing of his mitt. The next two batters walked, but a ground ball ended the threat.

The Braves finally scored the runs they needed in the fifth, but not without a struggle. Leadoff man Billy Bruton lined a Dickson pitch into the gap in right center. Speedy Richie Ashburn made a running, lunging catch to rob Bruton of a triple. The next batter, Danny O'Connell, hit one to the wall in left center, but Ashburn caught up to that one too. Mathews then found a place Ashburn could not reach—he stroked a double down the leftfield foul line. Rookie Henry Aaron rifled a fastball off the cement wall in left center for a double that drove home Mathews with the lead (and eventual winning) run. Adcock then bounced a base hit up the middle to score Aaron for a 3-1 Milwaukee lead.

With his fastball livelier than it had been in some time and his control sharp, Spahn made the lead stand up, helped by some sterling defense. In the seventh Ashburn laid down a bunt along the third base line. Mathews charged the ball, barehanded it, and fired a strike to Adcock to nip the Phillies' speedster. Then in the last of the ninth, Mathews made the play of the day. After one out, Danny Schell and Earl Torgeson both singled. With the tying run on base, Willie Jones ripped a savage one-bouncer toward left field. Mathews speared the ball on a short hop, ignored the runner sprinting to third, and turned the Phillies' hardest-hit ball of the day into a crisp five-four-three double play to end the ballgame. The slugger was now a ballplayer.

August 3, 1954

MILWAUKEE	AB	R	H	BI	PHILADELPHIA	AB	R	H	BI
Bruton, cf	5	0	1	0	Ashburn, cf	4	0	1	0
O'Connell, 2b	5	0	0	0	Morgan, ss	4	0	0	0
Mathews, 3b	4	1	1	0	Lopata, c	3	0	0	0
Aaron, lf	4	1	3	1	Hamner, 2b	3	0	0	0
Adcock, 1b	4	0	2	1	Ennis, rf	3	0	0	0
Pafko, rf	4	1	2	1	Schell, lf	4	1	2	1
Logan, ss	4	0	1	0	Torgeson, 1b	4	0	2	0
Crandall, c	2	0	0	0	Jones, 3b	4	0	1	0
Spahn, p	3	0	0	0	Dickson, p	1	0	0	0
					Clark	1	0	0	0
					Wehmeier, p	0	0	0	0
					Kazanski	1	0	0	0
					Konstanty, p	0	0	0	0
Totals	35	3	10	3	Totals	32	1	6	1

Clark flied out for Dickson in fifth; Kazanski
popped out for Wehmeier in seventh.

```
MILWAUKEE .....................  0 1 0  0 2 0  0 0 0--3
Philadelphia .................  0 1 0  0 0 0  0 0 0--1
```

E--Jones. 2B--Adcock, Mathews, Aaron. HR--Pafko,
Schell. DP--Jones, Hamner, and Torgeson; Mathews,
O'Connell, and Adcock. Left--Milwaukee 9, Phila. 7.
BB--Dickson 3, Spahn 3, Wehmeier 1. SO--Dickson 2,
Spahn 4. HO--Dickson 8 in 5; Wehmeier 1 in 2; Kon-
stanty 1 in 2. R-ER--Dickson 3-3, Spahn 1-1. W--
Spahn (11-10). L--Dickson (7-12). U--Barlick, Dixon,
Ballanfant, Jackowski. T--2:28. A--13,899.

SEVEN

Losing a Friend

It was a total shock! It happened a week before Christmas Eve. I had been out shopping for presents or something, and when I walked into my mother's house in Santa Barbara, she said, "Mr. Miller has been killed." This was just six months after my dad had died, and I was still trying to deal with that. Now another tragedy.

The Mr. Miller she was referring to was Fred Miller, the president of the Miller Brewing Company in Milwaukee. The news reports were vague and sketchy at first, but within a day or so we learned the terrible facts about his death. He had been in an airplane that crashed and burned shortly after taking off from Milwaukee's Billy Mitchell Airport. He and his 20-year-old son, Fred Jr., had been headed for their hunting cabin in Canada along with two pilots employed by the brewery. The airplane was a converted bomber that Fred had bought for the company from the Canadian Air Force. One of the engines failed, and all four people on board died. Fred Sr. was actually rescued from the burning plane by people living nearby, but he died a few hours later at a local hospital.

More than anybody else, Fred Miller was responsible for the Braves moving from Boston to Milwaukee. He was the driving force behind the construction of County Stadium, which made it possible for the club to move there. He put the support of his brewery and all their advertising dollars behind the Braves and persuaded Lou Perini to make the shift. In fact, as far back as 1950 Miller had attempted to buy the St. Louis Browns with the hope of moving them to Milwaukee. To do that he tried to get the help of his old friend Bill Veeck.

Veeck had bought the Milwaukee Brewers of the American Association after the 1941 season, ten years before I joined them. Veeck sold the Brewers after the war, but when he first arrived in Milwaukee, Veeck used to play handball at the firehouse with a guy he knew only as "Fritz." Fritz turned out to be Fred Miller, and Veeck soon contracted with Miller Brewing Company for radio broadcasting rights to the Brewers' games, as well as beer sales at Borchert Field. Thus was a friendship born, a friendship that lasted ten years.

In 1951 Veeck himself bought the St. Louis Browns, with the promise to keep the club in St. Louis. Fred Miller felt he had been betrayed, and he never forgave Veeck. When Veeck attempted to move his team to Milwaukee for the 1953 season, Miller offered him no support, no advertising revenue, no assistance of any kind. Instead he lobbied Lou Perini and used Veeck's attempted move to Milwaukee to induce Perini to move. Miller also received an agreement from Perini, as I understood it--although I can't prove it--that if Perini ever sold the Braves, Fred would have the first shot at buying them.

As soon as we heard the Braves were moving from Boston to Milwaukee, we began to hear about Fred Miller--or Mr. Miller, I guess I should call him. He was only 48 when he died, but he was older than I was and a lot more important. At all the welcoming ceremonies for the Braves, Fred Miller was there. Whenever there was a photograph of team officials and civic leaders in the newspaper, Fred Miller was in it. At the big celebration in the Milwaukee Arena the night before our opening game in 1953, the person who got the biggest ovation was not the mayor or the governor or Lou Perini or Charlie Grimm or one of the ballplayers--it was Fred Miller.

It would be hard to overstate how much Fred Miller had meant to the city of Milwaukee. His grandfather had immigrated from Germany a century earlier with a few thousand dollars in gold and founded the brewery. It was still a fairly small company until Fred became president in 1947. In a few years, though, it grew to be one of the biggest in the country. As sales increased, so did the civic role of Fred Miller.

Besides being a national leader in the brewing industry, he seemed to be everywhere in the community, spearheading the campaigns for a new stadium, an arena, an air terminal, a library, a legitimate theater, and a Catholic orphanage. He served on the boards of directors of the Milwaukee Red Cross,

122

the Marquette University Medical School, the local chapter of the USO, and at the time of his death he was president of the Milwaukee Association of Commerce.

I met Mr. Miller at one of the welcoming ceremonies when the Braves first arrived in Milwaukee. We bumped into each other a number of times after that. One day we were standing around talking, and the subject turned to handball.

"Do you play handball, Eddie?" he asked.

I said, "Sure, my cousin Gene Bowman and I play a lot back in Santa Barbara."

"Great," he said, "we'll have to get together and play sometime."

So I got to know Fred Miller the same way Bill Veeck did--on the handball court. Veeck had both of his legs at the time, of course, before he went to war, but I doubt if it would have made much difference against Fred Miller. He was a hell of a handball player, a southpaw. I was much younger than he was and in pretty good shape, but he was a former handball champion and a terrific athlete.

Charlie Grimm sits atop the dugout, flanked by (L. to R.) Fred Miller and Lou Perini. (Miller Brewing Co.)

123

Fred Miller, in fact, had been an All-American football player at Notre Dame. He was a tackle, and he played three years for the legendary coach Knute Rockne. He was the captain of the Notre Dame team that won the most famous football game of all time--the one where Knute Rockne gave his half-time speech about "Win one for the Gipper." After that speech Notre Dame went out and upset the undefeated Army team in from of 80,000 people at Yankee Stadium. Ironically, Rockne died three years later the same way Fred Miller did, in a plane crash.

As a businessman Mr. Miller obviously recognized the advertising potential that sports held for his product, but his interest in sports went far beyond that. When the Green Bay Packers were threatened with bankruptcy in the early '50's, he bought stock and sponsored radio broadcasts and helped sell tickets. He did the same for the Milwaukee Hawks pro basketball team. The Hawks struggled to keep going while Fred Miller was alive, but they moved to St. Louis (and later Atlanta) the season after he died. Mr. Miller also helped bring minor league hockey (the Milwaukee Chiefs), pro golf, and the Western Open tennis tournament to Wisconsin. Miller High Life also sponsored teams outside of Wisconsin, like the football New York Giants and Philadelphia Eagles, but Fred Miller's loyalty was always to Milwaukee. If he had lived, there's no way the Braves would ever have left Milwaukee.

After I had my little brush with the law for running a stop sign, and after the sportswriters had taken a few potshots at me for doing so, I received a letter that was written to bolster my spirits. It said that "there will always be some who are ready to criticize and are not sincere Braves or Eddie Mathews backers anyway. Don't pay any attention to any of them." It went on to encourage me to answer my so-called critics by good hitting and fielding--"Just like when I was playing football at Notre Dame--when the other side played dirty against us, Rockne used to tell us to take it out on them in harder blocks and tackles." The letter concluded by saying, "Keep up the good work, Eddie. We are all for you and are following every inning of every game." It was signed, "Sincerely, Fred Miller."

I have never been a collector of memorabilia or souvenirs, but that letter from Fred Miller is something I have always treasured and kept in a safe deposit box. When Mr. Miller's plane crashed, the sports world and the Milwaukee community lost a great leader and a remarkable citizen, and I lost a dear friend.

I have one other similar possession that I prize. Near the end of our first season in Milwaukee, I received a very nice letter from Ty Cobb. He was living in Nevada at the time, but he wrote to express his admiration for my ability and to offer me some fatherly advice about how to conduct myself in order to achieve success in my career. He reminded me that we had met in Atlanta (as if I would forget!) and encouraged me to visit him if I were in his area. The letter was warm, thoughtful, and sincere, in stark contrast to Cobb's public image as a cold, cruel, and friendless fanatic. He expressed his wish that his letter receive no publicity, so in deference to that wish, I will not quote from the letter, even 40 years later, but merely acknowledge its receipt and how much it meant to me.

Speaking of warmth and sincerity, what could be less warm and sincere than Hollywood? Early in 1955 I got a telegram from some Hollywood film producer, asking me if I would consider an audition to be the new Tarzan. No kidding. I'm sure I was exactly what Edgar Rice Burroughs had in mind when he created the character. Me Eddie, you Jane. I never called him and he never called me, so that was the last I heard of it. I did get a big kick out of it, though. I walked around making Tarzan sounds and showing the telegram to all the guys. I saved the telegram for a while, then threw the damn thing away. Somehow none of us could picture me swinging through the jungle holding onto a chimpanzee. Plus I couldn't even swim.

It was probably just as well that I didn't get involved in the Hollywood scene. I got into enough trouble just in baseball. I suppose the closest I got to being in show business was doing a couple of commercials, although that never really worked out either. There weren't many opportunities available to athletes at that time, nothing like they have now. Today every ballplayer has his own agent. At that time we had one agent for the whole major leagues. That was Frank Scott, the guy that arranged the trips with Eddie Lopat's All-Stars. He was the only guy floating around who would come up with these little deals. And he came to you--you didn't go to him.

Actually, the first time I ever got anything for any appearance was with Howard Cosell. Howard had a little league radio program in New York in the early 1950's. He would

It was great to be young and a Milwaukee Brave. (Frank Stanfield photo)

interview you on the air and then take you out to dinner afterwards. That was it. But Howard was really something. He truly had a photographic memory. He was very impressive. I always liked Howard.

Of course once we got to Milwaukee, all the Braves started doing endorsements of various kinds, little local businesses like grocery stores and certain brands of food and maybe restaurants. They never really paid anything, though, just a few dollars or maybe some merchandise. As I said, we didn't get paid at all for our public appearances. Virjean and I did a newspaper ad for Kroger Food Stores, I remember, and I think I did one for some kind of wieners. These things were usually pretty amateurish. Hank Aaron did a radio commercial that became a local classic. It was for a lumber yard, and he ended by saying, "And that ain't no Baltimore bloop."

I did a Gillette ad once, for newspapers and magazines, and I got paid $250. I also did one for Chesterfield cigarettes, and I didn't even smoke at the time. They took a picture of my face and then had an artist draw in a cigarette between my lips. Stan Musial did one of those too. Lots of guys did.

I also tried a couple of television commercials, but they never made it onto the air. One was for Viceroy cigarettes. They had a voice singing: "Smoother, smoother, smoother taste. Viceroy's got more flavor than any filter cigarette." Then I was supposed to exhale this big puff of smoke out of my mouth--but I couldn't do it. I must have done at least thirty takes, and I couldn't get it right. Either I'd cough or it would come out my nose or it just wouldn't look right. I did the last take, and I threw up all over the floor.

Another TV commercial I made was for Ovaltine, but that never was used either. While I was doing that one, though, they were filming a commercial on the same set for some kind of oatmeal. They had a kid about ten years old who was going to eat a big spoonful of the stuff and then smile or say something, I don't remember which. Well, sometimes oatmeal can be a little cool on the top and hot on the bottom. They told him to dig down and put it in his mouth, and it burned the top of his mouth. He spit it out and screamed, "You son of a bitches!" That film ended up the same place as my Viceroy commercial.

Nineteen fifty-five was a crazy year for me and for the Braves. There was no pennant race. Brooklyn won 20 out of 22 games and it was all over. The Dodgers clinched the pennant in Milwaukee, and it was right after Labor Day. The Braves finished second, but way back.

Maybe there was something in the air that year, I don't know. Maybe the Russians were bombarding us with gamma rays. In Milwaukee a guy stayed up on top of a pole almost all season. He wasn't going to come down until the Braves won seven in a row, which we never did. Sorry, buddy. One day about 500 people from some little town showed up at County

Stadium in costumes, all dressed like people in pioneer days with fake beards and the whole nine yards. And all summer, everywhere you went, all you heard was the same song--"Davy, Davy Crockett, king of the wild frontier."

My season personally was unusual, too. For the month of April I hit about two bucks and no home runs. I thought I was swinging okay, but the hits weren't dropping and the long fly balls were caught. One day in Forbes Field in Pittsburgh I came to bat against Vern Law with the bases loaded and nobody out. I hit a shot, right on the screws, toward right field. It was one of those low screamers that just keep rising and carrying. I hit a bunch of those for home runs. On this one Dale Long, their first baseman, jumped up and caught it and turned it into a triple play. That's how things were going.

I finally started hitting, I mean really hitting, about the second week in May, but I wasn't feeling right. My stomach was bothering me. I didn't know what an ulcer felt like or even what an ulcer was, really, but I thought I had one. I started asking other guys about ulcers, and of course they didn't know anything either. Finally the pain was so terrible that I said, "I've got to find out what's going on."

I went to see our team doctor, not at the ballpark but at his private office. He gave me a funny little test. He had me lie down on a table, and he pushed in on my stomach and let out real quick. Well, that damn near put me on the ceiling. He said right away, "You're going from here to the hospital."

Fifteen minutes later I was at Milwaukee Hospital getting prepped for emergency surgery to remove my appendix. They said it was close to being a burst appendix, so I was just in time. I was in the hospital for several days, but a week after the operation I was working out with the ballclub. I was a fast healer, plus the doctor said that because I was in good shape he did not have to make as big an incision, and it was all muscle.

Even though they wouldn't let me play for a while, I traveled with the ballclub on the next road trip. We had a doubleheader in Cincinnati, then a day off, and then a game in Brooklyn. In those days, though, the players didn't have a union, and the front office didn't understand the concept of a day off. Today they have a limit on how many days in a row a ballclub can play, but when I played we didn't. I think one time in the mid-'50's the Braves played 47 straight days, if I'm not mistaken. Well, to fill in the gap between Cincinnati and

128

Brooklyn, we flew up to Quebec to play an exhibition game against the Braves' farm club there.

Quebec was the Braves' Class D affiliate, managed by my old Boston teammate, Sibby Sisti. Sibby, by the way, for all you cinema buffs, played the part of the opposing manager in the climactic scene of *The Natural*. He was the guy that changed pitchers right before Robert Redford hit the home run into the arc lights. Sibby lost that night in Quebec, too, not that anyone cared. The Braves used a different pitcher every inning, and I believe one of the coaches might also have pitched. The main reason I remember that game--the only reason I remember that game--is I started at third base, my first game after the appendectomy. I was called out on strikes twice--it hurt too much to pull the trigger--and then I was taken out. I pinch hit in Brooklyn and got a home run off Billy Loes, and the next day Charlie Grimm put me back in the lineup.

Despite my early season difficulties, the fans of the National League voted me into the lineup of the All-Star Game, which was played at County Stadium. A bunch of Braves played in the game--Johnny Logan, Hank Aaron, Del Crandall--and Gene Conley wound up being the winning pitcher. We fell behind 5-0 and then tied it up, and Stan Musial hit a home run in the twelfth inning to win it. It was really an exciting finish. I wish I could have seen it. In the sixth inning Al Kaline smashed a line drive off my wrist. The ball really nailed my thumb. I had to get out of the game and go to the hospital and have it X-rayed. I listened to the last few innings in the doctor's office at Milwaukee Hospital, which was rapidly becoming my second home.

My first home, at least in Wisconsin, was a small house that Virjean and I bought in Brookfield, a semi-rural suburb west of Milwaukee. That was before we had kids. Then later I became acquainted with a guy who became one of my best pals, and he was a contractor. We went into the construction business together. We did that for maybe ten years or so--nothing fancy or big, but we did pretty well. We built houses, and we did some of the store fronts at Mayfair Shopping Center. After the kids started coming along, Virjean and I bought some land a little farther out from the city, still in Brookfield but really rural. We built a real nice home there. I had my own outfit do the work, so that saved us some money. And that's where we raised our three kids.

On August 2nd I went under the knife again. This time, though, I performed the surgery myself, and it was not a complete success. What happened was, I came home from a night game after hitting two home runs against the Dodgers. To celebrate our victory over Brooklyn I decided to treat myself to a sandwich. As I was cutting a big piece of meat, the knife slipped and the big piece of meat I sliced was my index finger, almost down to the bone. It was pretty nasty. I missed a couple ballgames because of it.

Two days later I was back in the hospital. This time was different, however. About 2:30 in the morning Virjean and I arrived at Milwaukee Hospital, and about five hours later she gave birth to the most beautiful baby boy the world had ever seen, an eight-pound, ten-ounce apple-cheeked matinee idol named Edwin Lee Mathews, Jr. The following night I was back in the lineup. Before the game the Brookfield Kiwanis Club presented me with a $25 savings bond for Eddie, Jr.

Eddie, Jr. at the 1958 World Series. It's gotta be the shoes. (Frank Stanfield photo)

June 2, 1955

The slowest start of Eddie Mathews' baseball career occurred in the 1955 season. During the month of April, a span of 15 games, the leading home run hitter in the major leagues for the 1952-1954 triennium batted .216 and hit no home runs. In fact the hardest ball he hit in the first month of the season was turned into a triple play by the Pittsburgh Pirates. He finally hit his first home run in Brooklyn on Sunday, May 1. The next Sunday he hit his second one, in St. Louis. The following Sunday he slammed two more, this time against the Phillies. Three days later he underwent an emergency appendectomy.

With Mathews in the lineup, the Braves, like their third baseman, had been struggling. Without him, the club was pathetic. In their first four non-Eddie games they scored a total of seven runs and lost all four contests, dropping to fifth place. Of course it hardly mattered—the Dodgers had already run away from the pack, winning 22 of their first 24 ballgames to destroy any pretense of a pennant race. Nevertheless, if doctors' initial estimates were correct and Mathews missed a month of the season, it would be a long summer in Milwaukee.

But rumors of Mathews' demise were greatly exaggerated. On Tuesday, May 31, just 13 days after his surgery, the Braves traveled to Quebec on an off-day to play an exhibition with their Canadian farm team. Mathews not only accompanied his teammates but also pinch hit, unsuccessfully, in the game. The next day in Brooklyn he tried pinch-hitting for real but grounded out for Burdette in the eighth. Now on June 2nd the Braves and Dodgers were finishing up their brief two-game series at Ebbets Field.

The afternoon's pitching matchup was ominous for Braves fans. The Dodgers offered Milwaukee nemesis Billy Loes, who had beaten them five times in 1953 before the Fourth of July. Meanwhile the Braves' hurler was Mathews' roommate, Bob Buhl, who had won 13 games as a rookie in

1953 but had endured almost a year and a half of failure since pitching in Puerto Rican winter ball after his rookie year. A year hence Buhl would be the biggest Dodger-killer in captivity, beating them eight times in one season. Today he was merely rehearsing for that role.

Actually Buhl pitched well, striking out nine in seven innings, at least one in every inning. He made only two bad pitches, but they hurt him. In the second inning he gave up a triple to Sandy Amoros, leading to a run, and in the third he served up a two-run homer to Duke Snider, the fourth four-bagger in two days for the Duke. Loes, meanwhile, was as tough as ever. The Braves came to bat in the top of the eighth trailing 3-0. Charlie Grimm had no choice but to send a pinch-hitter for Buhl, scheduled to lead off. He sent Eddie Mathews, the recent invalid.

Mathews cranked the first pitch out of the park to pull the Braves closer at 3-1. As things transpired, though, Grimm might have done better to let Buhl stay in the game and fail at bat. In the last of the eighth Dave Jolly relieved, and the Dodgers ate him for lunch. Jolly faced six batters and allowed three hits and three walks. His relief, Roberto Vargas, did a little better—he faced five men and got one out. Finally bonus baby John Edelman, a 19-year-old English major from West Chester (Pa.) College, made his big league debut and, after giving up a pair of hits, retired Gil Hodges and Jackie Robinson to end the inning at ten runs.

Johnny Logan added a solo home run in the ninth, but the final score was an embarrassing 13-2. The news was not all bad, though. Mathews was back. He started at third base against the Phillies the next night, two weeks ahead of the doctors' predicted timetable, and he slammed four home runs in the Philadelphia series.

June 2, 1955

MILWAUKEE	AB	R	H	BI
Bruton, cf	3	0	1	0
Tanner, rf	4	0	0	0
Aaron, 2b	4	0	0	0
Crowe, 1b	4	0	1	0
Logan, ss	4	1	1	1
Thomson, lf	4	0	2	0
O'Connell, 3b	4	0	0	0
Crandall, c	2	0	0	0
Buhl, p	2	0	0	0
Mathews	1	1	1	1
Jolly, p	0	0	0	0
Vargas, p	0	0	0	0
Edelman, p	0	0	0	0
Totals	32	2	6	2

BROOKLYN	AB	R	H	BI
Gilliam, 2b	5	1	1	2
Reese, ss	4	3	2	1
Snider, cf	4	3	3	2
Campanella, c	4	1	2	2
Amoros, lf	5	2	4	2
Hodges, 1b	3	1	0	0
Robinson, 3b	4	1	0	1
Furillo, rf	3	1	2	2
Loes, p	2	0	0	0
Totals	34	13	14	12

Mathews hit home run for Buhl in eighth.

```
MILWAUKEE ................... 0 0 0  0 0 0  0 1 1-- 2
Brooklyn  ................... 0 1 2  0 0 0  010 *--13
```

E--None. 2B--Bruton, Amoros. 3B--Amoros, Gilliam.
HR--Snider, Mathews, Logan. S--Campanella, Loes 2.
DP--Reese, Gilliam, and Hodges. Left--Milwaukee 5,
Brooklyn 6. BB--Buhl 3, Jolly 3, Loes 2. SO--Buhl 9,
Edelman 1, Loes 6. HO--Buhl 5 in 7; Jolly 3 in 0
(faced six batters in eighth); Vargas 4 in .1; Edel-
man 2 in .2. R-ER--Buhl 3-3, Jolly 6-6, Vargas 4-4,
Edelman 0-0, Loes 2-2. WP--Buhl. W--Loes (6-2). L--
Buhl (1-4). U--Gorman, Engeln, Pinelli, and Boggess.
T--2:25. A--5,301.

EIGHT

... but No Cigar

Now I was a family man. I made up my mind to play that role to the hilt--station wagon, big dog, puttering around the house in my bedroom slippers, no more partying past curfew, certainly no more embarrassing headlines in the newspapers to upset the front office.

I was also resolved to have the best year of my baseball career in 1956. I worked out over the winter, watched my diet, played a lot of handball. Usually I arrived in spring training about ten pounds overweight and needed to sweat it off. Not this time. When I stepped on the scale in Bradenton, I weighed the same as I had in high school football. I did my running, took extra batting practice, took ground balls after practice. When we broke camp and started to work our way north, I was hitting well over .300 for the spring, and I had the most homers on the club and more RBI's than anyone except Aaron.

On Easter weekend we made our customary stop in my old stomping grounds, Ponce de Leon Park in Atlanta, for a series with the Crackers. I always enjoyed that little jaunt because I still knew quite a few people in Atlanta, and they always treated me really well. On Saturday we had just walked onto the field to begin our pregame routine when a guy walked over to me. He held out a piece of paper folded in thirds and said, "Mr. Mathews, this is for you."

I figured he wanted an autograph. He didn't. It was, of all things, a subpoena. Somebody wanted $15,000 from me. At that same moment Charlie Grimm was being served with a similar paper saying they also wanted $15,000 from the Milwaukee Braves. Charlie was given the papers as a representative of the ballclub.

The piece of paper said I had committed "violent assault and battery" against a representative of the Southern Railway on March 27, 1955. It went on to say that my assault--excuse me, let's make that "alleged assault"--had caused his face to be "bruised, contused, and lacerated." I laughed when I read that phrase, but it wasn't funny. Then it said his lips were "cut and bleeding" and his arms and body were "bruised and contused." How about getting screwed and tattooed? Finally, the paper they gave to Charlie named the Braves as co-defendants because "they did not provide a suitable guardian for Mathews." Maybe they thought I escaped from a chain gang.

My reaction to being sued was total disbelief. Needless to say, Charlie Grimm was a little bit taken aback by the process as well. I missed infield practice that day although I did play the ballgame and hit a home run. Here's how that whole thing came about.

The previous year the Braves had played the Crackers, as we did every year on our way up north. Actually we usually played in Atlanta, then went south again, and then made our way north. Anyway, after we played in Atlanta we were going to take an overnight train to Jacksonville, Florida. We might have stopped for a drink first, but Atlanta was a dry county on Sundays, so before we left Atlanta, some of us thought we would get some food to take along on the trip. I knew this restaurant near the train station that had great ribs. I went with Chet Nichols and Bob Buhl and somebody else to get some ribs.

We bought a couple loaves of bread and a sack of ribs--a big sack of ribs--that we were going to pass out to the troops when we got on the train. The problem was, we didn't know which train the Braves were on. The depot in Atlanta had a ramp and then stairs going down on either side. We didn't know which stairs to take to get to our train. We were walking along the ramp, and I saw a passenger agent. He was a pretty good-sized guy for a passenger agent. I said to him, "Which ramp goes down to the Braves' train?"

He said, "You go back the way you came, all the way down to the other end." So we went back up the stairs and all the way to the other end and started back down the stairs.

We got down there and there was no train. I asked somebody, "Where's the train going to Jacksonville?"

The guy said, "Oh, you're in the wrong place. You go way

135

back the other way."

All right. We went back the other way to where we started out and headed down the stairs. Here was the same passenger agent standing there smirking. He gave us a little laugh and said, "I guess you didn't find your train."

I said, "What the hell's the matter with you? Where is the Braves' train?"

"Forget the Braves' train," he said. Then he stuck out his chin and said, "Get the hell outta here."

I don't know what was bugging him. Maybe he thought we were giving him a hard time or razzing him. I just don't know. At that point Chet Nichols knew exactly what to do. He said, "Eddie, give me the ribs." He knew what was going to happen. When the passenger agent saw me pass the ribs to Nichols, he shoved me. That was a mistake. When he shoved me, I hit him. Then he swung at me and I hit him again. It only lasted a minute. He got marked up a little bit. He hit me too, but it didn't cut me or anything.

We had a train to catch, and we didn't figure we'd get much help from the passenger agent, so we decided to just go down this one flight. As it turned out, that's where the Braves' train was. We went with the ribs into the compartment and started passing them out to the guys. We were sitting down and just starting to eat when the passenger agent came into the car with two cops. He spotted me and pointed me out to the officers. Then Charlie Grimm came running and said, "Eddie, what the hell did you guys do?" They handcuffed me and drove me and the passenger agent down to the jail. Nichols and Buhl stayed on the train and ate the ribs.

When we got to the police headquarters, the guy behind the desk was a cop that used to work at Ponce de Leon Park when I played down there. He saw me and asked, "Eddie, what happened?"

"We got in a little scrape," I told him.

The passenger agent started screaming, "I want this guy put in jail. He assaulted me."

I said, "That's not exactly the way it worked."

The cop said, "If he wants to press charges, Eddie, I guess you're gonna have to go in and we've gotta book you." The passenger agent did have a couple of marks on him, and his lips weren't working right. And then the cop said to me, "But don't you want to file assault charges against him?"

I got the hint. I said, "Yeah, I sure do."

The cop said, "Okay, then we'll put you both in jail."

Well, the passenger agent didn't care for that idea at all. "I'm not going to jail!" he yelled.

The cop came right back. "Well, you wanna drop the charges?"

He thought for a few seconds and then said, "Yeah, okay. Let's just forget the whole thing."

The cop told him that was the best thing for everyone involved. Then he said, "Why don't you two guys shake hands, and that'll be the end of it." We did. Then the cop said, "Eddie, you stay here for a minute." After the passenger agent left, the cop said, "I'll get one of the officers to drive you back to the train station. We'll let that son of a gun walk."

So one of the cops drove me back, and Duffy Lewis had held the train until I got there. This whole thing had taken about an hour. Nobody saved me any ribs, though. We went on to Jacksonville, and that was the end of the little brouhaha with the passenger agent, or so I thought.

I gave my subpoena to Charlie Grimm. He turned it over to the higher-ups, who turned it over to my old friend, Crackers owner Earl Mann. Earl said he would give the papers to his club's lawyers and they would take care of the whole deal. He said not to worry. About a year or so later they contacted me and said I should pay the passenger agent a few thousand dollars to settle out of court. They said it would cost me more than that to go back to Atlanta and go through the whole legal rigamarole. I hated to settle, first because he started it, and second because I would have liked to ask that jerk why he wouldn't tell us where the Braves' train was. But I wrote the check--what the hell.

It's not an original thought, but ballplayers have to put up with a lot from people, as do all so-called celebrities. If two people are involved in any altercation and one of them has a famous name, guess which one will be blamed, and guess which one will be sued? That same day I got into the hassle with the passenger agent, Casey Stengel was charged with assaulting a photographer in St. Petersburg.

At Al Lang field in St. Pete, they always let the photographers go on the field during the ballgames in spring training. That used to be common throughout baseball in the 1920's and '30's, but by the time I played I think Al Lang Field was the last

137

place where they allowed it. Well, a photographer was setting up to take a picture about six or eight feet from home plate. They let them get that close. The problem was he was blocking Casey's view of the game. Casey told the guy to get the hell out of the way, although he probably used stronger language. They got into an argument on the field. Later the photographer pressed charges against Casey, claiming he had cursed him and kicked him in the leg. Casey got off with an apology, though. He was smarter than me. He didn't leave any marks.

Later on in 1956 I was involved in another incident, but I was an innocent victim. Really. No one would ever believe that, of course. It was really nothing anyway. This one happened in Cincinnati in a bar called The Clock. It's not there anymore. About eight of us were sitting in there after a ballgame, rehashing the game and unwinding with a beer or two. A gal came in wearing a big white hat with a big brim.

That happened to be right at the time when everybody was talking about flying saucers. The year before it was Davy Crockett; this year it was flying saucers. Anyway, we were seated on kind of a raised level in this bar, looking down to where this woman was sitting. She looked a little bit tipsy. One of the ballplayers in our group started doing an announcer routine: "Ladies and gentlemen, may I have your attention please. You see before you the world's largest flying saucer. It will be taking off from earth in ten seconds."

We were all laughing to beat hell. Then he started a countdown: "Ten...nine...eight..." By "eight" we had all joined in. At "six" she picked up her glass and turned to throw it. I don't know if she singled me out and had an accurate arm or if she could even see me clearly, but she caught me on the side of the face with it. It cut me open pretty good. There was a big to-do, and as it turned out, it was a woman that was supposed to meet a well-known National League umpire in that bar. He's deceased now, but I still won't mention his name.

The next time we were in New York I was invited (ordered) to pay a visit to the office of the league president, Warren Giles, to discuss the incident. He started digging into me, telling me I had to be more careful about where I socialized and with whom and blah blah blah.

"Wait a minute," I said, "do you know who that woman was with?"

"No, who?"

"One of your umpires," I said, and I identified him. "That was his lady friend."

The league president gave me one of his stern looks and said, "Well, this time I'll let it pass, but don't let this happen again." Case closed.

On the baseball field our main focus was finding a way to beat the Brooklyn Dodgers. They were the reigning world champions now, with Johnny Podres and Sandy Amoros the heroes of the World Series, so of course they were the team to beat. Ever since the Braves had moved to Milwaukee, though, the Dodgers had been our main rival. They were the only club that had a winning record against us, plus we always seemed to get into some kind of fight or controversy when we played Brooklyn. There was just some kind of chemistry.

One of the Braves' ballplayers who seemed to be involved in a lot of the scraps with Brooklyn was Lew Burdette, and there was a simple reason: he was a competitor. Lew would do what he had to do to beat you. I mentioned the time in 1953 when Campanella started after him with a bat, but there were other times too, some of them involving Jackie Robinson. Jackie and Lew were both fierce competitors, and neither one would ever back down from anybody. It didn't have anything to do with race, though. When Burdette was out there pitching, he didn't think about what color you were. I've known Lew a long time, and I have never seen any prejudice in him.

Burdette pitched tight. He had to--that was his way of pitching. He never had a greatfastball, an overpowering fastball. Lew beat you with control and by keeping you off the plate. He'd put one under your chin if he had to, and occasionally one might get away. Also, pitchers absolutely protected their teammates, or at least most pitchers would. Not Warren Spahn. And it had nothing to do with Spahnie. He didn't want to or need to brush anybody back or throw at them. He was like Koufax--if one got away from Sandy, he would yell, "Look out!" It was their way.

I'd say most pitchers, especially the hard-throwing guys, didn't need or want to retaliate just for the sake of retaliation. Some of them did, though, and Lew Burdette was one. So was Bob Buhl. That was their way of working a ballgame. If you hit their guy, they would hit your guy. Or you--pitchers had to bat too, so they would get hit or knocked down.

We had a weird game against the Dodgers in Milwaukee

139

in 1954. We were rained out after five innings and the Dodgers beat us by a run. I hit a grand slam that night, but Brooklyn score five runs in the fifth inning to take the lead, and rain washed away the last four innings. Two things stand out about that game. First, Burdette got drilled his first two times at bat. Don Newcombe and Bob Milliken both nailed him, probably in retaliation for Lew throwing at one of the Dodgers. That was how you sent a message.

The second thing was, Johnny Logan drew a walk with only three balls in the count. Everybody in the press box agreed that the umpire, Lee Ballanfant, lost track of the count. The Dodgers yelled and screamed for 15 minutes, but he wouldn't change his call. Logan was surprised, but his walk loaded the bases, and then I hit a grand slam. Then the Dodgers really went nuts. Eventually Jackie Robinson got thrown out for arguing. As he left he threw his bat. It bounced into the seats and hit a couple fans.

We caught Jackie right at the end of his career. By then he had a lot of animosity. He'd had enough of the aggravation. Of course Burdette pitching the way he did, and as competitive as he was, he didn't like Jackie either, not because he was black, but just because he didn't like him. To Jackie, though, everything was racist. He had gained a little weight toward the end. Somebody yelled, "What time did that watermelon get cold?" He thought the person was saying it because he was black, but it was because he had that big belly. When he was playing second base, between innings when he took grounders, he'd throw the ball wide of the first baseman and into our dugout, either nail somebody or clean us out. That was one way he would get even.

Naturally we all heard stories of how it was for Jackie when he first broke the color line, all the crap he took from Ben Chapman and some of the southern guys. The only thing I actually heard--I'll never forget this--was in Boston in '52, somebody yelled, "Pitch the son of a bitch under his lips." When Milwaukee played Brooklyn, though, at least from my point of view, we went at it because it was part of the game, not because of race. I always admired Jackie. We all did. He was a hell of a ballplayer. He was the best baserunner I ever saw, the way he could start--stop--start, and then reach full speed in a split second from a flat-footed stance.

We were in Ebbets Field one time, having one of our usual go-rounds with the Dodgers. Burdette hit Robinson with

140

a pitch. Johnny Podres was pitching for Brooklyn that day, and I was the first batter in our half of the inning. I KNEW I was going down, so I turned to Campanella and said, "If he hits me, I'm hitting you."

Campy talked with that real high voice, and he said to me, "Damn, Eddie, I'm not throwin' the ball."

Sure enough, Podres unloaded on me, and I don't know how, but I spiked myself on my left knee getting out of the way. But nobody got mad--that was just part of the game.

Probably the most famous ballgame we ever played with the Dodgers was in Ebbets Field on July 31, 1954, when Joe Adcock, who was still sharing an apartment with me in those days, hit four home runs and a double. To this day nobody has surpassed that performance. Joe got so many calls that night from reporters that he had to hide out in Andy Pafko's room to get some sleep. The next day he hit another homer. Then he got beaned by Clem Labine and had to be carried off on a stretcher.

If Joe had been hit somewhere other than the head, he might have taken off after Labine. The way it happened, though, we weren't thinking about hitting Clem Labine in the mouth; we were worried about Joe. It's the guy that gets hit, the guy that's all upset, that starts it, not some guy in the on-deck circle or in the dugout. Once it starts you'll jump in, but Joe wasn't around to start anything. After everybody was out on the field, Jackie Robinson said something to Burdette and then got on Charlie Grimm about something. Then I got in Jackie's face. I said, "If you wanna talk to somebody, talk to me. You wanna beef, let's beef." It didn't lead to anything. That's the only confrontation I had with Jackie. I was just a Johnny-come-lately.

In 1956 Adcock did go after a pitcher, but not a Dodger. Ruben Gomez of the New York Giants nailed Joe on the arm. Joe started down to first base rubbing his bicep and mumbling to himself. About halfway there, Gomez for some reason started screaming at him. That just triggered Joe. As big as he is, Joe is like Ted Kluszewski. He was never going to start anything. But whatever Gomez said to him--it ticked him off because he charged the mound.

The mistake Joe made, though, was that Gomez had reloaded. The umpire had given the catcher the ball, and the catcher had already thrown it back to Gomez. When Joe charged the mound, Gomez cranked up and hit him again with the damn thing, harder than the first time but this time on the front of his thigh. Then Gomez took off like a halfback. We had a guy named John Riddle coaching at third base. When Gomez came by the foul line at third, Riddle took a dive at him and tore his shoulder up. Gomez just gave a little hip and went into the dugout and up into the clubhouse. That was it.

We faced Gomez only one more time after that, and he didn't have much success. He was such a laughing stock because he couldn't stand and take a punch or just move around and dance around Joe. Instead he ran like a raped ape.

Expectations were high for the Braves in 1956, both our own and the fans'. We thought we had as good a team as Brooklyn, or better. For about the first month and a half we stayed in first place or very close. Then for two weeks or so we just stunk. Rumors started flying, which they often do, that the Braves were going to fire Charlie Grimm. A lot of speculation centered around Fred Haney, the ex-Pirate manager who had been hired as a Braves coach before the season. He had experience as a manager in both the minor and major leagues, and he was already with us. Some people were guessing that Haney would finish the season and then Leo Durocher would be hired as manager. Leo had been replaced by Bill Rigney with the Giants, and so every time a managing job opened up, Durocher's name would pop to the surface.

The Braves were playing in Brooklyn, a four-game series. We lost the opening game on a bases-loaded single with two outs in the ninth, a real tough loss. We were in fifth place at the time, although not many games behind. Now the rumors were really strong. The next afternoon we lost again by one run, with two of the Dodger runs unearned. That was it. As soon as the team bus returned after the game to the Commodore Hotel, the microphones were set up and Charlie Grimm held a press conference and told the reporters he was resigning "for the good of the team," that old song and dance. Fred Haney was our new manager.

Nobody was surprised, but we felt bad for Charlie. We all loved him. He'd grown up in an era when baseball was for fun, and he always told us to go out and have fun. That was his lifestyle, when he played and when he managed. He enjoyed life. When we would go into St. Louis to play, he'd have us out to his farm outside of town for barbecues. At the end of our first year in Milwaukee, Charlie had the whole team out to his place, and he even had a little five-piece combo playing music. I sat in with

142

them for a little while and played the guitar and sang. Charlie played the banjo. We had a great time. I can play the guitar in different keys, but I'm not really a guitar player. I'm not really a singer either, but I'll sing at the drop of a hat. I usually carry a hat around with me. I just have fun, and that's how Charlie was. He made baseball fun. That really meant a lot to me, his approach to baseball. Don't take yourself too seriously. Enjoy life. Somebody gave you a gift--enjoy it. He'd sit down with us on the train and drink beer.

Charlie Grimm loved to have fun. (Frank Stanfield photo)

That was his weakness. He was probably a little too easy for a bunch of young guys. He wasn't really a manager; he was more of a pal. And he wasn't a tactician. He didn't change pitchers very much. Warren Spahn would walk up to Charlie and say, "I want 35 starts and I want to pitch nine innings." That's the way he thought, and Burdette and Buhl were the same way. And that was fine with Charlie. Spahn and Burdette were both good hitters, so that made it easier to keep them in the game. Buhl couldn't hit me with a bat if I ran across the plate, so he got pulled out faster.

143

We liked Fred Haney. After we got to know him, we had a lot of respect for him. Any new manager that comes in tries to establish himself, lay down the law, show he can be tough. That's how Fred tried to be.

Haney had had an interesting career, both as a ballplayer and then later on. He was a teammate of Ty Cobb for several years in Detroit and also of Charlie Grimm for a short time with the Cubs. He received a telegram from Cobb congratulating him for becoming manager of the Braves. Fred liked to tell the story of how one time in an exhibition game he was walked intentionally to get to Cobb. That was his proudest achievement, he said. After he retired as a player, he managed in the majors and the minors and then became a broadcaster on the West Coast. He was the radio man for the Hollywood Stars for a number of years. They loved him out there, so much that they talked him into managing the club. He did a good job at that, so he got promoted to the big league club, which was the Pittsburgh Pirates. In Pittsburgh, though, the cupboard was bare.

Fred was Mr. Hollywood. He knew everybody out there. He liked to bring in movie stars to talk to us, I guess to impress us. Right after he became our manager, we were playing at the Polo Grounds. Bob Hope sat behind our dugout and talked to Fred between innings. Then one time he brought Pat O'Brien into the clubhouse to give us the Gipper speech from *The Knute Rockne Story*. But all managers did stuff like that. Charlie Grimm brought in the best banjo player in the country. His name was Eddie Peabody. After that the big joke was, "And now, Eddie Playbody will pee on his banjo." After the Dodgers left Brooklyn and we went out to Los Angeles, it was natural that we got a little more of that star stuff, not so much in the clubhouse, but afterwards, at parties or on off-days.

We did have some changes with Haney. He managed entirely different from Charlie. He used the bunt and the hit-and-run more. He went to the bullpen a little more. Our club never did steal many bases, so that didn't change. A lot of times a new guy comes in and the ballplayers haven't been playing well, but the new guy gives the players confidence. That's why they hire new managers. In Fred Haney's case, it worked. The best example of how it worked was Joe Adcock.

Joe had been struggling at the plate. Charlie Grimm's way of handling that was to platoon Joe, just use him against lefthanders or have him sit out a few ballgames. Joe hated being

144

platooned. He wanted to play every day, like everybody wants to. When Haney took over, he told Joe, "You're my regular first baseman." The next day we won a doubleheader from the Dodgers, and Joe hit three home runs. One of them went over the leftfield grandstand. Joe killed the Dodgers. He had 13 home runs against them that year, which tied the record.

Sweeping the Dodgers that day gave us confidence, and all of a sudden we couldn't lose. We won our first eleven games for Haney. Everything worked for us. We stayed in first place up until the middle of September, and then it was touch and go until the end of the season. We went into St. Louis the last weekend with a one-game lead over the Dodgers and three games to play. We lost the first game with Buhl pitching, so now we had to win and hope the Dodgers lost a game.

In the second-last game, Spahn pitched a hell of a game, and we should have won, but we couldn't get any runs. The Cardinals had a centerfielder named Bobby Del Greco, and he went crazy against us, making all kinds of outstanding catches. I had two line drives that he made diving catches on, and he caught a bunch of others too, including one that Jack Dittmer hit. He just turned into El Freako that particular night. We finally lost in the 12th inning, and the play where they beat us was kind of a fluke. Stan Musial was on second, and Rip Repulski hit one right off the end of the bat toward me, one of those funny topspin bouncers All I was trying to do was get in front of it to block it. I didn't know where the hell the bounce was going to come. It hit my knee and bounced into foul territory and over to the stands. Musial scored and they beat us.

After the game we were extremely disappointed. None of us except Spahn had been in a situation to win a pennant before, and we were so close. The feeling in the clubhouse--and we talked about it a lot--was that the Dodgers weren't going to lose the next day. They were playing Pittsburgh, and they had handled the Pirates pretty well all year. We had done the best we could. We thought we should have won that game except Haney kept bunting. He was trying to get one run to win, so he had everybody bunting to move the runner over. We thought, for chrissake--are we a bunting and running team? He had Aaron bunting, he had me bunting... Very rarely in my career did the ballplayers blame the manager for losing a game, but we felt that Mr. Bunter cost us that one.

As soon as Musial scored the winning run, fans started

running onto the field. One of them ran up to Spahn and said, "Ha ha, we beat you!" Spahnie took off his glove and threw it at that lame-brain.

Later on after we showered and dressed, Spahn was still upset. He, Burdette, Buhl, a kid named Toby Atwell, and myself went out to drown our sorrows, and we were all totally pissed. We got fairly drunk. We all had on white shirts and ties, which we generally wore on the road. Spahn decided that Toby Atwell's shirt pocket didn't look quite right, so he just ripped it off. That started it. Pretty soon we were all ripping each other's pocket off. Then we got a knife from behind the bar and we all cut each other's tie off. We were walking around with our shirts torn and our ties cut.

We ended up in a White Castle. This was maybe two o'clock in the morning, and we were going to order hamburgers. There was a guy sitting by himself at the counter. Right out of the blue he said, "Well, if it ain't the lousy Braves."

We started in a little mouthy contest with the guy. He kept it up, so Burdette picked up a bottle of ketchup and poured it all over this guy's head. We were laughing and raising hell, and then we ate our hamburgers and went back to the hotel.

What we didn't know was, this guy was a relative of Lou Perini, the Braves' owner. He called Perini, and then he called John Quinn, the general manager, and the next day at the ballpark Fred Haney called in Burdette and me. Spahn had pitched the night before, so he wasn't going to play. Buhl had pitched the previous night, and Toby Atwell wasn't going to play either, so Haney just called Burdette and me.

"You two idiots aren't playing today," he said.

We didn't know what the hell was going on. "What are you talking about?" I asked him.

Then he told us who the ketchup man was and started screaming his head off.

"Look, Fred," I said, "this is going down to the wire. There's nothing wrong with us. You've got to at least give us a shot."

He did. We talked him into letting us play. Burdette was the starting pitcher, and I was at third base. The first pitch Burdette threw was a triple over my head by Don Blasingame. I walked in to the mound to talk to Lew. We looked over and there were Lou Perini, John Quinn, and our traveling secretary, Donald Davidson, right in the front row. I said, "Lew, if we

146

don't do good, we're in big trouble."

Well, Lew shut them out for the first six innings--Blasingame never scored from third. I had a home run and a double, and we won the ballgame. At the same time, though, the Dodgers won, so they went to the World Series and we didn't.

John Quinn came into the clubhouse after the game and said, "I don't know how you SOB's do it, but you're the two luckiest guys in the world."

Maybe, but we didn't win the pennant.

June 25, 1956

After Fred Haney replaced Charlie Grimm as manager, the Braves went on a tear. They had lost their last two games under Grimm, both one-run defeats in Brooklyn. Under Haney, they swept a doubleheader from the Dodgers, powered by three home runs from resurgent Joe Adcock, one of them the first home run ever to clear the roof in Ebbets Field. Then they moved on to Pittsburgh and swept a four-game series from the league-leading Pirates, a series in which the Braves' bullpen worked exactly one-third of an inning. Then they traveled to the Polo Grounds and swept four from the Giants, with Milwaukee hurlers allowing a total of five runs in the entire series.

The Braves' ten straight wins equalled their franchise's longest winning streak in the twentieth century, going back to their days as the Boston Beaneaters. The 1954 club had won ten in a row three times but could never win the eleventh. To achieve that mark now, Haney's team needed to win in Philadelphia against one of their toughest foes—Stu Miller. The willowy junk man had beaten the Braves eight times in ten decisions and compiled a 1.56 earned run average against them. Haney called on Bob Buhl to oppose Miller.

The Phillies staked Miller to a 1-0 lead in the first inning, but Bobby Thomson tied it in the second with a home run. Eddie Mathews put Buhl up a run with a solo shot in the top of the fourth, his 12th of the year and number 165 of his career. Philadelphia tied it again in the fifth, but Mathews scored the go-ahead run again in the sixth. He doubled and

147

scored on a Thomson base hit, and Milwaukee led, 3-2. Then in the top of the eighth the Braves appeared to put the game safely out of reach.

Leadoff man Danny O'Connell drew a base on balls, advancing to second on a perfect sacrifice bunt by Billy Bruton. Mathews also drew a walk, putting men on first and second. Hank Aaron then ripped Miller's slow curve toward the 447-foot sign in center field. Mathews, sure it was an extra-base hit, rounded second and headed for third. O'Connell, thinking that Richie Ashburn might flag it down, stopped midway between second and third. O'Connell, it turned out, was right. As Ashburn made a spectacular one-handed catch, Mathews and O'Connell collided. Mathews retreated quickly to first base, failing to touch second as he passed. O'Connell returned to tag up and headed for third, making it safely when the cutoff man threw wildly, and Mathews tagged and went to second.

A long rhubarb followed. Phillies manager Mayo Smith protested that Mathews had passed O'Connell and also failed to touch second in returning to first. The umpires dismissed the complaints. The argument took on greater significance after Thomson walked and Frank Torre, in the game for defensive purposes, singled home O'Connell and Mathews to put Milwaukee ahead 5-2.

Buhl couldn't hold the lead, though. After Mathews' throwing error put Del Ennis on base, Buhl hit Elmer Valo with a pitch and gave up a three-run homer to Puddin' Head Jones. The game was tied at five. Having lost a three-run lead, the Braves produced another.

Johnny Logan doubled off the concrete wall in left to start the ninth and finish Stu Miller. Facing reliever Harvey Haddix, pinch-hitter Andy Pafko tried to sacrifice but bunted so well that he got a base hit. O'Connell fanned. Del Crandall, on the bench because Del Rice usually caught Buhl, came in to bat for Bruton. He swung and missed the first pitch, then shocked everyone with a suicide squeeze bunt, the first he had ever attempted. A walk to Mathews, a sacrifice fly by Aaron, and Thomson's fourth hit of the day produced an 8-5 lead. Taking no chances, Haney brought in ace starter Warren Spahn, who retired the Phillies in order in the ninth. The Braves had their longest winning streak ever.

148

MILWAUKEE	AB	R	H	BI	PHILADELPHIA	AB	R	H	BI
O'Connell, 2b	4	1	0	0	Ashburn, cf	5	1	2	0
Bruton, cf	3	0	0	0	Blaylock, 1b	4	0	1	1
Mathews, 3b	3	3	2	1	Lopata, c	4	0	1	1
Aaron, rf	4	0	0	1	Ennis, lf	3	1	0	0
Thomson, lf	4	1	4	3	Valo, rf	2	1	0	0
Adcock, 1b	3	0	0	0	Jones, 3b	4	1	1	3
Torre, 1b	2	0	1	2	Kazanski, 2b	4	0	0	0
Rice, c	4	0	0	0	Smalley, ss	2	0	0	0
Logan, ss	4	1	2	0	Hemus	1	0	1	0
Buhl, p	3	0	0	0	Burk	0	0	0	0
Covington	0	0	0	0	Hamner, ss	1	0	1	0
Pafko	1	1	1	0	S. Miller, p	2	1	0	0
Crandall	1	1	1	1	Haddix, p	0	0	0	0
Spahn, p	0	0	0	0	Greengrass	1	0	0	0
					Seminick	1	0	0	0
Totals	36	8	11	8	Totals	34	5	7	5

Hemus singled for Smalley in seventh; Burk ran for
Hemus in seventh; Covington appeared for Buhl in
ninth; Pafko singled for Covington in ninth;
Crandall singled for Bruton in ninth; Greengrass
grounded out for Haddix in ninth; Seminick fouled out for Blaylock in ninth.

```
MILWAUKEE ................... 0 1 0  1 0 1  0 2 3--8
Philadelphia ................ 1 0 0  0 1 0  0 3 0--5
```

E--Mathews 2, Kazanski. 2B--Lopata, Mathews, Logan.
HR--Thomson, Mathews, Jones. S--Bruton. SF--Aaron.
DP--Logan, O'Connell, and Adcock. Left--Milwaukee 7,
Philadelphia 6. BB--Buhl 3, S. Miller 3, Haddix 1.
SO--Buhl 2, S. Miller 2, Haddix 1. HO--Buhl 7 in 8;
Spahn 0 in 1; S. Miller 8 in 8; Haddix 3 in 1. R-ER--
Buhl 5-4, S. Miller 6-6, Haddix 2-2. HBP--Valo (by
Buhl). W--Buhl (8-3). L--S. Miller (3-4). U--Dixon,
Gorman, Pinelli, Boggess. T--2:39. A--14,467.

NINE

Top of the World

It was a long winter. When you come close to winning a pennant and don't win it, everybody wants to ask you why you didn't win, or how it feels to get so close but lose. Nobody wants to know about the 92 games you won or all the great things you did; they want to know about the one terrible game you lost. It's natural. You can't blame them. The first few dozen or few hundred times somebody says "What happened in that game you lost in St. Louis?" you try to answer with patience and understanding. It gets old, though, talking over and over about the same moment of disappointment in your life. You want to say, "Hey, a month before that I beat the Cardinals with a three-run homer," but nobody cares about that. Instead they want to know, "What happened on that ball Repulski hit to you? Couldn't you at least knock it down?" Like I said, it was a long winter.

Spring was different. We started the season with five straight wins. In that fifth one we beat the Cubs, and three of our runs scored after their centerfielder dropped an easy fly ball. His name was Bobby Del Greco, just traded from the Cardinals. Back in September when it mattered, the guy was like flypaper. Now he had five thumbs and a hoof. That's life.

We actually won nine of our first ten games, and six of those wins were against the Cincinnati Redlegs. We always got into fights and rhubarbs with those guys, but we also had a lot of success against them. We played them in our home opener and Burdette beat them, 1-0. Throughout the whole game--in fact the whole season--the Reds were screaming and moaning about Burdette's spitters. They insisted he was juicing up the ball, which he was. Birdie Tebbetts was their manager, and he complained to the umpires about Burdette all the time. The Cincinnati hitters would ask the umpire time and time again to check the ball. Tebbetts even had movies taken of Lew when we were in Cincinnati, but they never figured him out or proved he was throwing a wet one. I never found out either how he got his spitball going. He never would tell me. The CIA couldn't have found out. To this day Lew won't tell me.

Back then we had an eight-team league. That meant we played each team 22 times. We only lost four to the Reds all year, but we still had some battles. Johnny Logan usually seemed to be at the center of things whenever we played Cincinnati. He and Johnny Temple, their second baseman, had kind of a continual skirmish going. A few years earlier Logan and Temple got into it a little bit in Crosley Field, and Logan was thrown out of the game. On his way out, he and Jim Greengrass of the Reds started jawing. Two seconds later they got into it. Logan won both fights, by the way.

This time Logan got matched up with my old nemesis, that nasty so and so, Hal Jeffcoat. Logan was covering third after a run-down. Jeffcoat slid underneath him and Logan fell on top of him. They were kind of wrestling around when I came over to break it up. Jimmy Dykes, the Redlegs' third base coach, tried to stop me. I think I might have knocked him down. By that time there were several people pulling on everybody to break it up. Jeffcoat and Logan got kicked out. The runner they sent in to take Jeffcoat's place was my old Navy buddy, Pete Whisenant. And the only person who got hurt was me--somehow in the struggle I sprained my right wrist. I missed the next two ballgames, and I kept it taped for two or three weeks.

I'll give just one example of how we stood with the Redlegs. Early in the year in Crosley Field we were pounding the crap out of them, and the number one crap pounder was Joe Adcock. Joe always hit home runs in streaks and bunches; right at that time he was in one of his streaks. He hit two home runs in that game, one of them a grand slam. I don't remember their starting pitcher, but Hershell Freeman, their ace relief man, came in late in the game. Freeman was a big guy, about Joe's size, maybe a little heavier. Everybody was expecting him to deck Adcock, and he did. His first pitch was up and in, not at his head but way inside. Joe got out of the way. The next pitch was in about the same spot. Joe didn't have the quickest reflexes, but he was expecting it, so he got out of the way again. The third pitch was the same, but he missed him again. Now it was three-and-oh. If he threw it down the middle, Joe would crush it and have three home runs. Rather than waste the pitch, Freeman threw at him again and this time nailed Joe on the leg. Freeman was obviously under orders to hit him. Tebbetts would never have admitted that, however.

A couple weeks after Logan and Jeffcoat got into it, Logan got into it again, this time against the Dodgers. Don Drysdale was pitching. He was tough for a lot of people to hit against, especially righthanded batters. He was tall and he threw hard, and with that big sidearm delivery of his the ball seemed to come out of the third base grandstand. Drysdale was only 20 years old at that time, but he already had a reputation for being mean, like Early Wynn. He had hit Logan earlier in the year. This time he threw a fastball behind Johnny that drilled him in the back of the rib cage.

I was watching from the on-deck circle. Logan trotted down to first base, no problem. Johnny was also a tough guy. As he got to first base, I saw Walt Alston strolling out toward the mound, signaling for a new pitcher. I figured I'd go back into the dugout and sit down for a minute while the new pitcher came in. I hadn't taken more than two steps when I heard Logan and Drysdale hollering at each other.

"Try coming into second base some time," Logan yelled, adding a few choice phrases regarding Drysdale's ancestry.

"Why wait?" Drysdale answered. "Let's do it now."

Logan threw down his batting helmet and went after him. When I got to the mound, they were duking it out. Somebody pulled Logan backwards and I stepped in and took a swing. I got Drysdale fairly good, enough to spin his head around and knock him off balance. I still had a bandage on my wrist at the time from the Jeffcoat incident, but it didn't bother me. As Drysdale hit the ground, I kind of dived and was pushed on top of him. I got in another punch or two. By then, though, there was a pile of bodies. The next thing I knew somebody had a hold of my ankles and was dragging me, face down, away from the mound area. It was Gil Hodges, who was a pretty tough hombre. Somebody in a Dodger uniform came by and deliberately stepped on my hand. I'll never know whose foot it was. What I do know is that it opened a three-quarter-inch cut on

152

the back of my left hand.

When I got off the ground, I saw Don Newcombe holding Drysdale around the waist, carrying him off the field like a sack of groceries. I made a mental note to stay on Newcombe's good side. Logan got thrown out, and after the game he was sporting a good-sized cut above his eyebrow. Asked about the fight by a reporter, Johnny said, "It was a baseball fight. It's over and done."

He was right. That's the attitude the ballplayers had. We didn't carry grudges. Later on Drysdale and I became good friends. When he was broadcasting in California and I was scouting, we used to run into each other a lot and socialize together. He was heavy duty. I had more fun with Don. His recent death was a real shock.

A sportswriter asked me after the game, "How many times did you hit Drysdale?"

"Hit him?" I said. "I never hit anybody."

The next day the newspapers carried a series of wire-service photographs showing me winding up and punching Drysdale. Okay, so I lied.

A couple days later the Braves acquired Red Schoendienst from the New York Giants. John Quinn had been trying to trade for a second baseman, and Red was the one he wanted most. Quinn was willing to give up Bobby Thomson and Danny O'Connell to get the Redhead. The Giants also wanted a pitcher, though. They wanted either Buhl or Gene Conley, and that Quinn would not do. It looked like the trade would not be made. Then at the last minute before the trading deadline, the Giants agreed to take Ray Crone instead. We got ourselves a terrific second baseman, a real veteran, and a super-nice guy. Red was given a lot of the credit for our winning the pennant, and deservedly so. He made a big difference in our club.

But no sooner do you solve one problem than another one pops up. A week later Joe Adcock broke his leg in Milwaukee sliding into second. Frank Torre took over at first base, but to back him up Quinn purchased Nippy Jones from the Pacific Coast League. Nippy did a decent job for us, especially his big moment in the World Series. Then right after the All-Star break our next crisis occurred. Felix Mantilla and Billy Bruton collided, putting Bruton out for the season, making Hank Aaron a centerfielder, and leaving a huge hole in our outfield.

153

With the trading deadline long past, the only choice was to bring somebody up from the minors. The Braves' Triple-A farm club was in Wichita. They had already sent us Wes Covington and Don McMahon; now John Quinn needed another outfielder. His first choice was Earl Hersh. When Quinn called Wichita, though, he was set straight: "The guy you want is Bob Hazle." The man who offered him that advice was Ben Geraghty, the Wichita manager.

Ben Geraghty was a great person. He could have managed in the big leagues. He was in the Braves organization a long time. Ben drank a little bit, but hell, we all did. If anybody had reasons, he sure did. He grew up in an orphanage, and when he was in the minor leagues, out on the West Coast, the team bus went off the side of a mountain and killed half the team. Ben got his head split open and his knee smashed and was lucky to survive. He never got over that. Later he was Hank Aaron's manager at Jacksonville. Hank thought the world of him. One of Ben's dreams was to manage in the big leagues. Unfortunately he died at the age of 48 without ever realizing that goal. But Ben knew baseball and he knew talent. He told John Quinn, "The man you want is Bob Hazle."

What can you say about Hurricane Hazle? He came up to the Braves at the end of July, and for the rest of the year nobody could get him out. I've never seen a guy as hot as he was--ever. He was something else to behold. He hit over .400, and regardless of the rest of the team, he really put us on the A track or whatever you call it. He got it started, and he kept us going.

I remember one Sunday afternoon we were playing in Philadelphia, in Connie Mack Stadium. The wind was blowing straight in from right field. I was a pull hitter, but they had a tall, tall fence there in right field, and that wind was strong. I thought I was going to be smart and hit to left, which I did. I think I got a double out there. Hazle walked up to the plate--he was a lefthanded batter too--and hit a home run against that wind. A couple innings later he did the same damn thing, in almost the same spot. I don't know what happens to suddenly make a minor league ballplayer into Babe Ruth, but Hazle was right out of "The Twilight Zone." We were hanging in there pretty well before he arrived, but he just picked us up.

A few days after Hazle joined the club, we were in second place, a game behind the St. Louis Cardinals. We won the next

154

ten games, averaging over nine runs a game, and that was about it for the pennant race. It wasn't over, but it might as well have been. During those ten games Hank Aaron, Wes Covington, and I each hit four home runs. Covington's last one was a grand slam in Cincinnati. The next day he was drilled on the elbow by--guess who?--nasty old Hal Jeffcoat.

The last month of the season was fun. We knew for a number of years we had a good team, but we just hadn't put it together. This year we did. We lost enough ballgames in September to keep it interesting, but we felt pretty confident we were going to win the pennant. Even when we lost some games, nobody was upset or panicked. We just had a certain confidence that somebody was going to do something good whenever we needed it.

The night we clinched the pennant, that somebody was Hank Aaron. He hit a home run off Billy Muffett in the 11th inning, and we carried Hank off on our shoulders. We felt good to bring a pennant to the loyal fans of Milwaukee. I learned one thing that night--that when you go in the clubhouse after an event like that, everybody should take their spikes off. Everybody was stepping on everybody's feet and hugging each other and throwing all their stuff around. I got spiked--I'm not sure how, but we were jumping up and down like a bunch of kids. But what the hell--then came the celebration, and it did not hurt one bit. I could take that.

After the ballgames, win or lose, we always went to Ray Jackson's, which was a restaurant and bar near the ballpark. We started going there the first year the Braves moved to Milwaukee, and we kept going there as long as the team was in town. Ray himself instigated it. He started bringing food down to the clubhouse for us after the ballgames. He had a real nice place, so our wives could wait for us there. A lot of the ballplayers stopped there before the games, too, to get something to eat. Ray and his wife LaVerne made everybody comfortable. He had a bar on the main floor, plus he had a bar upstairs that was basically for us. Usually if you had a good night you stayed down with the fans; if you went 0-for-4 you went upstairs. That night I think about a dozen of us and our wives ended up at the one upstairs, and the downstairs was jammed. That was the "in" place for Braves fans. I don't know how long I stayed there, but it was a happy night, and they told me I had a good time. God almighty!

155

We were excited about playing the Yankees, but they didn't scare us one little bit. We were a confident bunch of ballplayers. We got our scouting reports. Our pitchers got their reports--how to pitch each of their hitters. We were all told basically how to play them. We knew we could win. When the Yankees came to Milwaukee, one of them--maybe it was Casey Stengel--saw all the excitement and called it "bush." That did not bother the ballplayers, but it bothered the fans. I guess it made winning that much sweeter.

New York won two of the first three games. I was doing okay with the leather, but I didn't get a hit in those three games--five walks, but the hits weren't falling. In game four in Milwaukee I finally got a double off Tom Sturdivant. Spahnie had a 4-1 lead in the ninth with two outs and nobody on base. It looked like we would tie the Series. Then Spahn gave up two singles and a three-run home run by Elston Howard.

The Yankees took a 5-4 lead in the top of the tenth. Then Nippy Jones pinch-hit for Spahn and became a famous name in Milwaukee history. As every Wisconsin baseball fan knows, Nippy got hit on the foot with a pitch and was awarded first base after he showed Augie Donatelli the shoe polish on the ball. If that ball had hit my shoe, you wouldn't have known it. As long as I could put them on and tie them up, I didn't care what they looked like. Nippy was different. He was very meticulous about his uniform and how he looked, including his shoes. He insisted that the clubhouse boys polish his shoes before every game. Good thing he did.

After a pinch runner, a sacrifice, and a double by Johnny Logan, the game was tied. I was the next batter. Bob Grim was pitching, a righthander, and first base was open, so I figured they might walk me and set up a force or a double play. Aaron was hitting behind me, though, so I guess they didn't want to. Maybe Stengel figured he could get me out and then walk Aaron. Whatever he was thinking, he let me hit.

Before the game I had been thinking about Gil Hodges going 0-for-21 in the 1952 World Series. I was 0-for-8 at the time and starting to get concerned. A Milwaukee sportswriter handed me three pennies and said, "Put these in your pocket for good luck." I wasn't the slightest bit superstitious, but what the hell, I put them in my uniform pocket. I wasn't hitting worth two cents, so maybe three would help. I also changed bats. Mine had a bigger knob at the end; it was rubbing on a blister on my

156

right hand. Instead I borrowed a bat from my old roomie, Joe Adcock, and told him I'd buy him a whole box of them if it worked.

Batting against Grim, I felt relaxed and confident. I was not thinking home run. All I wanted was a pitch that I could hit hard, a fastball in the strike zone. I could hit the curve, but basically I made a living hitting fastballs. Grim threw me one, belt high, and I jumped on it. At the moment of contact I thought it was going out. Then I was worried for a second when I saw Hank Bauer in front of the rightfield fence, pounding his glove like he was going to make the catch. Bauer was just being a smart guy, though. I didn't see the ball go into the seats, but the crowd reaction left no doubt that it was a home run.

My feelings at that moment are hard to describe. I suppose it's like the feeling that long-distance runners get, the high from endorphins being produced in the brain. I know I told reporters that as I circled the bases I felt at least ten feet tall. We hadn't won the World Series or anything, but we were even again. That short sequence of events--hitting Grim's fastball, running the bases, fighting through a mob of Braves to find and jump on home plate, being pummeled by joyous teammates--is like a slow-motion video in my mind. It's indelible. I'm not the type of person who says, "This was my biggest thrill in baseball," or my happiest moment, or any of that kind of baloney. Let's just say we had a hell of a good time at Ray Jackson's after that ballgame.

The next day wasn't bad either. Lew Burdette was outstanding, beating Whitey Ford, 1-0, allowing no extra base hits and no walks. It was Burdette's second win of the Series, and it put us ahead, three games to two, going back to Yankee Stadium. I scored the only run of the ballgame. The interesting part of that is what it shows about the limitations of scouting reports. With two out in the sixth I hit a bouncer to second baseman Jerry Coleman. I've talked to Coleman since then. He told me their scouting report hadn't mentioned that I could run, so he laid back to get the higher hop instead of charging it and playing the short hop. That gave me enough time to beat it out. I think whoever did the scouting probably saw my stats and said, "He doesn't steal bases; he probably doesn't run that well." After that Aaron and Adcock both singled. Lew had the only run he needed.

We lost game six in New York, so we had to play a

seventh. If you're going to play a big game, what better place than the most famous ballpark in the world, "The House That Ruth Built." Spahnie was supposed to pitch, but he came down with the flu, so Burdette was called on with two days' rest. Stengel decided on Don Larsen, which was an interesting choice. Larsen was not their best pitcher and probably not their best pitcher available. However, he had been the hero of 1956 with his perfect game against the Dodgers, and Stengel had faith in him. He just liked the guy. When Larsen drove his car into a telephone at four-thirty in the morning, instead of ripping him in the press or threatening to fine him, Stengel told reporters, "He was either out pretty late or up pretty early."

Against us he was out pretty early, namely the third inning. I drove in the first two runs with a double. The first run--as it turned out, the deciding run of the Series--was scored, appropriately, by Bob Hazle. Aaron drove me in, then he scored, and Burdette was working with a four-run cushion. Crandall hit a home run later to make it 5-0, and that's how it stood in the ninth inning. Then the Yankees used three singles to load the bases with two out and Moose Skowron at bat.

Skowron was not a pull hitter. He pretty much hit straight away, or at least that's what our scouting reports said. I knew, however, that Burdette was going to throw him a wet one. I moved about one-and-a-half steps over toward the foul line. Sure enough, Lew threw him a spitter and Skowron pulled it, a hard smash down the third-base line. I backhanded it and tagged third base to force Coleman for the final out. A second later I was hugging Burdette and Crandall. Pretty soon everybody was hugging everybody.

Every time I see Skowron, he says, "How could you play me like that?" It's simple--I knew who was pitching, and I knew what he was going to throw.

The play I made on the ball Skowron hit seemed to call attention to a fact that many people had overlooked--I had worked very hard to become a good fielding third baseman. I was not an exceptional fielder, like a Brooks Robinson, but I was now a good one. The writers generally agreed I was the defensive star of the Series. At least people were starting to recognize that I wasn't out there wearing a chest protector while I played third base.

From what I understand, the celebration in Milwaukee started as soon as I stepped on third base for the final out. They

After tagging third for the final out of the '57 Series, I moved in to hug
Crandall and Burdette. (UPI/Bettmann)

closed some of the bars and took the beer kegs right out onto
the street. The whole town went crazy, jamming the downtown
area. We flew back to Milwaukee soon after the game ended.
Once again they had a parade planned for the ballclub, to take
us from the airport, through downtown, and finally to County
Stadium. They had to change their parade route, though--Wisc-
onsin Avenue was solid people. The police chief said it was the
biggest crowd in the city's history, twice as big as the one

Wisconsin Avenue celebration of '57 Series victory, joyful but peaceful. The sign says "Mathews for Vice-President." (Milwaukee Journal photo)

celebrating the end of World War II.

Even though our parade missed the biggest crowd, there were still plenty of people along the way, cheering and waving. The whole city seemed to be outside. People were just having fun. I had bought my wife a poodle in New York. We walked by a pet store and she pointed and said, "I have to have that dog." It was a little baby snookums. So she got the dog, and she took it to the ballgame, and then she took it on the airplane. When we got off the plane, it was kind of cold--this was at night in the middle of October. John Quinn's wife--the general manager's wife--took off her fur coat and gave it to Virjean to wrap the dog in for the parade. So we rode in an open convertible from the airport to County Stadium with Virjean holding that little poodle wrapped in a fur coat. I don't know what Mrs. Quinn did to keep from freezing.

All along the way we saw hand-lettered signs: "Burdette for President," "Mathews for Vice-President," "Spahn for Mayor," and "We love you, Bush Leaguers." When we reached County Stadium, they ushered us through another crowd and

160

inside the ballpark. The problem was, now we were trapped. We had to get a police escort, one at a time, to get to our cars parked outside. I didn't have my car, so Virjean and I (and the poodle) caught a lift home from the police chief of Brookfield in a patrol car. When we got home, our neighbors had decorated the outside of our house with streamers and bunting and pennants and ribbons. A big sign on the lawn, probably twelve feet long, said, "Welcome Home, Eddie." After we arrived they built a big bonfire on the street and partied the night away. We joined them for a while and then later drove to the team party at a private club near downtown. It was a night to remember-- although I don't remember most of it.

The big hero, the Series' most valuable player by a long shot, was Lew Burdette. The Braves only batted a little over .200 for the seven games, but Old Nitro pitched three brilliant complete games and 24 consecutive scoreless innings. He was the man of the hour. The next morning he was interviewed by Dave Garroway on "The Today Show." Two nights later he and Hank Aaron appeared with Steve Allen on his TV show. A couple weeks later Lew made a recording with Teresa Brewer. Everybody loves a winner, and Lew sure earned it.

I spent part of the off-season working with a friend of mine who had a trucking company, making calls and taking guys out to lunch. I had a favorite tavern, Stoll's, out near where I lived, so I spent time in there. I'd always meet Johnny Logan down at the Athletic Club. I played a lot of racquetball at that time. And I did my hunting with Buhl. It was a good winter.

September 22, 1957

Baseball fans old enough to remember the Milwaukee Braves' first pennant remember vividly the night Hank Aaron hit the home run off Billy Muffett to clinch it. What they may not remember, though, is how the Braves arrived at that clinching game.

After sweeping a Labor Day doubleheader from the Chicago Cubs, the first game by the football score of 23-10, the Braves led the National League by eight and a half games. Two weeks later, on the morning of September 16, following three straight losses, the Braves' lead was two and a half games. Terrible nightmares of 1956's final weekend collapse began to recur among the Milwaukee faithful. And then suddenly the pitching staff revived: Bob Buhl, Bob Trowbridge, and Lew Burdette won complete games, Warren Spahn won his 20th game with help from Don McMahon, and Buhl won another. On Sunday, September 22, 1957, the Braves arrived at Wrigley Field for their final road game of the season, bolstered by thousands of Wisconsin fans within the ivied walls.

Sporting a five-game winning streak, the Braves sent Bob Trowbridge to the mound looking for number six. Trowbridge had pitched masterfully to beat the Giants five days earlier, but against the Cubs he never got out of the first inning. He faced six men, allowing four hits and one walk, retiring only Bob Will. Taylor Phillips replaced him and gave up two more singles, and the Cubs led, 4-0. The lead held up until the fourth inning.

In the fourth Hank Aaron homered off Cubs starter Dick Drott, tying Ernie Banks for the league lead with 42. Wes Covington singled, Joe Adcock walked, Bob Hazle singled in a run, and Del Crandall doubled home two more to tie the score at 4-4. The Cubs reclaimed the lead in the next inning, however, against lefty Juan Pizarro. The key to the inning was Johnny Logan's error on a sure doubleplay ball with the bases

162

loaded and one out. One run scored, and then ex-Brave Chuck Tanner doubled home two more to make the score 7-4.

Once again the Braves fought back. Covington led off the sixth inning with his 21st home run of the year (amazingly, he hit only four doubles all season). Adcock and Hazle singled. Crandall advanced them both with a sacrifice. Carl Sawatski (Mathews' old rival from the Southern Association) batted for Pizarro and grounded out as Adcock scored to make it 7-6. That's where the score stayed until the ninth, but it should not have. In the eighth the Braves loaded the bases with one out. Logan, though, popped up an attempted squeeze bunt (Haney loved bunts), and Hazle was doubled up after straying too far off third. ("I couldn't think quick enough," Hazle said after the game.)

With the Braves trailing by one and three outs to go, Eddie Mathews led off the ninth against Turk Lown. Mathews swung hard at an outside pitch and rode it into the leftfield bleachers, his 32nd homer of the season and 222nd of his career. Sensational rookie Don McMahon held the Cubs scoreless in the last of the ninth. Then in the tenth Hurricane Hazle atoned for his earlier baserunning boner. The rookie wonder already had three singles in the game, but he outdid those with one swing. He slammed a Lown offering into the rightfield bleachers to give the Braves an 8-7 lead. After McMahon walked, Red Schoendienst singled, and with two out, Mathews singled home McMahon with an insurance run.

The Cubs put two men on base against McMahon in the bottom of the tenth. To save the game Haney brought in Joey Jay, who had not pitched in the majors in more than a year. Jay served up two straight ground balls, and the Braves had a 9-7 victory, McMahon's first win after 31 sparkling relief appearances. The Braves' winning streak remained intact as they returned home for their date with destiny. Take it, Henry.

September 22, 1957

MILWAUKEE	AB	R	H	BI
Schoendienst, 2b	5	0	2	0
Logan, ss	6	0	1	0
Mathews, 3b	5	1	2	2
Aaron, cf	4	1	1	1
Covington, lf	4	2	2	1
Adcock, 1b	3	2	1	0
Hazle, rf	5	2	4	2
Pafko, rf	0	0	0	0
Crandall, c	4	0	1	2
Trowbridge, p	0	0	0	0
Phillips, p	0	0	0	0
Hanebrink	1	0	1	0
Pizarro, p	1	0	0	0
Sawatski	1	0	0	1
Johnson, p	0	0	0	0
DeMerit	0	0	0	0
Torre	1	0	1	0
McMahon, p	0	1	0	0
Jay, p	0	0	0	0
Totals	40	9	16	9

CHICAGO	AB	R	H	BI
Goryl, 3b	6	2	2	0
Will, cf	6	1	2	0
Banks, ss	4	2	1	0
Long, 1b	4	1	0	0
Moryn, rf	4	1	2	3
Tanner, lf	5	0	2	3
Morgan, 2b	3	0	1	1
Bolger	0	0	0	0
Fanning, c	4	0	0	0
Haas	1	0	0	0
Drott, p	3	0	0	0
Brosnan, p	0	0	0	0
Lown, p	1	0	0	0
Elston, p	0	0	0	0
Littlefield, p	0	0	0	0
Speake	0	0	0	0
Totals	41	7	10	7

Hanebrink singled for Phillips in third; Sawatski grounded out for Pizarro in sixth; Torre singled for Johnson in eighth; DeMerit ran for Torre in eighth; Bolger walked for Morgan in tenth; Haas fanned for Fanning in tenth; Speake walked for Littlefield in tenth.

```
MILWAUKEE .................... 0 0 0   4 0 2   0 0 1   2--9
Chicago ...................... 4 0 0   0 3 0   0 0 0   0--7
```

E--Logan 2. 2B--Crandall, Tanner, Logan. HR--Aaron, Covington, Mathews, Hazle. S--Crandall. DP--Logan, Schoendienst, and Adcock; Goryl, Morgan, and Long; Banks, Morgan, Long, Fanning, and Long; Lown and Goryl; Will, Banks, and Long. Left--Milwaukee 10, Chicago 10. BB--Trowbridge 1, Drott 4, Pizarro 2, Brosnan 2, McMahon 3, Lown 2. SO--Drott 2, Pizarro 4, Brosnan 1, McMahon 4, Lown 1. HO--Trowbridge 3 in .1; Phillips 2 in 1.2; Pizarro 3 in 3; Johnson 2 in 2; McMahon 0 in 2.1; Jay 0 in .2; Drott 8 in 5 (faced two batters in sixth); Brosnan 4 in 2.1; Lown 2 in 2; Elston 1 in .1; Littlefield 1 in .1. R-ER--Trowbridge 4-4, Phillips 0-0, Pizarro 3-2, Drott 6-6, Johnson 0-0, Brosnan 0-0, McMahon 0-0, Lown 3-3, Elston 0-0, Littlefield 0-0, Jay 0-0. W--McMahon (1-3). L--Lown (5-7). U--Burkhart, Dixon, Gorman, Sudol. T--3:20. A--25, 651.

TEN

Almost Heaven

Baseball clubs are not sentimental. Three weeks into our new season, the world champion Milwaukee Braves were playing the Cardinals in St. Louis. It was still very early, but we had been playing decent ball. We were a half-game out of first place, behind the Chicago Cubs--as I said, it was still very early.

Our outfield was thin. Billy Bruton remained sidelined from his collision with Felix Mantilla almost ten months earlier, so Aaron was still in center field. Bob Hazle was our rightfielder, and Wes Covington had recently returned from a knee injury and was in left. Wes was in and out of the lineup with that bad wheel. All year the outfield was a matter of "Who can play today?" One day Haney had seven infielders in the starting lineup, with Adcock, Mantilla, and Harry Hanebrink playing outfield. At least I didn't have to.

Getting back to the Cardinals, we climbed all over them in the first inning. Herman Wehmeier was pitching. Wehmeier was the guy who pitched the game of his life to beat Spahn in 12 innings in the second-last game of 1956. In this game he got exactly one batter out--me. Schoendienst led off with a hit, Logan singled, and I flied out. Then Aaron doubled, Frank Torre doubled, and Covington parked one in the seats. Six batters, five hits, five runs, and so long, Herm. Fred Hutchinson brought in a new pitcher, Larry Jackson.

Bob Hazle was the next hitter. Jackson's first pitch caught Hazle right behind the ear. It made an awful sound, like thumping a watermelon only louder. You could actually see the imprint of the stitching of the ball on the side of his head. Bob never lost consciousness, but some of the guys--Don McMahon,

165

Del Rice, Ernie Johnson--had to carry him to the clubhouse on a stretcher. He was rushed to the hospital, and he stayed in there for several days.

That's how baseball was played. Five hits, Covington's home run, bang--you knew somebody was going to hit the deck. Jackson didn't have a reputation as a headhunter, but he pitched tight. I've talked to Larry since then. I don't think he was exactly trying to hit Hazle in the head. I don't feel any pitcher wants to nail somebody in the head with a 90-mile-an-hour fastball. They assume they can throw it and the batter will duck away from it. When they throw behind and a little below your head, though, sometimes you dive right into it. I don't think Jackson wanted to hit him, or at least wished he hadn't. He figured he'd get out of the way.

Hazle suffered a concussion but no permanent damage. That came two weeks later--the Braves sold Hazle to the Detroit Tigers! The other ballplayers were completely stunned and upset about it. We thought it sucked. Here was a guy who came out of nowhere and led us, not singlehandedly, but led us to our first World Series. He was in a slump for the first month of 1958, but he'd had some ankle trouble in spring. We figured the ballclub owed him more than that. He was 27 years old and a super-nice kid. After he came up in 1957 he was just a part of us. Whenever we'd go out, he'd come with us, just a nice, quiet guy, what I would call a good old Southern boy, fun, laughs, the whole bit. Of course, I never understood a lot of stuff that went on in baseball, but we were pretty disappointed when Hazle was dumped. We all said, "What the hell did he do wrong, have an affair with the general manager's wife?"

Basically 1958 was a disappointing year. I wasn't hitting well. It was my worst season since Boston. The Braves were pretty much expected to win the pennant again, which we did. Hank had a good year for us, and Frank Torre did too, filling in at first base. Covington hit great when he was healthy. Spahn and Burdette had their usual years, both winning 20 games. Burdette won seven just in August as we built up a good lead over Pittsburgh and the Giants. Buhl didn't work much because of shoulder problems. I hit four home runs the first two days, but after that I just couldn't find my stroke.

As a team we didn't hit as well as in 1957, but I'd say our pitching was better. Bob Rush came over from the Cubs and won some games, and we had Don McMahon in the bullpen for the whole season. We played the same kind of ball as the year before, which was to put men on base and drive them in with home runs. That was the kind of club we had, power but not much speed. We set a record for the fewest times caught stealing because we never tried to steal bases. We were last in the league in that category. We were also last in triples--we didn't get one until the middle of May. With power and pitching, though, we didn't need to run.

Another thing that was the same was our rivalry with Cincinnati. We didn't have any particular brawls that made headlines that year. The intensity and the knockdown pitches were there, though. Early in the season we played them in Cincinnati. Crandall got drilled twice, by Brooks Lawrence and Harvey Haddix, and Haddix also nailed Torre in the same game. Both Crandall and Torre missed a few ballgames because of it. I thought Fred Haney was going to have a stroke, he was so mad. The players weren't too happy either. I don't remember who was batting, but one time I moved up on the edge of the infield grass and yelled to Don McMahon, who was the hardest thrower on our club--and I yelled it loud enough for the batter to hear it--"Knock this son of a gun on his butt. I guarantee he'll never reach the mound." When we played the Reds, the fists and the beanballs were always flying.

Speaking of flying, that was the year I started--piloting, that is. During the winters I had been working for a trucking company. They had a Cessna 310, and they would fly me places, like down to St. Louis, to call on customers. On one trip I started thinking--which is always dangerous for me--about how vulnerable we were, how dependent I was on this pilot. So I asked him, "What happens if something happens to you while we're up here?"

He laughed. "Whatever happens to me," he said, "is gonna happen to you."

I started paying attention to what he was doing and saying. Then I took flying lessons. I ended up buying my own airplane, a Bonanza, after I got down to Atlanta, but in Milwaukee I used to rent them by the hour. The team officials never discouraged me from doing it. When I was coaching in Atlanta, that's when I bought the plane. I finally gave it up because I wasn't doing enough flying to be real comfortable. I wasn't even getting ten hours a month, and that's kind of the minimum if you're going to fly. And it got to be an expense.

167

I enjoyed flying, though. I did that for quite a few years. One time in Milwaukee I told Hank Aaron, "Hey, Hammer, bring your kids and I'll take you out flying." He and his kids came over and we went up. We flew right over his house. His wife was waving at us, and we all got a big kick out of that. We landed and went back to our homes. That night when I got to the ballpark, I had a message to report to the front office. John McHale was the general manager at that time. He got right to the point.

"I understand you and Hank went flying today," he said.

"Yeah," I told him, "we had a great time."

McHale just said, "We don't mind you flying, but don't take Hank with you."

A couple years later I had another experience. Bob Uecker was a neighbor of mine, which is an experience in itself. We got together all the time. In fact, we roomed together for two years. If I hadn't done that I might have been able to play longer.

Well, we decided to fly up to the Tri-Cities for a banquet, Uecker, Logan, and myself. I flew them up, got there, then went out and partied. We were leaving the next morning. On the way home Logan said, "I was watching this movie the other day, a war movie, and they were strafing people. What the hell is strafing?"

I chopped the engine a little bit and went zzzoooom, and Logan threw up all over the plane. God, did we laugh!

Quite a few ballplayers have been pilots. Johnny Sain was one. He learned to fly in the service during the war, with Ted Williams and Johnny Pesky. Later on he flew his own plane. Sain said he thought learning to fly helped him a lot as a ballplayer. He said flying an airplane was similar to walking out on the mound--"If you can't think, you can't pitch; if you can't think, you can't fly." I don't know if flying did me any good as a ballplayer, but I enjoyed it.

Starting that season I also got a lot of flying hours as a passenger. The National League expanded its territory when the Dodgers and Giants moved to California. We missed our old haunts in Manhattan, but we quickly made friends on the West Coast and located new watering holes in the desert climate of Los Angeles. We still had a hell of a time beating the Dodgers, though.

Our old Brooklyn adversaries hit rock bottom in their

168

new home town, dropping to seventh place. They still had some power, but their pitching was terrible. They couldn't beat anybody--except us. Don Drysdale was 7-13 against the rest of the league but 5-0 against us. Maybe it was a jinx, but more likely it was their funky ballpark. We only won three games there all season.

The Los Angeles Coliseum should never have been used for baseball. The Braves were the last team in the league to play there, but it was still too soon. We lost several games there because of cheap home runs called "screenos" over their 42-foot screen in left field, 250 feet from home plate. Then in right field you needed binoculars to even see the fence. It was almost 400 feet at the foul line. I was the third batter to hit a home run over the rightfield fence, and that was after the All-Star break.

In both 1956 and 1957 the Dodgers played one game against each National League club in Jersey City. We split the two games. The ballpark there, Roosevelt Stadium, had been a minor league park. I hit a home run in both games we played there, which was amazing because the lights were so bad. The place was a W.P.A. project built during the Depression on a landfill. It was in every sense a dump, but it was better for baseball than the Los Angeles Coliseum. In San Francisco the Giants played in a minor league park, Seals Stadium, which was okay but small, about 25,000 seats, I think. The Dodgers could have done the same, but they went for the 90,000 seats in the Coliseum. I hated the place. We all did.

As much as I disliked the Coliseum, I enjoyed going to L.A. For one thing it was near my hometown and I could visit my mother, or she could come down and see me play. For another thing the social scene in southern California was a nice change for us. Quite a few of the movie stars and other show business people were baseball fans. Some of them were friends of Fred Haney's, like Jack Webb, the guy who played Sgt. Joe Friday on "Dragnet"--"I just want to get the facts, ma'am." Frank Lovejoy was another one, and then Desi Arnaz and the actor who played Fred Mertz on "I Love Lucy."

Aside from Haney, though, we met lots of show business people just because they came to the Coliseum. Actor Jeff Chandler was one of those. He was a big baseball fan. Another one was Sammy Cahn, the songwriter. He was the guy who wrote "Three Coins in the Fountain" and a bunch of Frank Sinatra songs, plus that Christmas song with the line, "Let it

169

snow, let it snow, let it snow." He probably wrote a thousand songs. He loved to perform in private, too. Well, his son was our batboy when we were visiting Los Angeles.

Sammy and his wife Gloria became big baseball fans. Several times they threw parties for us--maybe receptions is a better word. They were a lot of fun. They would pick a night when we had the night off and invite the team out to their house in Beverly Hills. They would also have a lot of celebrities there, movie stars, all of whom were very nice to us. Spencer Tracy sat and talked with my mother for quite some time. Billy Wilder, the director, was there, and Kirk Douglas couldn't have been nicer. On one side of the Cahns lived Lauren Bacall--that was after Humphrey Bogart had passed away, I didn't meet him--and on the other side was Art Linkletter and his family. This happened several times. I wasn't there all the time--some of them involved the single guys. They got to know the Hollywood set.

The Braves' most notorious Hollywood misadventure happened that year but--thank goodness--I was three thousand miles away, with reliable witnesses. Spahn and I were at the All-Star Game in Baltimore, along with boss Fred Haney. Aaron, Logan, and Crandall were all-stars, too. The incident in Hollywood involved four Braves: Frank Torre, Lew Burdette, Gene Conley, and, of all people, straight shooter Red Schoendienst. As I said, I wasn't there, but Burdette has told me the story often enough that I think I've got it down pat.

What happened was, an actor that Torre had gone to school with invited him to a party at the Bel Air mansion of a movie producer out there. Torre and these other three guys went there to check it out. Two of the guys had on swimming suits and the other two had their street clothes on. The host of the party threw a girl in the swimming pool with her clothes on, and he thought that was funnier than hell. Gene Conley saw that, so he picked the next girl that he saw and pushed her in the pool. It turned out to be the host's girlfriend. The host got mad and asked him to leave. Well, old Stretch is six-foot-eight and doesn't like to be told what to do. As he was leaving, he saw a baby grand piano on the deck near the pool. He reached down to the front leg of the piano and tore it right off. The piano collapsed forward with a crash.

Frank and Lew and Red finally succeeded in getting Conley outside and into the car. Gene was sitting in the front

170

passenger's seat of this rented car. All of a sudden he went nuts. The dashboard just went "tilt," and then he broke the glass right out of the car. Now they drove the car back to the hotel and turned it in. They told the car rental guy, "Somebody tried to break into this car."

The guy looked at it and said, "No, somebody tried to break out of it."

At this point Conley looked across the street from the hotel. There was a squad car parked there. This was a nightmare. Gene ran across the street and tried to tear the red light off the police car. The three other ballplayers finally grabbed him and pulled him off the car and dragged him up to his room.

Needless to say the incident, or series of incidents, made the headlines in Los Angeles and Milwaukee and maybe some other places. When Spahn and I got into L.A. and saw the newspaper, I said, "Spahnie, I'm glad we were at the All-Star Game, for crying out loud." The next night the last-place Dodgers kicked the crap out of us.

The Bel Air brouhaha took a couple weeks to blow over, but eventually it did. Haney handled it well. He called a team meeting and warned us about the dangers lurking in the jungles of Hollywood. As a longtime Hollywood man, he knew the drill. He told the press he had investigated and found there was no drinking at the party. Right, Fred, no drinking at a party in Beverly Hills. He also told the reporters, "We don't have any playboys on the Braves." And then he added, "Every club has a few beer drinkers, but we don't have any real hell-raisers." He sounded almost like he meant it, too.

A week after the swimming pool caper the Braves played in St. Louis, working our way back east to Milwaukee. The Cardinals had a good club and were hanging within a few games of us in the standings. While we had been in Tinseltown, the Cardinals had purchased a lefthanded pitcher from the Washington Senators by the name of Chuck Stobbs. He pitched 15 years in the big leagues, but if you could find ten people who remember Stobbs, nine would probably remember him because he gave up Mickey Mantle's 565-foot home run in Griffith Stadium in 1953. He had never pitched in the National League, so he didn't know the hitters and we didn't know him. I met him in a hurry, though.

Stobbs threw a fastball at my head. Maybe it was because I had two home runs that night, one of them off him.

171

Maybe he didn't like my looks. Maybe his dog had just died. Whatever the reason, he tried to stick it in my ear, and he came close. Now, if a batter can't tolerate an occasional duster, he doesn't belong in baseball. Period. It goes with the territory. But this one really got my goat. Maybe it was because I didn't know him. Maybe I didn't like his looks. My dog was okay. Whatever the reason, I decided to get him.

When this happens today, the batter charges the mound. Maybe it's from watching too many cartoons on TV--I'm no sociologist. In my day that was almost never done. We had two ways to get even. You could slam a line drive up the middle and try to make him a soprano, but that's tough to do. The usual way was to drag a bunt down the first-base line and spike the pitcher as he made the play. Ty Cobb did it. Enos Slaughter did it. In seven years in the big leagues I had never retaliated against a pitcher, but you have to start sometime.

So I drag bunted down the first base line. When Stobbs covered, I stepped on his foot and twisted my ankle. I missed the whole next series with the Cubs. That was the last of that happy stuff. I felt like Earl Torgeson.

A lot of fights came from things that happened on the base paths. A couple weeks after I hurt my ankle, Mel Roach was playing second base for us. Mel had been a bonus baby, so he wasted two years just sitting on our bench and watching. He was just starting to play up to the club's expectations. In fact, he hit home runs the two previous days. Then Daryl Spencer of the Giants came into him at second, not with a hard slide, but with a roll. Mel tore up his knee, and he was never the same after that. Rolling into somebody is not a legitimate way to break up the double play.

I had a personal experience with Daryl Spencer a few years later. He came flying into me at third base in a game in Milwaukee with his spikes about two feet off the ground. He cut my knee--really opened me up. I turned around to go after him, and he was rolling on the ground holding his knee. He had popped his kneecap doing it, so we didn't fight that time. After I saw he was hurt too, I went in and pulled my pants leg up--I didn't want Spencer to know I was hurt--and the trainer put two butterfly bandages on there real quick. I finished the game and then went to the doctor and got it sewn up. I needed about 20 stitches. I was out about two or three days after that.

I had my construction company at that time. I went

home and got a pair of my spikes and took them to the foreman. I was going to pull a Ty Cobb. I had those spikes sharpened so you could shave with them. I carried them with me for a long time, but Spencer never played the infield against us after that. I never got a shot at him. That's one of the few times I held a grudge. There is a difference between playing hard and playing dirty. Spencer was dirty. He came in with his spikes up on me. I'll never forget that. I held that grudge a long time.

We kept a comfortable lead throughout August and September and finally clinched our second pennant in Cincinnati a week before the end. Our victory celebration wasn't as high-spirited as the year before. That first one is always special, plus the visiting clubhouse in Crosley Field was the size of your bathroom. We were also a long way from Ray Jackson's, although we had some spots in Cincinnati.

My hitting was down all year, but near the end I really fell into a slump. I went to Haney and said, "Fred, we're going to the World Series. I'm not hitting. I think a couple days off would help."

He said, "I can't do it. We'll be playing the Reds, and they have a chance to end up third. It wouldn't be right."

I said, "Fred, what about us?"

"Don't worry," he told me, "you'll be all right. Just keep swinging the bat."

I wasn't all right. My confidence was down. I went into the World Series, and I could not hit a baseball. It was a disaster. I hit .160 and set a record for a seven-game Series by striking out 11 times. I definitely was not all right.

We won the first two games in Milwaukee. Spahn won the first; Burdette won the second. In game two we scored 13 runs. Little did we know that was more than we would score in the other six games combined. We thought we were on our way, but after that--pffttt.

Leading two games to none, we went to Yankee Stadium feeling very good. During my first time at bat, the crowd gave a standing ovation. I thought maybe they were giving me some shit--you never know in New York--but it had nothing to do with me. Roy Campanella was being carried in to his box seat by his attendants. I struck out. The next time up I struck out again. And the next time. The guy who struck me out all three times was Don Larsen. He had been bothered by elbow problems much of the season. In a must-win situation, though,

173

On June 29, 1966, for three innings, Mickey Mantle and I were tied with 483 career home runs. (Author's collection)

Casey Stengel called on him, and he shut us out for seven innings. Maybe Casey was a genius.

Spahn was brilliant in game four, pitching a two-hit shutout, and we were up three games to one. Even if we lost in the fifth game, we could go back to Milwaukee to finish up. We could not have been in better shape. Burdette had one bad inning in game five, but we got shut out, so it didn't matter. And we still had two more chances, both at home.

Our last two games were pathetic. Spahn deserved to win

174

game six, but we failed at the plate and lost in extra innings. I batted five times in that ballgame and never got the ball out of the infield. Twice I left runners in scoring position. In the tenth inning I struck out in the middle of a rally. It was so bad that the next day Haney dropped me down to sixth in the batting order. I couldn't blame him at all.

In the deciding ballgame we were tied after seven innings but lost it. Give the Yankees credit for a great comeback to win the Series, but we beat ourselves. Our defense was sloppy, and we couldn't hit. I couldn't hit. If I had been hitting just a little bit, we would have beaten them. When you have a guy who can hit home runs, he literally can carry a club, if he's hot, for two or three days. We had men on our club capable of doing that, like Aaron and Adcock and me, but nobody was hot. We were just pecking around. The Braves only hit three home runs in the entire World Series. They came from Del Crandall; Billy Bruton, who only had three home runs all year; and Lew Burdette, who had hit five in his life.

I think in 1957 the country wanted us to win the pennant and beat the Yankees. In 1958 I think they expected it. We let them down.

The ballclub pretty well split up and headed home the next day. There was no hanging around. It wasn't like if we had won it. Then most of the guys would have hung around for a couple days. But the fans were great. I remember going home and finding my house decorated with a big banner--"Congratulations, Champs!" They were anticipating us winning the Series. I don't think they would have done that if they knew we were going to lose. We did have a little bit of a party at the house, but it was pretty much dampened.

The very next evening I had to leave. Burdette and I were going to play in Hawaii against the St. Louis Cardinals, who were on their way over to Japan. Lew and I supplemented the Hawaiian team for a couple games. I got to the airport and realized I had forgotten my duffel bag at home. I had to call the police department in Brookfield from the airport. They sent a cop over to my house to get it. He put on the siren and brought it to me at the airport. Brookfield was a smaller town then, a lot different in those days. They treated me very well.

Against the Cardinals in Hawaii, I hit a home run. Talk about being a day late and a buck short! Like I said, 1958 was a disappointing year.

April 17, 1958

Eddie Mathews had a reputation as a slow starter, and the Milwaukee Braves always won the home opener—until 1958. On April 15 the Braves lost to the Pittsburgh Pirates, 4-3, in 14 innings. Milwaukee's main bright spot was Mathews, who hit two home runs.

Actually Mathews' reputation was somewhat unfounded. In 1953 he had hit six home runs in his first eight games; the next year he slammed two homers on opening day in Cincinnati. (In fact, Mathews and Willie Mays hold the NL record for opening day home runs with seven.) Following the Braves' victory in the 1957 World Series, though, Mathews was determined to have a big year. He quit smoking during the off-season and worked harder than ever at Bradenton, bringing his weight down under 195, his lightest in the major leagues. Perhaps not coincidentally, he enjoyed his best spring.

Despite the opening-day defeat, Mathews and his champion teammates were confident and loose before their second game, on April 17. Zany Warren Spahn and Lew Burdette clowned and cavorted in the pregame warmups in record 84 degree heat. Spahn posed for photographers by demonstrating his high leg kick to Helga, the 23-year-old German ice-skating champion appearing in Milwaukee as the featured performer in the Ice Capades. Helga had never seen a baseball game before; as she said, "I think I'd get real excited if I knew more about it."

Once the game started, Burdette was, of course, all business. The Pirates knew that—he had beaten them nine straight times. The World Series hero was a fierce competitor with pinpoint control and the ability to throw ground balls. Characteristically, he gave up two base hits in the first inning but worked out of it unscathed by feeding a doubleplay ball to Ted Kluszewski. The game stayed scoreless until the bottom of the third, when Burdette singled home Johnny Logan.

Pittsburgh finally scored in the fifth inning. Roberto Clemente banged a triple to the bullpen in right center and scored on a sacrifice fly by second baseman Gene Baker. The tie was short-lived, though. In the Braves' half of the inning, with two out and nobody on base, Red Schoendienst lined a single to right field. Hurricane Hazle drew a base on balls. Then on Vernon Law's first pitch to Mathews, the Braves' slugger clubbed a three-run homer deep into the bleachers beyond the rightfield fence. The home run was Mathews' 225th of his career, and his team led, 4-1.

Mathews had one more time at bat, in the last of the seventh. Once again two men were out, and once more Schoendienst was on base, with his third single of the afternoon. Vern Law had been replaced by rookie Bennie Daniels. Mathews took the first pitch for a ball, then lined a shot into the left-centerfield bleachers for career home run number 226. The blast gave Mathews a record four home runs in the first two games of the season and a .400 batting average—four hits in ten at-bats, all the hits being home runs.

Burdette shut out the Pirates in the last two innings and won, 6-1. After the game Mathews modestly downplayed his fast start. "There's nothing to be excited about. Not quite yet, anyway." He also said he planned to play the season "like the managers—one game at a time."

The last word on Mathews, however, belonged to figure-skater Helga: "He beats the ball better than any of the players."

April 17, 1958

	PITTSBURGH					MILWAUKEE			
	AB	R	H	BI		AB	R	H	BI
Virdon, cf	4	0	2	0	Schoendienst, 2b	4	2	3	0
Groat, ss	4	0	0	0	Hazle, rf	3	1	0	0
Skinner, lf	4	0	1	0	Mathews, 3b	4	2	2	5
Kluszewski, 1b	4	0	1	0	Aaron, cf	4	0	1	0
Thomas, 3b	4	0	0	0	Torre, 1b	4	0	2	0
Clemente, rf	3	1	2	0	Pafko, lf	4	0	0	0
Baker, 2b	2	0	0	1	Logan, ss	4	1	2	0
Foiles, c	2	0	0	0	Crandall, c	4	0	2	0
Kravitz, c	0	0	0	0	Burdette, p	4	0	1	1
Law, p	1	0	0	0					
P. Smith	1	0	1	0					
Daniels, p	0	0	0	0					
Freese	1	0	0	0					
Powers	1	0	0	0					
Perez, p	0	0	0	0					
Totals	31	1	7	1		35	6	13	6

P. Smith singled for Law in sixth; Freese flied out
for Foiles in eighth; Powers flied out for Daniels
in eighth.

```
Pittsburgh ..................... 0 0 0  0 1 0  0 0 0--1
MILWAUKEE ...................... 0 0 1  0 3 0  2 0 *--6
```

E--Mathews. 2B--Logan. 3B--Clemente. HR--Mathews 2.
DP--Schoendienst, Logan and Torre 2; Logan, Schoendienst
and Torre. Left--Pittsburgh 4, Milwaukee 6. SF--Baker.

	IP	H	R	ER	BB	SO
Law (L, 0-1)	5	9	4	4	1	0
Daniels	2	2	2	2	0	0
Perez	1	2	0	0	0	0
Burdette (W, 1-0)	9	7	1	1	0	1

U--Jackowski, Landes, Delmore, Barlick. T--1:51.
A--12,854.

ELEVEN

Dead Heat

I enjoyed Hank Aaron. I hit it off with him right away. When I say hit it off, I mean we were very much at ease with each other. We didn't really socialize a lot. We moved in different social circles, you might say, mine being mainly Buhl, Burdette, and Spahn.

Before every ballgame, though, for a long time, Hank and I would play casino. We had so much fun doing that. It was a fairly even game as far as who won or lost after we were through for the day. But it got so bad that the manager finally told us, "Damn it, the game's starting. Put those stupid cards down and get your butts out there. From now on you guys quit 15 minutes before the game starts." We'd get so wrapped up in the cards that we would lose track of the time. We'd be the only two guys in the clubhouse, playing casino.

Hank was a sensitive type of guy. He was quiet and private and liked to mind his own business. He was never comfortable chit-chatting with the sportswriters and talking about his own accomplishments. In other words, he was just like me. Maybe that's why we got along so well. I didn't communicate with the sportswriters too well, so they said I was temperamental. It was probably my fault. At that time I was a little more sensitive than I am now, but I think the accusation of being temperamental or moody was unfair, at least partially. I can be moody, but everybody is moody to an extent. We all have our ups and downs. When you just struck out three times or lost a ballgame, you're not going to feel like turning cartwheels or yakking with some reporter.

In Hank's case, of course, there was another factor. Until

he got into organized baseball he had never lived with white people or associated with them. Alabama was completely segregated at that time. Some people were harder than others for Hank to deal with. A good example would be Warren Spahn. Spahn was an agitator but he wasn't a good kidder. Some guys kid and you know they're kidding, just having fun. I don't think Hank knew what to think of Spahn, or didn't understand him. I don't think he disliked him. In the years I was with the Braves, I don't ever remember anyone having an argument--well, very few anyway. There was an awful lot of kidding and joking and agitating, but everybody got along well.

That doesn't mean that nothing was ever said by a slip of the tongue that might have been racial or insulting, but it was not malicious, or it wasn't directed at anyone in particular. There were things said, though, that were embarrassing and shouldn't have been said. I remember one spring we were playing in Memphis, and they had very small dugouts. A bunch of black people, kids I think, were pushing in on us during the game, trying to see into the dugout. I forget which player it was, but one of the guys on the bench said, "Somebody get these niggers out of here!"

Well, whoever said it was sitting next to George Crowe. He turned and said, "I'm sorry, George, I didn't mean it the way it sounded."

George looked at him. "Okay, I understand." It slipped out. It never should have been said. The person who said it was embarrassed. People talked like that in those days, and I guess some still do. But it was never a cause of any friction on the ballclub.

I've heard and read that some people, including some of my teammates, thought Aaron and I had a competition going to see who could hit more home runs. In a way that might have been true. When Hank started he was a spray hitter, a line drive hitter. As he got more confidence, he started to pull the ball more and hit more home runs. He became pretty much a dead pull hitter. He may have thought, what the hell, Mathews is getting all that attention for hitting home runs, so I'll hit home runs. I know Spahn said he felt Aaron always wanted to hit more home runs than I hit. If Spahnie was right, Hank sure as hell succeeded, didn't he?

As good a hitter as Hank was, if he had tried to just get base hits and not hit home runs, he probably could have hit .350

180

The team of Aaron and Mathews was hot in 1959, producing 85 home runs.
(The Sporting News)

every year and broken Ty Cobb's hit record instead of Babe
Ruth's home run record. That's how good Hank was. As it
turned out, I was a home run hitter, and he was a home run
hitter. I suppose that means we had a natural rivalry going. It
was like when Burdette pitched a no-hitter, Spahn went out and
pitched a no-hitter. But with Hank it wasn't "I gotta beat Eddie
in home runs this year," or vice versa. Neither of us ever
thought stuff like that. I don't think that even Hank would go
up and try to hit a home run because when you try to hit them,
they don't come that often. Home runs just happen.

Hank and I played together on the Braves for 13 years,
12 in Milwaukee and one in Atlanta. As teammates we hit 863
home runs, more than any two teammates including Ruth and
Gehrig. I would have to say that was my proudest accomplishment in baseball, not just because of the number or because no
one else did it, but because I shared the accomplishment with
Hank. He was the best. He wasn't flashy like Willie Mays, but
he did everything well. I never saw Aaron throw to the wrong
base, never saw him overthrow the cutoff man, but he did it so

181

easily that nobody noticed. Maybe because his cap didn't fly off.

Another guy that never got attention was Roberto Clemente. He was something else. He had a great arm and he could hit. He was a little more flamboyant than Hank, but not like Mays. Willie constantly threw to the wrong base, though, or overthrew the cutoff man to show off his arm. We always kept running on Willie. Don't get me wrong, he was a great player, but I would take Aaron and Clemente over Mays any time. But then I'd take Mays over me, so...

In our 13 years with the Braves, Hank and I had our best year together in 1959. Hank hit over .500 for April, and he was over .400 well into June. He ended up winning the batting title with .355, his highest in the big leagues. I hit .306, my highest in the big leagues, in fact my highest outside of Class D with the Hi-Toms. I hit 46 home runs, one less than 1953, and Hank hit 39. Hank led the majors with 400 total bases; I was second with 352. We both drove in over 100 runs and scored over 100 runs. Between us we had 405 hits, both of us getting our highest totals in our careers. We just had a hell of a year.

One of the strangest things that happened that year was the finish of Harvey Haddix's 12-inning perfect game against us. Haddix really had it that night. After 12 perfect innings we finally got a man on base. Felix Mantilla led off the 13th with a ground ball to Don Hoak at third, but Hoak threw it in the dirt, so Mantilla was safe. I was the next batter, and I was supposed to sacrifice him to second. I had never been asked to bunt very often until Haney started managing the Braves, but I was a decent bunter. I got the first pitch down and moved Felix up to second.

Aaron was up next. He was the hottest hitter in baseball, plus first base was open, so Haddix really had no choice but to walk him intentionally. Then Joe Adcock hit one over the fence and things got crazy. Aaron touched second, he saw Mantilla score, and he headed for the dugout. He hadn't seen the ball clear the fence, but he was watching the winning run. All he cared about was winning the game. Adcock knew he had hit a home run, so he kept running and passed up Aaron. The big commotion at the end was about the final score--was it 3-0, 2-0, or 1-0? It didn't matter to anyone except Joe, who naturally wanted that home run. What the controversy did was distract people from the important issue--Harvey Haddix had just pitched a perfect game, but Lew Burdette beat him. Lew had to pitch with men on base in almost every inning. He never gave in. That was the real story. Burdette was a sleeper. He never got enough credit for the type of pitcher he was, as good as he was. "Old Nitro"was probably one of the best competitors baseball has ever seen.

Another good competitor on our club was Red Schoendienst, but in 1959 he had tuberculosis and couldn't play. Losing Red really hurt us. It would be hard to overstate how important he was in our winning the pennant in 1957. Leadership is hard to define. It involves clutch hitting, turning the key double play, a whole list of things. Red did them all. He was already starting to get sick in 1958, but he still helped us win another pennant. Without him we had a real deficiency at second base. If Red had stayed healthy, I really believe we would have run away from the pack in 1959. He made that much of a difference.

Red had played about a year with the New York Giants, so he knew his way around Manhattan a little bit. One time when we were in New York, Red said to me after a ballgame, "Let's go to Toots Shor's."

I said, "Okay." I had never been there, but I knew about it, of course. A lot of celebrities hung out there, show business people and sports figures and so forth.

We went down there, and Red said, "The reason I'm doing this is Toots always comps the ballplayers."

"Great," I said. Then we sat down and snorkled up. I mean, we ate good. Red kept looking around. "What's the matter?" I asked him.

He said, "I don't see Toots." Well, he wasn't there. I think it ended up costing us about $40 apiece.

In 1959 I had another experience in a fairly well-known watering hole. In July we were in St. Louis. It was a Saturday night, and we had lost our ballgame with the Cardinals that afternoon. The losing pitcher was Bob Buhl. We had been playing shit ball. That day's loss was something like our fifth in a row. We were about at our low point of the season. Buhl and I were in the Zodiac Lounge, which was the bar and restaurant upstairs in the Chase Hotel, where we stayed. We were sitting there having a beer and crying on each other's shoulder.

A group of four guys were sitting near us. I don't know if they had lost money on the game or what, but they started in on us. We sat there for about ten or fifteen minutes, trying to

183

ignore them, but they just would not stop. It was all zingers, not directly to us but loud enough for us to hear. "That rotten Mathews stinks!" That type of thing. "Buhl can't pitch worth crap!" Finally I turned around and looked at them.

This guy said to me, "What the hell are you looking at?"

I turned back to Bob and said, "Are we gonna do something or are we gonna get up and leave?"

Bob said, "Let's get the hell out of here."

I said, "I agree."

These guys were sitting next to a pillar. As we got up to leave and started walking out, one guy stood up to challenge Bob and blocked his way. I don't know what the guy's problem was, but that was a mistake. I came around the other side of the pillar. I hit the guy, and he went through some fake stained glass, not really glass but plastic, that went out into the hall where the elevators were. We just walked out, got in the elevator, and went down. That was the end of it. Nobody said a word. One of the unfortunate parts of being in the public eye is that some jerks always want to give you a hard time or show somebody how tough they are. It happens to athletes more times than they can count. A lot of strange things happen.

I had a weird experience involving a fan in Philadelphia sometime back in the mid-1950's. This one happened to be a woman. The situation was reminiscent of the Eddie Waitkus incident, so it was a little bit spooky. What happened was, a woman named Margaret (I won't use her last name) started writing me letters about every other week or so. Now, I was accustomed to getting fan mail, and a lot of it came from women--"You're my favorite ballplayer, blah blah blah," or "You're so handsome, and I love you," that type of thing. Ballplayers always get that stuff.

Margaret's letters, though, were different. They were goofy, kind of over the edge--"I love you and I can't live without you. You're my only desire, etc." And they were consistent. She just kept sending them. This went on for about a year. Then all of a sudden each of the letters started arriving with a five-dollar bill enclosed. I didn't know what the hell to do, so my wife, just for the fun of it, talked to our local priest. I'm not Catholic, but Virjean was. Her priest contacted a priest in Philadelphia, and he found out this gal had a little history of a mental problem. That's when I decided to put a stop to it.

I contacted the Philadelphia police. They assigned a

184

couple of plain-clothes detectives to do a little snooping around on this gal. In the meantime, on our next trip into Philadelphia, this woman showed up knocking on the door of our hotel room. Buhl and I were both in the room. I had never seen her before, so I didn't know who she was, but she identified herself. I just caught a quick glimpse, but I would say she was in her 30's. I said, "You can't come in here."

She didn't. She stood in the hall and reached inside her coat and said, "I have something for you." This was where Eddie Waitkus flashed across my mind. Then she said, "I just want to give you this," and she took a small package and handed it to me. Then she left.

This was getting very strange. I opened the package, and inside was a religious statue. Then I went and called the detectives. I had already talked to them, but after I told them what had happened, they took it more seriously. I never heard from the woman again, but I did hear that she had been institutionalized prior to that, and the family was looking for a reason to put her back. From what I understand, they did put her back in. I really wasn't looking at this as a life-threatening situation, even though I knew about Waitkus getting shot. He had had a working arrangement with that gal, though, that he was shutting off. I had never even met this woman. Even so, I was relieved that I never heard from her again.

After we left St. Louis, the Braves started to play a little better, but we never really got it going. We stayed near first place but not in it until the final week. The critical game for us was in Los Angeles in mid-September, a game we actually won but got screwed out of by a stupid umpire's decision. Since we ended up tied for first with the Dodgers, that ruling in effect cost us the pennant. What happened was, Adcock hit a ball that hit the stanchion above the leftfield screen. It was a home run. It hit the stanchion, though, and dropped right down behind the screen. The umpire, Vinnie Smith, first signaled a home run and then changed his call. He finally said the ball had gone through the screen, which was ridiculous to anybody who was watching. We appealed, but naturally the league president said, "Well, I'm going to listen to the umpire. It went through the screen." That thing really cost us.

After the ballgame we went back to the Ambassador Hotel and packed up to go to San Francisco. Across the street from the hotel was a place where we used to hang out. We were over there, getting ready to go back on the airplane, so we thought we would load up with some beer. I think we had told the bartender we needed four cases. Just then Jeff Chandler, the actor, came in and said, "I'm buying."

I said, "You're buying because the Dodgers beat us."

He said, "That's right." By God, it was just a couple years after that that he died on the operating table. He was a good guy and a good friend.

That umpire's decision upset us, but I've seen a lot of stupid calls. One time Del Crandall and I worked a pickoff play at third against Philadelphia. I had Art Mahaffey, their pitcher, out by a mile. He was lying stretched out with his hand a foot from the bag. I tagged him and the umpire called him safe--and he would not change it. Another time when I was managing in Atlanta, somebody hit a ball that bounced over the fence. We had a little wire screen fence, too. The umpire called it a home run. There's not a thing in the world you can do, either. Talk about frustration.

Thanks to Vinnie Smith, then, the Braves went into the final weekend of the season a game out of first, behind the Dodgers. The situation had certain similarities to 1956, except now we were a game behind instead of a game ahead. We were playing in Milwaukee, against the Phillies, instead of in St. Louis. Haney used the same three starting pitchers, of course-- the Big Three: Buhl, Spahn, and Burdette--but in reverse order. Each one did the opposite of what he had done three years before: Burdette lost the series opener, Spahn won the middle game, and Buhl won the last day to put us in a tie with Los Angeles.

We started the playoffs in Milwaukee and we lost, although hardly anybody saw us. After playing in front of big crowds for so many years, we came to a championship playoff and County Stadium wasn't even half full. It was weird. Maybe the fans were all waiting for us to play the World Series. I didn't do a thing at bat. Nobody did. We lost, 3-2.

The next day we played in the L.A. Coliseum. We had the game won, but we didn't hold them. I hit a home run off Drysdale that put us ahead by two runs. It was number 46 for me, one more than Ernie Banks. As I came into the dugout, I said, "Banks, you are number two" to Johnny Logan.

"That's right," Johnny said. "That's right."

We led 5-2 going into the last of the ninth. Burdette was

pitching and it looked like we were going to be tied at a game apiece, but we didn't win. The Dodgers loaded the bases, Haney took Lew out, and...everything fell apart. They tied it up, and we lost on a throwing error by Felix Mantilla in the twelfth inning. Nobody blamed Felix. It was just a throw in the dirt that Frank Torre couldn't scoop out. Those things happen.

The play that really irritated a lot of the Braves happened in the seventh inning. Dodger outfielder Norm Larker took out Johnny Logan with a block at second base trying to break up a double play. Logan was carried off on a stretcher. Mantilla took his place at shortstop, and later he made the crucial error. Quite a few of my teammates felt that Larker's dirty play cost us the game.

I saw it differently. I thought what Larker did was just a hard slide. That's aggressive baseball. I blamed Haney for taking Logan out. He wasn't injured; he got a few bruises and he got the wind knocked out of him. He got hit pretty good, but Johnny's a tough son of a gun. Give him a couple minutes and he would have finished the game. He could have stayed in. But no, bang, Haney took him out. I'm not saying it would necessarily have made a difference in the outcome, but Johnny would have wanted to stay in the game, and he should have.

Fred Haney had a different way of managing. I don't think he adapted to the players that we had on the ballclub. He was going to manage his way regardless of what we had going out there, and I think that did hurt us.

That was pretty much of a general feeling among the ballplayers. It's just like when you're a hitting instructor, you don't try to tell everybody, "This is the way it's supposed to be done." Every hitter is different. We had a different type of talent on that club. As I said earlier, Haney bunted us out of the pennant in 1956. That's just the way he was. I won't say he mismanaged, but he could have adapted to the type of club we were better than he did. We didn't have a base-stealing club. We had a power-hitting club, and he had everybody bunting. He left a lot to be desired because he wouldn't adapt. Whether part of that was because his coaches wouldn't help him and talk to him, I don't know. I'd say part of the problem may have been his age. Fred was 61 at the time and pretty much set in his ways.

As far as handling pitchers, Fred saw to it that Spahn and Burdette and Buhl got their turns in the order. A guy like Juan Pizarro, though, would pitch a great game and then not work again for two weeks. Haney was over-managing. He had me hitting second in the order. His theory was that I would get up to bat more often. That's my point--certain managers, and Haney was one, think they're going to win the games with their mind. I liked and respected Fred, but he may not have been the perfect match for our ballclub.

We probably should have won four pennants in a row, 1956 through 1959. We naturally were disappointed, but at the end of a season, as many games as you play, you're starting to wind down, and it happens so fast, so you just accept it. We had given it a damn good shot. When you're in professional sports, it's a little different. You can't be a winner without being a loser. The good athlete can accept defeat without busting up and crying in his beer. We were all upset to a point. We wished we had won, but what are you going to do?

The flight home was dreary. Then what happened after I got home was incredible. I started getting hate mail! It seems some people were unhappy because the home run I hit in the playoff game counted toward the home run championship. They didn't think that was fair to Ernie Banks. Well, I looked it up. Banks played in seven more games than I did that year. The Cubs played 155 games because of one tie, which was one more than the Braves played not counting the playoffs. Is that fair? Give me a break.

September 21, 1959

That abominable word "three-peat" was still three decades in the future, but in 1959 the Milwaukee Braves expected, and were expected, to win another National League pennant. With Hank Aaron hitting over .400 until mid-June, the Braves creaked along in first place, barely, leading by percentage points at the first All-Star break. Eddie Mathews hit a home run in the National League's 5-4 victory, but the next day the Braves lost to the Dodgers and fell out of first place.

They stayed out until the day after the second All-Star game, when they took the lead by .001. The following day they lost and fell out again, dropping as far back as five games. The next time they were able to enjoy the view at the top came on the night of September 21 in Pittsburgh's Forbes Field. That evening they pulled into a tie with the idle L.A. Dodgers—but it wasn't easy.

Beginning a three-game series with the fourth-place Pirates, Milwaukee jumped on top with a pair of runs in the first inning, with Aaron's triple sandwiched between base hits by Billy Bruton and Lee Maye. Pittsburgh tied the game with single runs off Warren Spahn in the third and fourth. The latter inning was highlighted by a melee featuring Pittsburgh's 220-pound first baseman Dick Stuart and Milwaukee's 160-pound shortstop Felix Mantilla. The two exchanged punches and wrestled briefly, but neither was seriously injured or ejected.

Mantilla led off the next inning, serenaded by a loud chorus of boos and catcalls. He silenced his critics by bouncing a base hit into left field. After one out Al Spangler batted for Bruton, who had injured himself sliding in the first inning, and also singled. Then with two out Mathews smashed an enormous home run off Bob Friend. The ball cleared the roof of the double-decked rightfield grandstand, 86 feet high, carrying an estimated 500 feet. Mathews described the blow after the game as the longest he had ever hit. It was the sixth ball ever to clear the roof of the 50-year-old ballpark. The first had been hit by Babe Ruth on May 25, 1935, the Babe's final home run.

Mathews' blast put his team ahead, 5-2. Each club added a run in the sixth. After two scoreless innings, Spahn led off the ninth by grounding to Dick Stuart, Mantilla's sparring partner. The hulking first-sacker demonstrated the fielding skills that would, a few years later, earn him the nickname of "Dr. Strangeglove"—he booted the ball and Spahn was safe. The error proved costly when, a few moments later, Mathews belted his second homer of the night, this one off reliever Bennie Daniels. It was Mathews' 43rd of the season and 296th of his career.

An 8-3 lead in the ninth inning looked safe for Spahn, but it was not. Two singles and a double brought in one run and Don McMahon. A base hit by Roberto Clemente scored another run, and after Stuart popped out, Smoky Burgess stroked a sacrifice fly to make the score 8-6. Don Hoak represented the tying run at the plate, but he looked at a called third strike to end the ballgame. McMahon saved his 13th game, and Spahn received credit for his 20th win, his tenth time reaching that mark. Spahn's victory was also the 266th of his career, tying Eppa Rixey for the most wins by a National League lefthander.

Most important, though, after a seven-week struggle and with just five games remaining, the Braves were back in first place.

September 21, 1959

MILWAUKEE	AB	R	H	BI	PITTSBURGH	AB	R	H	BI
Bruton, cf	2	1	1	0	Skinner, rf	4	1	2	1
Spangler, cf	2	1	1	0	Groat, ss	5	1	2	1
Mathews, 3b	5	2	2	5	Clemente, rf	5	0	2	1
Aaron, rf	5	1	3	1	Stuart, 1b	5	2	1	0
Adcock, 1b	5	0	0	0	Burgess, c	4	0	0	1
Torre, 1b	0	0	0	0	Hoak, 3b	5	0	2	0
Maye, lf	5	0	3	1	Mazeroski, 2b	4	0	2	2
Avila, 2b	3	0	0	0	Mejias, cf	4	0	0	0
Schoendienst, 2	1	0	0	0	Friend, p	1	1	1	0
Crandall, c	3	1	1	0	Porterfield, p	0	0	0	0
Mantilla, ss	4	0	1	0	Bright	1	0	0	0
Spahn, p	4	2	1	0	Gross, p	0	0	0	0
McMahon, p	0	0	0	0	Stevens	1	0	0	0
					Daniels, p	0	0	0	0
					Schofield	1	1	1	0
Totals	39	8	13	7	Totals	40	6	13	6

Spangler singled for Bruton in fifth; Bright flied out for Porterfield in fifth; Stevens grounded out for Gross in seventh; Schofield singled for Daniels in ninth.

```
MILWAUKEE .................... 2 0 0  0 3 1  0 0 2--8
Pittsburgh ................... 0 0 1  1 0 1  0 0 3--6
```

E--Avila, Mejias, Stuart. 2B--Crandall, Friend. 3B--Aaron. HR--Mathews 2. Left--Milwaukee 7, Pitts. 9. SB--Bruton. S--Avila, Spangler. SF--Burgess.

	IP	H	R	ER	BB	SO
Spahn (W, 20-15)	8	12	6	6	1	3
McMahon	1	1	0	0	0	1
Friend (L, 8-19)	4.1	8	5	5	0	2
Porterfield	.2	0	0	0	0	1
Gross	2	1	1	0	0	1
Daniels	2	4	2	1	0	1

Spahn faced three batters in ninth.
HBP--By Gross (Crandall). U--Secory, Jackowski, Gorman, Donatelli. T--2:55. A--17,205.

TWELVE

Travels with Charlie

Maybe the novelty had worn off. I don't know. The Braves' season attendance dropped about a quarter-million, but it was still higher than any other team except the Dodgers in that big Coliseum. We had all been a little surprised when our first playoff game against Los Angeles drew less than 20,000 people. It was a Monday, though, with no presale. The day before that, when we beat the Phillies to tie the Dodgers and get into the playoffs, the crowd was the largest the Braves ever had in Milwaukee.

The opening day crowd in 1960 was right around 40,000, a nice crowd on a warm, sunny day, but not a full house. Spahnie pitched, we came from behind and beat the Pirates, the fans made lots of noise and saw an exciting game, but you could look around and find empty seats. In the early sixties the Braves' attendance began to fall off. For one thing the team was changing. For another, the local Dutchmen got all upset because they couldn't carry beer into County Stadium anymore. Imagine that in Milwaukee?

I blame that on the local city fathers, or maybe the county fathers. It certainly was not the fault of the ownership because Lou Perini didn't give a damn. The people on the county board, which controlled the stadium, got greedy. It's that simple. They decided they could make some money by banning carry-ins and making the fans buy beer from the concession stands and vendors, at a big mark-up, of course. General manager John McHale went along with it, so Perini received a lot of the blame. Perini was already a villain to some people because he wouldn't televise any ballgames. The beer

191

ban wasn't Perini's fault, though, it was the politicians'. They claimed it was for safety, so fans couldn't throw bottles or cans, but I never saw that happen. It was money. They should have raised the rent or something against the ballclub, not punished the fans. In the good days, two guys would come to the ballpark and buy three seats--one for each of them and one for the beer cooler. What the hell difference did it make?

When attendance started to decline, the drop was pretty gradual at first. The ownership tried to stop the decrease in attendance with gimmicks. That might have worked for Bill Veeck, but he was a genius, and remember, when he set all those attendance records in Cleveland in 1948, he had a terrific ballclub that won the pennant and the World Series. When he tried similar tricks in St. Louis, people still didn't go to the ballpark because the Browns were a terrible team.

The Braves tried all kinds of promotional deals to attract customers. They set up a picnic area near the leftfield bleachers. They had a little German band playing in the stands between innings. Professional golfer Patty Berg put on a demonstration before one of the games. They had Milwaukee's first Old-Timers' game, with guys ranging from "Unser Choe" Hauser, who was in his sixties, to Jack Dittmer, who was only a few years older than I was, and people like Sid Gordon and Kenny Keltner in between. That was fun, seeing those guys. Whether it brought in any extra fans, I couldn't say.

Later on in the season they had a special Cranberry Night. What that had to do with baseball, I'm not sure. We played the San Francisco Giants that night, I know. They had a fireworks display after the ballgame, and before the game they held a little ceremony near home plate in which they had about six or eight of us ballplayers--me, Adcock, Bruton, Logan, and a few more--receive and put on Indian head-dresses. We looked like a bunch of stupid turkeys. The whole affair was sponsored by the state's cranberry industry. It was nothing more than cheap advertising for cranberries. The ballplayers always went along with these shenanigans pretty good-naturedly, but some-times we felt silly doing it. And what was the point? Attendance was lower that night than the previous night or the following night. In fact, the actual attendance that night was lower than the pre-sale of tickets.

I can just imagine some guy getting ready to go to the ballgame with his wife. "Hurry up, Honey," she says, "we don't want to be late for the game. It's Cranberry Night."

The guy would probably say, "Wouldn't you rather go bowling?"

The following year, during the winter, the Braves went a step further to reach out and bring in fans from around the state of Wisconsin. They organized their first "Hi, Neighbor" trip, in which a group of ballplayers, coaches, broadcasters, and front office personnel traveled around the state in a chartered bus to promote the Braves. The tour lasted about a week to ten days. Hank Aaron and I both lived in the Milwaukee area year-round, so we joined the tour, and so did Del Crandall and Joe Torre. Our radio announcing team, Earl Gillespie and Blaine Walsh, went along, plus Andy Pafko and Birdie Tebbetts and John McHale and a few others. We stopped in different towns--Racine, Oshkosh, Sheboygan, Manitowoc--and went to factories and Kiwanis Club meetings and so forth to drum up interest in baseball. We toured the plant in Kohler where they make all the toilets and bathtubs, and we shook hands with every Moose, Lion, and Elk we could locate. We were just like a bunch of guys running for public office. We met some wonderful people, but I don't ever want to look at chicken and peas again. And as with Cranberry Night, I'm not sure how much it did to put fannies in the seats.

Baseball, like cheese or cranberries or toilet paper, is a product. If you offer a good product, people will go out of their way to buy it. Declining attendance said the Braves' product had lost some of its zest. After the end of the 1959 season, the Braves' front office wanted to fire Fred Haney and bring in a new manager. The problem with firing him, of course, was that Haney had been so successful. During his three-and-a-half seasons the Braves had won more games than any other club in the big leagues. Also, Lou Perini was very fond of Haney and had said the job was his as long as he wanted it. The night after the Dodgers beat the White Sox in the third game of the World Series, in Los Angeles, Haney solved their dilemma by announcing his retirement. Whether it was his decision I don't know. Nobody said anything about it. My own opinion? I think they made a change.

For the next few weeks rumors were flying about who would replace Haney. A lot of speculation centered on Leo Durocher, who was available, but that would have been a nightmare. I don't think there would have been any chance for

193

Durocher with our team. Mainly the problem was his arrogance, but also he wore so much cheap perfume you could smell it right in your mouth. He must have taken a bath in it. Anyway, when John McHale announced our new manager, it was Charlie Dressen. We knew of Dressen, but we didn't really know him. He had managed the Brooklyn Dodgers in 1953, so we had gotten into some brawls with his club before. He was a feisty little bugger. More recently he had been a coach with the Los Angeles Dodgers for the previous two years, which meant we saw him a lot, but as I said, we didn't really know him.

After the Dodgers won the pennant in '53, Dressen had insisted on a two-year contract. Walter O'Malley refused. Walt Alston was hired instead, to the first of 23 one-year contracts with the Dodgers, and Dressen went to the Pacific Coast League to manage. When the Braves hired Dressen, the contract was for two years, breaking a policy they had established after they fired Charlie Grimm during his three-year contract.

Wherever he was, Dressen was always controversial, always flamboyant and outspoken. He had a well-deserved reputation for using the pronoun "I" more than anybody else, seemingly at least once in every sentence. He thought he could win every game with his mind. Probably his most famous statement came when he was managing the Dodgers: "Just hold them for a few innings, fellas, I'll think of something."

Charlie was cocky to the point of being almost comical. When the Braves first hired him, he said, "I don't think it will take much help for the Braves to win enough games to win the pennant." Just like that--nothing to it.

One time Dressen was talking to Warren Spahn, going over the other team's lineup and how to pitch to the different hitters. Spahn at that point had won over 300 games in his career and was probably the greatest lefthanded pitcher of all time. Charlie said, "I could tell you how to get this guy out if you had a curve ball, but you don't have a curve ball." He was not trying to be funny, either.

Every manager who joins a new ballclub seems to feel he has to establish himself. He wants to prove to the front office that he can be tough and control the ballplayers. Dressen was like that. He prided himself on being a disciplinarian anyway, and the Braves had a reputation for being kind of high-spirited, maybe even a little wild under Haney. Charlie figured his job was to come in and make rules. He started out pretty heavy

Dressen tells Spahn, "If you had a curve ball..." (Frank Stanfield photo)

duty. Eventually he loosened up a little bit as we got to know him and vice versa.

Charlie's big bag was cooking chili. He loved to cook, and chili was his specialty. After a game he would come into the clubhouse with a big pot of it, so we all had a little bowl. He was so proud of that stuff, and it sucked.

Later on I saw Dressen off the field quite a bit. We both liked to shoot. I didn't hunt with him, but we had a mutual friend who owned a shooting preserve outside of Milwaukee. The guy was a well-known dog trainer, and he would invite us out to his shooting preserve. That's really how you get to know a guy like Dressen. If you only saw him at the ballpark, you would never even get acquainted with him. Johnny Logan said he never even had a conversation with Dressen the whole time he was with us.

Dressen was all business around the clubhouse and on the field. He was considered a good baseball man, and he was. He was stubborn, though. He was an older guy, the same age as

195

Haney, and there was only one way--his way. A few years earlier when he managed the Washington Senators, he told his Cuban ballplayers, guys like Camilo Pascual and Pedro Ramos, that they had to learn to speak English. "What am I going to do," he said, "send over to the United Nations for an interpreter every time I want to give some signs?" That's the way Charlie was. He always had his way of doing things.

More than anything else, Charlie Dressen was obsessed with curfews. We had heard stories about him giving a baseball to the elevator operator in the hotel where the ballclub stayed. The elevator man would have the ballplayers autograph the ball when they came in after one o'clock. Charlie would get the ball from the guy in the morning and see who came in late.

We had our own curfew experiences with Dressen. I roomed with Bob Buhl when we traveled, and one night in San Francisco, for some reason, Bob had gone up to the room early and gone to sleep. At some point he accidentally knocked the phone off the hook. When Charlie started doing his room checks, ours didn't answer because the phone was off the hook. Pretty soon we got this banging on our door.

"You guys aren't in there," this loud voice said. It was Charlie, of course.

I said, "I'm standing right here."

He said, "Then Buhl's not in."

I opened the door without turning on the light. "He's sleeping right there on the bed. Come in and check."

Charlie recoiled like I was a spitting cobra. "Forget it. I wouldn't walk into that room with a machine gun with you two loonies." I'm not sure what he thought we had cooked up, but he didn't trust us. Then he said, "I've been in baseball for 40 years, and we've got the four worst offenders on this club that I've ever met--Spahn, Burdette, Buhl, and Mathews."

The next morning I told the others what Charlie had said. The four of us went out and had our picture taken, all cutting up for the camera. Then we gave a nice eight-by-ten of it to Charlie. On the bottom we wrote, "From the four worst offenders in baseball," and we all signed it. That's still my favorite photograph. I have a copy of it on my bedroom wall.

Another time we were in Los Angeles, staying at the Ambassador Hotel. Our rooms were out in this wing of the hotel, and in front of that wing were some large, large shrubs. That was how we could sneak in if we were out late. We walked

196

through the shrubs. It was like a maze. You had to walk through them and around them. Somehow Charlie got wind of our late-night secret entry way, so he decided he was going to stand out there in the middle of these shrubs and catch us in the act.

What happened, though, was that Spahn found out about Dressen's little trap and set up his own plan of attack. Spahnie located the controls for the sprinklers, and at curfew time he went and turned all the sprinklers on. There was Charlie, lost in this maze of shrubs, soaked to the skin and fit to be tied. We were all standing off to the side watching this little drama unfold. We thought it was hilarious. Right at that moment Dressen probably realized he wasn't going to reform us all in one night.

After the initial break-in period, most of the players liked him okay. He was a fun guy and a dedicated baseball man. He believed in some things we were not accustomed to, like stealing bases and the hit-and-run. His theory was that if a team could score four runs every game, they would win the pennant easily. And if you look at it, put it into a computer, he was right. They would win the pennant. We weren't able to do that with Charlie, but we adapted to each other pretty well. You know, you can't live with people and walk around with a chip on your shoulder all the time. We all learn to adjust.

The ones who never adjusted were the Milwaukee fans. They just did not warm up to Dressen the way they had to Charlie Grimm or even Haney. The media played a big part in that, I think. The writers did a lot of second-guessing, especially about the way he handled the pitching staff. We had a young pitcher named Don Nottebart who made his big-league debut in a game in St. Louis. He got roughed up pretty good, but Dressen let him go a long time before he even warmed anybody up. Nottebart finally left with the Cardinals leading 7-0. It was like Dressen was almost conceding the game by leaving him in there so long. We were right in the thick of things at the time, right behind the Pirates. The worst of it was we came back and tied the score, 7-7, but then lost in extra innings. The sportswriters really got on Dressen for that one, for leaving Nottebart in.

The writers also stirred up a feud between Fred Haney and Dressen during the early part of the year. They would print something Haney supposedly said about the way the Braves were being managed. Then they would show the quote to Dressen and get his comments and go back and forth. To clear the air, Haney and Dressen went on a panel show on TV together. Joe Adcock and I were on there too for some reason, and the Braves' radio announcer, Earl Gillespie, was the moderator. The main topics of discussion were whether I should be batting second or third in the order, and whether the Braves had enough speed to be a hit-and-run ballclub.

"Mathews gets more walks than anybody on the team," Haney said, "so I wanted him batting number two."

Dressen said, "I'm a hit-and-run man. I don't like hitting into double plays, so we're going to run. Aaron and Mathews can both move okay."

Then they asked me what I thought. "I'm not paid to manage, just to play ball," I told them. I wasn't trying to be diplomatic, just honest. Adcock and I couldn't wait for the program to end so we could get a beer.

We had our disagreements with Dressen, over bedtimes and lots of other little items. One time on a bus in Philadelphia we had a little fire started in the back, and that made the local press. Charlie was upset at the time, but the whole incident was blown out of proportion. When you would catch a guy reading a newspaper, you would take your cigarette lighter and you'd light the paper on fire. That was something we had done while Charlie Grimm was the manager. He enjoyed jokes and pranks and so forth. We were always doing that. It just continued on through the rest of the managers. Dressen was not quite as amenable to it. After that bus incident he changed some guys' roommate assignments and cut our meal allowance for a while.

On the field, though, Dressen backed every one of us to the hilt. That included the so-called Frank Robinson incident, which was probably my most notorious fight in baseball, so I suppose I should at least mention it. We were playing the Reds in Cincinnati when Robinson hit a blooper down the rightfield line. Nobody could get to it, and Robinson got an easy double out of it. He kept running, though, trying to stretch it to a triple. Adcock ran the ball down and threw to me at third. Robinson wasn't even close to third yet, so he was an easy out. All I had to do was wait for him and put the tag on.

Well, we all knew Frank. He was not a dirty player, but he could be rough. Sometimes he was too aggressive. We'd had a couple of run-ins before. This time when he came around second he made a mistake. I had him out by a mile. I didn't go out to confront him. I stayed on the bag, and he came barreling into me. As he slid in, hard, he swung his arm up and caught me on the side of the head. He was always doing stuff like that when he slid.

"Frank, don't come in here like that," I told him. "I've had enough of that garbage."

He responded with some very unfriendly phrases.

I threw my glove down and we went at it. Now, most baseball fights aren't one on one. Usually ten people step in and break it up right away. This time, though, it happened so fast. We were there by ourselves when it started. Mel Roach, our second baseman, had tried to catch Robinson's blooper, and he ran into the railing and fell into the box seats. Apparently everybody was looking at that. Then when I got the ball, everybody had moved away from us. I swung at Frank and got him pretty good. I knocked him down, and then I landed a couple more good ones. His face got messed up, and I hurt my right hand. I felt like I had punched a bowling ball. My one knuckle still sticks up further than the others to this day.

I got ejected from the game, and they took Frank to the clubhouse for repairs. This was the first game of a doubleheader, though, and the funny part was he came back for the second game and beat us. I hit a ball down the leftfield foul line, which in Crosley Field went right to the edge of the grandstand. Frank ended up in the third row, but he caught the ball and took away an extra-base hit. He also got a double and a home run in the second game, even though he had to stop at bat a couple times to wipe the blood away from his eye.

The manager of the Reds at that time was Fred Hutchinson, and Freddy and I were good friends. About a week or so later, after Robinson had gone on a little tear, Fred sent me a telegram.

"Thanks for waking Frank up," it said.

The next year I sent Fred a telegram: "All it takes is plane fare." I never received a response, but the Reds went on to win the pennant.

After my little bout with Robinson, Mel Roach moved over from second base and took my place at third. Hank Aaron finished up the ballgame as the second baseman. The league never fined me for the incident--they said it was just a normal fight. The Reds protested that decision because Billy Martin, who was playing for Cincinnati then, had been fined and suspended about a week before that for punching Jim Brewer and breaking his cheekbone. They said if Martin deserved a fine, so did I. They lost, though.

When Charlie Dressen came into the clubhouse after the ballgame, which we lost, all he did was slap me on the back and say, "Nice punchin', Eddie. That SOB had it coming."

July 13, 1960

All ballplayers have slumps. Sometimes they deny it, as Yogi Berra once did: "Slump? I ain't in no slump. I just ain't hitting." But the numbers don't lie.

In the weeks before the 1960 All-Star games (yes, they were still playing two), Eddie Mathews was truly in a slump. When he arrived in Kansas City for the first All-Star contest on July 11, he had hit successfully in only eight of his last 65 at-bats (a .123 clip). What's more, he had not homered in his last 19 games, the longest power outage he had ever experienced. In Kansas City his bad luck continued. Against American League hurlers like Bill Monbouquette and Jim Coates, Mathews went hitless in four trips and kicked in two errors to boot although the Nationals won, 5-3.

Two days later, in baseball's only attempt at back-to-back All-Star games, the two clubs traveled to Yankee Stadium for the sequel. The fans were underwhelmed. In the nation's most populous city, in the 67,000-seat House That Ruth Built, only 38,362 paying customers bothered to show up to watch. What they saw for their money was a one-sided game utterly devoid of suspense. The Kansas City game had been won by Pittsburgh's Bob Friend; this one was won by his fellow Pirate Vernon Law. (This was, of course, the year of the Pirate—Bill Mazeroski's dramatic home run would make the Bucs the champions of the World Series.)

Whitey Ford worked the first three innings for the host league. Ford would win 236 games in the American League and retire with the best winning percentage ever, but in All-Star competition he was strictly a pigeon. He had earned the defeat in the first All-Star game last year—today he wore the brown helmet again, thanks to two bad pitches. The second of
200

those was a gopher ball to Willie Mays in the third inning.

An even more damaging blow had been struck in the previous inning. After Ford served up a single to Joe Adcock, Mathews' ex-roommate in Milwaukee, Mathews slammed a 3-2 pitch 20 rows deep into the seats in right field for a two-run lead. The blast gave the National League a lead they never relinquished. Six pitchers combined to shut out the junior circuit in a 6-0 victory, giving the Nationals a sweep. Despite lacking excitement, though, the game featured some interesting moments.

The game's most conspicuous flop had to be Yankee outfielder Roger Maris, in the midst of his first of two consecutive MVP seasons but hampered by sore ligaments in his wrist. Maris left seven men stranded, twice leaving the bases loaded and grounding out with a runner on base to end the game. Two old superstars, though, did themselves proud. In the top of the seventh, 39-year-old Stan Musial took a strike, then ripped a home run off former teammate Gerry Staley, his sixth in All-Star competition, to establish a record that still stands. Then in the bottom of the seventh, 41-year-old Ted Williams, in his final All-Star appearance, batted for Minnie Minoso. "The Kid" received a huge ovation from the once-hostile New Yorkers and rewarded them with a base hit.

After the game Mathews spoke of his three-week-long slump as if it were history: "That must have been the granddaddy of all slumps. I didn't even hit a ball good." If he thought his batting drought was over, he was right. The next night, in Pittsburgh, Mathews banged out three hits, including a home run. He also homered in two of his next three ballgames. Then after a three-game respite, he homered again two days in a row. The stroke was back.

July 13, 1960

NATIONAL LEAGUE	AB	R	H	BI	AMERICAN LEAGUE	AB	R	H	BI
Mays, cf	4	1	3	1	Minoso, lf	2	0	0	0
Pinson, cf	0	0	0	0	T. Williams, ph	1	0	1	0
Skinner, lf	3	0	1	0	B. Robinson, 3b	1	0	0	0
Cepeda, lf	2	0	0	0	Runnels, 2b	2	0	0	0
Aaron, rf	3	0	0	0	Staley, p	0	0	0	0
Clemente, rf	0	0	0	0	Kaline, lf	1	0	1	0
Banks, ss	3	0	1	0	Maris, rf	4	0	0	0
Groat, ss	1	0	0	0	Mantle, cf	4	0	1	0
Adcock, 1b	2	1	1	0	Skowron, 1b	1	0	1	0
White, 1b	1	0	0	0	Power, 1b	2	0	0	0
Larker, 1b	0	1	0	0	Berra, c	2	0	0	0
Mathews, 3b	3	1	1	2	Lollar, c	2	0	1	0
Boyer, 3b	1	1	1	2	Malzone, 3b	2	0	0	0
Mazeroski, 2b	2	0	0	0	Lary, p	0	0	0	0
Neal, 2b	1	0	0	0	A. Smith, ph	1	0	0	0
Taylor, 2b	1	0	1	0	Bell, p	0	0	0	0
Crandall, c	2	0	0	0	Hansen, ss	4	0	2	0
S. Williams, p	0	0	0	0	Ford, p	0	0	0	0
Musial, ph	1	1	1	1	Kuenn, ph	1	0	0	0
Law, p	1	0	0	0	Wynn, p	0	0	0	0
Podres, p	0	0	0	0	Fox, 2b	3	0	1	0
Burgess, c	2	0	0	0					
Jackson, p	0	0	0	0					
Henry, p	0	0	0	0					
McDaniel, p	0	0	0	0					
Totals	34	6	10	6	Totals	33	0	8	0

```
NATIONALS  ......................  0 2 1   0 0 0   1 0 2--6
Americans  ......................  0 0 0   0 0 0   0 0 0--0
```

E--None. 2B--Lollar. HR--Mathews, Mays, Musial, Boyer. Left--Nationals 5, Americans 12. DP--Law, Banks, and Adcock; Banks, Neal and White; Fox, Hansen, and Power. SB--Mays. S--Henry.

	IP	H	R	ER	BB	SO
Law (W)	2	1	0	0	0	1
Podres	2	1	0	0	0	1
S. Williams	2	2	0	0	1	2
Jackson	1	1	0	0	1	0
Henry	1	2	0	0	0	0
McDaniel	1	1	0	0	0	0
Ford (L)	3	5	3	3	0	1
Wynn	2	0	0	0	0	1
Staley	2	2	1	1	0	0
Lary	1	1	0	0	1	0
Bell	1	2	2	2	1	0

U--Chylak, Boggess, Honochick, Gorman, Stevenson, Smith. T--2:42. A--38,362.

THIRTEEN

Breakin' Up Is Hard To Do

Things started to deteriorate. We were beginning to run out of gas. When I say we, I certainly include myself in that category. I wasn't doing what I thought I should have been doing, and I had company.

In my tenth year in the big leagues, everything was flip-flopping. We were all getting older. It was inevitable that something like that would happen, but you still hate to see it happen. Ever since the Braves moved from Boston, our lineup had been pretty much the same, very consistent. Second base and left field were never really settled, but every other position was solid and predictable: Del Crandall catching, Joe Adcock at first base, Johnny Logan at shortstop, I was at third, Billy Bruton played center field, and Hank Aaron was in right. The core of the pitching staff stayed the same that whole time, too: Warren Spahn, Lew Burdette, and Bob Buhl. In Milwaukee you really could tell the players without a scorecard.

We had a lot of success together, a lot of good times. It couldn't go on forever, though. The Braves were probably too slow in making changes. John Quinn had gone to the Philadelphia Phillies after our second World Series, in 1958, to be replaced by John McHale as general manager. Many people thought Perini made a big mistake letting Quinn go. He was a good baseball man. He might have made the necessary changes in personnel, which some of the ballplayers would not have liked, or some of the fans either for that matter, but which would have helped the ballclub.

McHale didn't do that--until after the 1960 season. Then right after the World Series, the Braves released Red Schoen-

203

dienst. That move made no sense to us. They didn't trade him for anybody; they just let him go. Red was getting up in years, but he had some baseball left. He went back to the Cardinals, and for the next couple years he was the best pinch hitter in the league. Red was not too pleased when they gave him his walking papers, but he was really upset a few weeks later when McHale bought Billy Martin from Cincinnati. Red thought that was an insult to him, and it was, especially after what Schoendienst had done for our ballclub during the two pennant years. But that's baseball. There is not a lot of loyalty and there never was.

Billy Martin fell right into place with us. He had been one of my best pals ever since our Japanese trip with Eddie Lopat's All-Stars. Billy wasn't a wild man, which most people seemed to think. As far as the fights that he had, like the marshmallow salesman and so forth, Billy wasn't a big guy, but he had a reputation for fighting. These guys would always start something, and Billy would not back off. That's how a lot of those happened. He never walked up and chose a fight, but he wouldn't back away from one. As he said, "I don't throw the first punch. I throw the second four punches."

Of course he had his share of baseball fights, too. He got in a couple with catcher Clint Courtney of the St. Louis Browns, and another one under the grandstand at Fenway Park with Jimmy Piersall before a ballgame. A week before my little tussle with Frank Robinson, Billy broke Jim Brewer's cheek-bone in a one-punch affair on the pitcher's mound. Later when he was managing the Twins he punched out his own pitcher, Dave Boswell, in a scuffle in the alley outside the Lindell A.C. sports bar in Detroit. Billy was not an instigator, though. He just couldn't back down from anybody.

Ninety-nine percent of the time, Billy was a quiet, kind, generous, fun-loving guy. He always liked to have his pals around him--Lee Walls, for example--and they pretty much watched out for him. I don't mean they were his bodyguards, don't get me wrong, but if somebody was starting to zing Billy, his pals would back him off or talk to him to settle him down. Billy was a drinker. He was a good drinker, if there is such a thing. Sometimes when he was in bars, though, people would recognize him and cause trouble, challenge him or whatever. It's amazing how many people will do that. I say that from experience because it happened to me many times. Billy and I were alike in a lot of ways, which I suppose is why we hit it off so well. Billy was always a winner, but he was his own worst enemy. I know what that's like, too.

What many people don't know, or what they forget, is that Billy was funny. The sportswriters loved to quote Billy. A little while after he broke Jim Brewer's cheekbone, Brewer sued him for a million dollars. Billy learned about it from a reporter. He asked the guy, "How does he want it, cash or check?"

To me, the best way to remember Billy is in that beer commercial he did where he was sitting at the bar with his back to the camera, dressed in western clothes. Then he turned around with kind of an innocent grin and said, "I didn't punch no doggie." He was like that. He could laugh at himself and poke fun at his public image. If you backed him into a corner, though, he'd punch your lights out.

Billy was also a hell of a ballplayer. He made that famous catch that saved the final game of the 1952 World Series. The next year he set all kinds of batting records in the Series. By the time he got to Milwaukee, though, he was about at the end of the line as far as his playing days. A few days after the Braves bought Billy, we got Frank Bolling in a trade with the Detroit Tigers. Bolling had such a good year for us that Billy just rode the bench. He only batted a few times and never got a base hit in a Braves uniform. In mid-season he was sold to Minnesota. While he was there he met Art Fowler, my old running mate from the Atlanta Crackers, in a bar in St. Paul. Art was pitching for the Los Angeles Angels at the time. When Billy met Art, it was the beginning of a beautiful friendship.

Billy told Art Fowler that if he ever became a manager, he would hire Art as his pitching coach. He did. Everywhere he managed, he took Art along with him. It was Art who introduced Martin to Bill Reedy, the owner of Reedy's Saloon just down the street from Tiger Stadium in Detroit. I knew Reedy very well. He used to come to spring training. Tragically, Reedy was there when Billy's pickup truck crashed and killed Billy on Christmas Day, 1989, in upstate New York. Both of them had been drinking; that I know. The controversy was about who was driving, Martin or Reedy. Reedy at first said he was, but later he said he had lied to protect Billy. Reedy was tried and convicted of drunk driving.

Now, I wasn't there, so obviously I don't know for sure who was driving. I was shocked when I heard that Billy was killed. It's too bad that all the trials and lawsuits and other

205

foolishness took place. Regardless of who was driving or what happened, it was an accident. But I know this--I never knew Billy, when there was a car or truck available, that he wasn't the driver. He always did the driving. It didn't matter how much he had been drinking. Unless this was some freak deal, Billy always drove.

As I said, Billy never got a chance to play with the Braves because Frank Bolling was having such a great year. Frank batted over .300 while Martin was there. Bolling helped the club a lot and made the all-star team, but to get him the Braves paid a price. They traded Billy Bruton, one of the most popular ballplayers in Milwaukee and the regular centerfielder from opening day in 1953. Bruton was very steady, a good hitter, an excellent fielder, and probably the best baserunner in the league when he was younger. Bruton was the first one of the longtime Braves to be traded. That was the first real sign that John McHale was going to clean house. With Bruton gone, Aaron became a centerfielder again, which was not his best position.

About a week after the Bruton deal, McHale traded Juan Pizarro and Joey Jay in a three-team exchange that brought us Roy McMillan from the Cincinnati Reds. Jay had been the Braves' first so-called "bonus baby" back in 1953. He had pitched real well for us at times, but overall he was a disappointment. He had spent a couple seasons in the minor leagues. Haney thought Jay was fat and lazy and out of shape, so he didn't get a lot of work. After he got traded to Cincinnati, Jay won 21 games and took them into the World Series. The next year he won 21 again. Sometimes a change of scenery will do that for a ballplayer. The Braves could have used those 42 victories.

McMillan was from Bonham, Texas, like my dad. Roy teamed up with Bolling to give us one of the better double-play combinations. He wasn't much with the stick, but he could play shortstop with the best of them. I would have to say I was a better third baseman playing alongside him. He was a good guy, too, a real character. One time Roy and his wife and my wife and I and another couple leased a yacht out of Miami to go over to the Virgin Islands. It was a big yacht. In fact, Elizabeth Taylor had leased it once, so we all took turns sleeping in the bed that she slept in. It was a stateroom. Every night we changed. On that trip we got caught in a storm. I won't say it was a hurricane because it wasn't that bad, but it was pretty choppy. Poor Roy got seasick and stayed sick during that whole trip. Jeez, he was a sick puppy dog. For the rest of us, though, it was a good trip.

A month into the season the front office traded Mel Roach to the Cubs. Mel had been the Braves' second "bonus baby," signed a week after Joey Jay. He hadn't played a lot for us either, but he would have if Daryl Spencer hadn't ruined Mel's knee with that rolling block of his. He never really came back from that injury. In the trade with the Cubs the Braves picked up Frank Thomas. He was a kind of serious guy. He hit quite a few home runs for us and gave us help in the outfield, which we needed. Then after the season the people upstairs sent him to the Mets. What their thinking was, I have no idea. John McHale did a lot of things I never understood.

Another player we lost, not through a trade but by injury, was Del Crandall. He had arm or shoulder problems and only played a few games all season. Losing Del hurt us. He was an all-star practically every year and a strong influence on our pitching staff. Del was a straight shooter and our team captain. Without him we were less of a team. His replacement was Charlie Lau. Charlie caught Warren Spahn's no-hitter, but that was about it. He only hit around .200. The ironic part of that is that Charlie later became a so-called expert on hitting.

All hitting instructors had the same theory except Charlie Lau. He had a ridiculous theory where you were supposed to let go of the bat with your top hand on your follow-through. Did you ever see Ted Williams hit? Did you ever see films of Babe Ruth or Rogers Hornsby or Paul Waner or Joe DiMaggio? They never hit like that, but here's Charlie Lau, who never hit more than six home runs in one season and who batted .200 for the Braves, writing a book on hitting and using this strange batting style. George Brett let Lau use him as an example, but Brett said, "I never hit like that." And he didn't. Lau's theory doesn't work. For all you kids out there, don't try this at home. If you want to learn to hit, who do you think you should try to copy, Charlie Lau or Ted Williams?

Lau couldn't hack it with the Braves, so they brought Sammy White of the Red Sox out of retirement. That didn't work out either, so they dipped into the farm system and found Joe Torre. That was kind of funny to see because Frank Torre had brought his little brother around many years prior to this.

I always enjoyed chatting with the Milwaukee fans, or as in this case, posing for pictures. Well, almost always. (Ernest W. Anheuser photo)

At that time he was just a chubby little Italian kid. Now here he was on our ballclub, and he turned out to be a hell of a ballplayer. Crandall got his job back the next season, but Joe stayed around, and by the next season Joe was the regular catcher. When he didn't catch, he played first base. He was such a good hitter that they had to keep his bat in the lineup every day.

I mentioned that Charlie Lau caught Spahn's no-hitter. That wasn't Spahnie's only big win of the season. In August he reached a milestone by winning the 300th game of his career. It was a very dramatic game at County Stadium in front of our biggest crowd in two years. I played a part in building up the excitement and suspense. With the Braves winning 2-1 in the ninth, two out, nobody on base, Ernie Banks bounced one to me at third. I was so psyched up I fired the ball six feet over Joe Adcock's head to put the tying run on base. Spahn ended the suspense by getting the next batter to pop one up to Aaron in right field.

Besides Spahn, the star of that game was Gino Cimoli.

He hit a home run in the eighth to give Spahn a one-run lead. He also made a sliding catch in center field in the ninth to protect the lead. Cimoli had only been with the Braves for a couple months. We got him in a trade with the Pirates right before the June 15 deadline. To get Cimoli the Braves peddled another longtime starter, a local favorite, and this time the trade hit home with me because he was one of my best friends--Johnny Logan, the only regular shortstop the Milwaukee Braves had ever known until we got Roy McMillan.

Johnny had been a pal of mine since the Boston days. We lived in the same house there, Madam DuBarry's, so we got to be good buddies. We used to get together after every ballgame. We'd catch a bus downtown when we had the chance and see the big city, maybe take in a movie. We weren't making any money, comparatively speaking, but you could buy a car for $1,500 then. Not that either one of us had one, though--hardly any of the ballplayers did. Spahn had opened up a diner right near the ballpark, and Johnny and I used to eat there sometimes. Mostly, though, we didn't do much of anything. We didn't have the experience or the guts or the opportunity to really do much. When we got on the road it was a little different. We were staying in a big hotel. We were big shots, Johnny and me.

I first got to know Johnny in spring training in 1952. He and I and my spring roommate, Pete Whisenant, ran around together. One day after the workouts, the three of us were in a local bar drinking beer and playing shuffleboard. Whisenant got mad at the shuffleboard game and threw one of the pucks, and it knocked a big hole in the wall. At that particular time he and Logan were playing; I was sitting in the back room of the place relaxing. The owner of the bar called the ballclub, and somebody--I forget who--from the front office came down. A couple days later Pete and Johnny were both cut from the Braves' roster. That was just at the time the club was cutting anyway, so I can't say the incident in the bar was the reason, but Johnny thought so. He was really unhappy about being sent down because he should have stayed. Instead they kept Jack Cusick. In June, though, when Charlie Grimm replaced Tommy Holmes as manager, he brought Logan with him to Boston. Johnny never went back to the minors.

My family and Logan's family did quite a bit together. We both lived in the Milwaukee area year-round, so we socialized a lot. Johnny and Dottie were close friends of ours. When Johnny was traded, it hurt all of us.

Nineteen sixty-one was the first year in a long time when we were never in the thick of the pennant race. We just could not get anything going or keep it going. We still had our usual scuffles with clubs like the Redlegs and the Dodgers, of course, but no big deal. In one ballgame against Cincinnati we had Jim O'Toole picked off third. When he came back he took a whack at me, trying to make me drop the ball. There was really no fight. I just threw my glove down and grabbed him. We kind of rassled our way to the ground. A lot of people jumped on top and started pulling us apart. Nobody got hit. If I remember right, I think my old buddy Pete Whisenant might have gotten his face scratched or something in the ruckus. Really not much happened. Those things happen like that. You can't stand there at third base and let somebody whack you. My God--they'll chase you out of the league.

I got thrown out of the game, though. Hank Aaron took my place at third base. I was always helping him find a new position to play. With Hank, as good an athlete as he was, you could put him damn near anyplace and it didn't matter.

At the start of the Labor Day weekend, everybody on the ballclub received a shock--Charlie Dressen was fired. Usually when those things happen there are rumors, some hints that a change is going to take place. This time--boom, there was nothing. Clean out your office, Charlie, thanks a lot, 'bye. Just like that. We finished the ballgame, walked into the clubhouse, and heard that John McHale was having a press conference up in the employees' dining room on the second floor of the Stadium.

As I said, some of the ballplayers didn't care too much for Dressen. Every manager, every leader of any organization, makes enemies, but the way it was handled, you had to feel bad for him. Baseball can be a cold business. It can also be a strange business. If you ever figure it out, call me and let me know. A perfect example would be the manager the Braves put in to replace Dressen--none other than Birdie Tebbetts.

Birdie Tebbetts had managed Cincinnati from 1954 until 1958. He was the skipper of the club, or one of the clubs, that the Braves were constantly getting into fights with. Tebbetts was the guy who was always protesting something in our games, especially accusing Lew Burdette of throwing a spitter. Almost

210

every time Birdie stepped on the field during a ballgame in Milwaukee, the crowd got on him. He was disliked by the fans more than any other manager in the league. So when Tebbetts got fired by the Reds in 1958, who did the Braves hire as Executive Vice-President? Birdie Tebbetts.

A couple months after Tebbetts was hired by the Braves, John Quinn resigned and went to Philadelphia. Quinn had basically built our ballclub, first as general manager in Boston and then in Milwaukee. Quinn had been a loyal employee of Lou Perini's for many years, but Tebbetts was brought in basically as Quinn's boss. After Quinn left, Tebbetts hired John McHale. From that point on, the ballclub went downhill, attendance fell off, and eventually the ballclub left town. Did all that happen because Lou Perini hired Birdie Tebbetts? How the hell should I know? No one will ever know what effect that had. What I do know is that Tebbetts seemed like an odd choice for the Braves, first in the front office and then as manager, and I'm not the only one who thought so.

I had nothing against Tebbetts. We got along fine. He was probably the funniest manager as far as his theories about baseball. He pretty much felt he had invented the game. Between him and Dressen it would be a tossup. Birdie was another one that had lots of rules. He was curfew conscious and discipline conscious, but he loosened up once he got to know everybody and saw that we were not Peck's Bad Boys. I heard later that some of the black players thought Tebbetts was unfair to them, but I was never aware of that. I never heard Birdie say anything even close to that. He always had too many stingers in him. God, he could drink those stingers.

And Charlie Dressen? He landed on his feet. The next year he managed Toronto in the International League, but the season after that he was back managing in the big leagues, this time with the Detroit Tigers. He did that for about three years until a series of heart attacks made him quit and finally took his life. Five years after the Braves unceremoniously dumped him, he was dead. He died one day after the Atlanta Braves fired Bobby Bragan.

June 8, 1961

The Cincinnati Reds were on their way to their first pennant in more than two decades. The Milwaukee Braves were in sixth place, going nowhere. After eight years as pennant contenders or winners, the Braves had become also-rans under Charlie Dressen. The fielding, especially in the infield, was superb. Joe Adcock at first base, Frank Bolling at second, and Roy McMillan at shortstop each led the league at his position; third baseman Eddie Mathews finished second in the NL. The pitching, however, which had carried the club for so long, no longer could. One skill the Braves still had, though, was the ability to hit the long ball.

In 1961 only the record-setting Yankees of Maris and Mantle (61 and 54, respectively) hit more home runs per game than the Braves. No one from Milwaukee could rival the fabeled M & M boys, but the Braves boasted four big-time sluggers: Mathews, Adcock, Aaron, and Frank Thomas. The quartet of musclemen accounted for a career total of 1,889 home runs. That meant that collectively they covered more than 128 miles just in their home run trots. On the afternoon of June 8, the Braves' home run corps flexed their muscles in unprecedented fashion in Cincinnati's Crosley Field. If one game could characterize the entire Milwaukee season, it would be that game.

Forty-year-old Warren Spahn, starting on three days' rest, gave up an unearned run in the second, then tied the game himself with his 27th career home run in the next inning. This was not Spahn's day on the mound, however. Trying for his 295th victory, he left after working just five innings, having allowed five earned runs to go with the undeserved one in the second inning. After Spahn left, matters only got worse. Polish-born relief man Moe Drabowsky gave up four runs in just one inning of work, including a three-run-homer to Gene Freese and a solo shot by Gordy Coleman. By the time mop-up reliever George Brunet appeared, Milwaukee trailed 10-2.

In the top of the seventh, though, the Braves' offense sprang to life. Bolling led off with a single. Mathews then drove a Jim Maloney pitch into the rightfield pavilion, his 351st lifetime home run, to make it 10-4. Next up was Hank Aaron, who pulled a Maloney breaking ball against the screen in left field for a solo homer, making it 10-5. The back-to-back blasts irritated Cincy manager Fred Hutchinson, who yanked Maloney and called in lefthander Marshall Bridges (surprisingly, since the next four batters hit righthanded). Bridges enjoyed no more success than Maloney, or Drabowsky, for that matter. Adcock got a hold of a fastball and drove it over the wall in center field, a typical Adcock shot, to make the score 10-6.

Three times before this the Milwaukee club had hit three consecutive home runs: in 1956, 1957, and 1958. Each time both Mathews and Aaron had been among the trio of fence-busters, twice teaming with Wes Covington and once with Bobby Thomson. This time, however, the Braves outdid themselves. On a 2-1 pitch from Bridges, Frank Thomas clubbed a long fly ball to center that landed in nearly the same spot as Adcock's blast. The fourth consecutive home run was a major league first, and the score was 10-7.

Somehow Bridges regained his composure and retired the next three batters. He then left for a pinch-hitter. With two out in the eighth and nobody on base, Mathews faced his third pitcher of the day, Bill Henry. Mathews already had a single, double, and home run, so he needed a triple to hit for the cycle. He overshot the mark, though, belting another home run (career number 352) into the rightfield seats. After Mathews' second homer Jim Brosnan retired the last four Milwaukee hitters to hang a 10-8 loss on Warren Spahn.

After the game, Charlie Dressen said it all: "I've never seen anything like it in all my years in baseball. Imagine hitting four straight home runs and six altogether and still losing."

June 8, 1961

MILWAUKEE	AB	R	H	BI		CINCINNATI	AB	R	H	BI
Maye, rf	3	0	1	0		Blasingame, 2b	5	1	2	1
DeMerit, rf	1	0	0	0		Kasko, ss	4	1	1	0
Bolling, 2b	5	2	1	0		Cardenas, ss	0	0	0	0
Mathews, 3b	4	2	4	3		Pinson, cf	4	1	2	2
Aaron, cf	4	1	2	1		Robinson, rf	4	1	2	0
Adcock, 1b	5	1	1	2		Freese, 3b	4	1	1	4
Thomas, lf	5	1	2	1		Post, lf	4	2	1	0
Torre, c	4	0	1	0		Coleman, 1b	4	2	3	2
McMillan, ss	4	0	0	0		Zimmerman, c	4	1	1	0
Spahn, p	1	1	1	1		Maloney, p	2	0	1	0
Lau	1	0	0	0		Bridges, p	0	0	0	0
Drabowsky, p	0	0	0	0		Gernert	1	0	0	0
Taylor	1	0	0	0		Henry, p	0	0	0	0
Brunet, p	0	0	0	0		Brosnan, p	1	0	0	0
Totals	38	8	13	8		Totals	37	10	14	9

Lau flied out for Spahn in sixth; Taylor struck
out for Drabowsky in seventh; Gernert lined out
for Bridges in seventh; DeMerit grounded out
for Maye in eighth.

```
MILWAUKEE  ..................  0 0 2  0 0 0  5 1 0-- 8
Cincinnati  ..................  0 1 1  3 1 4  0 0 *--10
```

E--Maye, McMillan. 2B--Mathews, Aaron, Post. HR--
Mathews 2, Aaron, Adcock, Thomas, Spahn, Freese, Coleman. Left--Milwaukee 9, Cincinnati 11. DP--Blasing-
ame and Coleman; Freese, Blasingame and Coleman. S--
Maloney. SF--Freese.

	IP	H	R	ER	BB	SO
Spahn (L, 6-5)	5	8	6	5	4	2
Drabowsky	1	4	4	4	0	0
Brunet	2	2	0	0	2	0
Maloney (W, 4-2)	6	8	5	5	5	2
Bridges	1	2	2	2	0	1
Henry	.2	2	1	1	0	0
Brosnan	1.1	1	0	0	0	1

Maloney faced three batters in seventh. HBP--By
Maloney, Spahn. WP--Spahn. U--Donatelli, Conlan,
Burkhart, Pelekoudas. T--3:14. A--5,149.

214

FOURTEEN

Sublime to the Ridiculous

Okay, so it wasn't the breakup of Dean Martin and Jerry Lewis, or Huntley and Brinkley, or Richard Burton and Elizabeth Taylor. But after rooming with me on the road for over nine years, Bob Buhl left the Braves in a trade at the end of April, 1962. The Braves didn't get much for him--a lefthanded pitcher who won a few games and then disappeared. But at least Bob got a chance to pitch.

Bob and I had gone through a lot of stuff together--a lot. We were just damn close, the wives and everybody. Even though he lived in Michigan, he always had his family there in Milwaukee during the season. It wasn't as much fun after he left our club. But Bob didn't get along with Birdie Tebbetts, let's put it that way. John McHale had been trying to trade him, so there was no surprise involved. Bob was 34 years old, and they wanted to go with younger guys. He had a lot left in his arm, but he wasn't getting a chance anymore in Milwaukee. He almost got traded to Houston for Bobby Shantz, but Shantz came up with a sore arm and killed the deal.

We were on a plane going to Philadelphia when Bob went up and told Birdie, "I don't think you're gonna use me. I want you to trade me."

Birdie said, "I'll see what I can do."

The next morning Bob got a call about ten o'clock. It was Birdie. "I want you to come up and see me." When Bob got there, Tebbetts told him, "We traded you to Chicago for Jackie Curtis. You can get an airplane this afternoon and join the Cubs out in L.A." Bob thanked him, and that was it. He might have preferred going to the Detroit Tigers because he lived in

Michigan, but Chicago wasn't far away, and at least with the Cubs he had a chance to pitch. The next time the Braves played the Cubs, I hit a home run off my old roomie. He won the game, though. In fact, he beat us four times that year.

I first met Buhl in Bradenton in 1953. I pulled up to the Dixie Grande Hotel in my Mercury convertible, with my guitar in the back seat. I hadn't met Bob yet, but he saw me from the hotel window. I went up to the room and knocked on the door. I said, "I'm Eddie Mathews. I guess we're roommates."

At first he didn't say anything. Then he held out his hand and said, "Hi, I'm Bob Buhl. What the hell's this? Do you play the guitar?"

"No," I said, "I'm just practicing."

"Thank goodness for that. I hate the guitar," was his response. "I don't go for that hillbilly stuff." That was how we started out.

Bob and I did everything together--drank, talked baseball, got in fights, hunted. He was a more serious kind of guy than Spahn or Burdette, a quieter guy. Of course, next to Burdette, anybody was quiet. You have a tendency, when you're together for as long as we were, to think you're going to be together forever. Kind of like Ernie Banks--never leave the Cubs. Each time one of these guys left the ballclub--Logan, Buhl--it was a kick in the tail, but we still had to keep going.

Both Buhl and I came into the Braves organization in 1949. He got declared a free agent that year because he had signed originally while he was in high school. After that he signed a three-year contract with Milwaukee, the Braves' Triple-A farm club. He played at Hartford in the Eastern League for a year and then for Charlie Grimm in Dallas before going into the Army. When we got hooked up as roommates, we hit it off right away. As Bob said, we were two of a kind, both about the same size and just as hungry as anybody else.

One of the things Bob and I liked to do the most together was hunt. He had 160 acres of land in the northern part of the lower peninsula. It was mostly woods, with just a deer shack on it--two little bedrooms, a kitchen area, and a tiny living room--way out in the boondocks. Deer season would start in November. I would drive over to Bob's house every year a couple days before deer season, and then we'd drive up to his land and hunt.

One time we came back to the hunting shack late one

216

afternoon, right as it was getting dark. I walked in carrying part of a hind quarter from a deer I had just shot. There was this older lady sitting there. I didn't know who she was, and she didn't know me. I wasn't sure what I should do or say, so I put the deer's hind quarter on the table and said, "I shot this thing." The lady turned out to be Bob's mother-in-law. She had brought us a big pot of bean soup. We had a great time. The Buhls are wonderful people.

After Bob got traded, I didn't have a roommate, so they paired me up with a rookie catcher by the name of Bob Uecker. Little did I suspect what I was getting into. Actually, it was just by coincidence that I knew Uecker already. I knew his whole family. They only lived about five miles from me in Milwaukee. I lived in Brookfield, and he lived a little north of there. We'd gotten together a few times prior to this, so it was a natural thing for him to room with me. I didn't quite realize how funny or goofy he was, but I learned in a hurry.

Of course everybody in America knows Bob is a quick-witted, fun-loving guy from watching him in his TV series and seeing him in the movie *Major League* or listening to him do his "Mr. Baseball" routine on Johnny Carson's show or seeing him on all those great commercials. But he also was a pretty damn good catcher--not much of a hitter, but a damn good catcher. He puts himself down, but he handled the knuckleball as well as anybody. He probably would have made the club the year before except Charlie Dressen didn't like his attitude.

"There's no room in baseball for a clown," Dressen told him, and he sent him down to the minors.

Charlie would eat his shorts if he had lived to see Bob do those Miller Lite commercials--"I must be in the front row." I'm tickled to death that Bob has done so well because he really did not make any money in baseball when he was playing. He wasn't a regular. One Christmas he borrowed a hundred bucks from me to buy some presents for his kids. That's how tapioca he was. Come to think of it, I don't think he ever paid me back. What a hell of a guy, though. He'd go flying with me and work on my farm with me. He's a fat cat now--big boat, lots of money. But he's still a good friend, still a down-to-earth guy.

Bob came from a wonderful family. He was the first native of Milwaukee to actually play for the Braves, and his dad was so proud of him. I think his dad had diabetes, I'm not sure, but he had bad circulation in his legs, and he ended up with

217

both his legs amputated. I'd go over to their house to visit, and Bob would call his dad "Shorty." His dad would laugh until tears came out of his eyes. But Bob can do that--he can get away with stuff like that. He's got the knack for kidding and saying things so that people know that he's kidding and they don't take offense. And they say you don't ever kid anybody that you don't like.

Not many people are as witty as Bob Uecker, but I'll tell you one--his sister. I used to see her at Bob's house when I went to visit his dad. Then I didn't see her for a long time, maybe twenty years or so. I went back to Milwaukee for a baseball card show, and I was staying at this hotel. I went down to the bar to get a drink. I started talking to the gal that was tending bar.

"Damn it, you look familiar," I told her. That sounds like a pathetic pickup line, but she really did.

"I ought to," she said, "I'm Bob Uecker's sister." Then I could see the family resemblance, although she looked a lot better than Bob.

We had a real nice talk. Then I said, "Have you got Bob's phone number?"

"Yeah."

"Give it to me," I said. "I'm gonna call him."

I got his answering service. I said, "Bob, this is Eddie Mathews. I'm sitting here with your sister, and I'm gonna hit on her tonight."

I hung up. An hour later, she got a frantic call from Bob. "What the hell...."

Rooming with Uecker was like rooming with the Marx Brothers. I never knew what to expect. One time I came back to the hotel after we'd had a rainout. It was still drizzling out. Bob had taken the waste basket and filled it with water. We were on about the 18th floor, and he was throwing this water out on the pedestrians, but it kept blowing back against the building. He did this three times, and it kept blowing back.

I said, "You Punch-and-Judy hitter, gimme that thing. I'm a home run hitter." I filled the waste basket with water. I moved back a little bit from the window. Then I said, "Now, you tell me when."

He said, "Now."

I ran forward and went whoosh, and the whole thing slipped out of my hands. We watched that sucker tumble down--if it hit somebody, it might have killed them. Fortunate-

218

ly, it didn't. It hit on the hood of a cab and destroyed it. You could see the carburetor sticking up.

All I could say was, "Oh, my God!"

At that point I was just glad it hit the hood of the cab. Now people were pointing up at us, so we quick got the room list, and around the corner was another ballplayer. We went and banged on his door and got his waste basket and brought it back and put it in our room. Then we sat back and tried to relax like nothing had happened.

In about fifteen minutes we heard a knock on the door. It was two house detectives and a policeman. They said, "There's been an accident. Do you have your waste basket?"

I pointed and said, "It's right there, officer."

So we got away with it, but it was spooky after I thought about it. We started out having fun, but we could have ended up charged with murder. That might have been the dumbest thing I ever did.

Another time we were in L.A., and I had taken my mother and some of my relatives out for dinner. At the time I was in a little batting slump, so I had taken a couple of my bats back to the hotel to swing in front of the mirror. I was hoping to find out if I was doing something wrong in my swing. They always gave me a good room there at the hotel, and this one had a false fireplace in it.

When I got off the elevator to go to the room, I could smell smoke. I went into the room. There was Uecker, sitting with a tub of beer, and he was burning my two bats in the false fireplace. Smoke was pouring out of there.

Bob yelled, "Hey, Eddie! That's how much good your bats are doing you." He was something.

Uecker didn't get a chance to play very much, but he sure kept the ballclub in stitches. On the last day of the season he hit his first home run, his only one as a Milwaukee Brave. I hit one that day, too, my 399th. All winter Bob kept telling people, "My roommate and I have 400 home runs between us."

My home run in the final game was my 29th of the year, which broke my streak. I had hit at least 30 for nine straight years, the Braves' first nine years in Milwaukee. That's still the National League record, but it should have been at least ten. I got off to a hell of a good start. Birdie Tebbetts brought me in an old bat of Vern Stephens', a little longer than I normally used, and I used that thing to get off to a hell of a start. I hit six

219

home runs with it in the first two weeks. After that we went on a short road trip. When we returned to Milwaukee, we played a four-game series with the Houston club, one of the two new teams that year along with the Mets.

Against Houston, which was called the Colt .45's then, we played our first doubleheader of the year. We won the first game with Warren Spahn. In the second game Dick Farrell pitched for Houston. He had been a relief pitcher with the Phillies for years, and a damn good one. The Braves had tried to trade for him a couple years earlier to help in the bullpen. Houston made him a starter, though. He beat us that day and pitched his first complete game ever. He did more than that. In the first inning he threw me a high forkball that fooled me. I swung and fouled it off and tore all the ligaments in my right shoulder.

It hurt like hell. I felt a pop in my right shoulder, and I could hardly lift my arm. The trainer came out and massaged it a little bit. I tried to keep playing. I made a feeble swing at strike three and then left the ballgame. I was out for almost two weeks. After I came back I developed a habit of, instead of swinging my usual way, tucking my arm in to protect the shoulder. My swing was never the same after that. I didn't have a very good year, and I didn't get my 30 home runs. I probably should have laid out another week because the shoulder was really torn up. I actually had only one good year after that. I never really came back from that injury.

When I did come back 12 days later, I still couldn't make the throw from third to first. Tebbetts put me back in the lineup but as a first baseman. I had never played that position. I had to borrow a first baseman's glove. I hit a home run in my first game back, but I could hardly throw at all. I played first base for a week or so and then went back to third. My throwing motion was different, though, more from the side. To this day I've still got that atrophy in my shoulder.

I saw Birdie many years after that, and he said, "I've got one regret in baseball. That's letting you come back too fast after that injury." I wasn't ready. I couldn't throw, and I wasn't swinging right. I just went downhill from there.

With the Colt .45's in the league, it meant we had to play ball in Houston. I didn't mind going to Texas--it was my native state, and some of my relatives still lived down there. But playing in Houston was god-awful. It was like a nightmare--the heat, the humidity, the mosquitoes. The mosquitoes were whoppers. In fact, what we ended up doing was taking a piece of paper and putting it inside our outer socks because they could bite through those things. And even though they sprayed every day--took a jeep with a spray unit around there--it didn't help.

To top it off, what they had for a clubhouse was an old tin Army quonset hut. You'd take a shower in that place and before you could put your clothes on you were soaking wet. It was something. To me, it was hotter there than anyplace, and the mosquitoes were beyond belief. If Old Man Hofheinz hadn't built that domed stadium, baseball in Houston would not have lasted five years.

As early as May rumors were starting to pop up that Lou Perini was planning to sell the Braves or that he wanted out. A New York writer first wrote the story. He said the ballclub would deny it but that Perini would sell. The ballclub, specifically John McHale, denied it. Later on a Boston paper said the Braves were considering moving back to Boston. McHale denied that one too.

Perini at that time hardly ever came to Milwaukee to see the ballclub. He just let McHale run the show while he tended to his construction business back east. He did come to New York to see us play the Mets at the Polo Grounds. On one of those trips he was quoted as being disappointed with the club's attendance and saying he couldn't understand it. He insisted he did not want to sell the ballclub, though, and said nobody had tried to buy it.

The ballplayers never paid much attention to any of that stuff, one way or the other, but we did notice something. County Stadium didn't have skyboxes, of course, but they had a mezzanine under the edge of the upper deck. As the season went along, all of a sudden we started to see this group of guys up there and we began to wonder. The head of the group turned out to be Bill Bartholomay, and another guy that we recognized was Potter Palmer, the owner of the Palmer House in Chicago. These guys started showing up at our games, and that was when we were hearing all this happy crap about Perini wanting out.

A month and a half after the season ended, Perini did sell the Braves to those guys, all of whom were from the Chicago area. As we got to know them, beginning in spring training, we found out that individually they were all very nice. I mainly had contact with Bartholomay and Palmer, but there

221

The happy new Braves owners, November 16, 1962. John McHale is seated; Bill Bartholomay is second from right. (Ernest W. Anheuser photo)

were four or five others, including Fred Miller's nephew. Bartholomay was the guy who ran the show. He was a good man but a little bit aloof. Palmer, though, was a hell of a nice guy. In fact, he fit us like an old shoe. We all knew who he was and how much money the guy had, but he would come out and mingle, have a few drinks, and let loose. He would be one of the local people that we would run into down in Florida, and he'd have a drink with us or whatever. And he was a great baseball fan.

After the season we got a surprise. Birdie Tebbetts resigned to manage the Cleveland Indians. Two weeks later McHale announced that Bobby Bragan would replace Tebbetts. Oh, brother.

July 12, 1962

Eddie Mathews and Hank Aaron slammed more home runs as teammates than any other pair of hitters in baseball history (863), with Aaron supplying 442 and Mathews supplying 421. They hit home runs in the same game 75 times, and no tandem of sluggers has surpassed that figure. Hank and his brother Tommie also hold a career record for home runs by siblings--768, with Hank contributing all but 13. Three times the brothers homered in the same game, once in the same inning. On the night of July 12, 1962, in County Stadium, all of those records intersected.

On June 12th Mathews and the two Aarons had all homered in a 15-2 rout of the first-place Dodgers. Tommie's home run was only his second in the big leagues. Exactly one month later the Braves were hosting the Cardinals, with whom they were fighting for fifth place. Birdie Tebbetts' Milwaukee club had yet to climb over the .500 mark after losing their first five ballgames of the season on the West Coast. Now as they resumed league competition following the All-Star break, their record was 42-43 and they trailed St. Louis by five games.

The evening began badly for the Braves. Sophomore southpaw Bob Hendley failed to survive the first inning, allowing three runs on four hits before being rescued by Carl Willey. Not until the last of the fourth did Milwaukee get on the board. In that inning Mathews narrowed the lead to 3-1 with a bases-empty home run off Larry Jackson, his 17th of the year and the 387th of his career, tying him at that moment with Duke Snider for eighth place on the all-time list. In the fifth Mathews' new roommate, rookie catcher Bob Uecker, looped a pinch double, his first extra-base hit in the big leagues, but his teammates left him stranded. Milwaukee scored twice in the sixth and trailed by only 4-3 after seven innings, but four singles in the eighth off Claude Raymond gave the visitors a 6-3 advantage, which they carried into the last of the ninth.

223

The Braves needed a big inning, meaning they were in big trouble. Only two Milwaukee batters sported averages above .266, and one--Del Crandall--was not even in the lineup. Frank Bolling, the .266 hitter (batting eighth in the order) made the first out. With the pitcher due to bat, Tebbetts went to his bench and found Tommie Aaron, owner of a .199 average. On the first pitch Jackson threw him, Hank's younger brother ripped a home run into the bleachers in left center. It was 6-4, but the next two batters, the top of the order, hardly struck fear into pitchers' hearts. Leadoff man Roy McMillan had been the worst hitter in the league the previous year at .220, and he was only four points higher as he waited on-deck. After McMillan was Mack Jones, whose two strikeouts earlier in the game gave him 89 for the season, exceeding his total of base hits.

As Yogi Berra said, though, "In baseball, you don't know nothing." McMillan and Jones both singled, the latter against reliever Lindy McDaniel. Yet even then the prospects seemed dim. McDaniel had not allowed an earned run in his last 15 appearances, more than 30 innings. He worked carefully to the next batter--Mathews, who had two singles and a home run for his evening's efforts. McDaniel worked too carefully, walking Mathews to load the bases for Hank Aaron.

Aaron, the Braves' top hitter as usual, was playing with a heavily taped right ankle, but the infirmity never showed. He already had three hits in the game, and on a 2-1 pitch from Jackson he made it four--in a big way. Just trying to hit the ball hard, Hank drove one over 400 feet, near where his brother had hit his homer minutes before. Aaron's seventh career grand slam made Milwaukee an 8-6 winner. And according to Joe Dittmar's book *Baseball's Benchmark Boxscores,* his blast marked the first time since 1938 that brothers had hit home runs in the same inning. The previous brother act had been former Braves batting coach Paul Waner and his brother Lloyd.

ST. LOUIS	AB	R	H	BI	MILWAUKEE	AB	R	H	BI
Javier, 2b	4	1	2	1	McMillan, ss	5	1	1	0
White, 1b	4	1	3	0	Jones, cf	5	1	1	0
Flood, cf	4	1	0	1	Mathews, 3b	4	3	3	1
Boyer, 3b	3	1	2	1	H. Aaron, rf	5	2	4	4
James, rf	4	0	0	0	Adcock, 1b	4	0	1	0
Musial	1	0	0	0	Bell, lf	4	0	0	1
Smith, lf	5	1	2	1	Torre, c	4	0	0	0
Gotay, ss	3	1	3	1	Bolling, 2b	4	0	1	0
Schaffer, c	3	0	0	0	Hendley, p	0	0	0	0
Sawatski, c	1	0	0	0	Willey, p	1	0	0	0
Jackson, p	4	0	1	1	Uecker	1	0	1	0
McDaniel, p	0	0	0	0	Fischer, p	0	0	0	0
					Aspromonte	1	0	0	0
					Raymond, p	0	0	0	0
					T. Aaron	1	1	1	1
Totals	36	6	13	6	Totals	39	8	13	7

Uecker doubled for Willey in fifth; Aspromonte
grounded out for Fischer in seventh; Sawatski
struck out for Schaffer in eithth; Musial
flied out for James in ninth; T. Aaron homered for Raymond in ninth.

```
St. Louis ................. 3 0 0  0 1 0  0 2 0--6
MILWAUKEE ................. 0 0 0  1 0 2  0 0 5--8
```

E--Boyer. 2B--White 2, Boyer, Uecker, Bolling.
HR--Mathews, H. Aaron, T. Aaron. Left--St. Louis 9,
Milwaukee 7. DP--McMillan, Bolling and Adcock. S--
White. SF--Flood.

	IP	H	R	ER	BB	SO
Jackson	8 1-3	11	5	3	0	6
McDaniel (L, 2-4)	0	2	3	3	1	0
Hendley	2-3	4	3	3	0	0
Willey	4 1-3	3	1	1	2	1
Fischer	2	1	0	0	1	3
Raymond (W, 2-0)	2	5	2	2	1	1

McDaniel faced three batters in ninth. WP--
Willey, Jackson. U--Burkhart, Pelekoudas, Jackowski, Walsh. T--2:47. A--13,426.

FIFTEEN

Bye Bye, Birdie

Mention 1963 and most people who were around then think of John F. Kennedy. They can tell you where they were and what they were doing when they heard that he had been shot. I was in a truck on my way to northern Wisconsin to go deer hunting with my father-in-law when the news came. Regardless of politics,people were caught up in the whole Camelot thing. Here was a young, athletic, good-looking President with a glamorous wife and cute kids. The country was excited and optimistic. It was a shock when he was killed. I suppose that was the most significant event of the 1960's, or maybe since World War II. The country is still obsessed with that whole assassination story, the conspiracy and all that.

I never met Kennedy, but some of us on the Braves did become acquainted with his father during that spring before the President was shot. At that time the Braves had their spring training in West Palm Beach. We stayed at the Town House Motor Hotel there. Someone from the ballclub, probably one of the new owners, must have made the initial contact with the Kennedy family, but however it got started, a bunch of us--myself, John McHale, Spahn, Burdette, and a few others--paid a visit to old Joe Kennedy at their family compound in Palm Beach.

It was impressive. We drove over to this place, and of course they had Secret Service men all around there to protect the President's family. John Kennedy wasn't there, but just being in his house was an experience. We met both his father and his mother, Rose Kennedy. Neither one was in very good health, but they were very nice to us. We were introduced to

226

them, and then it was, "Hi, very nice meeting you," that type of deal. Joseph Kennedy had suffered a stroke, so he was incapacitated, in a wheelchair, but he seemed alert. We didn't stay long, of course, maybe half an hour. A week or so later we received a letter from President Kennedy, thanking us for visiting with his father. Also, while we were there we got acquainted with some of the Secret Service and FBI guys.

After that we went out a couple times on the President's boat, courtesy of the Secret Service. The boat was called the "Blue Something"--maybe the "Blue Marlin." We became good friends with some of the people guarding the President and his family, particularly one guy named Ham Brown. We'd go out on the boat, and we'd be introduced as junior Senators wherever we stopped. It was no big deal, but we had quite a bit of fun. Ham Brown had Joseph Kennedy's wheelchair in the trunk of his car, along with a walkie-talkie and a couple of guns, and he followed him around. When Ham got some time off, that's when we saw him.

Years later, when I was working as a scout for the Oakland A's, a bunch of us former ballplayers were called up to the White House to have lunch with President Ronald Reagan. If I remember right, we were all Hall of Fame members. When we got to the White House, who should be working on the President's security crew but my old buddy, Ham Brown.

We had an interesting luncheon with the President. I sat next to James Brady, the press secretary who was shot when that Hinckley guy tried to kill Reagan. Brady was just a super-nice person. He treated us like we were somebody important. We had all been around celebrities before, but no matter what you've done or who you've met, having lunch with the President of the United States puts you in awe. After we ate, they set up a kind of reception line to meet President Reagan. We would go up to meet him one at a time and shake his hand. Before we got to him, an officer in a Navy uniform asked each of us, "What's your name?" Then he would turn around and whisper the name to another guy, and he would whisper your name to the President. That way when you got to the front of the line, the President could greet you by name.

Before I went to the luncheon, I told Billy Martin that I was going. Billy was managing Oakland at the time. He gave me an Oakland A's jacket to take to the President. My wife Judy wrapped it, and I took it along. At the White House one of the

227

Secret Service men took it from me and gave it to the President, telling him it was a gift from Billy Martin. The President put it on, and everybody applauded. And I must say, it looked very good on him.

On our trip to the Kennedy compound to meet Joseph Kennedy, one of the other people who went along, for sure, was Donald Davidson. He probably made the specific arrangements, too. Donald always handled the arrangements for everything we did. He had replaced Duffy Lewis when Duffy retired as traveling secretary in 1960. Before that, Donald had been publicity director of the Braves. Before that he was an assistant PR man. Talk about working your way up from the bottom of the ladder--Donald had started out as a clubhouse errand boy with the Braves in Boston. Then he was Casey Stengel's bat boy in the late 1930's. In the history of baseball, Donald Davidson was unique. He was a legend.

When Donald was six years old, he had some kind of sleeping sickness that stunted his growth. He never grew taller than 48 inches (not four feet--he insisted he was 48 inches tall). They told him he would not live past the age of 30, but he lived more than twice that long. In high school he hung around both Braves Field and Fenway Park in Boston. Because he was so small, they made him their mascot. One year Joe Cronin, the Red Sox manager, tried to send Donald in to pinch hit for Moe Berg in an exhibition game, but the umpire wouldn't let him.

After high school Donald went into show business. He was the featured performer in a group called the Roller Skating Vanities. He would dance on roller skates. His big show-stopping number was "Me and My Shadow," and he was the shadow. He stayed with that for three or four years, and when the Braves won the pennant in 1948, Donald joined their publicity staff to help out at World Series time. He stayed with the Braves for the next 40 years.

Donald was a very talented guy. As a hobby he used to write song lyrics, and our farm director, John Mullen, wrote the music. Donald was also a good Cutty Sark man. We had a lot of fun with him. Burdette and Spahn and I used to pick him up and dunk him in the whirlpool. Then he would swear a blue streak at us. God, he could cuss. Even for baseball his language was exceptional. No one ever felt sorry for him because of his size, though, and he never wanted special treatment. Donald was tough. He really demanded respect, and he got it. And he

At press conference (L. to R.), Lou Perini, Donald Davidson, and Bill Bartholomay. (Ernest W. Anheuser photo)

would always get back at us some way or other.

As I said, Donald was a good Cutty Sark drinker. I forget what city we were in, but one night we were in our hotel room and it was pretty late. All of a sudden we heard this pounding next door, and Donald's voice yelling, "Let me in! Let me in!"

I got up out of bed and went to the door. I opened it, and there was Donald--and he was smoked. He was pounding on his own door--"Let me in, damn it!"

I went over and I said, "Donald, what's the matter?"

He said, "They won't let me in."

I said, "Donald, that's your room."

"Well, give me the key," he said.

So I tried to find his key. The problem was, he had all his clothes specially made because of his size, and he had a secret pocket put in his coat. I could feel the key from the outside, but I couldn't find the entrance to that secret pocket. I finally had to lay him down on the floor in the hallway and search him. If anybody had seen us, they would have thought I was rolling some drunk and called the house detective.

After about five minutes of poking and pulling I finally got his key. Any longer and we would have been engaged. I got the door open and helped him into the room. He flopped down on the bed like a corpse, fast asleep. The next morning I went over to check on him. There he was, bright-eyed and bushy-tailed, doing his thing, checking the hotel register. Oh, God, he was strong! He was heavy duty. He and Hank and I always hit it off. We did a lot of socializing with him in Milwaukee. We were probably closer to him than any of the other ballplayers were. Besides that, I'm pretty sure Donald saw more of Aaron's home runs than anybody else. They were with the Braves together for over 20 years.

Nineteen sixty-three was pretty much a lost cause for the Braves. How did that song go by Tennessee Ernie Ford--"...another day older and deeper in debt"? We were another year older and deeper in the standings. Birdie Tebbetts had been brought in to make changes in the ballclub, but now Birdie was gone. Instead of a transfusion of young blood, fresh talent, we got a new manager with an ego problem.

Bobby Bragan had been a below-average ballplayer with the Phillies and Dodgers. He managed the Pirates and Indians and was a loser in both places. In the three and a half years he managed the Braves, we never finished above fifth place. In his own mind, though, Bragan was Casey Stengel. He thought he was going to win ballgames by his shrewd manipulations of his team. He had a million ideas. Unfortunately, he never had a good one. He was a beauty.

Bragan's idea of keeping his players on their toes was to keep them wondering what the hell position they would be playing or where the hell they would be batting in the order. We had a new lineup damn near every day. One day I ran out to my position at third base before the start of the game and Denis Menke was standing there.

"I'm playing third today," he said.

Okay. Nobody told me. I went back to the dugout and said to Bragan, "Am I sitting out today, or what?"

He said, "Don't you read the lineup card?"

I said, "Not really. I've been playing third base for a long time."

I walked over and looked at the lineup card on the dugout wall. "Mathews, LF." Jesus Christ. I hadn't played the outfield in nine years. Even so, if Bragan had said to me, "I want you to play left field today; go take some fly balls," fine. I would have taken some fly balls. I never questioned any of the managers I played for. If they said "Squat," I said, "How

230

much?" Bragan never said a word. But then what can you expect from a guy who bragged about never even tasting a sip of beer in his life? Bragan was unique.

Besides getting Bragan as our manager, we also had a couple other changes. My old manager from the Crackers, Dixie Walker, came in as a coach. He and Bragan had been room-

Hank and I, with Bragan looking suspicious to the far right.
(Ernest W. Anheuser photo)

mates with the Dodgers back in the '40's. Bringing in Dixie might have been the best thing Bragan did for us. Old Dixie was a hell of a guy.

I suffered a couple losses, though, big losses. Lew Burdette was traded to the St. Louis Cardinals. Old Thirsty-Three and I had been teammates since Boston. He was a fun-loving guy. He didn't give a damn whether the sun came up or not. Along with Buhl and Spahn, we had been part of the same Rat Pack since we started in Milwaukee. We had more good times together--some bad ones, too, but mostly good--than I could even count. With Buhl and now Old Nitro leaving as well, I was starting to feel like a stranger on my own ballclub. Joe Adcock was also gone, traded to the Cleveland Indians. The only ones left from the old days were Spahnie and I and Crandall, and of course Aaron. Crandall didn't drink, so we only saw him at the ballpark. That basically left Spahn and me.

To compound the loss, the Braves shipped out my roommate, Bob Uecker. In the Burdette deal one of the players the Braves got was Gene Oliver. He was a catcher, so that made Uecker the odd man out, in every sense of the words. They packed him off to Denver or some damn place. Oliver ended up being my roommate. He was a good guy, but he was no Bob Uecker.

Gene was not a bad hitter--stronger than hell. He always came in right at curfew. Sometimes I might not be there, but sometimes I was and I'd be asleep. He always had a hamburger with him from someplace. He'd sit down on the little night table or whatever next to me. By that time, of course, I was awake. We'd start talking. Pretty soon he'd go to sleep, and I would end up eating the stupid hamburger. I lost Uecker, but I gained a lot of hamburgers.

And so it was Spahnie and I. He was 42 years old by then, but age to him meant nothing. He was a rubber band anyway. He was so effortless. He could take three warmup pitches and he was ready to go. There never was another pitcher like Spahn, and there never will be again. He had just a great year for us, too--23 wins and seven losses, the same as in 1953, which was his best year. He also threw eight shutouts, although he only received credit for seven.

Two of those were ballgames I will never forget, both on the West Coast, four days apart. The first one was in Dodger Stadium. Spahnie had never had much success against the

Dodgers, especially in Brooklyn. With all their righthanded hitters, he usually didn't even pitch against them. This year, though, he beat them four straight times. He hadn't beaten the Dodgers in their home park in 15 years, but this year he did it twice in L.A. The first one of those wins was a 1-0 game. Spahn had a perfect game going into the seventh inning, and he finished with a three-hitter. That was just the warmup.

Four nights later we went up to play the Giants at Candlestick, and as usual it was colder than the arctic. It seemed even colder that night than usual. Spahnie was matched up against Juan Marichal, who at that time was probably the best pitcher in the major leagues except maybe for Sandy Koufax. For me personally, I'd have to say Marichal was the toughest pitcher I faced. He wasn't tough in the sense of knocking you down or anything like that, but the hardest pitcher for me to hit, consistently, was Marichal. He had that big leg kick and that funny motion. You could never tell where the hell the ball was coming from because of his kick and his throwing motion, plus he had great control. Actually, he was a lot like Spahn except from the other side.

I didn't last long that night. I had been having some trouble with my right wrist. In fact, I hadn't started a game since Spahnie's last start in L.A. I played about four innings and struck out twice. I wasn't swinging the bat right. Bragan took me out and put in Denis Menke for the rest of the game. I sat and watched and froze my tail in the dugout.

What I watched turned out to be the best pitchers' duel I ever saw. Spahn and Marichal hooked up in a shutout that lasted until the 16th inning. Willie Mays finally won it for the Giants with a home run. Spahnie threw him a screwball that didn't break, and that was the ballgame. It was a tough one for us to lose but especially for Spahn. He pitched a hell of a game. He only walked one batter all night, and that was an intentional walk to Mays after one of our outfielders made a two-base error. We just couldn't get anything going against Marichal. We had a couple chances early in the game. Norm Larker tried to score from second base on a base hit, but Norm didn't run too well and Mays gunned him down at the plate. Later on Aaron hit a ball that actually cleared the fence in left field, but the wind brought it back and Willie McCovey caught it. Other than that the closest we came to scoring was when Spahn hit a ball off the top of the fence in right. A foot higher and it was a home run,

233

but all he got was a double, and we didn't score.

Both pitchers threw over 200 pitches. Can you imagine any pitcher going sixteen innings anymore? Of course the other guys played sixteen innings, too. People sometimes forget that. And what about the catcher? Del Crandall worked that whole game, and he had been hurting anyway. He hadn't played in over two weeks before that game. I respect any pitcher who goes the distance, but that poor catcher--I guess that's what they mean by the "tools of ignorance." Most of the attention focused on Spahn, though, and rightly so. He was amazing. In his next start, he pitched another shutout.

Near the end of the season the Braves honored Spahnie with a Warren Spahn Night at County Stadium. They sold buttons with his picture on them to raise money, and all the proceeds went to a college scholarship fund in his name. Before the ballgame, which was against the Giants, both clubs lined up along the foul lines and he received a few gifts: an oil painting of County Stadium, plus some other stuff. He also received a letter of congratulations from President Kennedy. Some former outstanding ballplayers flew in for the ceremony, including Lefty Grove and Carl Hubbell and Bob Feller and Johnny Sain. Spahn pitched that night, and wouldn't you know, he had his worst game of the season. He only lasted about three innings. We had our biggest crowd of the year, though, the biggest in a couple years.

At the time of Spahnie's "night," however, he was not the biggest baseball story in Milwaukee. Beginning at the All-Star break, rumors had been circulating that the Braves' new owners were planning to move the club to Atlanta. McHale and Bartholomay both denied that, but nobody believed them. By September we knew it was only a matter of time. For me this was a lot different than the move from Boston. I never had any roots in Boston, and most of us were young guys then. Now my family lived in the Milwaukee area. I liked Atlanta, and I had friends there, but I sure as hell didn't want to move there.

June 20, 1963

Eddie Mathews had been the National League's premier third baseman for a decade, a nine-time all-star. On May 9, 1963, without warning, Bobby Bragan made him a leftfielder. Actually, Charlie Grimm had tried the same experiment back in April of 1954—with disastrous results. In ten games as a fly-chaser, Mathews had committed two errors, batted .184, and climaxed the experience with one hit in his last 22 at-bats. Grimm promptly returned his leading slugger to his proper position.

Bragan, however, was not so easily daunted. He loved to tinker with his lineup, the way some men do with old cars. On May 9th Bragan announced that Mathews was in left field to stay—that the move would "take some of the defensive pressure off him." Bragan further stated that, by getting away from third base, Mathews would not "have to worry about bunts and difficult plays down the line." Mathews, batting cleanup, responded by going 0-for-3 and dropping a fly ball as the Braves got whomped by the Giants for the third straight day.

Six weeks later, on June 20, as the Braves hosted the Pirates in a battle for sixth place, Mathews was back at his accustomed spot in the infield. He was no longer batting fourth, though—he was now the Milwaukee leadoff batter! At age 31 and with more home runs than all but seven hitters in the history of the game, Mathews now came to bat once a game with the bases guaranteed to be empty. After that he followed the pitcher to the plate. By leading off with a slugger like Mathews, Bragan was following the teachings of Branch Rickey, but, in a batting slot that puts a premium on getting on base, Mathews was mired in his worst slump in years—maybe the worst since the first time he had played left field. He had just two hits in his last 31 times at bat, one in his last 23.

The Braves' starting pitcher for the game was 24-year-old lefty Denver Lemaster. Ten weeks into the season, Lemaster was the Braves' hard-luck hurler, sporting a 2-4 record despite an ERA just a shade above 2.00. In his last three decisions, his club had failed to score even one run. Through six innings today Lemaster's luck had not improved. He had allowed just one run, a third-inning home run by rookie catcher Ron Brand. Lemaster's teammates, however, could not score against Pittsburgh's Don Schwall. In fact their only base hit was a second-inning single by Mack Jones.

In the last of the sixth Schwall fanned Lemaster for the first out, but the Pirate pitcher suffered a back spasm in doing so and had to leave the game. Tommie Sisk replaced him. Mathews welcomed Sisk by driving his second pitch high into the rightfield bleachers for his ninth home run of the year and the 408th of his career. Mathews' blow tied the score at one, where it remained until the bottom of the eighth.

Lefthander Harvey Haddix came in to face Milwaukee in the eighth. Haddix knew about heartache in County Stadium, having pitched twelve perfect innings there in 1959 only to lose in the thirteenth. This time Haddix retired Denis Menke, bringing up Lemaster with one out and nobody on base. Lemaster was a fair hitter, good enough for the Yankees to scout him for three years as a first baseman back in high school. Like actor Ray Liotta playing Shoeless Joe Jackson in *Field of Dreams,* Lemaster threw lefty but batted righthanded. After taking a strike from Haddix, Lemaster pulled a line drive into the left-field corner, just inside the foul pole and just beyond the fence for his second home run in a week, putting him in the lead by 2-1.

Roberto Clemente led off the Pirates' ninth with a single, his sixth straight hit. With the help of a great play by Mathews, though, charging Donn Clendenon's slow roller, barehanding and throwing him out, Lemaster made the slim lead hold up. Ex-Brave shortstop Johnny Logan grounded out to Menke for the final out. Lemaster had a well-deserved victory, and Haddix had suffered another Milwaukee defeat because of one bad pitch.

After the game Lemaster talked happily about his hitting prowess, but he added, "I'm supposed to pitch and win games. They hire guys like Eddie Mathews to hit home runs, like he did today."

	PITTSBURGH					MILWAUKEE			
	AB	R	H	BI		AB	R	H	BI
Bailey, 3b	3	0	0	0	Mathews, 3b	4	1	1	1
Schofield, 2b	4	0	1	0	Bolling, 2b	3	0	0	0
Clemente, cf	3	0	3	0	H. Aaron, rf	3	0	0	0
Clendenon, 1b	4	0	0	0	Maye, lf	3	0	0	0
Savage, lf	4	0	0	0	Torre, c	3	0	0	0
Logan, ss	4	0	0	0	Jones, cf	2	0	1	0
Stargell, rf	2	0	0	0	Oliver, 1b	3	0	0	0
Brand, c	3	1	1	1	T. Aaron, 1b	0	0	0	0
Schwall, p	2	0	0	0	Menke, ss	3	0	0	0
Sisk, p	0	0	0	0	Lemaster, p	3	1	1	1
Lynch, ph	1	0	0	0					
Haddix, p	0	0	0	0					
Totals	30	1	5	1	Totals	27	2	3	2

Lynch fouled out for Sisk in eighth.

```
Pittsburgh ...................  0 0 1  0 0 0  0 0 0--1
MILWAUKEE  ...................  0 0 0  0 0 1  0 1 *--2
```

E--Logan, Schofield. 2B--Schofield. HR--Brand, Mathews, Lemaster. Left--Pittsburgh 5, Milwaukee 3.

	IP	H	R	ER	BB	SO
Schwall	5 1-3	1	0	0	1	5
Sisk	1 2-3	1	1	1	0	0
Haddix (L, 1-2)	1	1	1	1	0	1
Lemaster (W, 3-4)	9	5	1	1	3	6

WP--Lemaster. U--Harvey, Weyer, Vargo. T--2:12. A--6,496.

SIXTEEN

On Your Mark, Get Set . . .

Three Braves originals, no more Buhl or Lew;
Crandall got traded, and then there were two.

During the winter the front office took another step in the makeover of the ballclub by trading Del Crandall to the San Francisco Giants in a multiple-player deal that brought us Felipe Alou, Billy Hoeft, and Ed Bailey. Those were all good guys, but after playing eleven years with Del, I hated to see him leave. Del had been with the Braves since 1949, when he was 19 years old, although he was in the service during my rookie year in Boston. In his prime he was the best catcher in the National League, an All-Star just about every year. He had a few years left as a backup catcher, but his days as a regular were over. He was getting up in years--my goodness, he was a year older than I was!

That left Spahnie and me to hold the fort. I was coming off my worst season, at least as far as home runs. I had only hit 23. Spahn was coming off one of his best seasons, winning 23 games. At age 43, though, he should have been looking at retirement. He could have gone out on top, a 20-game winner 13 different times, leading the league in complete games his last seven years. What a hell of a way to end a career as a pitcher. He wouldn't do it, though. He's been one of my closest friends, but he's a proud man. He still thought he could go right on pitching. Actually, I don't think his arm ever recovered from that 16-inning game against Marichal.

Spahn and Mays both played over their time to the point where, in my opinion, they embarrassed themselves. Forget

238

Every Warren Spahn victory was a milestone. (Ernest W. Anheuser photo)

it--you had your day in the sun. If an athlete's ego won't let him accept the fact that it's time to retire, that's where the problem comes in. If he's still producing, great, but when he starts embarrassing himself in front of 40,000 people, it's time to find something else to do.

Most of the ballplayers that continue on too long don't do it because of the money. They just don't want to give up the ghost. They want to go back and be 25 years old again. There's 24 other guys on the team, and if one ballplayer can't pull his weight and won't admit that, then he's just being selfish. Spahnie pitched a few more good games, but mostly he got hit hard. It hurt me--it hurt all of his teammates--to watch him getting knocked around like that. He deserved a better finish.

Having Spahn around did one thing for the ballclub, though. He helped keep us loose by getting things going in the clubhouse. He was always one of the big agitators on the club, always up to something. I guess I was one too. It could be anything--dunking sportswriter Lou Chapman in the whirlpool with all his clothes on, or setting fire to Wes Covington's hat in

239

Ebbets Field. Everybody got involved in one way or another. One time somebody nailed my shoes to the floor in the clubhouse. I never found out who.

I'll give an example of what I mean by agitating. We had an outfielder named Lee Maye. We called him "Sharky." He was a good ballplayer and a hell of a rock 'n' roll singer. One day I walked by Hank Aaron and I said, "What's Sharky upset at you about?"

Hank said, "What did he say?"

"Well," I said, "I don't wanna say what he said, but he was pretty upset with you."

Hank looked over at Lee. Lee caught Hank looking over at him. About that time we had Buhl go over and say to Lee, "What's Hank mad at you about?"

Pretty soon Maye went over to Hank and said, "What did you say about me?"

"What did you say about me?" Hank said. Pretty soon they really got going. Meanwhile the rest of us were enjoying the show. It may seem ridiculous, but ballplayers--especially back then--spent a lot of time together, and we needed to agitate to keep everybody on their toes. With guys like Spahn and Burdette, we had very few dull moments.

As bad a year as Spahn had--and he only won six games--I didn't do much better. We were well into June before I raised my batting average above .200, and I went 32 games in a row without a home run, the longest dry spell of my life. I had some problems with a groin injury, and my arm bothered me for most of the season. It hurt to make the throw to first a lot of the time. Also Bragan kept me out of the lineup sometimes against lefthanders. I ended up hitting .233, the lowest of my career, and tied my lowest home run total with 23.

The ballclub struggled too. We were in ninth place for a while. We didn't really start to play ball until the last couple weeks of the season. We won 13 of our last 15 games and made up a lot of ground, but the best we could do was finish five games back. We swept four games from the Phillies to knock them out of first place, which helped the Cardinals sneak in and win the pennant by a game.

All season long most of the action took place off the field. The big story, of course, was the Braves' move to Atlanta, which by now was a foregone conclusion. The only question was when. But even though everybody knew the club was going, the front office kept denying it. The county government was threatening to sue the Braves if the team left. The chairman of the county board got into an ongoing debate with Bragan, claiming he wasn't trying very hard to win so the team would look bad. That, of course, was ridiculous. Despite what Bragan's ego seemed to believe, it was the ballplayers, not the manager, who won or lost games.

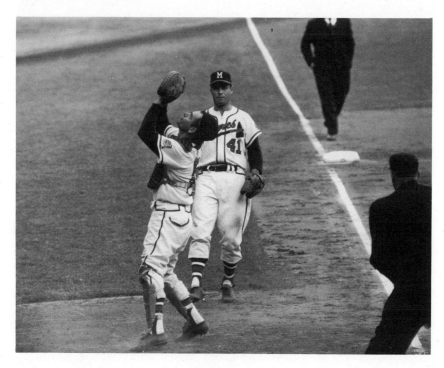
Backing up catcher Ed Bailey. (Ernest W. Anheuser photo)

After the season Billy Hoeft told a reporter that Bragan tried to lose by switching the lineup around so often. That I don't believe at all. I never had that impression or saw any sign of it. Bragan did his thing, right or wrong, but there's no way he was ever trying to lose. Absolutely not. He's not that kind of person. He could be very sarcastic, and quite honestly I didn't think he was a good manager, but as far as losing on purpose-- no way in hell. I like Billy Hoeft, but on that charge, I feel very comfortable saying Billy's off his rocker.

Every day, it seemed, we heard a new rumor about when the Braves would be leaving Milwaukee. Atlanta's new stadium wasn't ready yet, but we heard a story that we were going there anyway and that we would play our games in Ponce de Leon Park. It was about a third the size of County Stadium, plus the field was not major league caliber, but that was the rumor. We heard this stuff from the reporters and read the stories in the papers, but really, fans would be surprised how little attention the ballplayers pay to that sort of thing. We had a ballgame to play every day. That's all we cared about. Whatever the front office did or didn't do was beyond our control. We just played baseball.

At the end of the season we played the Pittsburgh Pirates in a three-game series at County Stadium. We had already been mathematically eliminated and the Pirates were in the second division, so the games really meant nothing. In that situation the teams will usually play a lot of rookies just to get a look at them. That's what we did. For the last game of the year, Bragan decided it would be a clever idea to have me manage the team while he sat in the stands and watched. That's what we did. I made out the lineup card and got my first taste of managing, although as I said the game meant nothing. I should have learned my lesson then about managing because I didn't like it.

For all we knew, this was going to be the Braves' final game in Milwaukee. We were winning going into the ninth inning, 6-0. I decided to put Hank and myself into the game for the last inning, along with a few other veterans, just to give the fans one last chance to see us. I also took out the pitcher, Bob Sadowski, even though he was pitching a shutout, and put in Warren Spahn to finish the game. He hadn't won a game in three months, but if we were leaving, who else would you want as the last Braves pitcher? The fans gave him a huge ovation. He didn't let them down, either. He gave up one hit but then struck out the last two batters he faced. Spahnie had a great finish, and I was undefeated as a manager.

July 9, 1964

From the time the Braves arrived in Milwaukee in 1953, the core of the ballclub—on the field, off the field, together and inseparable—was the fearsome foursome of Eddie Mathews, Bob Buhl, Lew Burdette, and Warren Spahn. The quartet was broken up at the end of April, 1962, with the trade of Buhl to the Cubs. Little more than a year later, Burdette was swapped to the Cardinals. By 1964 the rumors of the Braves' migration to Atlanta had become an accepted fact. Fans now focused their loyalty, what remained of it, on the last of the Milwaukee Braves originals—Spahn and Mathews.

Spahn had seemingly pitched forever. He had worked for Casey Stengel in Boston before serving in World War II. He had been a 20-game winner 13 times, including his 23-7 season in 1963 at age 42. He had won 355 games in a Braves uniform at the time of the 1964 All-Star game. Unfortunately, unlike the previous year and so many before it, Spahn had not earned a place on the National League squad. His record was 5-8, with a 4.89 earned run average.

Two days after Hank Aaron and Joe Torre represented the Braves in the 7-4 National League win, Bobby Bragan took his ballclub into Forbes Field to meet the Pirates. Bragan's team occupied seventh place, a performance so dismal that the chairman of Milwaukee's County Board publicly accused the ballclub's management of not trying to win, to make the city look bad in preparation for the move to Georgia. When he heard of the chairman's remarks, Bragan exploded. He told the team of the accusation before they took the field for the series opener in Pittsburgh.

The Braves' batters responded with an explosion of base hits. Mathews led off the game with a single off Vern Law. The next three hitters—Denis Menke, Hank Aaron, and Lee Maye—also singled, and the game was Lawless. Torre doubled off reliever Bob Priddy, Rico Carty singled home two more

243

runs, and Milwaukee had six hits before anybody was out. No one else scored, but Warren Spahn had been staked to a 5-0 lead.

The Pirates got two runs off Spahnie in the bottom of the first, but not to worry—Mathews singled to start a four-hit, three-run rally for the Braves in the second. Spahn got out of the inning with the help of a doubleplay. Then Mathews smacked a solo home run in the top of the third, the 432nd homer of his career, and Spahn had a 9-2 cushion. It wasn't enough.

The great southpaw threw back-to-back gopher balls to Bill Mazeroski and Gene Alley in the fourth inning. He still led 9-4 as he took the mound in the last of the sixth. When he walked the first two batters, though, he was relieved by Bob Sadowski, the tall righthander obtained in trade for Spahn's old running mate, Lew Burdette. Sadowski gave up a walk and a two-run single, both runs charged to Spahn. After that Sadowski retired ten batters in a row to earn the save. The final tally sheet on Spahn read: five innings, five hits, five walks, and six runs, all earned. Thanks to some lusty hitting by his teammates and a sterling relief job by Sadowski, Spahn received credit for the victory, but it offered little consolation. For the tenth straight time he had failed to complete a game. His earned run average had soared to 5.14. And although he had no way of knowing it, he would never win another ballgame in a Braves uniform.

Meanwhile a banner in the rightfield stands at Forbes Field offered an ominous message: "Scalp the Atlanta Braves."

July 9, 1964

```
           MILWAUKEE                          PITTSBURGH
              AB  R  H BI                        AB  R  H BI
Mathews, 3b    4  3  3  1    R. Bailey, 3b        5  1  2  2
Menke, ss      5  2  3  0    Mota, cf             5  1  1  0
Aaron, rf      5  2  2  1    Clemente, rf         3  0  0  1
Maye, cf       4  2  3  4    Clendenon, 1b        4  0  0  0
Torre, 1b      5  2  2  2    Pagliaroni, c        2  1  0  0
Carty, lf      4  0  1  2    Stargell, lf         3  1  0  0
E. Bailey, c   5  0  0  0    Mazeroski, 2b        3  1  1  1
Bolling, 2b    5  0  1  0    Alley, ss            4  1  2  1
Spahn, p       3  0  0  0    Law, p               0  0  0  0
Sadowski, p    2  0  0  0    Freese, ph           1  0  0  0
                            Lynch, ph            0  0  0  0
                            Virdon, ph           1  0  0  0
                            
  Totals      42 11 15 10      Totals            31  6  6  5
```

```
MILWAUKEE .................  5 3 1  0 0 0  2 0 0--11
Pittsburgh ................  2 0 0  2 0 2  0 0 0-- 6
```

E--Aaron, Stargell, Butters. 2B--Torre, Mota. 3B-
-Maye. HR--Mathews (10), Mazeroski (6), Alley (5).
Left--Milwaukee 7, Pittsburgh 5. DP--Milwaukee 1,
Pittsburgh 1. SF--Clemente.

```
                              IP   H  R ER BB SO
Spahn (W, 6-8) ................  5   5  6  6  5  1
Sadowski ......................  4   1  0  0  1  2
Law (L, 7-7) ..................  0   4  4  4  0  0
Priddy ........................  1   4  3  3  0  1
Sisk ..........................  1   2  1  1  1  0
Face ..........................  4   2  1  1  0  2
Butters .......................  3   3  2  1  2  5
```
    Law faced four men in first; Priddy faced two men
    in second; Spahn faced two men in sixth.
    WP--Spahn. T--2:40. A--9,295.

245

SEVENTEEN

End of the Innocence

"Now hear this! This is your captain speaking!" Yep, it's true. For the Braves' last season in Milwaukee, I was Captain Eddie. I really don't know what the hell that was about. Naturally it was Bragan's idea. Del Crandall had been the Braves' captain for a while, but he was no longer with the club. The job of team captain is strictly honorary anyway. You don't really do anything except deliver the lineup before the start of the game. It's just a way some teams have of recognizing the leadership qualities of a particular player. Pee Wee Reese was the Dodgers' captain for a long time, for example. Most teams don't even have a captain, though. I mean, what's the point? Maybe Bragan thought appointing me captain would make me get back before curfew. Wrong again, Bobby.

I also achieved another title. I was named the Braves' most valuable player of spring training. Now, being chosen most valuable player in games that don't count is like winning a big pot in a poker game where you're not playing for money. It did prove something, though--I was not dead yet. I could still play ball. After the season I had in 1964, some people were starting to wonder, including me. I kept looking to see if vultures were circling overhead. I won't say I had a great year in '65, but I hit over 30 home runs again, for the last time as it turned out, and I raised my RBI total and batting average.

There was no longer any question that we were the Atlanta Braves, just finishing up our time in Milwaukee. We played some exhibition games down in Atlanta, three of them at the end of spring training and one against the White Sox on an off-day during the season. The owners were anxious to move

246

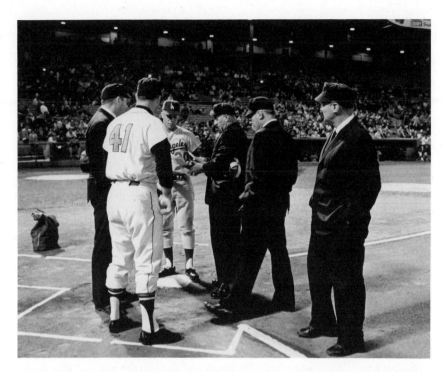
Delivering the lineup for the last Braves game in Milwaukee, on the night of September 22, 1965. (Ernest W. Anheuser photo)

the club--they had no competition down there. They had the whole Southeast for TV and radio. They knew they could make a whole lot of money. The problem was that Milwaukee County had a lease on the stadium that ran through 1965. The Braves' owners tried to buy their way out for a million dollars, but it was no deal. So we stayed.

That last year in Milwaukee was so different from the first. The crowds were gone. Most of the time at the stadium they didn't even open the upper deck. The people that did come to the ballpark still treated the players very well, but they booed the hell out of Bragan every time he left the dugout. The city set up a big promotion for opening day to try to fill up the stadium for the last time. They brought back a bunch of guys from the 1953 ballclub for the pregame ceremonies. We played the Cubs that day, so Buhl and Burdette were there. They also brought back Johnny Logan, Max Surkont, Andy Pafko, and some others. The attendance that day topped 30,000. That was the last time County Stadium was over half full for a Braves game.

Another guy from the 1953 club who returned for the

opener was Warren Spahn. The Braves had given up on Spahnie and let him go to the New York Mets to be Casey Stengel's pitching coach. The Mets let him come back for the opening day festivities, so we had a reunion of the Four Musketeers--Spahn, Burdette, Buhl, and me.

Spahn had been a teammate of ours since Boston, although I didn't get to know him or run around with him until the Braves hit Milwaukee. In Boston he was basically part of the "old guard," a different generation, and I came up as one of the bunch of young guys they brought in. I remember that the veterans resented us young kids--not that they gave us a bad time or anything, but they went their way and we went ours. Spahn fit in more with Earl Torgeson, Vern Bickford, Walker Cooper, and that crowd. Those three guys were more of what you might call team leaders than Spahn was. Spahnie was the best ballplayer on our team, but the team was so bad that even he didn't look good. He had a bad record even with an E.R.A. below 3.00.

By the time I joined the Braves in '52, Spahn had already been a 20-game winner four different times. I never held him in awe, though, mainly because I didn't know anything about what he had done. I didn't pay much attention to major league baseball until I got into it. Without television most people just followed their local team, and in California there were no big league teams. To me, Spahn was just another teammate, an older one that I didn't really talk to.

That changed right away in Milwaukee. Spahn started winning, the club started winning, and Spahn and Burdette and Buhl and I became almost inseparable. We enjoyed each other socially, and we enjoyed talking baseball together. The only on-going argument we had was about Spahn's aversion to tipping. He just did not believe in tipping anybody for bringing him a drink or a meal or carrying his luggage. It got to the point that, one time in Cincinnati, the bellboys wouldn't carry the bags up to the rooms because of Spahn. They knew about him, and it got that flagrant.

Spahnie used to say, "Look, you don't tip a gas station attendant. These guys are paid to do their job." That was one of his little quirks. You could say he was a little tight. His other flaw was, he pitched past his time. That's why the Braves let him go.

But even after that he wouldn't quit. He was 44 years old

248

but he didn't know it. He had been in World War II, with the combat engineers at the famous bridge at Remagen. Maybe he caught a piece of shrapnel in the part of the brain that tells you when to hang up your jock and be a coach. When the Mets made their first trip of the year into Milwaukee, in late May, Spahn wasn't coaching--he was their starting pitcher. The fans were excited to see him pitch again. After getting about 2,000 attendance the night before, the game where Spahn pitched drew close to 20,000, the biggest crowd since opening day. The people let everyone know they were there to see Spahn. They had banners welcoming him back home. They cheered whenever he threw a strike and booed if the umpire called one of his pitches a ball. They gave him a standing ovation when he came to bat. For him it was 1953 all over again.

My first two times at bat that old codger made me look sick. I mean, here was this old man--this coach--out on the mound, and I couldn't even make solid contact. He struck me out on a pitch way out of the strike zone one of those times. Actually, Spahn really was not a strikeout-type pitcher. He had an ability--a unique ability, which he and Buhl and Burdette and I talked about for many, many hours--to set up a hitter. He knew how to set them up because he wanted to get them out with a screwball. Hell, he would miss with a fastball, then miss with another fastball. You could see the batter thinking, "Here it comes, now I've got him." And then Spahn would just turn that thing over, and if the batter was lucky he got a little piece of it. Now here I was. I was the batter, and I was lucky to get a little piece of it.

I wasn't the only guy on our team that Spahn made look bad. We didn't get a hit off him for the first three innings. Bragan did his best to show Spahn up by having a couple guys bunt against him, but it didn't work. In the next inning we got a couple guys on base, but Spahn got out of it with a doubleplay ball. He had a shutout for four innings. The Braves' pitcher that night was Spahn's protege and former roommate, Wade Blasingame, who did even better. He had a no-hitter going at that point and finished the game with a one-hitter. Ron Swoboda singled in the seventh inning for New York's only hit. By that time, Spahn was in the shower.

We already had two runs in when I came to bat with the bases loaded in the bottom of the fifth. Nobody in the world knew me better, knew more about my hitting style and my

249

strengths and weaknesses, than Spahn. Hey, we had talked about it hour upon hour for I don't know how many years. I was a fastball hitter. I could hit the curve, but I made my living off fastballs. Spahnie had been juking me around with breaking balls, changing speeds and working the ball in and out. His first two pitches this time were both breaking balls, what he called sliders. One was a ball, one was a strike. He was setting me up. That was how he made his living, setting hitters up.

This time, though, he screwed up. He tried to sneak a fastball by me on the outside part of the plate. He knew I wouldn't be looking for the fastball, and actually I wasn't. But what happened was, he got the pitch right down the middle. My eyes must have lit up like a pinball machine when I saw that ball. I got the fat part of the bat on it and lined it over the fence in right field.

The crowd reaction was hard to describe. Most of the people in the stands were there to cheer for Spahn, of course, but at the same time they were still loyal to the Braves ballplayers. They hated Bragan and the front office, but they didn't hold any grudge against the players. They wanted Spahn to do well, to win the game, but they also wanted us to do well. It was a case of mixed loyalties, just as the whole season was in Milwaukee. When Spahnie walked off the field at the end of the inning, the fans stood up and screamed and yelled and clapped. They truly loved the guy. The rest of the night after Spahn left the ballgame, they rooted for Blasingame. They weren't being fickle, either. In Milwaukee the fans always supported their ballplayers, and in their hearts Spahn was still and always would be their ballplayer.

After the game a writer asked me, "What are your feelings about hitting a home run off your former teammate?"

I remember exactly what I told him. "Feelings?" I said. "I don't have any feelings. It doesn't matter whether it's Warren Spahn or anybody else. To me it's just a gray uniform."

That sounds cold, but it's true. He's out there doing his thing, trying to strike me out. I'm trying to get a hit. One of us is going to succeed and one isn't. Would I rather have him be successful than me? That wouldn't make any sense. Besides that, the Mets weren't going anywhere but last place. The Braves were trying to win the pennant. We were in third place, chasing the Dodgers and the Reds. Spahnie and I went out and drank together after the ballgame, but there was no sentiment

250

These young ladies gave me this cake, which read, "You will always be in our heart." (Ernest W. Anheuser photo)

while he was on the mound.

That home run really corked Spahnie, though, for a couple reasons. First of all, he made a bad pitch. He didn't get the ball where he wanted it to be. Second, he and Burdette and Buhl were constantly telling me to learn to hit the curve ball. Spahn used to tell me, "No pitcher in his right mind is going to throw you a fastball where you can hit it." We used to have arguments about that. I said I should wait for the fastball. Hell, if a pitcher could throw every pitch where he wanted it, there wouldn't be any baseball. Nobody would ever get a hit or score a run. Spahn just said, " Learn to hit the curve." So he threw me a fastball and I hit a grand slam.

The next time I faced Spahn I hit another home run off him. That one was about a month later at Shea Stadium in New York. The bases were empty that time, and he made a good pitch, low and away, but I got enough of it to hit it to the opposite field and clear the fence. He wasn't happy about that one either. We beat him that day, and he got hit pretty hard. As I said, he should already have hung it up. A few weeks later the Mets released him because he wouldn't just coach--he wanted to pitch. He signed with the San Francisco Giants and finished up there.

The Milwaukee ballclub played pretty well for most of the season. We hit a lot of home runs. In fact, we set a National League record for the most players with more than 20 home runs: Hank and I hit 32 each, plus Mack Jones, Felipe Alou, Joe Torre, and Gene Oliver all hit over 20. We stayed in contention until August, and then we got hot. We went into St. Louis and won three straight and finally got into first place. After Labor Day, though, the ballclub just died. We fell out of the race and finished fifth.

In mid-September we had our last homestand in County Stadium. We played our final game on a Wednesday night against the Dodgers. Sandy Koufax pitched for Los Angeles, but we knocked him out after about two innings. Frank Bolling hit a grand slam off Koufax, and big old Gene Oliver hit an inside-the-park homer off somebody. I got a couple hits. My last time up, though, Bragan had me bunting. After 476 home runs in the big leagues, my final plate appearance in Milwaukee was a puny sacrifice bunt to advance a runner who never scored in the tenth inning. We lost the game in the eleventh. We had a big early lead, but Bragan left Wade Blasingame in too long.

252

A thoughtful Milwaukee fan kept a scrapbook of my career and gave it to me before our final home game. (Ernest W. Anheuser photo)

As you might expect, that was a very emotional night. The reality of leaving Milwaukee was sinking in. Most of the ballplayers didn't want to go to Atlanta. Aaron and I had been around the longest, and we certainly didn't want to go. The fans cheered us all night, but when I came to bat in the last of the eighth, for what looked like the last time in Milwaukee, the fans gave me about a two-minute standing ovation. I was over-whelmed. My eyes filled up with tears. I tried to bat, but I had to step out of the batter's box three or four times. I know I finally did bat. I don't remember it, though. Everything was a blur.

With the game tied, I came to bat once more in the tenth inning. Again the fans stood and cheered for a long time. I felt very humble at that moment. Everyone should have a moment like that in his life. When the game ended and we lost, 7-6, the whole crowd stood and gave us the longest ovation on record. Many of us came out of the dugout and kind of doffed our hats to those wonderful folks. It was the end of an era and the end of probably the best years of my life.

My favorite photo—with Hank, in the tunnel after our Milwaukee finale.
(Ernest W. Anheuser photo)

August 16, 1965

One of the pleasures of the 1965 season was watching the Milwaukee Braves take batting practice. Baseballs flew out of the park like exploding kernels in a popcorn popper. That season the Braves not only led the major leagues in home runs but also set a record with six batters hitting more than 20 home runs: Eddie Mathews (32), Hank Aaron (32), Mack Jones (31), Joe Torre (27), Felipe Alou (23), and Gene Oliver (21). As St. Louis manager Red Schoendienst said, "I thought we had power when we won pennants in Milwaukee in '57 and '58, but this club has even more."

Schoendienst had reason to think that. On the night of August 16, the Braves arrived at old Busch Stadium (in its last full season) a game and a half behind the first-place Dodgers. Before the evening was over, the Braves would pummel four Cardinal pitchers and move within .002 of the league lead. And the man who led the pummeling was the hottest hitter in the National League: Braves' captain Eddie Mathews.

At the All-Star break Mathews had 16 home runs but only a .227 batting average. In the next month, however, he raised his average 32 points while smashing ten home runs and driving in 29 runs. In a doubleheader sweep on August 8 he slammed two home runs and drove in six, beginning a four-game winning streak. Entering St. Louis the Braves had won three in a row and seven of their last eight. They were facing a tough foe, however, in Bob Purkey, who had already beaten them four times this season.

In the first inning Mathews grounded into a force play at second as Mack Jones scored the game's first run, the only time all night Mathews would be retired. The Cardinals doubled it in their half of the inning to take the lead.

The Braves reclaimed the lead in the third. With runners on first and third and one out, Aaron grounded a sure double-play ball to shortstop Dick Groat, who tossed to second baseman

Phil Gagliano for the forceout. Gagliano, however, could not get the ball out of his glove to throw to first. The tying run scored, and Aaron was safe at first. The failure became even more costly when Mathews rode the next pitch onto the roof in right field for a two-run homer, his 27th of the season and 472nd of his career, leaving him just three behind Stan Musial. The Braves led again, 4-2.

The Cardinals scored twice in the fifth to tie the game at 4-4. Once more the Braves took the lead, and for the third time Mathews drove in the go-ahead run. Aaron singled and stole second. Mathews singled him home. Torre followed with a double, Gene Oliver drove in Mathews with a base hit, and Frank Bolling counted two more with a single. This time the lead was 8-4. Mathews tried to increase it with a two-base hit in the seventh, but the Braves could not score him.

The lead that had looked so secure vanished suddenly in the last of the eighth. After three singles off Phil Niekro loaded the bases, Bragan called on relief ace Billy O'Dell to stem the uprising. He failed spectacularly. Catcher Tim McCarver knocked O'Dell's first pitch into the pavilion in rightcenter field for his second career grand slam. The score was knotted, 8-8.

For the fourth time in the game, though, Mathews broke the deadlock. Felipe Alou singled off Nelson Briles and advanced on a wild pitch. Relief man Hal Woodeshick retired Mack Jones, then walked Aaron intentionally. That brought up Mathews. A passed ball let both runners move up and left first base open. Four days earlier in Milwaukee, in a similar situation, Bragan had sent Mike de la Hoz to pinch hit for Mathews against lefthander Woodeshick. De la Hoz had failed; this time Mathews batted. Schoendienst disdained the intentional pass. Woodeshick jammed Mathews, but he muscled a base hit up the middle to drive in two runs.

O'Dell held the Cardinals in the ninth, and the Braves had their fourth straight win, 10-8. And all Mathews contributed was two singles, a double, a home run, and six runs batted in. Mike de la Hoz did not play.

MILWAUKEE	AB	R	H	BI	ST. LOUIS	AB	R	H	BI
Alou, lf	5	1	2	0	Brock, lf	5	2	2	0
Jones, cf	5	1	0	0	Groat, ss	4	1	1	0
Aaron, rf	4	3	2	1	Flood, cf	4	1	3	2
Mathews, 3b	5	2	4	6	Boyer, 3b	2	0	0	1
Torre, 1b	3	1	1	0	White, 1b	5	1	1	0
Oliver, c	4	1	2	1	Gagliano, 2b	3	1	1	0
Bolling, 2b	4	0	1	2	Savage, rf	4	1	2	0
Woodward, ss	3	0	1	0	McCarver, c	4	1	1	4
Blasingame, p	0	1	0	0	Purkey, p	2	0	0	0
Carroll, p	1	0	0	0	Francona, ph	1	0	0	0
Cline, ph	1	0	0	0	Briles, p	1	0	0	0
Niekro, p	1	0	0	0					
Totals	36	10	13	10	Totals	35	8	11	7

```
MILWAUKEE .................  1 0 3  0 0 4  0 0 2--10
St. Louis .................  2 0 0  0 2 0  0 4 0-- 8
```

E--White, Jones. 2B--Brock, Torre, Mathews. 3B--Flood. HR--Mathews (27), McCarver (11). Left--Milwaukee 4, St. Louis 6. DP--Milwaukee 2, St. Louis 2. SB--Oliver, Aaron. S--Woodward. SF--Boyer.

	IP	H	R	ER	BB	SO
Blasingame	2 1-3	3	2	2	2	1
Carroll	2 2-3	4	2	2	2	2
Niekro	2	3	3	3	1	2
O'Dell (W, 9-4)	2	1	1	1	0	1
Purkey	5	8	8	7	1	1
Dennis	1	1	0	0	0	1
Briles (L, 1-2)	2	3	1	1	1	2
Woodeshick	1	1	1	1	1	0

Carroll faced four men in sixth; Niekro faced three men in eighth; Briles faced one man in ninth. HPB--By Purkey, Blasingame. WP--Niekro, Briles. PB--Oliver, McCarver. T--3:07. A--15,763.

EIGHTEEN

Are You From Dixie?

It took some time to get used to. After 13 years of saying "Milwaukee Braves," the words "Atlanta Braves" didn't exactly roll off the tongue. Maybe Spahn and Sibby Sisti and some of those guys had the same experience when they moved from Boston to Milwaukee.

I wasn't the only one who had the problem. The night before we opened the season, the mayor of Atlanta hosted a black-tie banquet for local big-shots and people from the ballclub. The main speaker was Dizzy Dean, the Hall of Fame pitcher who became famous for butchering the language as a broadcaster. As a banquet speaker, Diz was a great pitcher. "I'm real proud," he said, "to be invited to this dinner honoring the Milwaukee Braves." The audience kind of groaned, but Dean didn't realize what he had said. In fact, he said "Milwaukee Braves" two or three more times, finishing up by saying, "The Milwaukee Braves will win the National League pennant this year." Sure, Diz.

The other speakers all took their shots at Milwaukee and praised our new home town. John McHale, Bill Bartholomay, the mayor, the governor, all said the right things for the occasion. The mayor said this was "the beginning of a World Series year." The Braves had finished the exhibition season with three games in Atlanta against the New York Yankees, and the Yankees won all three. Bobby Bragan told the folks at the banquet, "I'd rather lose three games and open in Atlanta than win a lot of games and open in Milwaukee." That got a big round of applause.

All spring reporters had been asking everyone on the

club how they felt about moving to Atlanta. I guess they wanted us to bad-mouth Milwaukee, but Bragan was about the only one who did. Hank Aaron said, "Milwaukee is home to me. I came up as a kid there, and in the 12 years I was there they never booed me. I always felt I was a part of Milwaukee." I felt the same way.

After Bragan sat down, they asked me to say a few words, being the team's captain and senior statesman. What the hell can you say at a time like that? "Thank you for the hospitality you've shown us," I said. "We'll do our best to make Atlanta proud of the Braves. This is the best ballclub I have ever been with." You can take that a couple ways, of course. The Braves were the only ballclub I had ever been with.

Actually, it was funny being in Atlanta because it seemed like nobody knew us. Most cities we went to, in restaurants and hotels and other public places, people recognized the ballplayers and asked for autographs. In the lobby of our hotel in Atlanta, nobody even noticed us. The sportswriters commented on that. I remember telling one reporter, "Maybe it'll pick up when the season starts." It took quite a while.

The next afternoon they had about an hour-long parade through the downtown area along Peachtree Street. Actually it was a dual-purpose parade, in honor of the Braves and also Atlanta's annual Dogwood Festival. It was quite a shindig. All the light poles had flags on them with the words "Welcome, Braves" and a picture of an Indian's head. To make sure they got a good turnout, the mayor declared the day a legal holiday, so all the city employees and school kids could come out to greet the ballplayers. We rode in open convertibles in uniform, all except for Joe Torre, who heard a different drummer and wore civilian clothes.

It was a hell of a parade, if you like parades. Besides the dignitaries and the ballplayers, a bunch of Playboy bunnies in a jeep were there to turn people's heads. They also had the Shriners on their motorcycles and the Busch brewery's Clydesdales and the Georgia Chiropractic Association Posture Queen, along with the usual clowns and bands and floats.

Mayor Allen at one time had promised a dome over the new stadium, but that never happened. It was a beautiful park, built in less than a year in the middle of a huge traffic interchange in downtown Atlanta. When we first saw it, before we really got a chance to hit in there, we all figured it would be a tough place to hit home runs. We figured wrong.

Before the first game, Hank Aaron said, "It's a pitcher's park. The foul lines are good and deep center is good, but something happens to the ball when you hit in a closed-in place like this. It just doesn't travel." Then he added, "We'll get a lot of doubles and triples, but not too many over the fence."

Famous last words. As it turned out, of course, Atlanta-Fulton County Stadium came to be known as "The Launching Pad." Beginning the year I played there and ending the last full year I managed there, that ballpark led the National League in home runs in six out of eight seasons. What Hank and the rest of us didn't realize at the time was that the altitude in Atlanta was the highest in the league (until the Colorado Rockies came along). The ball carried better because of that, or so they say.

I think there's another factor, too. When you fly an airplane, you understand a little bit about the difference between humidity and denseness in the air. Humidity, even though it feels to you like it's heavy or hot, actually gives your airplane less lift because the air is less dense. That's just aerodynamics. It's always humid down there, so I assume that's another reason why the ball carries so well there.

The ball carried so well that Hank changed his hitting style. After a dozen years of hitting to right center, he became a dead pull hitter and started swinging to put it out of the park. His batting average dropped, but he led the league in home runs that year and the next. The rest, as they say, is history.

The Atlanta opener, the first regular season ballgame played in the Deep South, happened to fall on the anniversary of the attack on Fort Sumter, which was the start of the Civil War. We learned that from the scoreboard. Tony Cloninger, our ace pitcher now that Spahn was gone, pitched a good ballgame, but we lost to the Pirates in extra innings on a home run by Willie Stargell. I didn't do squat, a big oh-for-six. I had had a very decent spring, hitting almost .300 with a few home runs, but I hit nothing in the opener. The crowd was over 50,000, the biggest that had ever watched a Braves home game, not quite a full house. The next night Stargell hit another home run and the Pirates beat us again. This time the crowd was about 12,000.

During our last couple years in Milwaukee some people had speculated about what it would be like for the black ballplayers after we moved to Georgia. I think the colored

Hank and I in Atlanta. (Author's collection)

ballplayers themselves might have been uneasy or uncertain about it. Actually, the people of Atlanta were great. They treated all the ballplayers very well, although it wasn't the same kind of excitement or hero worship as it had been in Milwaukee. That's not to say that there were no problems at all. The sixties were wild all over the United States, including Atlanta. The civil rights movement was going on there hot and heavy. In September there was a race riot only a couple blocks from the ballpark. We were up north at the time, though, I think in Pittsburgh. When we got back to Atlanta, things had calmed down.

One incident did take place while we were playing at home. After the ballgame on July 30, in the area of the parking lot where the players parked their cars, Hank's wife Barbara Aaron was driving her car. Her sister-in-law, the wife of the Braves' assistant PR director Bill Lucas, was riding with her. A cop told Hank's wife she had to move her car. I wasn't there at the time, but the way we heard it, she refused to move, so the cop pulled out his pistol and pointed it at her and yelled, "I'll blow your brains out, nigger!"

Barbara Aaron was arrested. Later on the city suspended three police officers for the incident, and they considered firing the cop that pointed the gun. I don't remember if they did or not. Hank said it was a good thing he wasn't with her at the time because he didn't know what he might have done. He made a point of saying he didn't blame the city of Atlanta, that it could have happened anywhere. That incident really upset him, though.

The Braves were expected to be one of the better teams in the National League that year, but nothing fell into place for us. We hit a lot of home runs--more than any other club in the majors--but our pitching didn't come through the way we thought it would. I was part of the problem, too. I wasn't doing what I was supposed to. I only hit 16 home runs, half of what I hit the year before and my lowest total ever for a full season in organized baseball. Of course I played in the least number of games. Bragan had it in his mind that I couldn't hit lefthanded pitching, so I was getting platooned with Denny Menke at third base.

The ballclub got off to a decent start, although we lost the first couple of games in Atlanta. We put a little winning streak together in April and had a pretty good month. Then the bottom fell out. By the start of July we were in eighth place, quite a few games below .500. Bragan was starting to get booed just like he had in Milwaukee. He was still cocky, though. He told the press, "I'd rather be in eighth place in Atlanta than in first place in Milwaukee." He probably meant it, too. The rumors started that Bragan was on his way out, and frankly nobody was too worried about him. As I said, he never got close to the ballplayers. We never really knew him. He was arrogant and sarcastic and kept mostly to himself. Some people said he knew baseball. Maybe he did, but I never saw it. He always believed he could make a million lineup changes and win games that way, with his mind. Maybe that was why he never finished higher than fifth place as a manager.

At the All-Star break, with the ballclub in seventh or eighth place, John McHale gave Bragan a vote of confidence. "He'll be our manager for the rest of the season--period. No matter what." That kind of baloney is always the kiss of death. Bragan's case was no exception.

On a Sunday in early August we played the first-place L.A. Dodgers in Atlanta. Before the game a barbershop quartet was down on the field entertaining the fans. Bragan went over and joined right in and sang with them. The Braves were behind every team in the league except the expansion teams and the Chicago Cubs, who had the worst team in the majors, but Bragan was having a wonderful time singing harmony with four men in fake mustaches carrying little towels over their arms. I didn't play third base in that game even though the Dodgers started Don Sutton, a righthander. By that time I was on Bragan's permanent shit list, so I just went in to pinch hit near the end. The Braves won the game with four runs in the last of the ninth. The next morning Bragan was fired and Billy Hitchcock, one of our coaches, took over as manager.

We were all excited about Billy taking the job. First we were happy because Bragan had come to the end of his line, but everybody liked Billy Hitchcock. He was a laid-back kind of guy, easy to get along with. He had managed a couple years with the Baltimore Orioles, and he had been our bench coach, so he knew what it was about. We had a lot of respect for Billy. As soon as he took over, our season just turned right around. For the last seven or eight weeks of the season, whatever it was, we were the best team in baseball. We had the best record in either league during that time. Unfortunately we had been in seventh place when Billy started, so we only finished fifth even though we won almost two-thirds of our games with him managing.

I felt like I had just gotten out of jail. Billy said when he got the job that we were not a second-division ballclub, that we could win right away. He wanted to stabilize the infield--in other words, let people know where the hell they were going to be playing from one day to the next. After three-and-a-half years of Bragan's shenanigans, that was a radical change.

"Do you want to play every day?" Billy asked me.

"I sure as hell do," I said.

"Then you're my third baseman." He made Menke his everyday shortstop. He also put Felipe Alou, our first baseman, back in the leadoff spot.

Hitchcock's first game as the Braves' manager was one I will never forget. We played the Dodgers again, the defending world champions. Their starting pitcher was Sandy Koufax, the best pitcher in baseball at that time, having probably his finest year of his career, and also his last year, as it turned out. Koufax and Drysdale had held out together in the spring and gotten a pair of big contracts. Anyway, with Koufax pitching and Bragan gone, we had a sellout crowd that night, over 52,000, bigger than opening day. Alou led off the bottom of the first inning with a home run to put us ahead. It was kind of drizzling at the time, and in the fourth inning it rained like hell. The game was delayed for over two hours.

When it finally stopped pouring, we resumed the ballgame with the same two pitchers, Koufax for them and Denny Lemaster for us. Why Walter Alston left Koufax in the game after a two-hour rain delay I never understood. I suppose you could say the same thing in regard to Lemaster, but Lemaster wasn't the Cy Young Award winner, and Koufax had such a bad elbow problem anyway. Koufax was as tough as ever that night, but Lemaster was better. For the first seven innings Lemaster had a no-hitter and we were winning, 1-0.

Jim Lefebvre hit a home run off Lemaster in the eighth inning to break up the no-hitter and tie the game at one. By the time I came up to bat in the last of the ninth, the score was still tied, each pitcher had allowed three hits, and it was after midnight. Most of the crowd had stayed around despite the long rain delay. They were cheering louder than any Atlanta crowd I had heard. We had one out and nobody on base as I faced Koufax for the fourth time in the ballgame.

Koufax was winning the battle. Over the years I would say I had only had modest success in batting against him. Tonight was a disaster. I had faced him three times, and he had struck me out three times. I had never hit a home run off Koufax. I hadn't hit a home run off any southpaw all year, thanks to Bragan, and I only had seven home runs in the first two-thirds of the season. Not very promising.

He made a mistake, though. He gave me a breaking ball

264

where I could reach it. I didn't crush it, but I made good contact, good enough to carry it over the wall and into the rightfield stands. That was one happy moment. I felt good for Billy Hitchcock, and I felt good for Denny Lemaster, and I felt good for me.

In the clubhouse a sportswriter asked me the predictable question--"How did it feel to hit the winning home run to-night?"

Earlier in my career that might have seemed like a dumb question. I might not have known what to say about it. This time I had no trouble.

"I don't think any home run has meant as much to me," I said, "since the one that won the World Series game in Milwaukee in 1957."

We played good baseball for the rest of the season. As I said, we only got up to fifth place by the end of the year, but our strong finish made everybody optimistic about the future. Billy Hitchcock was a total gentleman; we liked playing for him. When he took over for Bragan, he told the press, "Mathews is an old pro with some good baseball left in him. He'll be his old self if he plays regularly."

Actually I did play better after he took over. I didn't set the world on fire, but I raised my batting average a little bit and I hit more home runs in seven weeks than I had in the previous four months under Bragan. In about Hitchcock's fifth or sixth game I hit another game-winning home run, this one into the fourth level of seats in the Astrodome off Chris Zachary. That was by far the longest ball I ever hit in that place.

Shortly after the season was over, back home on my little ranch in Brookfield, Wisconsin, I picked up a newspaper and read a statement from Billy Hitchcock: "Eddie Mathews will be my starting third baseman in 1967. You can't write him off. He's our captain, and pitchers still have lots of respect for him."

That made me feel good. I was 35 years old now, but I felt strong and healthy and figured I had a few more good years left. Obviously Billy Hitchcock thought so too. Stuff happens, though. On New Year's Eve my wife and I were getting ready to go out and welcome in the new year in the traditional fashion. The telephone rang. It was Lou Chapman, the baseball writer for the Milwaukee Sentinel.

"Hi, Eddie," he said, "how do you feel about the trade?"

265

"What trade?"

"The trade with Houston," he said.

It didn't register. "What the hell are you talking about, Lou? Who got traded?"

Lou paused for a few seconds. "You did," he said. "Didn't you even know about it?"

I was speechless. "Are you giving me a hard time, Lou?" I asked him, but I knew he wasn't. Lou was a good friend, a straight shooter.

"Jeez, I'm sorry," he said. "I thought you knew."

Well, now I did. Lou gave me the gory details. The Braves had traded me, along with a minor league pitcher named Arnie Umbach, plus the famous player to be named later (which turned out to be Sandy Alomar), to the Houston Astros for pitcher Bob Bruce and an outfielder, Dave Nicholson, who at that time was assigned to their minor league club in Oklahoma City. Bruce had been a decent pitcher a few years earlier, but he was over the hill. Basically, I was traded for nobody. In other words, I had been written off.

I was stunned. How did I feel about the trade? "I've been around long enough to accept these things," I told Chapman. "As a ballplayer, I just look at this as another challenge."

"Are you surprised that they traded you?" he asked.

"Not really," I lied. "I respect their right to make any deal they want involving me or anybody else. I don't argue with their reasons." Argue with them--I didn't know what they were. Nobody from the club had said a single word to me.

Chapman continued. "Are you surprised at the way the trade was handled?"

"I'm not only surprised," I said, "I'm shocked. It isn't the trade itself that shocks me. What the hell, I wasn't doing what I was supposed to be doing. They must have figured they could better the ballclub. Maybe I'm not of much value these days. I don't know the whys and wherefores."

After I got off the phone with Chapman, I cried. Forget all that macho, tough-guy garbage--I cried. After 18 years with an organization, you expect a little consideration, a little loyalty, a little common courtesy. Instead you find out from a reporter that you've been traded. That hurt.

Actually, I should have seen it coming. A month earlier the Braves had traded with the New York Yankees to get Clete Boyer, who was also a third baseman. Boyer was not an outstanding hitter, but he had a great glove, and he was about five years younger than I was.

A little while after Chapman hung up, I got another phone call. Another reporter. A little while later, another reporter. I never did get a call from the Braves' front office. John McHale was the president and general manager, and Paul Richards was in charge of personnel. Each one said the other was responsible for the trade, and each one blamed the other for not notifying me about the trade before it was made public.

The next day I read the newspaper and saw a quote from Richards, giving the reasons why I was traded. He said that they got Boyer to play third base, not sit on the bench. That meant the only thing left for me would have been pinch hitting. He also said they couldn't afford to pay my salary, which was $60,000, for a bench-warmer. I didn't enjoy being called a bench-warmer, especially after Hitchcock had announced that I was his third baseman for the next year. But what the hell, I was a grown-up. I could accept their reasons for trading me. As I told Lou Chapman, "The Houston Astros can be assured that I'll report to them in shape and give them the best I have." That goes with being a professional athlete.

After 18 years in the Braves organization, though, I thought I deserved the courtesy of a phone call. Even a collect call. Those turkeys didn't even have the decency or the guts to pick up a phone and say, "Eddie, we're going to trade you to Houston."

May 29, 1966

The Atlanta Braves made their first visit within a 100-mile radius of Milwaukee on Memorial Day weekend in 1966. Naturally the three-game series at Chicago's Wrigley Field attracted a certain amount of attention among Wisconsin fans. It also drew what Bobby Bragan called "crackpot and crank mail" addressed to the Atlanta skipper, much of it containing anonymous semi-threats along the lines of "Don't get caught in Wisconsin." Bragan had made numerous remarks critical of Milwaukee, calling it among other things a "two-bit town" and a "short-beer town." In the less violent world of the '60's the Braves made jokes about the threats—Coach Jo-Jo White told Bragan, "Do me a favor and don't stand too close to me while we're here." Bragan himself cracked, "Maybe I'll be remembered as the only baseball manager ever assassinated in Chicago." A quarter-century later he might not have been so cavalier.

For some of the Braves the trip was a return to familiar and friendly territory. Eddie Mathews and Hank Aaron still lived in Milwaukee suburbs, Brookfield and Mequon, respectively. The two stars were permitted to commute to their homes during the series. Mathews was stopped for speeding on his commute Friday, but the police officer recognized him and issued no ticket or even a warning, just socialized for a few minutes with the famous third baseman. As Mathews said later, "It made me feel right at home."

The seventh-place Braves won the series opener; the last-place Cubs won the Saturday ballgame on a 12th-inning home run by Ron Santo. For the deciding game on Sunday Hank Fischer of Atlanta was opposed by Canadian righthander Ferguson Jenkins of the Cubs, obtained a month earlier from the Phillies in a trade for Mathews' long-time roommate Bob Buhl. In the stands were 25 busloads of Milwaukee fans plus Allan (Bud) Selig, already hard at work trying to find a team to replace the departed Braves.

Fischer gave up a run in the first inning, then allowed none for the next five. Jenkins did even better, holding Atlanta scoreless through six innings and leading 1-0. The Cubs added another run off 38-year-old bullpen specialist Chi Chi Olivo in the last of the seventh without a base hit. Adolfo Phillips, obtained in the Buhl-for-Jenkins trade, took a pitch on the wrist, stole second, advanced on a wild pitch, and scored on a ground ball to make the score 2-0.

The Braves finally scored in the top of the eighth. Mack Jones led off with a single and moved to third on a base hit by Hank Aaron. On a 3-2 pitch to Rico Carty, with Aaron running, Carty fanned. Aaron was safe at second, and Glenn Beckert's throw to the plate was in the dirt as Jones stole home to make it 2-1.

Atlanta was still losing by that score when Mathews, in the ballgame replacing Woody Woodward, came to bat with one out in the ninth. Mathews hit a high fly ball into the rightfield corner. He thought the ball might be foul, and so did rightfielder Billy Williams. Mathews slowed down as he rounded first base, then began to sprint when he saw the ball bouncing away from Williams. Williams had tried to make the catch near the line and near the grandstand wall, but the ball hit off his glove and the wall and rolled away. Still thinking it had been foul, Williams retrieved the ball and made a leisurely throw to the infield. By the time the ball arrived, Mathews had scored the tying run on his 480th career home run, his first inside the park in his 15-year big league career (although he hit one in Pelican Stadium in New Orleans when he was an Atlanta Cracker).

Cubs manager Leo Durocher argued loudly that the ball had struck the grandstand first and was foul. Umpire Bill Engel disputed Durocher and threw him out for good measure. The point became moot in the next inning, though, when Santo hit his second extra-inning home run in two days, and the Cubs won, 3-2. As the Braves left the field, a sign in the upper deck proclaimed, "Bye Bye Bragan." It was prophetic—he was fired ten weeks later.

May 29, 1966

```
            ATLANTA                        CHICAGO
            AB  R  H BI                    AB  R  H BI
Alou, 1b     5  0  1  0    Phillips, cf     4  2  2  0
Jones, cf    4  1  2  0    Beckert, 2b      5  0  2  2
Aaron, rf    4  0  1  0    Williams, rf     5  0  0  0
Carty, lf    5  0  0  0    Santo, 3b        2  1  2  1
Torre, c     5  0  0  0    Thomas, 1b       4  0  1  0
Bolling, 2b  4  0  1  0    Browne, lf       4  0  0  0
Menke, 3b    4  0  1  0    Krug, c          2  0  1  0
Woodward, ss 2  0  0  0    Stewart, ph      1  0  0  0
Mathews, 3b  2  1  1  1    Hundley, c       1  0  0  0
Fischer, p   2  0  0  0    Kessinger, ss    4  0  1  0
Herrnstein, ph 1 0  1  0   Jenkins, p       3  0  1  0
Olivo, p     0  0  0  0    Hoeft, p         0  0  0  0
Geiger, ph   0  0  0  0    Estrada, p       1  0  0  0
Oliver, ph   0  0  0  0
O'Dell, p    0  0  0  0
             _____                   _____
Totals      38  2  8  1    Totals          36  3 10  3
```

None out when winning run scored.

```
ATLANTA .................... 0 0 0  0 0 0  0 1 1  0--2
Chicago .................... 1 0 0  0 0 0  1 0 0  1--3
```

E--Browne, Carty, Torre, Beckert. 2B--Phillips.
HR--Mathews (3), Santo (9). Left--Atlanta 9, Chicago
10. SB--Jones (3), Phillips, Aaron.

```
                          IP     H  R ER BB SO
Fischer ................. 6      7  1  1  2  2
Olivo ................... 2      0  1  1  1  0
O'Dell (L, 1-2) ......... 1      3  1  1  0  0
Jenkins ................. 8 1-3  8  2  2  1 10
Hoeft ................... 0      0  0  0  1  0
Estrada (W, 1-0) ........ 1 2-3  0  0  0  1  0
```
    HBP--By Olivo, Phillips. WP--Olivo. T--2:55.
    A--16,039.

NINETEEN

Deep in the Heart of Texas

One of the reasons the Houston Astros traded for me--maybe the main reason--was they were a young ballclub, and they thought maybe I could help them out with the mental aspect, not the physical part, kind of a player-coach. After so many years with the Braves, it felt strange to be the new kid on the block. I readjusted, though. The kids were all very nice to me. They had some excellent young talent--Joe Morgan, Jim Wynn, Rusty Staub. They all had damn good careers.

They weren't all kids, of course. When I first arrived in Houston, they had a couple of the old Dalton Gang from Philadelphia there--Jim Owens and Dick Farrell. Neither one stayed around long, but they were wild guys while they lasted, both dandies. I think Owens was released and Farrell was traded back to the Phillies. Farrell was the one who was pitching to me in 1962 when I tore up my shoulder.

Farrell came into the clubhouse one night with a big knot on his forehead. We asked him what happened, and he said, "I came home late, and when I opened the door, my wife hit me right there with a frying pan." We laughed like hell about that. After he was out of baseball, Farrell worked on an offshore oil rig in England. He was killed over there while he was driving his car on the wrong side of the road. He had forgotten what side of the road to drive on. It was a terrible thing. He was only about 43 years old.

Another guy on the Astros was Bo Belinsky. He had pitched a no-hitter with the Angels in the first month of his rookie year, and after that his career was never the same. After the no-hitter he told the reporters, "If I'd known I was going to

271

pitch a no-hitter today, I would have gotten a haircut." The writers fed off things that he said like that. He got the same kind of treatment from the sportswriters that movie stars get from the tabloids. He dated and then married Mamie Van Doren, and later on he married a very wealthy woman from Hawaii. Actually, though, Belinsky was a fairly quiet guy. He was kind of a loner, at least as far as his teammates. We only ran into him a few times. But when you drove out of the ballpark, back toward the hotel, on the marquee of this other motel was a big sign--"Bo Belinsky stays here." I guess he wanted a few phone calls or something. He wasn't a complete loner.

We definitely had some characters in Houston. Doug "Red" Rader was a rookie first baseman, and Norm Miller was one of our outfielders. Miller used to pester Rader something awful and drop in at his place unexpected. One time Norm went over with his wife, unannounced as usual, and Red saw him coming down the sidewalk. He took off all his clothes, and that's how he answered the door. Miller never came over again without calling first.

And speaking of characters, we also had a ballplayer, whose name I won't mention out of respect for his family, who was as goofy as they get, a real beauty. Nobody on the club has forgotten him, I guarantee. This guy caught a case of the crabs. Then he went and picked these crabs off and put them in everybody's shorts and jockstraps--well, not everybody's, because he didn't have that many. Damn near the whole team, though, came down with crabs. Then it spread to the wives. And this guy was so goofy that we couldn't even get mad at him. Fortunately, crabs are pretty easy to cure, or should I say clean up, but it took about four days. We bought jars of that blue ointment by the gross, and I guess gross is the right word.

Our ballclub was basically a mixture of young players who hadn't matured yet plus a handful of has-beens--Owens and Farrell, ex-White Sox outfielder Jim Landis, third baseman Bob Aspromonte. Aspromonte hit pretty well that year, but he couldn't throw the ball from third to first without bouncing it. And then me--I was going on 36 years old. As I said, they thought I could relate to the young ballplayers as an older player, let them know what the game of baseball is all about. Here's the attitude you should have, this is the way you should approach the game, that type of thing. Also, because I was

In the dugout with my Houston teammates. (Author's collection)

older, they got me fairly cheap, which I'm guessing was another major factor in the trade.

In all honesty, I did not arrive in Houston with the best attitude, or maybe I should say in the best frame of mind. It had nothing to do with Houston. I had always figured I'd wind out my career with the Braves. Relocating at that stage in my life just didn't excite me. Also, I had some problems in my life. I was in the process of a separation, so I was down there by myself, without any of my family. I never saw my wife from the start of spring training until the end of the season. I had a lot of adjustments to make. I was bitter about the whole situation with the Braves. For a number of years I had thought they hadn't treated the ballplayers fairly, as far as salaries, travel conditions, and what have you. The last straw was the way they handled the trade. I really resented it, but at that time, because of the way I had been brought up, I wasn't going to pop off. I went to Houston and gave it my best shot.

Everybody there was good to me. Grady Hatton, the manager, was great. So was the owner, Judge Hofheinz, and so were his daughter and her husband. The fans treated me fine, too. They were all nice, but the ballpark--that was something else again. The Houston Astrodome was called the "Eighth Wonder of the World," and it was. It was a hell of a place to have a tractor pull or a circus or a revival meeting. It just was not right for playing baseball, or at least not for me to play baseball.

I had a tough time adjusting to the Astroturf. Right at third base they had dirt. The ball would come off the Astroturf and then hit the dirt and take an entirely different hop. They also put me over at first base quite a bit. I never really got comfortable there. And when somebody hit a popup in that place, that was a real workout. If you lost it for a second it was gone--you would never find it.

The worst thing of all about the Astrodome was it was too big for me. When you've been a home run hitter for 19 years, you expect to hit home runs. In the Astrodome the power alleys were the deepest I ever hit in except for Yankee Stadium, and Yankee Stadium compensated with a short home run porch in right field. Houston had deep foul lines to go with the monstrous power alleys. To top it off, the ball simply does not carry in the Astrodome like it does in other ballparks. I don't believe they've ever figured out why, although some people blame the air-conditioning. I hit some balls that I started jogging on, but the outfielder just backed up to the warning track and made the catch. I hit a few home runs in there, but not many.

Regardless of what I thought of playing under the dome,

or what any of the ballplayers thought, that ballpark changed baseball forever. When it first opened in 1965, that place was beyond belief. It may not seem like such a big deal today, but at the time, putting a whole baseball stadium under a roof was mind-boggling. The place cost over $30 million to build, which today won't get you a good lefthand-hitting outfielder, but in the mid-sixties it seemed like the national debt. They had a huge scoreboard, all electronic, and they put cartoons on it to entertain the fans and get them to yell "Charge!" and all that good stuff. I don't know what it had to do with baseball, but the ballplayers were as impressed with it as the fans. Just like the space program, the Astrodome seemed exciting and modern, even futuristic. It had the first skyboxes in a ballpark. I hated the artificial turf, but to get away from the heat and humidity and mosquitoes outside, it was worth it.

The man responsible for the dome, of course, was Judge Roy Hofheinz. Old Man Hofheinz was smarter than anybody else I have ever met. Can you imagine somebody out of the clear blue sky saying he's going to build a domed stadium? He did it. Supposedly--and I don't know for sure if this is true or not--the Judge was on vacation in Italy and he visited the Roman Coliseum. The tour guide told him that the Roman emperors had some kind of covering, an awning or something, to protect them from the sun and rain. He figured if they could do it 2,000 years ago, he could do it in modern times.

Judge Hofheinz had done some of everything. He was elected judge when he was only 24 years old, after growing up basically in poverty. Later on he helped get Lyndon Johnson elected to the House of Representatives. After that he made a fortune in the oil business and got elected mayor of Houston. He was controversial and flamboyant, but mostly he was smart. It was his plan for a domed ballpark that impressed the National League owners and allowed Houston to get an expansion franchise along with the New York Mets.

Despite his power and wealth, Judge Hofheinz was very down-to-earth. When I got traded down there, he turned out to be a very, very nice friend of mine. I brought my mother down there, and the Judge treated her like a queen. He had an apartment up in the Astrodome where he slept sometimes and entertained visitors. Part of the entertainment was a bar that had all kinds of tricks. You could sit down on a barstool and he could make it sink into the floor. He even had a bowling alley in there. He gave my mother the royal tour.

He also took us down to Galveston. He had another house down there. He cooked dinner for just the three of us. He served okra, but he didn't fry it. It was that slime kind of okra. I watched my mother trying to eat that stuff. I wish I would have had a camcorder. I could have had the grand-prize winner on "America's Funniest Home Videos" with a tape of my mother chewing that okra.

That year in Houston, I was running out of gas. I wasn't playing every day, and when I was playing, I wasn't doing what I thought I should be doing. Some days I played third base, some days I played first base, some days I rode the bench. That wasn't all I rode. I bought myself a horse, an old stable horse. On days when I figured I wasn't going to be playing, against a lefthanded pitcher for example, I went out and rode the horse before I went to the ballpark, maybe for an hour or so. The ballclub didn't know about it. It wasn't any huge deal, but when I was with the Braves I would never have done anything like that. There was always a risk of injury.

At the end of my stay with Houston, I had this sixty dollar horse. So what did I do? I bought a $3,000 trailer and trailered the damn horse all the way up to Wisconsin to my farm in Brookfield. We had plenty of room for it--my kids had a Shetland pony and my wife had a horse--but we certainly didn't need it. And to show what a great equestrian I was, when I got the horse back home, I found out he only had one eye.

I didn't do a whole hell of a lot to help the Astros, not that one ballplayer could have made much difference on that club. Ty Cobb and Babe Ruth in their prime might have made us a .500 ballclub, but then again maybe not. We had the worst pitching in the major leagues. My only contribution to the club's highlight film occurred at Candlestick Park on the night of July 14. Facing my old nemesis, Juan Marichal, with Jim Wynn and Rusty Staub on base, I got around on a fastball and lined a three-run homer just inside the foul pole in right field. That made me the seventh player in the history of baseball to hit 500 home runs, preceded by Ruth, Foxx, Ott, Williams, Mays, and by a couple months, Mantle. Not bad company.

The ball I hit for number 500 was caught by a teenaged kid named Wayne Nichols. Somebody from the Giants organization brought him to the clubhouse after the game to meet me. They gave him $50 and a different baseball, which I auto-

276

graphed, in exchange for the one I hit. The ballplayers uncorked some bottles of champagne in the clubhouse afterwards to celebrate the occasion. During the celebration I got a phone call from a sportswriter.

"Eddie," he said, "we can't get down there, so I'm pooling what you say for the rest of the sportswriters."

"Yeah, okay. Fine," I said.

"What's your reaction after hitting your 500th home run?"

"I wish it would have come against the Braves," I told him.

"I can understand that," he said. "How do you feel otherwise?"

How do I feel? What the hell kind of question is that? "I feel great," I said. "Hit 500 home runs, what the hell--I feel great."

"How many of the guys ahead of you on the home run list can you pass up?" he asked.

"I'd like to pass up Mel Ott and Ted Williams, but I don't want to talk about that yet. That's not my immediate goal."

He said, "Okay. Thank you." Bam. That was the interview.

When we got back to Houston, Judge Hofheinz had a pregame ceremony honoring me for hitting 500 home runs. He had two big plaques made up that he presented to me: one of them spelled out "500" in silver dollars, and the other was engraved with the number, date, pitcher, and city of each of my 500 home runs. I donated both plaques to the Hall of Fame. They are both beautiful, very classy, typical of the man that Judge Hofheinz was.

I only hit three more home runs as a Houston Astro. On August 17 I was traded to the Detroit Tigers on a waiver deal. The Tigers were in the American League pennant race, and they needed a replacement for Don Wert, their third baseman, who was sidelined with a groin injury.

Even when I was leaving, the Houston organization was wonderful to me. Spec Richardson, the general manager, told me what a great job I'd done for the ballclub--which was not true, of course, because I hadn't done squat. It was nice of him to say, though. Richardson also announced to the press, "We wouldn't have traded Eddie anywhere except to a pennant contender. He deserves to be with a winning team."

The trade surprised me, and apparently it also surprised the Astros. After I hit my 500th home run, they had thousands of Eddie Mathews Little League bats made up, inscribed "500 Home Runs." They were supposed to be given away as a special promotion, but before they could give them away, I was a Detroit Tiger. So what did they do with the bats? They gave them away anyway. Business is business. What the hell.

Receiving 500-home run plaque from Judge Hofheinz. (Author's collection)

By joining the Tigers I was joining a winning team, but I was also moving into a war zone. A couple weeks before I arrived in Detroit, the city experienced the deadliest race riot in the history of the United States, at least up until the Rodney King riot in South-Central Los Angeles. I got there right after it quieted down, but still when there were no gas stations open and no bars open and everything was still iffy. On the ride from the airport, the cab driver showed me bullet holes and shell holes in the walls of the buildings. He pointed out where the National Guard came in and used machine guns to try to flush out a sniper. I really got the full-blown tour from the cab driver.

He had witnessed the riot, and he said it was like a war.

When I finally got to the hotel, the situation was desperate. There were about four or five ballplayers staying there, but with the bars closed, nobody could get a drink or a beer. That's when I made points with my new teammates right away. I put in a call to Liz Busch, the daughter of Gussie Busch, who owned the Busch brewery. Liz and I had been friends for years and years. I knew her brother, the guy that's the head honcho at the brewery now--Little Augie. He'd shoot me if he heard me call him that. I knew the whole family. They had a hunting lodge on the outskirts of St. Louis, and when the Braves were in town, we'd go out there during the day. That's how I became acquainted with the family. They were great people, and we had a lot of fun there.

Anyway, I called Liz. She had the Budweiser distributor deliver about a dozen cases to the hotel. They had to wrap them like Christmas presents, with a bow on them and the whole bit. Liz was a lifesaver. A decade later I married her.

I enjoyed Detroit. It's a tough town, but the sports fans are terrific. I really liked the people. It's funny how in certain towns it's easier to make friends. Detroit is like that. I didn't get downtown too often, mostly to the ballpark and then as far as the Lindell A.C., which is the local sports bar hangout. After that I went out the other way to Dearborn. I had a motel out there where I stayed. Some of the hockey players, the Redwings, stayed there too. I met all of them, Gordie Howe and so forth. That was a wild group, a fun bunch of guys. I have good memories of Detroit.

I also liked playing in Tiger Stadium. It's a great old ballpark. The fans are close to the playing field, so they're more a part of the game. And what a place to hit for a lefthanded batter--if I had played my career there, I might have hit 700 home runs. Those rightfield stands were very inviting. That's an example of why records don't mean very much. So much depends on where you play. Mel Ott hit most of his home runs into the short stands at the Polo Grounds. That's not to say he wasn't a great hitter, but he wouldn't have hit that many home runs in Comiskey or in the Astrodome.

After almost sixteen years in the National League, being in the American League was somewhat of an adjustment. The two leagues were almost completely different. I found out that the American was "Martini, please, with an olive"--clean. The

National League was "Gimme a shot and a beer." It was nastier, tougher, both during the game and after. Guys would slide harder in the National League, throw at your head more, all that happy stuff.

Right after the trade, when I first got to Tiger Stadium, they gave me a uniform and I put it on. Meanwhile the rest of the ballplayers were out on the field having batting practice. I hadn't even met them yet, although I knew who they were from spring training. I started walking down the tunnel toward the dugout. Somebody had written on the wall in chalk, "We'll win it despite Mayo." Mayo Smith was the manager. I walked back to the clubhouse and wet a towel down and started erasing it. As I was doing it, a couple ballplayers--I won't mention their names--came along and said, "That's how we feel."

I said, "Well, that's not the way I feel. You guys are feeling wrong." And then I said what I thought of them.

That little episode made me a friend of the whole team because some idiot had written that down there. Starting from that moment I was accepted right away. I had a good relationship with all those guys in Detroit. We were as close-knit as the Braves had been in our heyday. Mayo Smith was a hell of a nice guy. It was his first year with Detroit, and he did the best he could managing. One or two guys got their nose bent out of shape because they weren't playing enough, but otherwise everybody got along fine.

Because of Don Wert's injury I got in the lineup right away as the Tigers' third baseman. I made my American League debut in Tiger Stadium in a night game against the Indians. Chuck Hinton, the Cleveland rightfielder, was their leadoff batter. He bounced one to me at third base. I had just started to get the hang of the artificial turf in the Astrodome, where the ball came off fast but true. In Tiger Stadium the ball didn't bounce as high, and I kicked it. One batter, one grounder, one error. Good start. Hinton didn't score, though, and in the next inning, in my first American League at-bat, I singled home Willie Horton. We beat the Indians that night on a one-hitter by Mickey Lolich that was shortened by rain.

My teammates were beautiful. After a couple games with the Tigers, one of them (it might have been Norm Cash, I'm not sure) said to me, "Hey, Mathews, are you a home run hitter or not? When are you gonna hit one?" A couple nights later I did hit one against the Minnesota Twins. We knocked them out of first place that night. We were basically in a four-team race with Minnesota, Chicago, and Boston that went down to the last day of the season.

I was still having marital problems. In September the Tigers had a Monday off-day, so after our Sunday game I flew home to Milwaukee. I didn't have to be back in Detroit until the following night. I had my horse on my farm, and it hadn't been ridden for a while, so I went out to ride it. I rode him for about a half hour. When I turned him around to go back, I decided to let him gallop. What I didn't realize was, in that half hour of riding he'd lost enough to loosen the cinch. The saddle rolled on me, and I went off and landed on my hip.

I flew back to Detroit to see the doctor there. The hip was starting to fill with water. Every day before the game, the doctor had to drain that son of a gun. As a result I really was not performing well. I was hurting pretty bad. I didn't want to tell the club about falling off the horse, so I said I had fallen at home. The newspapers reported that I had tripped over a rug and fallen down some steps in my house, bruising my forehead

With my Tiger roommate, Stormin' Norman Cash. (The Sporting News)
281

and hip and tearing a ligament in my right thumb. I finally told Jim Campbell, the general manager, what really happened because they thought I was drunk and fell down the stairs. We ended up losing the pennant by one game. That was a shame because if I had been able to do anything at all, we could have won it. That stupid horse may have cost the Tigers the pennant. Funny the way it works.

It was a tough year. Being traded by the Braves had really hurt. I had felt bad when my friends like Buhl and Burdette were traded, but it didn't compare to how I felt when I was traded. Then when Houston traded me to Detroit, people thought I would be happy because I was going to a pennant contender. Actually, that was not any big deal with me. It's nice to win, sure, but I just went out and tried to do the best I could regardless of whether we were in contention or not. I didn't want to leave Houston, just like I didn't want to leave Atlanta.

This is me--I never liked to be traded. Period. I didn't like being fired, either, but I got fired quite often later on. I don't know why I didn't like being traded, any more than I know why I don't care about setting records and all that junk. That's just the way I am. That's why they make 31 flavors.

April 11, 1967

After 15 years as a Brave, after 2,223 games and 493 home runs representing the same franchise in three different home cities, Eddie Mathews began the 1967 season in a "foreign" uniform. Returning to the state of his birth, the 35-year-old slugger not only wore a Houston uniform but also found himself at an unaccustomed position: first base. Even more disorienting, after a decade and a half of being a crucial part of the heart of a fearsome batting order, Mathews found himself penciled in seventh on a ballclub that, during its five-year lifetime, would have been the most feeble in the National League but for the existence of the New York Mets.

Despite being in the state of his birth, Mathews could hardly have been further from his roots. In fact, his home field had no roots. Its playing surface had been produced not by germination but by Monsanto. Opening day for the Astros took place in their futuristic, space-agey, temperature-controlled pleasure palace named the Harris County Domed Stadium, which everybody called the Astrodome. This self-proclaimed "Eighth Wonder of the World" had conditioned air, which kept balls from carrying, and the deepest power alleys most hitters would ever see. Mathews was brought in to add power to a Punch-and-Judy lineup; it's unlikely, though, that The Babe in his prime could have hit homers under the roof.

The starting pitchers for Mathews' debut as an Astro were a pair of southpaws, Denny Lemaster for the visiting Braves and Cuban-born Miguel "Mike" Cuellar for the home club. Lemaster had been Mathews' teammate for most of five seasons and had been the heir-apparent to Warren Spahn. In the second inning Mathews faced Lemaster in his first non-Braves at-bat in the major leagues. With two out and nobody on base, Mathews bounced a single through the right side of the infield. That base hit, however, was the only one Lemaster allowed. For six innings Cuellar was equally effective, and the game remained scoreless.

In the top of the seventh the stalemate was broken. Clete Boyer, the Atlanta third baseman, slammed a solo home run near the leftfield foul line to put the Braves ahead. Boyer had been obtained from the Yankees after the 1966 season, making Mathews expendable and clearing the way for his trade to Houston. The Braves, however, had little time to gloat over their new third baseman's heroics.

Lemaster walked Bob Aspromonte to start the bottom of the seventh and, apparently fatigued, gave way to relief man Dick Kelley, who retired Rusty Staub. The next batter was Mathews. He promptly blasted a triple against the centerfield fence, driving home Aspromonte with the tying run. Atlanta manager Billy Hitchcock yanked Kelley and called on Clay Carroll to pitch, but with no success. He gave up successive singles to John Bateman, Mike Cuellar, and Sonny Jackson, with Mathews scoring the go-ahead run. Before the inning was over, another pitching change and two more hits had run the score to 6-1, Houston. Cuellar shut the Braves down, and the 6-1 score became final.

For Eddie Mathews, it was so long Braves, welcome to Houston.

April 11, 1967

ATLANTA	AB	R	H	BI		HOUSTON	AB	R	H	BI
Menke, ss	4	0	0	0		Jackson, ss	4	1	1	0
Alou, 1b	4	0	1	0		Morgan, 2b	2	0	0	0
Aaron, rf	4	0	1	0		Pointer, lf	3	1	1	2
Torre, c	4	0	0	0		Wynn, cf	4	0	1	1
Carty, lf	4	0	1	0		Aspromonte, 3b	3	1	0	0
Jones, cf	3	0	1	0		Staub, rf	3	0	0	0
Boyer, 3b	3	1	1	1		Mathews, 1b	4	1	2	1
Woodward, 2b	3	0	0	0		Bateman, c	4	1	2	1
Hernandez, p	0	0	0	0		Cuellar, p	4	1	1	1
Lemaster, p	2	0	0	0						
Kelley, p	0	0	0	0						
Carroll, p	0	0	0	0						
Millan, 2b	1	0	0	0						
Totals	32	1	5	1		Totals	31	6	8	6

```
Atlanta ..................... 0 0 0   0 0 0   1 0 0--1
HOUSTON ..................... 0 0 0   0 0 0   6 0 *--6
```

E--Jackson, Bateman. 2B--Jones, Pointer. 3B--Mathews. HR--Boyer (1). Left--Atlanta 4, Houston 6. DP--Houston 1. S--Staub.

	IP		H	R	ER	BB	SO
Lemaster	6		1	1	1	4	4
Kelley (L, 0-1)		1-3	1	1	1	0	0
Carroll	0		3	3	3	0	0
Hernandez	1	2-3	3	1	1	0	3
Cuellar (W, 1-0)	9		5	1	1	0	7

T--2:10. A--26,001.

TWENTY

Like a Tiger

I was eager to get started. After a disappointing finish in 1967, I was looking forward to better days and a full season in friendly Tiger Stadium. I worked a lot with Wally Moses, our batting coach, during spring training, and I felt good. After I tore up my shoulder against Turk Farrell back in 1962, I developed some bad habits. I started hitting defensively because I couldn't swing properly without pain. Wally worked with me to make sure I was swinging okay. When opening day arrived, I was ready.

Opening day wasn't. Out of respect for the funeral of the Reverend Martin Luther King, Jr., who had been assassinated five days before that in Memphis, all the major league baseball games were postponed. Instead we opened the season the next day, in Fenway Park. I say we opened the season, but I watched most of the game from the dugout. I finally got in to pinch hit for Daryl Patterson, our relief pitcher, in the ninth inning. I did not get a hit, and we did not win the ballgame.

During the first month of the season I didn't get to play very much. I played a little at third base, a little bit at first base, plus some pinch hitting. Don Wert was pretty much the everyday third baseman, and first base was between me and my roommate, Stormin' Norman Cash. I'm not sure why they had us room together--maybe they wanted to bunch us up or something. Norm was a good hitter, and he got the starting job at first base.

Around the middle of May I finally got in the game long enough to hit my first home run of the season, number 510 of my career. That meant my next home run would tie Mel Ott for sixth place on the all-time list. Al Kaline hit a home run in that game too, setting a new Tiger record for career homers. A week later in Anaheim Stadium, I hit two home runs off Sammy Ellis, the former Cincinnati righthander, to pass up Ott. Mayo Smith took me out of the ballgame after the second one and put in Cash for defensive purposes. We ended up losing in extra innings.

After the game Wally Moses came up to me and said, "Way to go, Slugger. Mayo said you've got the first base job for as long as you can hack it. Cash'll back you up for a while."

I felt terrific. I was swinging the bat well, the Tigers were in first place, and I was back in the lineup on a regular basis. We went out after the ballgame and had a few. Everything was great. The next morning I woke up in my hotel room and I could barely walk. I couldn't even straighten up. I don't know what the hell I did or what happened, but that was it. I flew back to Detroit with the club, but I was in quite a bit of pain. I went to see the team doctor. He put me directly into the hospital. I had a ruptured disk.

For the next eleven days they had me in traction. On the twelfth day I was ready to climb the walls. I said, "Forget this. Get me my clothes."

I hobbled out to the ballpark and put on a pair of shorts and my spikes. I had one of the groundskeepers throw me grounders, back and forth, back and forth, that I scooped up and tossed back to him. That seemed to work okay. Then I decided to try jogging. After about six steps I couldn't control my right foot. I kept falling down. The foot would catch under my leg and trip me.

I went back to the hospital and told the doctor what had happened. He gave me a very funny little simple test. He said, "Put your feet out. Now pull back on your right toes."

I couldn't. He said, "You've got a disk problem." The X-rays didn't show the disk problem, but his test did. "We've got to operate," he said. "There's no other choice."

The morning after the Fourth of July I went under the knife at Henry Ford Hospital. Dr. Robert Knighton removed the offending disk from my back. He did one hell of a good job, too, because 25 years later I've never had any more trouble with my back. They treated me just fine in that hospital, but I couldn't stand being in there. Two days after the operation I made a phone call to a friend of mine named Jimmy Butsicaris.

286

"Come up and see me," I told him, and he did.

Jimmy Butsicaris ran the Lindell A.C., which is the famous hangout for ballplayers near Tiger Stadium. Jimmy was Billy Martin's best man for one of his weddings, I think in Las Vegas. All the ballplayers knew Jimmy.

"I wanna get the hell out of here," I told him when he came to my hospital room. "Help me get dressed."

I couldn't bend at all, but with Jimmy's help I got my clothes on and made it out to his car. I felt like he was helping me break out of jail. We went to the Lindell A.C., and Doctor Butsicaris prescribed numerous shots of 86 proof anesthetic. They helped a lot. I couldn't sit on a barstool very well, but I stayed there until about two o'clock. After that Jimmy drove me back to the hospital.

When we got back to my room, there were two cops waiting. The hospital had sent out a goddam search party for me; the police had issued an APB (all points bulletin--I learned that from watching cop shows on TV). I hadn't told anybody I was leaving, so maybe they thought I had been kidnapped. Either that or they thought I was delirious and wandered off in a stupor. (Actually, I came back in one.) Whatever they thought, they were obviously worried about me. They even called my wife in Milwaukee, but they couldn't locate me. I was dead tired, so I got back into bed and slept. The next day I managed to get myself dressed and called a cab. This time I left a note, though, that said "I'll be back."

After I returned to the hospital, the doctor came to see me. This was three days after the operation. He said, "Eddie, how do you feel?"

I said, "I feel pretty damn good. I can't sit up or bend my back or anything, but I'm mobile."

He looked at me like I was nuts. "Okay," he said, "but don't do this anymore. Give yourself a little time."

I did. For the next two days I didn't leave the hospital. On the fifth day after surgery my doctor came in and gave me a bunch of tests. Then he said, "I've just written a paper for the medical society about your story because we've been approaching this thing all wrong." How about that--medical history. Then he added, "You're something else."

I decided to take that as a compliment. Then I told him, "Okay, then I'm getting the hell out of here." I stopped off at the ballpark to watch my teammates work out for a while. They were surprised to see me up and around, especially our team doctor, Clarence Livingood. He told the press, "I've never seen anybody so determined to get better fast." A couple weeks later Dr. Livingood checked into the hospital for a spinal disk operation of his own. It's a small world.

After I left the ballpark, I flew home to Milwaukee. I still couldn't bend or do very much, but I could walk. I had been home about three or four days when Jim Campbell, our general manager, called me.

"We're playing bad baseball," he said. I knew that already from reading the newspapers. "Can you fly to Baltimore and meet the club?"

I was still moving pretty slow, but I was able to get up and move around, so I flew to Baltimore to meet the team. I got to the hotel and checked in. It was maybe ten-thirty or eleven o'clock at night. I knew where those guys were going to be--in the bar of the hotel. I went in and ordered one for myself. There were no Tigers in sight. All of a sudden here they came walking in--Cash, Kaline, Freehan, the whole group. There must have been 10 or 12 of them.

"You jerks!" I said. "You got me out of my deathbed to come over and watch you play like bushers? Forget it!"

They won something like eight straight or eight out of nine or something like that. It was a coincidence, a freak deal. I couldn't play first base, but I was a hell of a mascot and a cheerleader.

After about a month I started pitching batting practice and running. I stayed with the club the whole year, by request of Jim Campbell. In late August the Tigers played a ballgame with the Chicago White Sox in Milwaukee. What happened was, the White Sox had a bad ballclub in those days, and they weren't drawing fans in Chicago. With the Braves in Atlanta, Milwaukee was trying to get a new ballclub. Arthur Allyn, the owner of the White Sox, agreed to have his team play one game in Milwaukee against each of the other nine clubs in the league. The Tigers were the last one. Earl Wilson pitched a shutout for us, and we drew a standing-room crowd to County Stadium. It was like the good old days when the Braves were in our heyday.

The biggest surprise of the night was that the Milwaukee Brewers, which was the name of the local group trying to get a new ballclub in Milwaukee, honored me with a pregame ceremony near home plate. They brought in Charlie Grimm and some

My "Night" in Milwaukee, August 26, 1968. From left, son Eddie, Bob Buhl,
my mom, me, my wife Virjean, son John, daughter Stephanie.
(Milwaukee Sentinel photo)

of my former teammates: Felix Mantilla, Bob Buhl, Johnny
Logan. Logan presented me with a plaque from the Wisconsin
Old Time Baseball Players' Association, and one of the local
sportswriters presented me with a beautiful portrait of myself
playing third base, painted by a local artist. My family was
there--Virjean and our three kids, Eddie Jr., John, and our
daughter Stephanie--and they had flown my mother in from
California.

It was a very emotional night. My mom was crying tears of joy as she came out of the dugout and gave me a big hug. They asked me to say a few words to the crowd, and about all I could say was, "All the good things that happened to me in baseball happened here in Milwaukee. Thanks for tonight and for all the other wonderful nights I've spent in County Stadium."

At the start of September, when the roster limit was increased, the Tigers took me off the disabled list and put me back on the active list. They also added Roy Face, who came over from Pittsburgh in a waiver deal. He pitched in maybe two games and I played in a few and pinch hit a few times, but neither one of us had any impact. But what the hell, the Tigers certainly didn't need us. They had Denny McLain.

Let's face it, 1968 was the year of Denny McLain. He had a year like nobody has had in the last 50 years or more. He had a terrific pitching coach in Johnny Sain. He had a manager, Mayo Smith, who was right out of the Charlie Grimm school of managing--"Give 'em a bat and a ball and a glove and leave 'em alone, let 'em have fun." That was a perfect fit for Denny's personality. Mayo liked Denny and didn't give a damn how outrageous or how flamboyant he was off the field. He let him do his thing. Denny dyed his hair red and bought an airplane and called the Detroit fans "the world's worst" and stayed out all night playing the organ (the musical kind), but Mayo never tried to interfere. The result was that Denny won 31 games and the Most Valuable Player and Cy Young awards.

I can only describe Denny's season as phenomenal. He lost his last two ballgames of the year by 2-1 scores, so he could very easily have won 33 games. He was something else. He had control of his pitches, good velocity, the breaking ball, the whole package. Everything he did worked for him. He was cocky, but his teammates all liked him, with the possible exception of Mickey Lolich. Those two just didn't get along. Denny didn't do any drinking--I've never seen him take a drink, but he would go to all the parties. He was just like everybody else, just a part of a very close-knit team. Everybody had fun together. Even though he didn't drink, he was a spender. He was very gracious that way.

Unfortunately for Denny, he got a little carried away at the time he was winning all those games. He kind of had the bit in his mouth and he was running with it. Some guys handle success better than others do. Denny didn't handle it well. The

290

first night of the World Series I left the hotel in St. Louis because there were so many fans in there. Denny went into the lounge and played the organ in there for about four hours. He never wanted to quit.

I don't know if Denny got in with the wrong crowd or just didn't know how to handle all of the success that he had. Near the end of the 1967 season he suffered a mysterious foot injury that made him miss his last five or six starts. One rumor that was going around--and I can't say if it was true or not--was that some loan shark stomped on his foot. We ended up losing the pennant by one game, so some of the fans blamed McLain. To me, though, he was an interesting guy, a hell of a nice guy. After he got out of baseball, of course, his problems really started. He was convicted of racketeering and drug smuggling and served a couple years in the penitentiary. In 1968, though, he was incredible. He could do no wrong.

With McLain pitching out of his tree and Willie Horton hitting home runs, the Tigers ran away with the pennant, winning by 12 games. We had good power and solid defense to go with the pitching of McLain and Lolich and Earl Wilson. We didn't have any .300 hitters, but nobody did. That was the year of the pitcher, and Carl Yastrzemski led the league with .301.

The Tigers' brass had to make a decision about who they should activate for the World Series roster. The choice came down to two people--myself and John Wyatt. One of us had to be cut. For some reason they cut Wyatt and kept me. I don't know what made their decision for them other than the fact that I had been a good cheerleader for them. I didn't expect to play, just be on the bench for moral support. I was feeling good and swinging the bat pretty well, but I knew my age. As it turned out, I did get into a couple games.

I got into the Series opener in St. Louis as a pinch hitter for Don Wert, but I might just as well have stayed in the dugout. Bob Gibson was pitching for the Cardinals, and he was bringin' it. He blew me away. When you aren't playing every day and then you face someone like Gibson, he just overpowers you. He put everyone away that day. He struck out 17, a World Series record. I was number 14. I helped him set that record, and he never even thanked me. McLain pitched for us, but Mayo pulled him after five innings. Denny was upset, but nobody could have beaten Gibson that day.

Back in Detroit in game four, McLain and Gibson

squared off again. I played the whole game at third base. My first time up I got a single off Gibson, which turned out to be the last base hit I ever got. Actually I almost had a home run off Gibson. I got around on a fastball and pulled it over the roof and out of the ballpark, but foul by a few feet. In this game Gibson didn't strike me out, and he walked me once. He only gave up one run, though, and the Cardinals ripped us, 10-1. The game was delayed by rain and interrupted for over an hour by rain. In fact it rained almost the entire ballgame. If it hadn't been the World Series, with millions of people watching on TV, I'm sure they never would have let us play it. They shouldn't have.

It was a weird game, a sloppy game. Late in the ballgame Lou Brock hit a double that could have been a triple, but he stopped at second. Then he stole third, and they were winning by about nine runs at the time. Usually you don't do something like that, show the other team up that way, but what the hell, he was trying to set the World Series record for stolen bases. I didn't care one way or the other if he stole the base, but let's just say Brock didn't make any friends on our club by doing it.

Then the next batter, Curt Flood, bounced one over third base, right along the foul line. I backhanded it and turned to throw to first. There was Lou Brock standing on third base, right in my way. I kind of leaned over and tried to throw around him. The ball fluttered off my hand and floated over in the direction of Norm Cash at first base. It probably made it on two bounces. Meanwhile, Flood was still standing near home plate, not even running. He thought the ball was foul. The third base umpire, Tom Gorman, gave a "safe" signal and yelled, "Foul ball." Well, what the hell--we looked like the Keystone Kops, for crying out loud. This was the World Series? I got into a little discussion with Gorman, but eventually the home plate umpire overruled him and Flood was out.

And that was it. That was the last ballgame I ever played, a 10-1 tail-whipping. As the man said, "Not with a bang, but a whimper." I spent the rest of the World Series cheerleading from the dugout. After the game Hubert Humphrey came into our clubhouse to do a little glad-handing. He was running for President against Richard Nixon. A month later Humphrey got his own tail-whipping. We were down three games to one, so I don't think we gave the Minnesota Senator a very cordial welcome.

My final game as a ballplayer, trying to put the tag on
the stealing Lou Brock in the 8th inning of Game Four of the '68 Series.
(UPI/Bettmann)

Game five was our last game in Detroit. Even though we
were facing sudden elimination, the ballplayers were still loose
and confident. Mickey Lolich was our starter, and he had won
our only game for us so far. Before the game Jose Feliciano, the
blind Puerto Rican guitar player, sang the national anthem. He
did it in kind of a soul version, slower but with kind of a beat to
it. He did a hell of a job, but the funny part was, none of the
ballplayers could stop wiggling. They were all out there making
their moves. We were standing along the base lines, and Jesus,
the whole line was moving. We laughed about that. Actually, it
was a good sign. It showed the team was still loose, not uptight.
The ones that were uptight were the people watching the game
on TV--thousands of them called up to complain about the way
Jose Feliciano sang "The Star-Spangled Banner." Personally, I
thought it was pretty good.

Once the game got started, things looked about as bad as
they could. Lolich gave up three runs in the first inning. What
happened was, they had started Feliciano singing the national
anthem about three or four minutes too early, so Lolich didn't
get all of his usual warmup time. Mayo stuck with him, though,

and he held them scoreless the rest of the way. Al Kaline drove in the tying and winning runs with a base hit, and we went back to St. Louis a game down but still alive. Everybody felt super-good for Kaline. He had waited something like sixteen years to play in a World Series, and he was an outstanding ballplayer, so he was the perfect guy to be a hero. Al had always said he wouldn't go to a World Series until he played in one, and he didn't.

Denny McLain won game six for us, with a lot of help that he didn't even need. The Tigers scored ten runs in the third inning to make his job easier. Jim Northrup hit a grand slam in that inning. He hit five of them during the season, all but one when McLain was pitching. Actually Denny almost didn't pitch. He had been having some trouble with his right shoulder. Before the game he took a shot of cortisone. Then he went out and held the Cardinals scoreless until the ninth. He was a gamer.

That left everything up to Lolich in game seven. He was working with only two days' rest, but he was the only choice to pitch the deciding game. It was the same situation as Lew Burdette in the 1957 Series. Gibson worked the game for St. Louis, but he wasn't as sharp as in his previous two starts. The key play in the ballgame came in the seventh inning. We had two men on base with two out. Northrup hit a long fly to center field that Curt Flood lost in the crowd or somehow misjudged. He took a few steps forward and then tried to go back on the ball. It could have been caught, but Flood screwed it up and we scored three runs.

As Flood was misplaying that fly ball, I was sitting in the dugout next to Mayo Smith. He was nervous as hell. All of a sudden he yelled out, "Oh, Jesus!"

I said to him, "Mayo, don't worry. We're gonna win this thing. Trust me."

He looked at me and said, dead serious, "You think so?"

I laughed. "Yeah," I said. And we did. That one little slip Flood made opened the door for us. Lolich shut them out except for a solo home run in the last of the ninth. After being down three games to one, we came back and won the World Series. Just like the Yankees did to the Braves in 1958. The big hero, of course, was our number two pitcher, Mickey Lolich, who won three games, three complete games. Just like Burdette. Deja vu all over again.

The celebration that night was something. The Tigers were a club with a lot of spirit, a bunch of great individuals. One guy that never received the credit he deserved was Mayo Smith. He was mainly a hands-off manager, not like Bragan or Haney, but he made the right moves in the World Series. The biggest one was he took Mickey Stanley out of the outfield and put him at shortstop for the Series. Stanley had only played there a few times, but Mayo benched the regular shortstop, Ray Oyler, and put Stanley there and put Kaline in the outfield. The result was that Kaline was the leading hitter in the Series in runs batted in, and Stanley did a decent job at shortstop. That move by Mayo probably made the difference for the Tigers. Mayo was a hell of a guy, and a good Scotch drinker.

For me, playing in another World Series--winning another World Series--was a thrill, but it couldn't match 1957 and 1958. It's completely different when you have a hand in winning it, when you really make a difference. This time I was a cheerleader. All I needed was the pompons and the little skirt. But I'm not putting it down--going out on top was terrific. We finished on top in Class D in my first year in organized baseball, and we finished on top my last year. What more can a ballplayer ask?

And so I quit. I told Jim Campbell, "That's it."

Campbell said, "We'll be glad to take you to spring training."

That's exactly the point. It was "We'll be glad to take you to spring training," not "We're planning on you in spring training." I was making a good salary at the time, but what the hell was I going to do, make a fool out of myself in front of 40,000 people? Spahnie didn't know when to quit. I wasn't going to be like that. My back was okay. I never had a bit of trouble with it after the operation. I played handball and racquetball after that. I could have played another year or two. I might have popped a few more home runs, but maybe I wouldn't have. Who knows?

Jim Campbell asked me again. He said, "We'll give you the papers if you want, but we'd like to see you in spring training."

I just said, "I don't think so."

Maybe I should have tried another year. Who knows. I don't have many regrets--some, but not many. I was having marital problems, and I had been offered a job opportunity back in Milwaukee. I thought, maybe if I can go back and settle down--which I'll never do--things might work out. What the hell's another couple home runs?

May 27, 1968

The 1968 Detroit Tigers were a rough-and-ready outfit. While fighting their way to their first pennant since World War II, the Tigers frequently demonstrated a willingness to defend their honor. Their most celebrated brawl occurred on a Sunday afternoon in Oakland. Actually, though, the trouble had begun the night before when a Lew Krausse fastball fractured Al Kaline's right forearm.

The next afternoon Athletics' relief pitcher Jack Aker hit Detroit outfielder Jim Northrup on the batting helmet. Northrup charged the mound and attacked Aker with a flurry of punches, and of course Aker fought back. Both dugouts emptied. Tiger outfielder Willie Horton, who had left the game two innings earlier with a leg injury, ran out of the clubhouse and onto the field in his stocking feet to join the brouhaha. For the next 10 or 15 minutes the combat continued. Umpire Ed Runge, a 15-year veteran, said after the ballgame, "This was the best fight I have ever seen on a baseball field. I mean, there were more punches thrown and landed." By all accounts, the best punch was thrown by Eddie Mathews, who came off the bench and delivered a hard left hand to the right cheekbone of Aker. Northrup was thrown out for fighting and was treated at a local hospital. Aker was not ejected but had to be removed, bruised and bleeding, his uniform nearly torn from his body.

The next night, May 27th, the Tigers played the Angels in Anaheim. Meanwhile 2,000 miles to the east, the National League's club owners were meeting in Chicago to select expansion cities for the 1969 season. After about 18 ballots they finally chose San Diego and Montreal, rejecting the bid of Milwaukee to return to the league. Back in California the Tigers found no more success than Milwaukee had, but Mathews did.

296

The Angels scored in each of the first three innings off Mickey Lolich to take a 3-0 lead. Then in the top of the fifth, after Willie Horton singled, Mathews belted a home run off Sammy Ellis to close the gap to 3-2. Mathews' blast was his second of the season and 511th of his career, tying Mel Ott for sixth on the all-time list. Mathews had played more games at third base than any man in the history of the game, but tonight he was a first baseman. Regardless of position, though, he had reached a slugging milestone.

California continued to tattoo Lolich, knocking him out of the game in the fifth with two more runs. Detroit got one back in the sixth when Northrup (apparently none the worse for his beaning) singled home Tom Matchick. Then in the seventh Mathews struck again. Leading off the inning, Mathews sent Ellis to the showers with his second home run of the night, number 512 in all, surpassing Mel Ott. It marked the 49th time he had hit two or more home runs in a ballgame.

Reliever Minnie Rojas replaced Ellis, but just long enough to allow a double by Don Wert and a pinch home run by Norm Cash. The Tigers had the lead, 6-5. After the inning Cash replaced Mathews at first base. The Angels then tied the game after the seventh inning stretch. It stayed tied until the 12th, when former University of Wisconsin football star Rick Reichardt singled and scored on Tom Satriano's double for a 7-6 Angel victory. The Tigers' lead over second-place Baltimore had been cut to a half-game.

The next morning some of the Detroit ballplayers went to Disneyland, near their hotel. Mathews did not. When he woke up he could barely walk. Two weeks later he was placed on the disabled list. On July 5 he underwent surgery for a herniated disk. He never hit another home run.

May 27, 1968

DETROIT	AB	R	H	BI	CALIFORNIA	AB	R	H	BI
Matchick, 2b	6	1	2	0	Schaal, 3b	6	1	2	0
Stanley, cf	6	0	1	0	Fregosi, ss	6	1	1	0
Northrup, rf	5	0	1	1	Hinton, 1b	5	2	3	1
Freehan, c	5	0	0	0	Reichardt, lf	6	2	3	2
Horton, lf	4	1	1	0	Morton, rf	5	1	3	2
Mathews, 1b	3	2	2	3	Trevino, cf	6	0	3	0
Tracewski, ss	2	0	1	0	Rodgers, c	4	0	0	0
Wert, 3b	5	1	1	0	Hall, ph	1	0	0	0
Oyler, ss	2	0	0	0	Satriano, c	1	0	1	1
Cash, 1b	3	1	2	2	Knoop, 2b	5	0	2	1
Lolich, p	2	0	0	0	Ellis, p	3	0	0	0
Dobson, p	1	0	0	0	Rojas, p	0	0	0	0
Lasher, p	0	0	0	0	Weaver, p	0	0	0	0
Price	1	0	0	0	Repoz, ph	0	0	0	0
Patterson, p	1	0	0	0	Wright, p	1	0	0	0
Totals	46	6	11	6	Totals	49	7	18	7

One out when winning run scored.

```
DETROIT ............... 0 0 0  0 2 1  3 0 0  0 0 0--6
California ........... 1 1 1  0 2 0  1 0 0  0 0 1--7
```

E--Freehan. 2B--Schaal, Hinton 2, Reichardt, Matchick, Wert, Trevino, Tracewski, Satriano. HR--Mathews 2 (3), Cash (2). Left--Detroit 5, California 11. DP--California 1. SB--Morton, Schaal, Repoz. S--Hinton.

	IP	H	R	ER	BB	SO
Lolich	4 2-3	10	5	5	0	6
Dobson	2	5	1	1	0	2
Lasher	2 1-3	1	0	0	1	2
Patterson (L, 1-2)	2 1-3	2	1	1	0	2
Ellis	6	5	4	4	1	4
Rojas	1-3	2	2	2	0	0
Weaver	1 2-3	0	0	0	0	1
Wright (W, 4-1)	4	4	0	0	0	2

HBP--By Patterson, Morton. Balk--Patterson.
T--3:33. A--8,712.

298

TWENTY-ONE

Out of My League

Things didn't work out. I went back to Milwaukee, where I had a job waiting for me. Once I was home every day, though, it only took about six months before Virjean and I both agreed, "This ain't gonna work out." Our marriage had been pretty much flopping around anyway, and that killed it. We had had a lot of good years together, and we had three great kids. The marriage just ran out of gas. There was no bitterness-- we're still friends today. We just couldn't keep it going.

The job didn't work out any better. I was selling nuts and bolts. I was a manufacturer's rep. I'd go in and talk a half hour of baseball and forget to mention the nuts and bolts. Seriously. I thought in Milwaukee I could open any door, but I really didn't know what I was talking about when it came to the products. The customers knew that. I'd say, "I'm working for Federal Screw Works," and they'd say, "Who was the toughest pitcher you ever hit against?" I didn't do very well. In fact, I didn't do squat, plus we were getting a divorce, so I was living in an apartment. I was not a happy camper.

To show how bad a salesman I was, I would drive around a plant where I was supposed to make a call and I'd hope there wouldn't be a parking place. Or if it was raining, I'd say to myself, "I can't get out in this rain and mess up my hair." I was not born to be a salesman. I didn't make anything. The only good thing about the job was it gave me something to do.

That was the situation I was in when Paul Richards called and asked, "You wanna come back with the Braves and do some coaching?"

I sure did. I was out of baseball for two years, 1969 and

1970. When Richards called me, I didn't ask about contract. I said goodbye to the screw works and got down to Atlanta as quick as I could.

When I saw Richards, he said, "We want you to coach first base and help out with the hitting."

I said, "Okay. How much are we talking about here?"

"Fifteen thousand."

I said, "I don't know, Paul, that's gonna be scraping the barrel."

"That's the best I can do," he said.

"I'll tell you what I'll do," I told him. "Give me seventeen thousand." I didn't need too much because I was just living in an apartment. "I'll move down here and I'll live down here and help you during the winter--sell tickets, public relations."

He said, "No, fifteen thousand."

Well, my wife had me tied up pretty tight. Even though I had money, in this divorce deal it was all locked up.

"Okay," I said, "I'll take it."

So I coached first base for the Atlanta Braves in 1971 for a lousy fifteen thousand dollars. Fortunately, I had a super, super friend in Atlanta that I'd known from way back. I had just rented an apartment, and I told him, "I need $10,000."

He said, "You got it."

He was a very wealthy guy. I borrowed the $10,000 to buy some furniture and get settled. Then a freak thing happened. In my apartment complex there was a bar. I walked into the place one night and sat down at the bar. The guy on the barstool next to me said, "Are you Eddie Mathews?"

"Yeah," I said.

His name was Sweeney. I can't remember his first name. He said, "What are you doing these days?"

"Well," I said, "I'm coaching for the Braves."

He said, "What are you doing during the day?"

I said, "Nothing."

"I run a small municipal bond company," he said. "Why don't you come down tomorrow morning? I think you could do some good with us."

I got up the next morning and went down there around ten o'clock. I had never heard of a municipal bond. He gave me a brief rundown on them. Then he asked me, "Where's the last place you played?"

I said, "Detroit."

300

He said, "Do you know anybody in Detroit?"

"No, not really," I said.

He brought out a book that had all the insurance companies--casualty companies are what you sell municipal bonds to, not life insurance companies.

I said, "What are you talking about?"

"Call 'em up and ask for the person that handles the portfolio, and introduce yourself."

So I called a casualty company in Grand Rapids, Michigan, and introduced myself. "I'm new at the business"--I laid it on the line--"I'm trying to get started in the municipal bond business. I represent a company called Sweeney Inc., in Atlanta. I'm still coaching, but..."

He said, "We're looking for 350 triple-A blah blah blah"-- I forget what all the details were. I was writing all this down.

I said, "May I get back to you if we can find some of these?" He said I could. I turned to Sweeney and said, "He wants 350."

Sweeney said, "That's $350,000 worth of these bonds." Then he got on the phone and started sniffing around, and he found them.

I called the guy back in about an hour and I said, "We found them," and I told him what they were.

"I'll take them," he said.

That year I made $50,000 selling municipal bonds, and I didn't even have a license. I finally got a license, and then when we were traveling I'd call different companies during the day--Argonaut, Fireman's Fund, you name it. I made a lot of money in that business, and that's the only thing that really got me off the hook financially. I never even met any of the people I was selling to. It was all done over the phone. What happens is, these guys have such huge portfolios of municipal bonds, which are tax exempt, and they keep rolling over, so as they roll over they get additional money and they have to reinvest it. They're forced to keep buying. I didn't sell everybody, but I sold a lot of them. I stayed with the municipal bonds until the Braves made me the manager. Then I started dropping off. When you're the manager, you're not as loosey-goosey or as free as when you're a coach. Later when the Braves moved me to California, that was the end of it. It lasted about four years, though, and it was just a freak thing.

I enjoyed coaching first base. It's like being a cigar store

Indian. There's nothing to it. You just stand there and say, "Hurry up!" or "Run fast." It's great. I didn't really want to manage. I wouldn't have been content with $15,000, but with the municipal bond thing I was fine. But then the following year I had a couple clandestine meetings with Bill Bartholomay, the Braves' president, because he knew he was going to fire Luman Harris. I didn't know, but he did. He wanted to know if I would run the ballclub. And I said, "Hell, I have a tough time running myself, for crying out loud!"

I had never had any ambition to manage. I really didn't want to, and I said so. I said, "I don't want the job. I'm very content. I think I'm a good coach. I don't want the job."

At our second meeting, though, Bartholomay kept insisting. He said, "Well, we're going to fire Luman, and we want you to take over. If you won't, we're going to have to get somebody else, but we'd prefer you."

I got to thinking--most of the time when a new manager comes in they'll fire the coaches, and I would be out of work. So I said, "Okay, I'll take the job." Then they fired Luman Harris and I took over. And I never did care for managing. I just never did care for it.

When I took over the club, I had to make a few changes. I had known all the players as a coach, but I had to firm up the team because under Luman Harris--and God love his soul, I liked Luman--it was so lax that guys were staggering in whenever they felt like it before a game. I told them, "You're gonna have to be here at 4:30 before a night game or there's a hundred dollar fine." Well, I collected $2,200 in the first two weeks until they realized I was serious. Then they accepted it.

I'm not a psychiatrist or an answer to a maiden's prayer, so I probably made mistakes. I had never managed before. I found out that managing requires you to deal with the temperament of each individual ballplayer, and I wasn't too good at that. I think you could take a good baseball fan and let him call when to hit, when to run, when to bunt, when to take, when to steal--the hard part is the off-the-field stuff, the clubhouse type thing.

When I managed, I would make a decision--"Okay, we're going to bunt." If it worked, fine. If the guy popped it up for a double play, then I was a dumb manager. I should have hit away or I should have hit and run. There is so much second-guessing in the game of baseball. There are always a whole bunch of ways to do things. That's not the problem, though. It's all in how you handle the ballplayers.

In my first game as the Braves' manager, we were playing in Cincinnati and big old Ron Reed was pitching. It was only the second inning and Reed was getting killed. I had never managed before, and I had never tried to handle ballplayers. I knew baseball--I wasn't concerned about that part of it. When it was time to take Reed out, though, I realized I was going to have to stay ahead of what was happening better because I was a little late in getting the relief pitcher ready. By the time I got Jim Hardin into the game, Reed had given up six runs, and we never caught up. We lost 9-1, and eight of the runs were driven in by two former teammates of mine, Denny Menke and Joe Morgan. But really, I didn't worry as much about my managing ability as I did about handling of the ballplayers and their wives, and their girlfriends, and their personality conflicts, and the curfews, and all the rest of the stuff that comes along with being a manager.

There was another time I took Ron Reed out. He had a one-hitter going, but he had been struggling the last three innings. We were leading by one run, and I took him out in the ninth inning. He got all upset. I told him, "Look, we wanna win the ballgame, and you've been struggling for three innings. You've got a guy on first base now, and it's as simple as that."

He didn't think it was simple at all. He got all upset. The pitcher always--I don't care who he is--always thinks he can get the next guy out. Somebody has to make those decisions, though, and that's the manager. That's a problem managers will always have. I tried to solve part of that by giving my pitching coach, Lew Burdette, complete charge of the pitchers. I told him, "You're gonna be my pitching coach. I'll be the hitting coach. You're going to set up the rotation, tell me who's right and who's wrong. If there's something that needs to be done, you do it." That's why you hire a pitching coach in the first place. You give him the authority. I have never seen anybody successful that doesn't have good people around him. If you don't trust or like the people you hire, or don't believe in them, why the hell would you hire them?

The winter before my last season as manager, I got called up to the Braves' front office. Eddie Robinson, the Braves' vice-president in charge of baseball operations, said, "We want you to fire Burdette."

I said, "Why?"

Robinson said, "We just don't think he's doing the job."

"Then you fire him," I said, "because I'm not going to."

Not long after that Lew came to me and said, "Guess what happened?"

I said, "I know, Lew." Oh, man, Lew and I both cried. I told him what Robinson had told me, and I told him I refused to fire him. I said Robinson would have to do it.

"He did," Lew said.

So then I hired Herm Starette. Did he do as well as Burdette? How the hell do you ever know? He worked well with the kids; they all enjoyed him. They liked Lew, too. If you could just point your finger at someone and give him an extra five wins, there would be a hell of a lot of better pitchers out there. It doesn't work that way.

Our ballclub had a lot of different personalities. We had Dusty Baker, Ralph Garr, Phil Niekro. Hank Aaron was never any problem, of course. I think he helped me in the clubhouse when I wasn't around, talking to the other guys. We didn't have many big conflicts, but, for example, sometimes there would be a guy who wouldn't run to first base. After the game I might say to a guy like that, "Why can't you run to first base?"

The answer would come back: "I couldn't get my head together."

I have no idea what the hell that means. I can't even begin to understand that person. Or I might ask an outfielder, "Why did you throw to that base when you should have known ahead of time what base you were going to go to?" And then the guy would look at me like I was from another planet or I had three nostrils.

Managing was very difficult, and obviously it's even tougher today. Every time I pick up a newspaper, some ballplayer has gotten into something or is creating a storm by talking about his own teammates or his manager. Everybody except the ground crew has an agent. It's insane. When I was playing, I wanted to play every game. Now the ballplayers say, "I'm tired. I need to sit out." How the hell can you be tired from playing baseball? Or if a guy has a bruise on his arm he's out for three days. Two things have changed since I played--money and players' attitudes, and I don't believe you can separate the two. With guys signing thirty million dollar contracts, there is absolutely no way to control the ballplayers now. They do

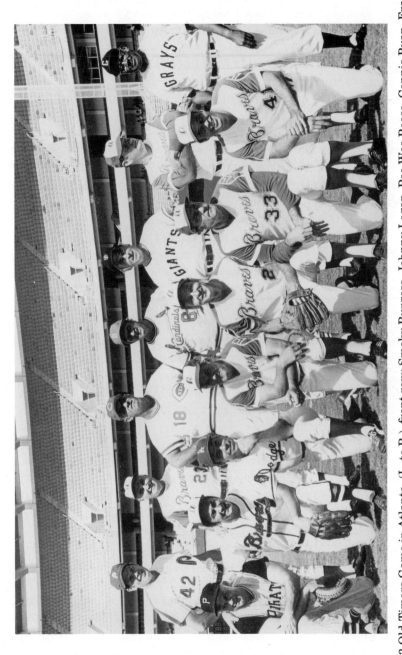

1973 Old-Timers Game in Atlanta. (L. to R.), front row: Smoky Burgess, Johnny Logan, Pee Wee Reese, Connie Ryan, Frank Bolling, Lou Burdette, Eddie Mathews. Back row: Robin Roberts, Tommy Holmes, Ted Kluszewski, Stan Musial, Sal Maglie, Billy O'Dell, Buck Leonard. (Author's collection)

exactly what they feel like doing. It wasn't that bad when I was managing, but it was bad enough for me. Casey Stengel said he respected anyone who lasted more than one year as a manager. I lasted longer than that, but not much longer.

It's been said many times, but I'll say it too--it's lonely at the top. As a ballplayer I did my share--all right, more than my share--of carousing and raising hell. I had no idea what the word curfew meant. Then when I became the manager, every-thing flip-flopped. I had to try to enforce the rules. I got all the middle-of-the-night phone calls--"Where the hell is my hus-band? What kind of club are you running?"

One time we had a catcher that everybody called "Mule." I was checking bedrooms one night, the usual rounds, and I had the club trainer, Dave Purseley, along with me. I made a rule of always having somebody with me so nobody could say I was lying or something. We finished checking, and Mule wasn't in his room. Dave and I decided to go out for a drink. I knew pretty much where the ballplayers hung out, so Dave and I walked into the place to have a beer. There was Mule sitting at the end of the bar. He was pretty well oiled. He got up to go to the bathroom, so I followed him in.

I was standing at the urinal next to him. I turned to him and said, "How you doing?"

Mule said, "I think I'm in trouble. Mathews is here."

He didn't even recognize me. I said, "Don't you think you better get back to the room?" I still see him once in a while and he laughs about that.

In the first ballgame I won as a manager, our winning pitcher--of all people--was Denny McLain. He pitched a hell of a game that night against the Houston Astros. He had a one-hit shutout for the first seven innings before giving up a few runs at the end, but he went all the way and we won. Denny had come over in a trade for Orlando Cepeda about a month or so before I took over the club. He had a sore arm which turned out to be a chronic sore arm. We found out later that he'd been going to his own doctor, getting cortisone shots to try to keep pitching. He wasn't the same Denny McLain that we had in Detroit. In fact, that game against the Astros was the last game he ever won in the big leagues.

During the off-season after my first couple months as manager we made a big trade with the Baltimore Orioles. We gave up a good catcher, Earl Williams, but in return we picked up two pitchers, Roric Harrison and Pat Dobson, plus a catcher, Johnny Oates, and second baseman Davey Johnson. The pitching didn't help us much, although Harrison won some games for us, but Oates was our starting catcher, and Johnson turned out to be a pleasant surprise. He had hit with some power in Baltimore, but in Atlanta he turned into Rogers Hornsby, at least as far as home runs. He tied Hornsby's home run record for second baseman.

Davey and I got along great except for one day. We played a doubleheader in Philadelphia, and Davey had evidently--I'm just guessing, I'm not accusing him of anything--taken some greenies to get him through the doubleheader or eaten too much sugar or something. Those greenies, if that's what it was, take away your appetite, almost like a diet pill, but they're also a pick-me-up. Anyway, for whatever reason, instead of coming back to the hotel and getting something to eat, he went back to his room. He was rooming with Mike Lum, and later on Mike wanted to get in the room. Davey opened the door and hit Mike Lum right in the face. Mike hit him back. Davey just had on a pair of pants--no shirt, no shoes, no socks--but he turned around and jumped out the window. They were on the second story, but fortunately he hit in the shrubs and broke his fall. Then he took off running, and it was raining like hell.

Now I got the phone call. I went down there to find out what happened. There were about eight ballplayers kind of walking around, trying to find out where Davey went, but they weren't going to go outside in the rain and look. I went down to the lobby and rented another room for Davey. I told the guys to get back to their rooms and go to bed. Then I took Dave Purseley with me and started meandering around the hallways. By now it was two o'clock in the morning.

All of a sudden I was walking down the hall, and around the corner, here came Davey. He looked like a wet cocker spaniel. I said, "Davey, wait a minute now. I've rented you a room. It's right down the hall here. Let's go down and get you settled in your room and relax, and we'll talk about this thing tomorrow."

We walked into his room. I said, "Davey, do me a favor. The next time you wanna hit somebody, hit me." BANG! He coldcocked me. I grabbed him and we went down on the floor. Purseley was there, and several ballplayers also rushed in and broke it up. Mike Lum was one of the players.

I said, "Okay, Mike and Davey, you guys come down to my room." Those two plus Purseley and myself went down there. Then I had Purseley call all the ballplayers' rooms and tell them to keep their big mouths shut about the incident. Then I told Lum and Johnson, "You guys go to your rooms and go to bed. I'll see you in my office at the ballpark tomorrow morning." I didn't even try to get them to shake hands because they were still pretty upset.

The next morning at the ballpark, Purseley brought Mike and Davey in to see me. I said, "I want you two guys to shake hands, and this thing is over." And that's the way it ended, right there. It didn't leak out until maybe a year and a half later. I don't think anybody other than myself and Davey and Mike actually knows what happened. I never made an issue out of it. I could have fined Davey and told the newspapers and gone crying in my beer that he hit me. Stuff like that did not really bother me, though. I got marked up a little bit, but what the hell, it goes with being a manager.

Without question, the biggest story during the time I was managing was Hank Aaron going after Babe Ruth's career home run record. He did it so gradually and so steadily that nobody seemed to even notice until the winter before he tied the record. Toward the end of 1973 he started getting close, but nobody came out to watch him. For one of the last ones--I think it was number 711--we barely had a thousand people in the stands in Atlanta. I don't think the excitement started until that winter. Then the hype started. Everybody knew he was going to do it. It was just a matter of time. I did what I could to protect him from what he was going through--threatening letters, really nasty racial stuff, plus everybody and his mother wanting interviews. Hank was really alone. He was the only one anybody wanted to talk to. I tried to yak with him, keep the writers away, give him as much support as I could.

The main problem began in mid-February when Braves owner Bill Bartholomay announced publicly that Hank would not play in the opening series in Cincinnati, that he would sit out until our first homestand. He had never discussed it with me, and I was the manager. Then a couple hot-shot New York writers picked up the story and said it would destroy the integrity of the game of baseball if Hank didn't play in Cincinnati. It would mean the Braves were not trying to win. From then on the media made a big issue out of worrying about

Hank, not the team--they didn't gave a damn about the Braves.

I agreed with Bartholomay. Loyalty was always a big thing with me. I figured the home fans should see Hank tie and break the record. If Hank didn't play in Cincinnati, we had an 11-game homestand right after that, and over half a million fans would have showed up to see him try for Ruth's record. Hank was 40 years old at that time, so let's face it, we knew he would not start every ballgame. He had sat out about a third of the games in 1973, so what was the big deal? Well, the big deal was the New York sportswriters. They got on Bowie Kuhn, the commissioner, so he figured he had to get involved. He contacted Bartholomay and basically said, I know you'll do what's right, which is to start Hank in Cincinnati. If Bartholomay had never announced his intentions, everything would have worked out fine.

When we went on our ticket-selling tour of the Southeast, in every town we went into, the first thing people wanted to talk about was Aaron going after Ruth's record. By the time spring training started, reporters were really pouring in from all over the world. They created quite a problem because they were very demanding. They would sit down and take up two hours of his time if he'd let them. Hank was super, very accommodating. I had to be the bad guy--which I didn't mind--and throw those guys out just so Hank could have some time to go out and hit.

No other athlete that I know of could have handled that situation as well as Hank. His temperament and his nature were perfect. It wasn't like poor old Roger Maris when he hit 61 homers--his hair fell out and he actually got sick. Hank handled it great, and the pressure was enormous. The club hired an Atlanta police detective to accompany him to spring training, and of course they had given him a private secretary long before that just to handle his calls and mail. We hired a private limousine to get him around. We had to hide him in the hotels under assumed names, sneak him in and out. It was hairy, but he handled it in stride.

During spring training every town on our schedule wanted to have a Hank Aaron Day. They were all calling to try to make sure Hank would play in their exhibition game, which of course was impossible. I tried to schedule it so he would play in most of the games in West Palm. Our final exhibition game was two days before the season opener. It was against the Orioles in old Rickwood Field in Birmingham, where both Hank and I had played more than twenty years earlier, and it was very nostalgic. I had played there with the Crackers, and Hank had played there with the barnstorming Negro team, the Indianapolis Clowns, when he was just out of high school. They had a pregame ceremony, and when Milo Hamilton, the Braves' announcer, introduced Hank, the fans stood up and cheered for a long time. They were there to see Hank hit one out of the park and he did, but it hooked foul.

We opened the season in Cincinnati on a Thursday. By tradition, the National League season always opened in Cincinnati because they had the first professional ballclub, back in 1869. I had talked it over with Hank, and I said, "I'd like to see you break the record in Atlanta."

Hank said, "Well, that's what I'd like to do, too."

"I'm not going to play you opening day," I told him. "I'll keep you as the Hammer. You can be ready to pinch hit." Hank agreed.

As it turned out, I did play Hank in the opener. I talked it over with Bartholomay and Eddie Robinson, but it was my decision. My thinking was, if it hadn't been for the record, I would have played him. He was in good shape and swinging well, so I put him in the lineup. The Vice-President, Jerry Ford, was there to throw out the first ball. By that time we had about 300 reporters traveling with us. It was really a madhouse. The first time Hank came to bat he got a little burst of applause but no big ovation. You could feel the excitement in the air, though. The count was 3-1 when Jack Billingham, the Reds' pitcher, threw him a low fastball. Hank swung--his first swing, actually--and lined it over the leftfield fence, way over Pete Rose's head, for home run number 714, tying the record. The game stopped for about five minutes for a little ceremony. Vice-President Ford congratulated Hank and called his home run "a great thing for baseball."

That was Hank's only hit that day. When he wasn't in the outfield, he stood and chain-smoked cigarettes in the stairwell below our dugout. After the game he posed for pictures and answered a thousand and one questions for the sportswriters. By the way, we blew a 6-1 lead and lost in extra innings, not that anyone noticed.

Friday was an off-day. I found out something from a reporter--that Hank was upset because he had asked, through our front office, to have a moment of silence before the game in honor of Martin Luther King, but the Reds refused. Jesse Jackson had called Hank with the idea because it was the anniversary of the assassination. When a reporter asked me my reaction, that was the first I had heard of it.

Before Saturday's game I called a news conference and made an announcement: "Hank Aaron will not play either today or tomorrow. His next game will be Monday night in Atlanta. We've been more than fair about this, but my thinking has changed since he hit the home run. Right or wrong, I'm the manager, and that's my decision."

Hank did not play Saturday and we won the ballgame. Afterwards, though, the trouble started. Sparky Anderson, the Reds manager, told the press he supported me, that I had handled it right. Everybody else took the opposing view. I was called into a meeting with Joe Reichler, the Assistant to the Commissioner, and Bartholomay. Joe said, "The Commissioner wants to talk to you over the phone."

First he talked to Bartholomay, then to me. What he said was, "If you don't play him, you're both going to be suspended."

My first reaction was, "Okay, Commissioner, why don't you make out the lineup for me." I was really steamed. I resented him telling me how to do my job. I still resent it. But I had no choice. The Commissioner had unlimited powers to impose penalties either on the ballclub or on individuals. I certainly didn't want to drag Hank into some ugly confrontation.

Before game three I read a statement that the club had prepared, explaining that, in the face of the threat of fines and suspensions, Hank would play in the game. He did, for seven innings, and then I put in a defensive replacement for him, which I had been doing for some time. Once again, though, I learned something from a reporter. In 1958 when Stan Musial was about to get his 3,000th hit, his manager, my old friend Fred Hutchinson, held him out of the starting lineup in Chicago so he could get number 3,000 at home. Nobody complained about damaging "the reputation of the game," as Bowie Kuhn put it. And by the way, Musial foiled the strategy by hitting a pinch double. Kuhn could have prevented the whole problem with Aaron by telling the schedule maker to have the Braves open their season in Atlanta. But that would have made too much sense.

I was glad to get the hell out of Cincinnati and start our

homestand. Big plans had been made for Atlanta's opening night, including performers like Pearl Bailey and Sammy Davis, Jr., and the usual politicians like Governor Jimmy Carter. The game was on national TV, of course, and every Braves game was going to be until Hank broke the record. All the baseballs for the game had been marked with a special ultraviolet dye to help identify the actual home run ball when it happened. We were all expecting Bowie Kuhn there. A writer asked me if I were looking forward to seeing Kuhn and I said, "Well, I'm not going to meet him at the airport."

Actually Kuhn never showed up. The biggest moment in baseball history--maybe in all of sports history--and the Commissioner didn't bother to make an appearance. That aggravated everybody. Personally, I didn't want to see Bowie Kuhn, but I thought he should have been there. What else did he have to do? He was speaking to the Wahoo Club in Cleveland. That says it all about Bowie Kuhn.

Of course, as the whole world knows, Hank broke the record that night. In his second time at bat, with Ralph Garr and Mike Lum on base, Hank pulled Al Downing's pitch into the bullpen in left field and trotted around the bases while the crowd went crazy. After they went crazy, they went home. When he hit the home run there were 52,000 people in the seats. Twenty minutes later there were 10,000. They came to see one thing. It's more than Bowie Kuhn did, though.

Around the middle of the game, Donald Davidson came to me in the dugout. "Where's Hank?" he said. "President Nixon is on the phone."

"Come on, Donald," I said, "he's out in left field."

We were ahead, so at the end of the half-inning I put in Rowland Office for defense, and Hank went with Donald to call Nixon back. We won the ballgame, and afterwards I got the news media mad at me again. I locked the clubhouse door to let us have a half-hour with just the team and the families, the wives and the kids. I wanted to let Hank have a chance to shift gears and just enjoy the moment. I climbed up on a table and gave a little talk about Hank, what he had accomplished and how much he had meant to me. After that we had some champagne and then let the press come in. Once they got in I really caught hell, of course. The players were all laughing--they loved to see me catch hell.

And then just like that, it was over. The sportswriters

and the TV cameras and the fans all left. No more reporters coming out of the rocks and peeking around trees. Three nights later when Hank hit number 716 to beat the Dodgers, we had 5,000 people in Atlanta-Fulton County Stadium. Everything was back to normal.

Hank's home run record overshadowed everything else in my managerial career, but it wasn't the only thing that happened. We had some good ballplayers and played good baseball at times, and we had some fun. One of the fun things happened during the offseason before Hank broke the record, on our ticket-selling tour of the South. Nashville was one of the cities we hit. We always visited the Grand Old Opry when we were there, and they let us go backstage. I sang with Roy Acuff, live on the air--"The Wabash Cannonball." God, it was great! I played the guitar, too--not very loud, of course. I've always loved to sing, not that I'm good at it, but that was a kick.

I got to know Roy Acuff a little bit, and through him we met a lot of the country singers. I sang with Loretta Lynn at home plate before a ballgame in Atlanta. All the Opry people were really nice, down-to-earth people. Later when I went to Nashville to do card shows, I'd call Roy Acuff and he would get

Singing with Loretta Lynn. (Author's collection)

313

passes for me and my wife. Roy was a good pal. So was Jim Ed Brown. He's got a small theater down there, and he gets me tickets too.

I have always enjoyed Nashville. When I played for the Crackers back in 1950, we always played night games, so we couldn't get to the Grand Old Opry. It was over before we could get there from the ballpark. What we used to do was go to a place called the Ernest Tubb Music Shop. He used to sing there after the Opry. I never got to meet him, but we listened to him a lot of times.

As I said, we had some fun, and we played some good baseball. In June we were eight or nine games above .500 and looking pretty good. Then we started to slip a little bit. On the Saturday before the All-Star Game, the Braves had a Hank Aaron Night to recognize Hank breaking Ty Cobb's major league record for most games played. We lost to the Pirates in extra innings. The next afternoon we lost to the Pirates again, and ten minutes after the game I was fired by Vice-President Eddie Robinson.

"After long and careful consideration and in-depth analysis of our team this year," his announcement said, "I've reluctantly come to the conclusion that a change in managers has to be made." He didn't announce a successor, but he said it would be on an interim basis.

A sportswriter asked me for my reaction. "It was a shock," I told him. "I had no inkling."

That was not entirely true. I had been told to start behaving myself about a month or so before that. The club was playing well at the time, so the warning had nothing to do with baseball. We had played in San Francisco, and Eddie Robinson had sent along a Mister Spy named Clyde King on the trip with us. King had been the manager of the San Francisco Giants about four years before that. I had known Clyde King, and I knew what he had done to other people, so when the front office sent him on that trip with us, I started thinking, oh oh, here we go. That was just the nature of the guy.

Actually the club had warned me even before that to slow it down. I had an expense account, and I know one off-day in St. Louis, at the Chase Hotel, I opened up the bar to all the sportswriters--they could go in and drink on my tab. Well, the people in the front office got a little angry at that move. I didn't know sportswriters could drink that well. It was just incidents like that. They'd had enough. It was my own fault.

On the Clyde King trip, we had played one of those businessmen's luncheon games, and we weren't flying out until about ten o'clock that night. What is there to do to kill time? As a result, the players and the coaches and myself were feeling no pain when we got on the airplane. This was one of those planes that have the cocktail lounge up on top, in the bubble. The sportswriters and I, plus a couple coaches, went up there and continued. We got back from the trip about five in the morning--and then our bus wasn't there.

I got upset with Donald Davidson, who was our traveling secretary. We waited around for about half an hour before the bus showed up. Donald and I got into a pretty good shouting match. One of the reasons it got a little vicious was it was so early in the morning and we were tired from being up all night. I thought he had screwed up by scheduling our return flight so late after an afternoon ballgame. Then on top of that, our bus wasn't there for us. It was a combination of things. Donald and I both got a little nasty.

Evidently Clyde King went back and turned in his report, which was not favorable. The reason was, he wanted the manager's job, which is neither here nor there. I blame no one but myself. To tell the truth, it didn't bother me that much. Of course nobody likes to be fired, but in baseball you're hired to be fired, unless you're Tommy Lasorda. They obviously didn't appreciate my behavior. Maybe they didn't think I was a very good manager, either. I don't know. Maybe they just thought the team should be playing better and a change of scenery would help. They never did say exactly why, and of course, I didn't ask them.

After we lost to the Pirates, Eddie Robinson and one of the owners came in and told me, "We're letting you go." They didn't announce it until the next day, but they gave the job to Clyde King.

I said to them, "Okay, I've had my day in the sun. I want to talk to the ballplayers for a minute."

I went into the clubhouse and told the kids what the hell was happening. I said, "You've got the All-Star break now. Get some rest. You're a good ballclub. Come back and give 'em hell."

I returned to my office. By then the two guys who had fired me had left already. Then one by one, each of the ballplayers came in there and shook hands and said they were sorry and all that happy stuff. And that was it.

Hank Aaron was asked by a sportswriter about my being fired. "It's their club and they can do what they want to, but personally, I thought he did a hell of a job. I've seen a lot of managers fired, but this one touched me especially hard."

Good old Hank.

September 29, 1973

If it is possible to sneak up on the most famous record in the history of professional sports, Hank Aaron did. For the first 16 or 17 years of his relentless assault on Babe Ruth's career home run mark, few people even noticed. Then as he closed in on the record, Aaron made the challenge during the football season and in the venue least likely to attract witnesses— Atlanta-Fulton County Stadium.

On Saturday night, September 29, 1973, the Atlanta Braves hosted the Houston Astros in the next-to-last ballgame of the season, a ballgame that scarcely mattered. In Eddie Mathews' first (and only) full season as manager, the Braves were ensconced in fifth place in the NL West, a notch below the Astros. The game's significance lay in Hank Aaron's possibilities—he entered the game with 712 home runs, two short of tying The Babe. The potential importance of this event was evidenced in two ways: a special VIP box next to the Braves' dugout contained 15 members of Aaron's family, and 17,836 fans had paid for admission into the stadium, meaning the park was uncustomarily only two-thirds empty.

The game matched pitcher Carl Morton of Atlanta against lefthander Jerry Reuss of Houston. Aaron had hit nine home runs in games Morton pitched this year; Reuss had allowed the first home run Aaron hit under the Mathews managership, back in August of 1972. Both facts were prophetic.

Reuss barely survived the first inning. With one out, Mike Lum doubled. A minute later he scored on Darrell Evans' 41st home run of the year. Evans had never hit 20 before that season, but he credited Mathews with teaching him to pull the ball and making him "a major leaguer." Aaron, batting cleanup, ripped a single to left field. The southpaw survived the inning, though, then carefully pitched around Aaron the next time by walking him in the third.

The score stayed 2-0 until the Braves exploded in the fifth inning. With one run in on an error, Mike Lum on third, and Evans on first, Aaron faced Reuss for the third time. Reuss' first pitch to The Hammer was a slow curve down around the knees, out of the strike zone. Baseball's most productive pair of wrists went down after the ball and propelled a towering fly ball far over the left-centerfield fence. The ball bounced against the huge message board that lit up the number of Aaron's home run—"713." Aaron said later he had guessed it would be a slow curve; as so many times before, Aaron was right.

While Aaron assumed his customary stiff-legged home-run trot, the crowd (mini-crowd) erupted in a standing ovation that continued long after Aaron completed his circuit and returned to the dugout. Aaron's jubilant teammates finally pushed the slugger out of the dugout to acknowledge the fans' cheering with several modest waves of his cap. Aaron's blast, his 40th of the season, established for the Braves a measure of home run slugging never achieved before or since: three teammates hitting 40 or more homers in the same season (Davey Johnson, 43; Darrell Evans, 41; Hank Aaron, 40).

A few minutes after play resumed, Dusty Baker completed the attack on Reuss by homering to make the score 7-0. Reuss then relieved his frustration in the time-honored way—by drilling next batter Davey Johnson in the back with a fastball. Umpire Satch Davidson assessed an immediate fine against Reuss, who finished the inning and then hit the showers $50 poorer.

In the seventh inning Aaron received one chance to tie Ruth. Against righthanded reliever Larry Dierker, Aaron worked the count to 3-2 before looping a single into short left field. That left the record safe for at least another day. The next day the Braves' star faced Dave Roberts in the season's final contest in front of the largest Atlanta crowd of the year, but he could produce only three singles in his four at-bats. With six hits in the final two ballgames, Aaron raised his season average to .301 (up from .255 at the All-Star break). He left himself six months, however, to agonize over the dramatic breaking of Ruth's magic 714 mark.

After the finale the sportswriters asked Eddie Mathews if he had considered having Aaron lead off in the final games of the year to give him a few extra times at bat. "No," Mathews said, "I haven't even thought of it. Hank hasn't wanted anything like that. We've just played the game as it was meant to be played."

Then he added, "Hank will get number 714 and number 715 and I don't know how many more. It'll be a great way for us to start out next season with a better ballclub."

September 29, 1973

HOUSTON	AB	R	H	BI	ATLANTA	AB	R	H	BI
Gross, rf	4	0	0	0	Perez, ss	5	1	1	0
Metzger, ss	4	0	0	0	Lum, rf	4	2	2	0
Cedeno, cf	2	0	1	0	Evans, 3b	4	2	2	2
Gallagher, cf	2	0	1	0	Aaron, lf	3	1	3	3
Watson, lf	4	0	0	0	Baker, cf	4	1	2	1
Rader, 3b	4	0	0	0	Johnson, 2b	2	0	0	0
May, 1b	3	0	1	0	Dietz, 1b	3	0	0	0
Sutherland, 2b	2	0	1	0	Tepedino, 1b	0	0	0	0
Jutze, c	3	0	0	0	Casanova, c	4	0	0	0
Reuss, p	2	0	1	0	Morton, p	4	0	0	0
Dierker, p	0	0	0	0					
Stewart, ph	1	0	1	0					
Upshaw, p	0	0	0	0					
Totals	31	0	6	0	Totals	33	7	10	6

```
Houston  ..................... 0 0 0   0 0 0   0 0 0--0
ATLANTA  ..................... 2 0 0   0 5 0   0 0 *--7
```

E--Casanova, Johnson, May. 2B--Lum, Baker, Sutherland, Perez. HR--Evans (41), Aaron (40), Baker (21). Left--Houston 5, Atlanta 6. DP--Houston 1, Atlanta 3. SB--Cedeno.

	IP	H	R	ER	BB	SO
Reuss (L, 16-13)	5	9	7	7	2	4
Dierker	2	1	0	0	1	3
Upshaw	1	0	0	0	0	0
Morton (W, 15-10)	9	6	0	0	1	3

HBP--By Reuss, Johnson. T--2:11. A--17, 836.

TWENTY-TWO

On the Road

I went home and the phone started ringing. I said, "This is for the birds." I called an old, old friend of mine that I'd played with when I was with the Crackers--Whitlow Wyatt. He had a farm about 40 miles out of Atlanta.

"Have you got room for a beat-up old third baseman and his wife for a few days?" (I had remarried several years earlier.)

"Sure," he said, "come on over."

We spent three days with Whitlow, three relaxing days where the sportswriters couldn't find me. Then I went back to Atlanta to pack up my stuff at the ballpark and get it out of the way. I had a message to go upstairs and see the front office-- Eddie Robinson.

"We'd like to keep you, Eddie," he said. "We'd like to give you an opportunity to stay in the organization."

They offered me two different choices. The first one was, the group that owned the Braves also owned a sporting goods company. I could have sold sporting goods in the Southeast. I had tried selling, though, and I knew it wasn't for me. The other choice was to become a scout.

I said, "Well, I think I'm going to move back to California."

Robinson said, "You can have a scouting job, southern California and Arizona." I went to work as a scout.

I became what they call a free agent scout, high schools and colleges. I didn't mind it, but it was a lot of work. In southern California I would go to maybe three games a day. The scouts out there were super good to me. I didn't know how to scout. I mean, I knew what to look for in a ballplayer, but I did

319

not know the mechanics of the job. I had this list of ballgames with me, and I'd always sit with the other scouts in the stands--all of us together--and they'd tell me, "Better get over here and see so-and-so," or "Don't worry about him." All the scouts help each other out in that respect.

Scouting involved an awful lot of traveling, especially since I had Arizona too. In southern California they play both day and night games, so what the scouts do is watch maybe three or four innings and see what they want to see, and if it's impressive enough, they'll make a point of going back. Then at night they'll go to another game. It took me a little time to get adjusted to it.

I found a kid from Dos Pueblos High School near Santa Barbara. His name was Donnie Young. This kid could catch, he could play first base, he could play the outfield, and he had a good arm. He was no Ted Williams; he was just the best I could find in the southern California area. I knew he wouldn't be a top draft choice. I figured he might fit in somewhere down our list, though, maybe in the third or fourth round. When we went back for the draft, all of the scouts were in there evaluating, and I said, "Well, I think he's available, and he's the best one that I've seen around here."

We made up a list of guys we were going to draft, and Donnie Young was about 16th on our list. On draft day all the teams got hooked up by telephone on a big conference call. Everybody could talk and everybody else could hear them. I think that was the first year they tried that. The Angels drafted first, and then the Padres, and so on according to their number. By the time the Braves got to make their pick, it was the 18th round and all of our top choices had been taken. I mean all of them. The highest person left on our list was Donnie Young. It put me in a spot.

"You're kidding me!" I said. "I never meant that he should be the number one choice in our organization."

But that's what happened. Now they sent me back out to Santa Barbara to sign him. I went to his house--I knew his parents anyhow--and would you believe it, he had an agent. I think it was a relative, but I'm not sure.

"Well, Donnie," I said, "you're number one." I explained to him that we didn't intend for him to be number one, but that's the way things worked out. Naturally his parents and everybody around there were as excited as hell--he was the

320

number one draft choice of the Atlanta Braves.

I said to the parents, "I guess we ought to talk money. I think because of the circumstances we'd probably be talking in the $30,000 range."

His agent said, "Thirty thousand? He's a first round draft choice. We're talking $100,000."

I said, "That's out of the question. I explained how this happened. I have a lot of respect for Donnie and I don't want to put him down, but.... Let me go back to the room and I'll call my boss and see what he says."

I called my boss, Eddie Robinson, and he asked me what I thought. I said, "If it were me, I'd go $40,000, but I wouldn't go any higher."

He said, "I think we should go that way."

I went back the next day and I said, "I got him to offer $40,000 in bonus."

The agent and the parents said, "We can't accept that."

I said, "Well, I can understand that. Maybe he's better off going to college and playing there. If he has a show there, maybe he can get more." I got up to leave, and I said, "Oh, by the way. Have you got a bat here?" They brought one out. "You've got a little thing you're doing," I said, "that you want to try to correct." He was breaking his front knee down instead of hitting against it. I said, "Work on that. I think it'll help you. I'm sorry we didn't work things out."

As I got to my car, the door of the house opened and a voice yelled, "Eddie, wait a minute." The dad and the agent said, "We'll take it."

I said, "I think you're doing the smart thing. If he doesn't really have an interest in college, he's got an opportunity in baseball to do well. That's my feeling."

We signed and I took him back to Atlanta for a tryout and to show him off to the front office and the sportswriters. He went to the Class A farm club and lasted a year and a half before he quit. Evidently he just couldn't hack it. It wasn't because of his ability--it was the lifestyle and everything that went with it. Some guys aren't cut out for it.

After scouting for the Braves for a year or so, I got a phone call one day from the Milwaukee Brewers. They had gotten permission from the Braves to talk to me, which they had to do, and they offered me a three-year contract for quite a bit more money than I was making with the Braves. The

Brewers wanted me to be kind of an advance scout and work with the general manager and work with the hitters in spring training. The Braves didn't mind and the money was good, so I said, "Sure."

With the Brewers I was doing a little bit of everything. Jim Baumer was the general manager there, and he talked about me going back to Milwaukee as his righthand man, his assistant. I sold my house in Westlake Village, near the Santa Monica Mountains north of Los Angeles, that I had bought when I was scouting for the Braves. I went over to Arizona to work with the kids as a hitting instructor for the instructional league. My wife went back to West Virginia to stay with her parents for a little while. Then I went to spring training with the Brewers, near Phoenix, to work with the hitters.

During spring training I was staying in a motel there. One day the phone rang, and it was Jim Baumer.

"Eddie," he said, "we're going to make some changes. Would you consider managing the Brewers?"

I didn't have to think about it for very long. "No," I told him. I had learned my lesson. I had never really wanted to manage, and my experience with the Braves reinforced that opinion. "Thanks for asking, but I really don't want to."

About two days later I got another call, from Baumer again. "Eddie, if we got Hank Aaron to manage, would you coach?"

This time I didn't have to think about it at all. "Yes, I would." Hank didn't have any experience as a manager, and I knew if he took the job he'd need somebody he could trust.

About two days later Baumer called me again. "Hank won't take the job either." It stayed like that. Baumer said, "Stick around there and do some scouting. When we need you, we'll give you a call and you can come to Milwaukee."

I bought a house in Scottsdale, and then my wife came back out there. We lived there for about a year, I guess. I ran around looking at the ballclubs and scouting in Arizona. But I never did get back to Milwaukee. Baumer got fired, and after about a year in Scottsdale I said, "To hell with this." I sold the house, got a divorce from Sue, and moved to San Diego. I didn't do anything except scout for the Brewers then, Arizona and southern California. At the end of my three years, the Brewers didn't renew my contract.

In the winter before my last year working for the

Brewers, I received the greatest honor of my baseball life. After a five-year wait, I was voted into the Baseball Hall of Fame in Cooperstown. To tell the truth, I thought it was overdue. I'm not saying I was the greatest ballplayer that ever lived because I wasn't. If you look at the records, though, Ernie Banks and I had almost identical careers. We hit the same number of home runs, and our batting averages were nearly the same. Ernie, though, was voted into the Hall of Fame his first year that he was eligible. With everything he accomplished, he certainly deserved it. But with the same numbers Ernie had, I was passed over four times. The year before, when Ernie was voted in and I was second in the voting but came up short, Ernie called me. He said, "Eddie, I'm sorry you didn't make it, but we'll get you in next year." That was funny. It was nice of him to call, and he was right--I did get in the next year.

Maybe I didn't get along with the sportswriters who were voting as well as Ernie did. In fact I know I didn't, which may have had something to do with my being passed over. Also for quite a few years it seemed like they hesitated to put in more than one player at a time, and some years nobody made it. In 1978 when I was voted in, I was the only one who went in who was alive. Larry MacPhail and Addie Joss also were inducted that year, but they were both dead and neither was voted in by the baseball writers. I was the only one. Only one third baseman was voted in before me, and that was Pie Traynor 30 years earlier. Plus a lot of great ballplayers had to wait years to get voted in, guys like Rogers Hornsby and Joe DiMaggio. Even so, I was disappointed that it took me five years.

The results of the voting for the Hall of Fame are always announced in New York in January. They called me in California and told me to be ready to take a red-eye special to be there for the press conference if I made it. They knew the results, but they wouldn't give them out. I said, "Forget this baloney. I'm going to New York for the announcement. If I don't make it, I don't make it." I was married then to Liz Busch. She was at her farm in Virginia at the time, so I flew there first and we flew up to New York together.

Liz, of course, was the daughter of August Anheuser Busch, Jr., the owner of the St. Louis Cardinals and the man who turned a small family business into the biggest brewery in the world. Before we left Virginia, she called her brother, Augie the third, and he made the reservation for us at the Waldorf

Astoria. I'm not sure why he did it instead of her--I guess he had more clout, plus he was going to pay for it. It wasn't like she couldn't afford it, though; she was an heir to the family fortune herself, worth who-knows-how-many millions. We had a pre-nuptial agreement that separated our finances, so I never concerned myself with the numbers. Really, the difference in our economic classes was the reason our marriage only lasted a couple years. We didn't have any particular problem between us, but we moved in different social circles. We had very little in common.

When we got to the reservation desk at the Waldorf, I said, "I'm Eddie Mathews, and this is my wife, Elizabeth Mathews." She always called herself Elizabeth Busch Mathews.

The guy behind the desk said, "I'm sorry, but we don't have a reservation in that name."

I tried to explain that Augie Busch had made the reservation for us, but they weren't buying that. They couldn't make the connection between his name and mine. That's when Liz got a little haughty and said, "I'm Elizabeth Busch, and my brother made this reservation, and if you don't get our bags up to that room immediately..." She had to get a little nasty and then show them some ID. They apologized and showed us to our suite. They still didn't trust us, though.

That night we were asleep in bed when we were awak-ened by somebody knocking on the door. It was midnight, and here were two house detectives with the hotel manager pound-ing on the door. They gave us some cockeyed story about the previous guest in our room leaving some diamonds. Well, we didn't believe that for a second--I mean, the room had been cleaned--but these guys went through the motions of searching the room. What they were doing was checking us out. They must have thought we were imposters trying to rip somebody off in the hotel. It was some night.

At the time we checked into the hotel I still didn't know if I had made the Hall of Fame or not. So who gave me the news? My mother. She was living with us in California at that time. When the call came through from New York, she was there to take it. I called her, and she told me I had made it. She also told me where to go the next morning for the press conference, which was the Americana Hotel. They made the official announcement, and then it was just a formality of waiting until August for the induction ceremony.

When you get to Cooperstown, it's a totally different atmosphere, particularly on the night of the banquet. They have just the Hall of Famers there for dinner, along with the Commissioner and the two league presidents, in a private room. It's a humbling experience to be sitting down to dinner in the company of people like Stan Musial and Joe DiMaggio and Ted Williams. You begin to realize what an honor this is.

At the ceremony in the afternoon, sitting under those trees on that platform, my mind was mostly on the little speech I had to give. Bowie Kuhn was the master of ceremonies. About 20 or 25 Hall of Famers from previous years were there: Musial, Roy Campanella, Ernie Banks, plus some of the old-time ballplayers that I didn't know at all. They also presented awards to two famous announcers, Red Barber and Mel Allen.

When it was my turn to speak, I said, "I'm glad Mel Allen and Red Barber are here to do the talking because this beat-up old third baseman isn't going to give you much."

I told the story of my mom pitching to me and making me a pull hitter. That got a big laugh. I also said, "I'm just a small part of a wonderful game that is a tremendous part of American life. Baseball has been so good to me. Everything I've got I owe to baseball. I always tried to give it all I had."

Finally, I told them, "Being chosen for the Hall of Fame is the greatest honor of my career." It wasn't an original thought, but it was sincere. After that I let Mel Allen talk. How 'bout that!

I finished up the 1978 season scouting for the Brewers and then spent a year out of baseball. I was looking for a job, and of all people, the person that hired me was Eddie Robinson--the guy who had fired me in Atlanta. He had been fired himself by the Braves, but he hooked on with the Texas Rangers. He hired me for Texas, but that only lasted a year. Then Corbett, the owner, decided to sell the ballclub to Eddie Chiles, and when Chiles came in, he cleaned house.

I kind of had an inkling when I saw they were going to change ownerships. Then I ran into Billy Martin in Texas when he was down there with the A's to play the Rangers. Billy was the manager and general manager of Oakland at that point. We went out after the ballgame and had a drink.

I said, "You know, I'm gonna get fired."

Billy said, "You've got a job if you want one."

"Well, I might need one," I told him.

The Rangers let me go and I called Billy, and he gave me a job. He said, "Come down to spring training and we'll do all the paperwork down there." He told me how much I was going to make. I went down and stayed with the club through spring training. Then he wanted me to do advance scouting for him, so I did that for maybe a month into the season.

Billy was riding high. He was head honcho, both general manager and manager. Spring training was a blast. All the ballplayers loved him. Everybody loved him. It was a neat organization. But Billy started to pull some of his tricks, and then the strike came. When that happened, he said, "Come on, we're all going to Hawaii." He took me and his coaches--about ten of us--over to Hawaii for a damn week. That was another wild time. I think we saw one minor league ballgame that whole week. Billy had an unlimited expense account, or at least it looked like it to me. He could get away with stuff like that, though, because the A's were winning. They were just awful the year before Billy got there. Then Charlie Finley hired Billy and they finished second, although Finley sold the club to the Levi Strauss people before the season was over. In the strike season the A's finished in first place for the first half of the year. Everything was great.

In 1982 it all started to fall apart. The club wasn't winning, and Billy wasn't getting along with the owners. He wanted a contract extension, plus he was having trouble with the IRS that he wanted the club owners to take care of, but they refused. Everything came to a head in August after a game the A's lost to the Milwaukee Brewers. I had watched from the stands; I was scouting then. After the game I went down to Billy's office, which I often did. When I got there, Billy was going nuts. He took his office and absolutely, totally destroyed it. He had a refrigerator in there--he tipped that thing over. He broke the walls. He smashed whatever he could get his hands on. I think they ended up with about $10,000 worth of damage. Billy said, "I finally learned to punch something that won't sue me." Two months later the A's fired him with two years to go on his contract.

Billy was a funny guy. He could go a year or two and really do a number. But then after that he started---I don't say losing control, but getting too out of line. The ownership or the front office decided they just couldn't control him. He was like that everywhere he went--Minnesota, Detroit, New York, Texas, Oakland. But he was one of my closest friends, and a damn good manager. He could bring it out in ballplayers if anybody could. He was a feisty little guy, and he would never back down. He was a winner.

I stayed with Oakland for one more year after Billy left. Then they called me and said, "We're not renewing your contract." They did an amazing thing, though. They paid me for the following year when I wasn't even working for them. That's the first time in baseball that's happened. That might be a Guinness Book of Records deal. They were good people to work for, the Levi Strauss people.

After that I was out of baseball about four years. I went to Atlanta to play in an old-timers' game. Out of the blue, Bobby Cox said to me, "We'd like to have you come to work for us."

I said, "Doing what?"

He said, "We'd like you to come down to spring training for two or three weeks, be in the instructional league for two-three weeks, be around the ballplayers, do some hitting instruction, and what have you."

"Well, okay," I said. I told him what I thought I needed in terms of money, and he agreed. I went to work for the Atlanta Braves again.

As it turned out, the job was a lot more involved than Cox had said. I was in spring training damn near six weeks. They asked me to start doing some hitting instruction with their minor league clubs, which were Richmond, Greenville, and Durham. I didn't get home all summer. Then they wanted me to come back down for instructional league, which was another four or five weeks. I was gone the better part of the year. I stayed in that until they didn't renew my contract.

In all I spent about ten years in baseball as a scout plus I don't know how many as a minor league hitting instructor. After all those years, one thing I can say for sure is that the attitude of a lot of kids has changed, for whatever reason. It's not just in baseball or in sports, but in everything. I've never done anything to try to hurt a kid in baseball when I was instructing him. I think I was a good hitting instructor. Other people told me that, and I believe that. But in the last ten or fifteen years, when you try to show a kid something and say, "This will help you," he seems to resent it for some reason. He wants to do it on his own--he wants to do it his way or no way. I

327

The wise old hitting instructor, 1987. (Atlanta Journal-Constitution)

don't know why.

Up to a point I can understand it. I was pretty much natural in my hitting. I would listen, though, and appreciate when someone tried to help me, and I would try what they suggested, like when Paul Waner worked with me with the Braves. Today's kids have a tendency to say, "Forget you, I'm going to be a great hitter doing it my way."

I worked with a lot of kids. I worked with Jose Canseco when he was scared to even open his mouth, when I was with Billy Martin at Oakland. They called from Miami and said, "We've got a kid here that might be able to play. Would you work with him?"

Canseco at that time was a skinny kid, tall and gawky, but the minute I saw him swing a bat, I knew he would be a hitter. He needed some polish or refinement, or at least something that would get him going quicker than just throwing him down in the low minors. We took him to instructional league the year I was in charge of it and we worked with him. He came on real fast. But there was never any doubt that he would make it. He could run, he could throw--he even looked good in the lobby. And because he was so shy in those days, he didn't resent what you said to help him, unlike most kids.

Of course, as the roving hitting instructor with the Atlanta Braves' minor league clubs, I worked with quite a few of the ballplayers from their pennant-winning teams of the early nineties, some good young players. I worked with David Justice, Jeff Blauser, Ron Gant, and so forth. Then at the start of 1989 the Braves thought my drinking was getting a little out of hand. They gave me an ultimatum--they said if I didn't go into a detox center, they wouldn't renew my contract. So I went into a detox center for a month down in West Palm Beach. I wanted one more year in baseball, so I went along with their ultimatum and got myself clean. After a whole month in the drunk tank, I came out and had a very dry martini. I worked for the Braves for one more year, but I was still drinking. I was going out to the ballpark and doing what I was supposed to do, but I was still drinking. They didn't renew my contract again, so I hung them up.

I have been a drinker all my life. There's no question about that. I love it. I enjoy bars and I enjoy drinking. It's just been a way of life with me since I was old enough to drink legally, or actually a little before. Like anything, it can progress

329

if you let it, but when I was playing ball, it stayed fairly level. Then as I took the uniform off, it started getting a little worse. Now that I'm retired, if I feel like having a drink in the morning, I'll have one. If I feel like having one in the afternoon, I'll have one. Booze has never gotten to the point where I don't fulfill commitments or do what I'm supposed to do.

I have never wanted to quit drinking. I'd like to quit smoking, but not drinking. I guess the average person would consider me an alcoholic. I saw that list of ten questions, and if you answer any of them yes, they consider you an alcoholic. So I'm considered an alcoholic, but I don't really feel like I am. I just enjoy drinking. I enjoy the social life of it. Maybe it's hereditary. My dad was an alcoholic--no doubt about it. He had little bottles hidden all over the house.

I don't know how to explain why I enjoy drinking so much. It's really not the taste. Maybe it's the feeling. Or maybe it's more of a habit. My friends all drink. I think the way it got started--and this isn't an alibi or anything--but when you travel in strange towns, which I've done all my life, you don't know where to go or what to do. That's I think why so many athletes drink, and sportswriters too. Total non-drinkers were unusual. Probably half the ballplayers drank but not heavily. The other half were good drinkers. On the Braves, the best ballplayers were mostly the best drinkers. And if you go back 40, 50, 60 years, some of those guys were heavy duty--Ruth, Foxx, Hack Wilson, Paul Waner. Those guys were legendary, on and off the field.

Drinking did not affect my playing career. When I say drinking, I'm talking about after a game, or during the winter. During the season, we'd get out of the ballgame, get showered and shaved and back to the hotel, and it was usually 11:00 o'clock at night by then. We had an hour or two or three to go out and party or play. That's what we did. I don't know what guys do now after the game. Society has changed. I don't relate to cocaine or marijuana or steroids or pep pills. We didn't have any of that crazy stuff.

Up until I was about 33, I was strictly a beer drinker. Then I roomed for a little bit with Danny Osinski. He was a martini drinker. He told me, "You oughtta drink martinis--or vodka. You oughtta drink vodka. Nobody can smell it."

What I say to that is, "You can't smell it, but you lose your wife, you lose your house, you lose your money, you lose

330

your job; but nobody can smell it."

Speaking of losing jobs, I did. Drinking was a big contributing factor in my losing the manager's job in Atlanta. No question about it, along with an assist from Clyde King. The next one was the job in Oakland. The other one, of course, was the last one working for Atlanta's minor league clubs. I was ready to hang it up after that anyway, but to be completely honest, drinking probably cost me three different baseball jobs. It's not a good habit, and I wouldn't recommend it for anybody. I don't feel I'm a bad guy, though, just because I drink. It's my life. That's just me. I'm still trying to learn to spell "moderation."

As far as my life, I've been blessed. I've got three great kids, all of them doing well, and seven wonderful grandkids. I've been lucky as far as the people I've known and the ballplayers I played with and against. It was a privilege to play ball with someone like Hank Aaron because he's a legend. There's no question about that. My proudest accomplishment in baseball was the record he and I set, 863 home runs as teammates. Then I was fortunate to be his manager when he broke Ruth's record. Most of all, though, I'm proud to call Hank my friend.

Life has been good. Despite three divorces, I have all the money I'll ever need--not like today's millionaires, but all I need. I have always been very financially conservative. I'll spend money in a bar, but as far as gambling it away, that never happened. I was never a high roller. I never had to support an agent, either. I have a wonderful wife, Judy, who helps me enjoy life. We take our RV down to Mexico or to various other places, and we live the way we want to live. I do a little gardening, and when I feel like it, I sign autographs at baseball card shows around the country. I still enjoy talking baseball with people. Amazingly, I still get five or ten letters a day from fans--and I haven't played baseball in over 25 years.

My health is pretty good. You could say I'm in good shape for the shape I'm in, but you can't grow old and be a sissy. If I "went south" tomorrow, though, I'd go with no regrets. My only request is that, when it's my time, I want a couple weeks just to apologize to everybody.

EDDIE MATHEWS' HOME RUN CHRONICLE
(Source: Society for American Baseball Research)

HR #	DATE (G)	PITCHER (Team)	SITE	INN.	ON
1	4-19-52	Ken Heintzelman (Phi)	PHI	8	2
2	4-23-52	Hoyt Wilhelm (NY)	NY	6	1
3	4-30-52	Murry Dickson (Pit)	PIT	5	0
4	5-04-52 (1)	Gerry Staley (StL)	StL	1	0
5	5-04-52 (2)	Cliff Chambers (StL)	StL	9	0
6	5-10-52	Jim Hearn (NY)	BOS	4	0
7	5-13-52	Howie Pollet (Pit)	BOS	1	0
8	6-01-52 (2)	Harry Perkowski (Cin)	CIN	4	0
9	6-06-52	Turk Lown (Chi)	CHI	9	0
10	6-15-52 (1)	Paul Minner (Chi)	BOS	6	0
11	6-19-52	Bubba Church (Cin)	BOS	2	0
12	6-23-52	Bob Friend (Pit)	BOS	6	0
13	7-01-52	Hal Gregg (NY)	BOS	5	0
14	7-04-52 (1)	Karl Drews (Phi)	BOS	11	0
15	7-20-52	Wilmer Mizell (StL)	StL	5	2
16	7-24-52	Turk Lown (Chi)	BOS	1	0
17	7-30-52	Joe Presko (StL)	BOS	4	1
18	8-13-52 (2)	Jim Konstanty (Phi)	PHI	8	0
19	8-27-52	Bubba Church (Cin)	CIN	3	1
20	9-03-52	Preacher Roe (Bro)	BOS	2	0
21	9-06-52 (1)	Robin Roberts (Phi)	PHI	8	0
22	9-14-52 (1)	Johnny Klippstein (Chi)	BOS	9	0
23	9-27-52	Joe Black (Bro)	BRO	3	1
24	9-27-52	Ben Wade (Bro)	BRO	6	0
25	9-27-52	Ben Wade (Bro)	BRO	8	0
26	4-17-53	Howie Judson (Cin)	CIN	1	1
27	4-22-53	Bob Rush (Chi)	CHI	3	2
28	4-22-53	Johnny Klippstein (Chi)	CHI	4	1
29	4-23-53	Warren Hacker (Chi)	CHI	4	0
30	4-25-53	Herm Wehmeier (Cin)	MIL	1	1
31	4-25-53	Herm Wehmeier (Cin)	CIN	5	1
32	5-13-53	Dave Koslo (NY)	MIL	1	0
33	5-23-53	Paul Minner (Chi)	CHI	5	1
34	5-25-53 (2)	Harry Perkowski (Cin)	MIL	1	2
35	5-25-53 (2)	Herm Wehmeier (Cin)	MIL	4	1
36	5-29-53	Gerry Staley (StL)	StL	7	0
37	5-30-53 (2)	Jack Faszholz (StL)	StL	5	1
38	5-31-53 (1)	Bubba Church (Cin)	CIN	1	1
39	5-31-53 (2)	Harry Perkowski (Cin)	CIN	4	0
40	6-03-53	Joe Black (Bro)	BRO	5	1
41	6-07-53 (1)	Steve Ridzik (Phi)	PHI	3	0
42	6-08-53	Al Corwin (NY)	NY	8	1
43	6-10-53	Jim Hearn (NY)	NY	1	0
44	6-12-53 (1)	Murry Dickson (Pit)	PIT	6	0
45	6-16-53 (1)	Steve Ridzik (Phi)	MIL	6	1
46	6-30-53 (2)	Jackie Collum (Cin)	CIN	8	1
47	6-30-53 (2)	Jackie Collum (Cin)	CIN	10	1
48	7-01-53	Joe Nuxhall (Cin)	CIN	3	1
49	7-05-53 (1)	Gerry Staley (StL)	MIL	5	1
50	7-07-53	Turk Lown (Chi)	MIL	6	0
51	7-10-53	Alpha Brazle (StL)	StL	5	1
52	7-12-53 (1)	Gerry Staley (StL)	StL	2	3
53	7-18-53	Jim Waugh (Pit)	PIT	1	0
54	7-21-53 (2)	Steve Ridzik (Phi)	PHI	9	0
55	7-24-53	Billy Loes (Bro)	BRO	5	1
56	7-27-53	Al Corwin (NY)	MIL	4	3
57	7-27-53	Monte Kennedy (NY)	MIL	8	0
58	8-01-53	Karl Drews (Phi)	MIL	8	0
59	8-06-53 (1)	Billy Loes (Bro)	MIL	1	0
60	8-08-53	Bob Hall (Pit)	MIL	4	1
61	8-09-53 (1)	Paul LaPalme (Pit)	MIL	5	0
62	8-14-53	Warren Hacker (Chi)	CHI	1	0
63	8-18-53	Bob Kelly (Cin)	CIN	6	1
64	8-21-53	Turk Lown Chi	MIL	8	0
65	8-25-53 (1)	Robin Roberts (Phi)	PHI	1	0
66	8-30-53 (1)	Johnny Lindell (Pit)	PIT	3	0

HR #	DATE (G)	PITCHER (Team)	SITE	INN.	ON
67	8-30-53 (1)	Roger Bowman (Pit)	PIT	8	2
68	8-30-53 (2)	Paul LaPalme (Pit)	PIT	3	1
69	9-03-53	Carl Erskine (Bro)	BRO	8	2
70	9-06-53 (1)	Joe Presko (StL)	MIL	1	0
71	9-16-53	Roy Face (Pit)	MIL	1	1
72	9-22-53 (1)	Stu Miller (StL)	StL	3	0
73	4-13-54	Joe Nuxhall (Cin)	CIN	6	0
74	4-13-54	Joe Nuxhall (Cin)	CIN	8	0
75	4-21-54	Johnny Klippstein (Chi)	MIL	5	2
76	4-25-54	Alpha Brazle (StL)	StL	9	1
77	5-05-54	Jake Thies (Pit)	MIL	7	0
78	5-12-54	Don Newcombe (Bro)	BRO	1	0
79	5-19-54	Murry Dickson (Phi)	PHI	7	1
80	5-22-54 (2)	Warren Hacker (Chi)	CHI	1	1
81	6-02-54	Bob Milliken (Bro)	MIL	4	3
82	6-06-54 (2)	Jake Thies (Pit)	MIL	3	3
83	6-07-54	Marv Grissom (NY)	MIL	8	0
84	6-17-54	Johnny Podres (Bro)	BRO	3	1
85	6-25-54	Steve Ridzik (Phi)	PHI	9	0
86	6-29-54	Paul Minner (Chi)	MIL	4	0
87	7-02-54 (1)	Corky Valentine (Cin)	MIL	7	0
88	7-02-54 (1)	Jackie Collum (Cin)	MIL	8	1
89	7-05-54 (1)	Brooks Lawrence (StL)	StL	2	0
90	7-05-54 (1)	Cot Deal (StL)	StL	7	0
91	7-09-54	Bud Podbielan (Cin)	CIN	9	1
92	7-15-54 (1)	Bob Milliken (Bro)	MIL	7	1
93	7-15-54 (2)	Billy Loes (Bro)	MIL	1	1
94	7-21-54	Robin Roberts (Phi)	MIL	9	0
95	7-22-54	Murry Dickson (Phi)	MIL	1	1
96	7-23-54	Ruben Gomez (NY)	MIL	4	0
97	7-24-54	Don Liddle (NY)	MIL	3	1
98	7-31-54	Don Newcombe (Bro)	BRO	1	0
99	7-31-54	Erv Palica (Bro)	BRO	3	0
100	8-01-54	Clem Labine (Bro)	BRO	5	2
101	8-07-54	Ruben Gomez (NY)	NY	3	0
102	8-08-54	Sal Maglie (NY)	NY	8	0
103	8-10-54	Ben Wade (StL)	StL	6	0
104	8-11-54	Brooks Lawrence (StL)	StL	5	1
105	9-05-54 (2)	Bud Podbielan (Cin)	CIN	3	0
106	9-05-54 (2)	Bud Podbielan (Cin)	CIN	7	1
107	9-06-54 (1)	Johnny Klippstein (Chi)	MIL	3	0
108	9-08-54	Dick Littlefield (Pit)	PIT	3	1
109	9-16-54 (2)	Marv Grissom (NY)	NY	6	0
110	9-19-54	Brooks Lawrence (StL)	StL	1	0
111	9-19-54	Alpha Brazle (StL)	StL	4	0
112	9-25-54	Joe Presko (StL)	MIL	8	1
113	5-01-55	Billy Loes (Bro)	BRO	3	1
114	5-08-55	Barney Schultz (StL)	StL	7	1
115	5-11-55	Ron Kline (Pit)	MIL	3	2
116	5-14-55	Jack Meyer (Phi)	MIL	5	0
117	5-15-55 (1)	Herm Wehmeier (Phi)	MIL	4	0
118	5-15-55 (1)	Herm Wehmeier (Phi)	MIL	5	2
119	6-02-55	Billy Loes (Bro)	BRO	8	0
120	6-04-55	Bob Kuzava (Phi)	PHI	3	1
121	6-05-55 (1)	Robin Roberts (Phi)	PHI	1	0
122	6-05-55 (1)	Robin Roberts (Phi)	PHI	3	0
123	6-06-55	Dave Cole (Phi)	PHI	1	1
124	6-11-55	Bob Friend (Pit)	PIT	4	0
125	6-13-55	Gerry Staley (Cin)	CIN	1	0
126	6-14-55	Robin Roberts (Phi)	MIL	8	1
127	6-21-55	Ron Kline (Pit)	MIL	3	1
128	6-24-55	Carl Erskine (Bro)	MIL	1	0
129	6-26-55	Jim Hughes (Bro)	MIL	8	2
130	6-29-55	Howie Pollet (Chi)	MIL	1	1
131	7-03-55	Joe Nuxhall (Cin)	CIN	3	1
132	7-04-55 (1)	Tom Poholsky (StL)	MIL	1	0
133	7-06-55	Bob Rush (Chi)	CHI	3	1
134	7-08-55 (1)	Art Fowler (Cin)	MIL	6	1
135	7-19-55	Vern Law (Pit)	PIT	1	0
136	7-20-55	Max Surkont (Pit)	PIT	6	1
137	7-28-55	Murry Dickson (Phi)	MIL	5	0
138	7-30-55	Ramon Monzant (NY)	MIL	7	0
139	8-01-55	Billy Loes (Bro)	MIL	6	0
140	8-02-55	Roger Craig (Bro)	MIL	1	0
141	8-02-55	Roger Craig (Bro)	MIL	8	1
142	8-13-55	Sam Jones (Chi)	CHI	1	1

HR #	DATE (G)	PITCHER (Team)	SITE	INN.	ON
143	8-15-55	Willard Schmidt (StL)	StL	1	1
144	8-17-55	Luis Arroyo (StL)	StL	3	1
145	8-23-55	Murry Dickson (Phi)	PHI	1	1
146	8-28-55 (1)	Dick Hall (Pit)	PIT	4	0
147	8-31-55	Carl Erskine (Bro)	BRO	3	1
148	9-04-55	Johnny Klippstein (Cin)	MIL	3	0
149	9-10-55	Vern Law (Pit)	MIL	1	1
150	9-10-55	Vern Law (Pit)	MIL	4	1
151	9-16-55	Brooks Lawrence (StL)	MIL	1	0
152	9-23-55	Tom Poholsky (StL)	StL	4	0
153	9-24-55	Lindy McDaniel (StL)	StL	3	0
154	4-20-56	Tom Poholsky (StL)	StL	4	0
155	4-20-56	Tom Poholsky (StL)	StL	6	0
156	5-01-56	Murry Dickson (Phi)	MIL	3	1
157	5-12-56	Brooks Lawrence (Cin)	CIN	7	1
158	5-22-56	Clem Labine (Bro)	BRO	7	0
159	5-30-56 (1)	Russ Meyer (Chi)	CHI	1	0
160	5-30-56 (2)	Warren Hacker (Chi)	CHI	6	0
161	5-31-56	Warren Hacker (Chi)	CHI	5	0
162	6-05-56	Roger Craig (Bro)	MIL	1	0
163	6-13-56	Ron Negray (Phi)	MIL	4	1
164	6-22-56	Ruben Gomez (NY)	NY	3	0
165	6-25-56	Stu Miller (Phi)	PHI	4	0
166	7-08-56	Bob Rush (Chi)	MIL	1	1
167	7-15-56 (1)	Laurin Pepper (Pit)	MIL	1	1
168	7-21-56	Harvey Haddix (Phi)	MIL	5	1
169	7-22-56 (1)	Robin Roberts (Phi)	MIL	5	1
170	7-22-56 (2)	Ron Negray (Phi)	MIL	1	2
171	7-25-56	Al Worthington (NY)	NY	4	0
172	7-30-56	Roger Craig (Bro)	BRO	3	0
173	7-31-56	Carl Erskine (Bro)	BRO	9	0
174	8-03-56	Vern Law (Pit)	PIT	2	0
175	8-04-56	Fred Waters (Pit)	PIT	8	1
176	8-05-56 (1)	Gonzalo Naranjo (Pit)	PIT	7	0
177	8-05-56 (2)	Bob Friend (Pit)	PIT	5	1
178	8-11-56	Hal Jeffcoat (Cin)	MIL	3	1
179	8-17-56	Larry Jansen (Cin)	CIN	1	1
180	8-19-56	Tom Acker (Cin)	CIN	6	0
181	8-20-56	Brooks Lawrence (Cin)	CIN	3	1
182	8-21-56 (1)	Ruben Gomez (NY)	MIL	1	2
183	8-24-56	Robin Roberts (Phi)	MIL	7	1
184	8-28-56	Dick Hall (Pit)	MIL	1	1
185	8-28-56	Dick Hall (Pit)	MIL	4	0
186	8-29-56	Vern Law (Pit)	MIL	2	0
187	8-31-56	Herm Wehmeier (StL)	MIL	7	2
188	9-11-56	Sal Maglie (Bro)	BRO	2	0
189	9-17-56 (2)	Marv Grissom (NY)	NY	8	0
190	9-30-56	Wilmer Mizell (StL)	StL	6	1
191	4-24-57	Herm Wehmeier (StL)	StL	5	2
192	5-06-57	Don Drysdale (Bro)	BRO	1	0
193	5-06-57	Don Drysdale (Bro)	BRO	6	0
194	5-10-57	Hoyt Wilhelm (StL)	StL	6	1
195	5-12-57 (2)	Willard Schmidt (StL)	StL	4	2
196	5-16-57	Bob Friend (Pit)	MIL	9	0
197	5-22-57	Robin Roberts (Phi)	MIL	5	2
198	5-26-57 (2)	Elmer Singleton (Chi)	CHI	1	0
199	6-10-57	Don Newcombe (Bro)	BRO	4	1
200	6-12-57	Ed Roebuck (Bro)	BRO	9	1
201	6-20-57	Curt Barclay (NY)	MIL	1	0
202	6-23-57 (2)	Turk Farrell (Phi)	MIL	7	0
203	6-26-57	Don Newcombe (Bro)	MIL	3	2
204	6-26-57	Don Newcombe (Bro)	MIL	5	0
205	6-29-57	Johnny O'Brien (Pit)	MIL	6	0
206	6-30-57 (2)	Luis Arroyo (Pit)	MIL	13	1
207	7-04-57	Tom Acker (Cin)	CIN	6	0
208	7-10-57	Bob Purkey (Pit)	PIT	1	1
209	7-26-57	Ruben Gomez (NY)	MIL	4	0
210	8-04-57	Sal Maglie (Bro)	MIL	1	1
211	8-09-57	Lloyd Merritt (StL)	StL	8	0
212	8-11-57	Willard Schmidt (StL)	StL	5	0
213	8-15-57	Hershell Freeman (Cin)	CIN	5	0
214	8-18-57 (1)	Herm Wehmeier (StL)	MIL	1	0
215	8-27-57	Al Worthington (NY)	NY	6	1
216	8-28-57	Curt Barclay (NY)	NY	3	0
217	8-30-57	Bud Podbielan (Cin)	CIN	1	1
218	8-31-57	Tom Acker (Cin)	CIN	2	1

HR #	DATE (G)	PITCHER (Team)	SITE	INN.	ON
219	9-02-57 (1)	Elmer Singleton (Chi)	CHI	9	1
220	9-04-57	Herm Wehmeier (StL)	StL	5	0
221	9-10-57	Whammy Douglas (Pit)	MIL	4	0
222	9-22-57	Turk Lown (Chi)	CHI	9	0
223	4-15-58	Bob Friend (Pit)	MIL	1	0
224	4-15-58	Bob Friend (Pit)	MIL	3	0
225	4-17-58	Vern Law (Pit)	MIL	5	2
226	4-17-58	Bennie Daniels (Pit)	MIL	7	1
227	4-26-58	Ray Semproch (Phi)	MIL	4	0
228	4-29-58	Dave Hillman (Chi)	CHI	8	1
229	5-03-58	Taylor Phillips (Chi)	CHI	3	2
230	5-17-58	Turk Lown (Cin)	CIN	5	0
231	5-18-58	Bob Purkey (Cin)	CIN	1	0
232	5-23-58	Johnny Antonelli (SF)	MIL	1	0
233	5-26-58	Moe Drabowsky (Chi)	MIL	8	0
234	5-31-58	Ron Kline (Pit)	PIT	1	0
235	6-12-58	Moe Drabowsky (Chi)	CHI	7	0
236	6-20-58	Sam Jones (StL)	MIL	1	1
237	6-24-58	Stu Miller (SF)	MIL	1	0
238	7-01-58	Harvey Haddix (Cin)	MIL	4	0
239	7-11-58	Don Drysdale (LA)	LA	4	0
240	7-16-58	Sam Jones (StL)	StL	1	0
241	7-16-58	Chuck Stobbs (StL)	StL	5	0
242	7-23-58	Larry Jackson (StL)	MIL	2	2
243	7-30-58	Sandy Koufax (LA)	MIL	8	0
244	8-05-58	Ron Kline (Pit)	MIL	3	1
245	8-07-58	Bob Friend (Pit)	MIL	7	1
246	8-09-58	Curt Simmons (Phi)	PHI	5	1
247	8-13-58 (2)	Alex Kellner (Cin)	CIN	6	0
248	8-26-58	Ruben Gomez (SF)	SF	7	0
249	8-26-58	Marv Grissom (SF)	SF	9	0
250	8-29-58	Bob Friend (Pit)	MIL	9	0
251	8-30-58	Curt Raydon (Pit)	MIL	3	1
252	9-06-58	Bob Friend (Pit)	PIT	5	0
253	9-23-58	Jim Owens (Phi)	MIL	1	1
254	4-10-59	Bob Friend (Pit)	PIT	6	1
255	4-11-59	Vern Law (Pit)	PIT	3	0
256	4-16-59	Robin Roberts (Phi)	MIL	6	0
257	4-23-59	Ray Semproch (Phi)	PHI	3	1
258	4-24-59	Don Newcombe (Cin)	CIN	4	0
259	4-24-59	Jim O'Toole (Cin)	CIN	8	3
260	4-25-59	Bob Mabe (Cin)	CIN	9	1
261	5-02-59	Jack Sanford (SF)	MIL	5	1
262	5-04-59	Johnny Podres (LA)	MIL	3	1
263	5-08-59	Brooks Lawrence (Cin)	MIL	8	0
264	5-10-59 (1)	Don Newcombe (Cin)	MIL	1	1
265	5-11-59	Moe Drabowsky (Chi)	CHI	5	0
266	5-12-59	Bob Anderson (Chi)	CHI	5	0
267	5-14-59	Jim Brosnan (StL)	StL	8	0
268	5-27-59	Vern Law (Pit)	MIL	5	0
269	5-30-59	Don Cardwell (Phi)	MIL	3	1
270	6-02-59	Stu Miller (SF)	MIL	1	0
271	6-03-59	Jack Sanford (SF)	MIL	6	1
272	6-03-59	Al Worthington (SF)	MIL	7	1
273	6-08-59	Seth Morehead (Chi)	MIL	3	0
274	6-12-59	John Buzhardt (Chi)	CHI	3	0
275	6-12-59	Bill Henry (Chi)	CHI	9	0
276	6-28-59	Dave Hillman (Chi)	MIL	4	0
277	6-30-59	Bob Purkey (Cin)	CIN	3	2
278	7-03-59	Red Witt (Pit)	PIT	6	0
279	7-12-59	Jack Sanford (SF)	MIL	3	2
280	7-13-59	Sam Jones (SF)	MIL	3	1
281	7-18-59	Dick Ricketts (StL)	StL	1	0
282	7-19-59	Marshall Bridges (StL)	StL	9	0
283	8-01-59	Marshall Bridges (StL)	MIL	7	2
284	8-09-59	Art Fowler (LA)	LA	4	1
285	8-12-59	Jim O'Toole (Cin)	CIN	1	1
286	8-12-59	Jim O'Toole (Cin)	CIN	3	1
287	8-17-59 (1)	Sandy Koufax (LA)	MIL	2	0
288	8-30-59	Glen Hobbie (Chi)	CHI	6	0
289	9-01-59	Don Cardwell (Phi)	MIL	3	0
290	9-12-59	Don Newcombe (Cin)	MIL	8	1
291	9-13-59	Bob Purkey (Cin)	MIL	4	0
292	9-17-59	Jack Sanford (SF)	SF	5	2
293	9-17-59	Jack Sanford (SF)	SF	7	1
294	9-20-59	Robin Roberts (Phi)	PHI	3	1

335

HR #	DATE (G)	PITCHER (Team)	SITE	INN.	ON
295	9-21-59	Bob Friend (Pit)	PIT	5	2
296	9-21-59	Bennie Daniels (Pit)	PIT	9	1
297	9-23-59	Ron Kline (Pit)	PIT	8	1
298	9-25-59	Don Cardwell (Phi)	MIL	1	0
299	9-29-59	Don Drysdale (LA)	LA	5	0
300	4-17-60	Robin Roberts (Phi)	PHI	7	1
301	4-20-60	Jim Brosnan (Cin)	MIL	1	1
302	4-23-60	Bennie Daniels (Pit)	PIT	4	0
303	5-11-60	Lindy McDaniel (StL)	MIL	3	0
304	5-11-60	Bob Duliba (StL)	MIL	6	0
305	5-12-60	Larry Jackson (StL)	MIL	8	0
306	5-17-60	Don Drysdale (LA)	MIL	6	1
307	5-27-60	Bob Purkey (Cin)	CIN	1	0
308	5-27-60	Bob Purkey (Cin)	CIN	5	1
309	5-29-60	Jay Hook (Cin)	CIN	1	1
310	6-04-60	Don Newcombe (Cin)	MIL	3	0
311	6-14-60	Glen Hobbie (Chi)	MIL	9	0
312	6-15-60 (2)	Bob Anderson (Chi)	MIL	3	2
313	6-15-60 (2)	Moe Drabowsky (Chi)	MIL	7	0
314	6-23-60	Sam Jones (SF)	MIL	1	1
315	6-23-60	Sam Jones (SF)	MIL	6	1
316	7-14-60	Harvey Haddix (Pit)	PIT	5	1
317	7-16-60	Robin Roberts (Phi)	PHI	7	0
318	7-17-60	Jim Owens (Phi)	PHI	7	1
319	7-22-60	Don Elston (Chi)	CHI	9	0
320	7-23-60	Don Cardwell (Chi)	CHI	1	0
321	8-03-60	Larry Jackson (StL)	StL	2	2
322	8-08-60	Don Drysdale (LA)	MIL	5	1
323	8-09-60	Johnny Podres (LA)	MIL	9	0
324	8-10-60	Stan Williams (LA)	MIL	4	0
325	8-14-60	Sam Jones (SF)	MIL	1	2
326	8-19-60	Art Mahaffey (Phi)	MIL	8	1
327	8-21-60	John Buzhardt (Phi)	MIL	6	0
328	8-23-60	Ed Roebuck (LA)	LA	6	0
329	8-24-60	Johnny Podres (LA)	LA	1	1
330	8-31-60 (2)	Mel Wright (Chi)	CHI	7	0
331	9-05-60 (1)	Bob Friend (Pit)	PIT	1	2
332	9-07-60	Jack Sanford (SF)	MIL	1	0
333	9-08-60	Mike McCormick (SF)	MIL	1	1
334	9-08-60	Mike McCormick (SF)	MIL	2	2
335	9-10-60	Roger Craig (LA)	MIL	3	2
336	9-14-60	Don Cardwell (Chi)	MIL	1	0
337	9-25-60	Roy Face (Pit)	MIL	10	1
338	9-28-60	Jim Owens (Phi)	PHI	1	1
339	4-11-61	Ernie Broglio (StL)	MIL	4	0
340	5-12-61	Billy O'Dell (SF)	SF	9	0
341	5-13-61	Eddie Fisher (SF)	SF	5	0
342	5-14-61	Billy Loes (SF)	SF	3	1
343	5-15-61	Jim Golden (LA)	LA	5	1
344	5-15-61	Larry Sherry (LA)	LA	9	0
345	5-20-61	Ken Hunt (Cin)	CIN	2	1
346	5-21-61	Joey Jay (Cin)	CIN	6	0
347	5-27-61	Turk Farrell (LA)	MIL	8	0
348	6-02-61	Ray Sadecki (StL)	MIL	4	0
349	6-03-61	Bob Miller (StL)	MIL	8	0
350	6-05-61	Joey Jay (Cin)	CIN	1	1
351	6-08-61	Jim Maloney (Cin)	CIN	7	1
352	6-08-61	Bill Henry (Cin)	CIN	8	0
353	6-09-61	Joe Schaffernoth (Chi)	CHI	8	0
354	6-10-61	Jim Brewer (Chi)	CHI	5	1
355	6-11-61 (2)	Jack Curtis (Chi)	CHI	8	1
356	6-27-61	Curt Simmons (StL)	StL	6	1
357	7-02-61 (1)	Jim O'Toole (Cin)	MIL	1	0
358	7-02-61 (2)	Bob Purkey (Cin)	MIL	7	1
359	7-18-61	Jim Brosnan (Cin)	CIN	9	1
360	7-23-61 (1)	Harvey Haddix (Pit)	PIT	3	0
361	8-13-61	Jim Brewer (Chi)	MIL	6	0
362	8-14-61	Bobby Shantz (Pit)	MIL	8	1
363	8-20-61 (1)	Chris Short (Phi)	MIL	5	0
364	8-29-61	Dick LeMay (SF)	MIL	13	0
365	9-12-61	Bob Gibson (StL)	StL	1	0
366	9-19-61	Jack Sanford (SF)	SF	5	1
367	9-23-61	Jack Curtis (Chi)	MIL	1	1
368	9-23-61	Jack Curtis (Chi)	MIL	3	1
369	9-26-61	Ray Sadecki (StL)	MIL	3	0
370	9-29-61	Jack Sanford (SF)	MIL	3	1

336

HR #	DATE (G)	PITCHER (Team)	SITE	INN.	ON
371	4-11-62	Billy O'Dell (SF)	SF	4	0
372	4-18-62	Jack Sanford (SF)	SF	4	0
373	4-19-62	Juan Marichal (SF)	MIL	1	2
374	4-19-62	Juan Marichal (SF)	MIL	9	1
375	4-24-62	Art Mahaffey (Phi)	MIL	7	0
376	4-25-62	Chris Short (Phi)	MIL	3	2
377	5-18-62	Roger Craig (NY)	MIL	8	0
378	5-24-62	Bob Buhl (Chi)	MIL	8	0
379	5-30-62 (2)	Moe Drabowsky (Cin)	MIL	4	0
380	6-10-62 (1)	Tom Sturdivant (Pit)	MIL	9	1
381	6-12-62	Johnny Podres (LA)	MIL	2	1
382	6-19-62	Roger Craig (NY)	NY	4	0
383	6-22-62	Stu Miller (SF)	SF	5	0
384	7-02-62	Ray Sadecki (StL)	StL	5	3
385	7-03-62 (2)	Curt Simmons (StL)	StL	9	1
386	7-06-62	Don Cardwell (Chi)	CHI	10	1
387	7-12-62	Larry Jackson (StL)	MIL	4	0
388	7-15-62 (1)	Jim Maloney (Cin)	MIL	1	0
389	7-25-62	Roger Craig (NY)	MIL	1	1
390	7-25-62	Roger Craig (NY)	MIL	5	1
391	7-28-62	Jim O'Toole (Cin)	CIN	1	0
392	8-05-62	Dennis Bennett (Phi)	MIL	3	0
393	8-25-62	Glen Hobbie (Chi)	CHI	8	0
394	9-04-62	Jim O'Toole (Cin)	MIL	1	0
395	9-04-62	Jim O'Toole Cin)	MIL	5	1
396	9-10-62	Bob Miller (NY)	NY	7	1
397	9-12-62	Art Mahaffey (Phi)	PHI	3	1
398	9-23-62	Bob Friend (Pit)	PIT	1	0
399	9-30-62	Al McBean (Pit)	MIL	5	0
400	4-16-63	Jack Hamilton (Phi)	MIL	7	1
401	4-22-63	Don Drysdale (LA)	LA	3	2
402	4-24-63	Turk Farrell (Hou)	HOU	4	0
403	5-11-63	Art Mahaffey (Phi)	PHI	6	0
404	5-16-63	Ray Washburn (StL)	MIL	1	2
405	5-19-63 (2)	Barney Schultz (Chi)	CHI	5	0
406	6-08-63	Vern Law (Pit)	PIT	1	1
407	6-10-63	Ray Culp (Phi)	PHI	6	1
408	6-20-63	Tommie Sisk (Pit)	MIL	6	0
409	6-24-63	Hal Brown (Hou)	MIL	6	0
410	7-15-63	Joe Nuxhall (Cin)	CIN	6	0
411	7-17-63	Jack Warner (Chi)	CHI	6	0
412	7-30-63	Bob Buhl (Chi)	MIL	3	0
413	8-02-63	Al Jackson (NY)	MIL	3	1
414	8-04-63	Roger Craig (NY)	MIL	1	0
415	8-11-63	Ken MacKenzie (StL)	MIL	7	2
416	8-21-63	Gaylord Perry (SF)	SF	1	0
417	8-21-63	Gaylord Perry (SF)	SF	5	0
418	8-23-63	Dick Calmus (LA)	LA	1	1
419	8-26-63	Don McMahon (Hou)	HOU	3	2
420	9-05-63	Tom Parsons (Pit)	MIL	3	2
421	9-25-63	Jim O'Toole (Cin)	MIL	2	0
422	9-27-63	Cal Koonce (Chi)	MIL	6	0
423	4-15-64	Jack Sanford (SF)	SF	7	1
424	5-02-64	John Boozer (Phi)	MIL	5	1
425	5-07-64	Art Mahaffey (Phi)	PHI	8	2
426	5-10-64	Bob Friend (Pit)	PIT	1	2
427	6-12-64	Bobby Bolin (SF)	SF	4	1
428	6-23-64	Howie Reed (LA)	MIL	8	0
429	6-26-64	Tracy Stallard (NY)	MIL	7	0
430	6-29-64	Bob Gibson (StL)	StL	9	0
431	7-03-64	Bob Buhl (Chi)	MIL	3	0
432	7-09-64	Roy Face (Pit)	PIT	3	0
433	7-12-64 (2)	Jack Baldschun (Phi)	PHI	9	0
434	7-14-64	Juan Marichal (SF)	MIL	6	1
435	7-15-64	Billy O'Dell (SF)	MIL	8	1
436	8-01-64	Larry Jackson (Chi)	CHI	1	0
437	8-05-64	John Tsitouris (Cin)	CIN	8	1
438	8-12-64	Hal Brown (Hou)	MIL	3	0
439	8-15-64	Jim Duffalo (SF)	SF	4	1
440	8-16-64 (1)	Gaylord Perry (SF)	SF	7	2
441	8-19-64	Phil Ortega (LA)	LA	5	0
442	8-25-64	Rick Wise (Phi)	MIL	5	1
443	8-30-64 (1)	Bobby Bolin (SF)	MIL	1	0
444	9-04-64	Joey Jay (Cin)	CIN	6	1
445	9-19-64 (1)	Larry Jackson (Chi)	MIL	4	1
446	4-12-65	Jim O'Toole (Cin)	CIN	6	1

337

HR #	DATE (G)	PITCHER (Team)	SITE	INN.	ON
447	4-18-65	Bob Buhl (Chi)	MIL	1	0
448	4-21-65	Bob Purkey (StL)	StL	4	0
449	4-27-65	Bob Purkey (StL)	MIL	4	0
450	4-30-65	Ray Herbert (Phi)	MIL	3	2
451	5-04-65	Bob Bruce (Hou)	MIL	3	0
452	5-08-65	Jack Fisher (NY)	NY	8	1
453	5-20-65	Warren Spahn (NY)	MIL	5	3
454	5-24-65	Bob Shaw (SF)	SF	3	2
455	5-25-65	Ron Herbel (SF)	SF	1	0
456	6-03-65	Masanori Murakami (SF)	MIL	3	1
457	6-04-65	Bob Miller (LA)	MIL	9	2
458	6-15-65	Art Mahaffey (Phi)	MIL	3	0
459	6-29-65	Warren Spahn (NY)	NY	2	0
460	7-02-65	Don Cardwell (Pit)	PIT	5	1
461	7-09-65	Jim Maloney (Cin)	CIN	2	1
462	7-15-65	Vern Law (Pit)	MIL	1	1
463	7-18-65 (1)	Tom Parsons (NY)	MIL	2	0
464	7-18-65 (1)	Tom Parsons (NY)	MIL	6	0
465	7-19-65	Jack Fisher (NY)	MIL	4	0
466	7-23-65	Ron Herbel (SF)	SF	2	0
467	8-01-65 (2)	Jack Sanford (SF)	MIL	3	2
468	8-08-65 (1)	Don Nottebart (Hou)	MIL	5	1
469	8-08-65 (1)	Don Nottebart (Hou)	MIL	7	2
470	8-10-65	Bob Gibson (StL)	MIL	5	1
471	8-13-65	Bob Buhl (Chi)	CHI	5	1
472	8-16-65	Bob Purkey (StL)	StL	3	1
473	8-20-65	Don Cardwell (Pit)	PIT	8	1
474	8-24-65	Jim Maloney (Cin)	MIL	4	0
475	8-31-65	Roger Craig (Cin)	CIN	8	0
476	9-16-65	Lew Burdette (Phi)	PHI	2	2
477	9-25-65	Bobby Bolin (SF)	SF	8	1
478	5-09-66	Joey Jay (Cin)	ATL	4	0
479	5-14-66	Bob Gibson (StL)	StL	8	0
480	5-29-66	Ferguson Jenkins (Chi)	CHI	9	0
481	6-12-66	Don Cardwell (Pit)	PIT	2	3
482	6-12-66	Tommie Sisk (Pit)	PIT	4	0
483	6-28-66	Don Lee (Chi)	ATL	8	0
484	7-16-66	Turk Farrell (Hou)	ATL	4	0
485	8-09-66	Sandy Koufax (LA)	ATL	9	0
486	8-15-66	Chris Zachary (Hou)	HOU	7	1
487	8-28-66	Dennis Ribant (NY)	ATL	1	0
488	9-02-66 (1)	Larry Dierker (Hou)	ATL	1	1
489	9-02-66 (1)	Ron Taylor (Hou)	ATL	7	0
490	9-03-66 (1)	Dave Giusti (Hou)	ATL	1	0
491	9-04-66	Bob Bruce (Hou)	ATL	1	0
492	9-05-66 (1)	Vern Law (Pit)	PIT	8	1
493	9-11-66	Dick Selma (NY)	NY	4	0
494	4-14-67	Mel Queen (Cin)	CIN	7	2
495	5-14-67 (1)	Gaylord Perry (SF)	SF	1	1
496	5-30-67 (2)	Roy Face (Pit)	PIT	8	1
497	6-01-67	Tom Seaver (NY)	HOU	8	0
498	6-17-67 (2)	Bob Bruce (Atl)	HOU	9	0
499	7-08-67	Ray Culp (Chi)	HOU	6	0
500	7-14-67	Juan Marichal (SF)	SF	6	2
501	7-16-67 (2)	Jim Brewer (LA)	LA	5	0
502	7-18-67	Bob Hendley (NY)	NY	5	1
503	7-19-67 (1)	Jack Fisher (NY)	NY	8	0
504	8-22-67 (1)	Ron Kline (Min)	DET	8	0
505	8-25-67	Chuck Dobson (KC)	KC	7	0
506	9-06-67 (1)	Catfish Hunter (KC)	DET	4	0
507	9-06-67 (1)	Lew Krausse (KC)	DET	7	1
508	9-08-67	Tommy John (Chi)	CHI	2	0
509	9-24-67	Phil Ortega (Was)	WAS	4	0
510	5-19-68 (2)	Camilo Pascual (Was)	DET	4	2
511	5-27-68	Sammy Ellis (Cal)	CAL	5	1
512	5-27-68	Sammy Ellis (Cal)	CAL	7	0

ALL-STAR HOME RUNS

	DATE	PITCHER	SITE	INN.	ON
	7-07-59	Early Wynn (Chi)	PIT	1	0
	7-13-60	Whitey Ford (NY)	NY	2	1

WORLD SERIES HOME RUN

	DATE	PITCHER	SITE	INN.	ON
	10-06-57	Bob Grim (NY)	MIL	10	1

338

INDEX

Fricano, Marion 30
Frick, Ford 58-60, 85, 92, 107
Friend, Bob 189, 200

Gagliano, Phil 256
Ganss, Bob 35
Gant, Ron 329
Garcia, Mike 93
Garr, Ralph 304, 312
Garroway, Dave 161
Gehrig, Lou 92, 181
George, Homer 3
Geraghty, Ben 103, 154
Gibson, Bob 291-292, 294
Giles, Warren 85, 138, 185
Gillespie, Earl 81, 107, 193
Gillooly, John 57
Gomez, Ruben 142
Gordon, Sid 74, 89, 98, 105-6, 192
Gorin, Charlie 37, 50
Gorman, Tom 292
Gray, Pete 32
Greene, Carl 14
Greengrass, Jim 151
Grim, Bob 156-157
Grimm, Charlie 5, 45, 47, 50-1, 53,
  65, 69, 71-3, 81, 83, 89, 91-2,
  98-9,101, 107-8, 122-3, 129, 132,
  134-7, 142-4, 147, 194, 197-8,
  209, 216, 235, 288-90
Grissom, Marv 99, 113
Groat, Dick 255
Grove, Lefty 234
Gruzdis, Jimmy 13-15

Haag, Sgt. Howard 109-110
Haddix, Harvey 148, 167, 182, 236
Haggerty, Pat 33
Hajduk, Chet 26
Hamilton, Milo 310
Haney, Fred 29, 142-8, 163, 167,
  169-71, 173, 175, 182,
  186-8, 193-5, 197-8, 206, 295
Hardin, Jim 303
Harrington, Fred 39
Harrington, Vann 13, 18
Harris, Luman 302
Harrison, Roric 307
Hatfield, Fred 27

Hatton, Grady 274
Hauser, "Unser Choe" 192
Hazle, Bob 154, 158, 162-3, 165-6,
  177
Hearn, Jim 98-99
Heintzelman, Ken 71
Helga (ice skater) 176-177
Hemingway, Ernest 27, 56
Hendley, Bob 223
Henencheck, Al 39
Henry, Bill 213
Herman, Billy 56
Hersh, Earl 154
Higgins, Pinky 39
Hinckley, John 227
Hinton, Chuck 280
Hirshberg, Al 56, 58
Hitchcock, Billy 263-5, 267, 283
Hoak, Don 182, 189
Hodges, Gil 76, 132, 152, 156
Hoeft, Billy 238, 241
Hofheinz, Judge Roy 221, 274-278
Holmes, Tommy 9, 61, 64, 71-2, 74,
  76, 107, 209, 305
Hooper, Harry 62
Hoover, Dick 26, 50, 71
Hope, Bob 144
Hopper, Jim 18-19
Hornsby, Rogers 86, 107, 207, 307,
  323
Horton, Willie 280, 291, 296-297
Howard, Elston 156
Howe, Gordy 279
Howell, Dixie 53
Hubbell, Carl 14, 18, 234
Hughes, Jim 74
Humphrey, Hubert 292
Huntley, Chet 215
Hurth, Charlie 32, 48
Hutchinson, Fred 165, 199, 213, 311
Hutson, Don 107

Irvin, Monte 63-64

Jackson, Jesse 311
Jackson, Larry 165-166, 223-224
Jackson, Ray 155, 157, 173
Jackson, Shoeless Joe 62, 236
Jackson, Sonny 283

345